PC Magazine
Guide to C
Programming

*PC Magazine
Guide to C
Programming*

Jack Purdum, Ph.D.

Ziff-Davis Press
Emeryville, California

Editors	Deborah Craig, Terry Somerson
Technical Reviewer	Dana Lukken
Project Coordinator	Sheila McGill
Proofreader	Pat Mannion
Cover Design	Gary Suen
Book Design	Laura Lamar/MAX, San Francisco
Technical Illustration	Cherie Plumlee Computer Graphics & Illustration
Word Processing	Howard Blechman and Cat Haglund
Page Layout	Sarah Tucker and Anna L. Marks
Indexer	Valerie Robbins

This book was produced on a Macintosh IIfx, with the following applications: FrameMaker®, Microsoft® Word, MacLink® *Plus*, Aldus® FreeHand™, Adobe Photoshop™, and Collage Plus™.

Ziff-Davis Press
5903 Christie Avenue
Emeryville, CA 94608

ISBN 1-56276-069-6
Manufactured in the United States of America
10 9 8 7 6 5 4 3

In memory of my best
friend—Paul O. Pfeiffer

CONTENTS AT A GLANCE

TABLE OF CONTENTS

ACKNOWLEDGMENTS

NO BOOK IS WRITTEN WITHOUT THE HELP OF OTHERS. IN PARTICULAR, I would like to thank David Cooper, Don Dudine, David Fenoglio, Carl Landau, Chuck Lieske, Davie Reed, and Jim Rheude for their comments and suggestions. Also, numerous editors, artists, and other individuals at Ziff-Davis Press have made many valuable contributions to this book. To each of them, my sincere thanks.

INTRODUCTION

WHEN I FIRST STARTED LEARNING C 15 YEARS AGO, PERSONAL COMputers with 64k of memory and one floppy-disk drive running the CP/M operating system were state-of-the-art machines. There were only two or three C compilers available, and most of them did not support the full C language.

C has matured over the years, partly due to changes in hardware and system software, but also in response to the programmers' needs. These evolutionary changes in C have been formalized by The American National Standards Institute (ANSI), which has defined a formal specification for the C language. The purpose of this book is to teach you how to program using ANSI C.

About This Book

This book has a number of features and conventions that were designed to help you learn C programming.

First, each major C topic is covered in its own chapter. This approach allows you to read and understand each topic in small, manageable time periods. Most people remember a concept better if the material is presented in small, easily digested portions. You should be able to read almost any chapter in this book in less than an hour. Also, the sequence of topics is such that you will build a solid foundation for understanding C.

Second, though the material is presented in easily manageable chunks, each C topic is discussed thoroughly. Particular attention is given to those areas where beginning programmers often have problems. In some cases, a C topic is separated into two chapters simply because of the volume of material that must be covered. (There are two chapters, for example, that discuss C pointers and another two chapters devoted to disk file I/O.)

Third, we have used program examples as a teaching aid for each major topic area. Each example is purposely kept as short as possible to encourage you to type in and experiment with the examples. You will learn C faster and understand it better if you do this.

Fourth, each chapter has a section of skill-checking questions that will help you judge your progress. Although each question is answered in the text, answering the review questions on your own will point out areas where you need further work. Understanding the review questions will enable you to proceed to the next chapter with confidence.

Fifth, the book is sprinkled with programming tips and techniques that will help you to understand C better. Some of these tips are designed to help you avoid common C programming mistakes. Other tips simply show you a better way to accomplish some specific task in C. All of them should help make you a better C programmer.

Finally, you will learn to think about C not only from the programmer's perspective, but also from the point of view of a compiler, the program that translates C code into the machine code that makes your programs run. You will be amazed how studying things from the compiler's point of view helps clarify what a C program statement does. Understanding what the compiler is doing will make both writing and debugging C programs easier.

Why C?

With all of the languages that programmers now have available to them, why has C become so popular? First, C is a sound and versatile language that can be used to write just about anything you want. Whether you want to write an operating system or an accounting package, C gives you the resources necessary to get the job done.

Another important advantage is that C source code is *portable* across different computing environments. That is, code written for one machine can be moved to different machines and recompiled with few, if any, changes. Be warned that bad coding practices can reduce the portability of a program. I will show you how to make your code more portable as you proceed through this book.

Because C is a portable language, it is often one of the first languages available when a new machine is introduced. Because C compiler manufacturers adhere to the ANSI standard, you can move to a new system without having to learn a new dialect of the language.

C is also an extendible language. If a function provided with your compiler doesn't suit your exact needs, you can write a new function to fill the shortcoming. You can, of course, reuse these new functions in other programs. Over time, these new functions make developing new programs a much easier task.

C also lends itself to structured programming techniques. You will learn to think of a program as a series of tasks, each of which is solved by a C function. A C program involves little more than arranging these functions in a way that solves the problem at hand. Using structured programming techniques makes it easier to debug and maintain a program, too.

C is not a stagnant language, and can be shaped to fit very specific programming styles and environments. In recent years, C has been extended to encompass object-oriented programming with the introduction of the C++ programming language. Generally, however, you will find it easier to learn C before you tackle C++. Also, knowing C is very useful if you plan to program under Microsoft's Windows operating system.

Finally, C is an enjoyable language. Once you've mastered some of its fine points and have become comfortable with it, you'll agree that though C is not perfect, it's way out in front of whatever is in second place.

A Little C Background Information

When I was first introduced to personal computers about 15 years ago, I had two programming languages from which to choose: assembler or BASIC. Quite honestly, I was not a great assembly language programmer, so I relied more and more on BASIC for program development. In 1977, one of the first commercial programs our firm marketed was a statistics package named Microstat. By 1978, it became clear that BASIC had too many shortcomings for our needs. The search for a better development language was on.

As fate would have it, one of our distributors from England visited us and suggested that we investigate a "new" language named C. After a little digging, we found that C was a language that was an outgrowth of ALGOL 60, CPL, and BCPL. Ken Thompson of Bell Labs developed the B language in 1970. Dennis Ritchie, also of Bell Labs, developed the C language about two years later. Ritchie's goal was to design a compact, yet robust, language that could be used for systems development. (Indeed, most of the UNIX operating system now is written in C.)

The more we investigated C, the more it appeared that it was a perfect fit with our product development goals. The problem was, we weren't writing programs for the UNIX operating system. We were involved with personal computers (PCs) using the 8080, Z80, and 6502 processor chips. When we first began searching for a suitable C compiler in the late 1970s, there were only two choices, both for the CP/M operating system. One choice was a C interpreter named tiny C, which was written by Tom Gibson. The other choice was a C compiler from a firm that rewrote their minicomputer C compiler for the PC market.

Unfortunately, tiny C did not support the floating-point data type, which was a critical limitation for our statistical package. The other product had all C data types, but it was awkward to use and the generated code ran only slightly faster than BASIC.

We solved our problem by writing our own C compiler for the Z80 processor and the CP/M operating system. When the IBM PC appeared, we moved our compiler to the 8086 processor family running under PC-DOS and MS-DOS.

Meanwhile, two things happened in the late 1970s that had a profound impact on the popularity that C enjoys today. First, Leor Zolman began marketing the BDS C compiler for the CP/M operating system. The compiler was very fast (it was written in assembler), generated good code, and was relatively inexpensive. A lot of people learned C with that compiler.

The second factor affecting C's growth was an article by Ron Cain in the widely read *Dr. Dobbs Journal*. In the article, Cain gave the complete source code for a small C compiler. Although it did not support all of C's data types, giving the source code made it possible to extend the compiler. In fact, Jim

Hendrix has spent years refining Cain's small C compiler and still markets it today.

By the mid-1980s, there were over 20 full C compilers available for MS-DOS. Clearly, there were a lot of people using C by that time.

With more than 20 vendors vying for the programmers' dollars, each vendor was trying to outdo the other by adding new features and enhancements to the language. Such competition has both a good and bad side to it. The good side was that the consumer was getting a better product at a lower price. Plus, some of the enhancements were quite useful. The bad side was that, without a formal set of specifications, or a *standard*, the language was headed toward a fragmentation that might split C into "dialects." Each new "enhancement" meant that code for one compiler would not compile with another vendor's compiler.

Since its publication in 1978, *C Programming Language* by Brian Kernighan and Dennis Ritchie (Prentice Hall) had been considered the only specification of the C language. (In fact, many programmers still refer to some compilers as a "K&R compiler." This is a compliment, as it means that the compiler conforms to all of the specifications contained in the Kernighan and Ritchie book.) However, with the growing number of C vendors, the K&R "standard" for C was disintegrating.

The risk of "dialectizing" C was sufficiently real that a group of C programmers, led by Jim Brodie, petitioned the American National Standards Institute (ANSI) for a committee to create a standard for the C language. In 1982, a standardization committee was formed to write a standard definition for the C language. The outcome of the committee's efforts was the American National Standard X3.159–1989. This standard is what most programmers refer to as "ANSI C."

Today, there are fewer than a half-dozen major vendors of C compilers left in the PC market. Those compilers that do remain, however, are almost fully ANSI-compliant. That is, the compilers meet almost all of the standards set forth in the X3.159–1989 document. The programming tools that come with these compilers are an order of magnitude better than they were a decade ago. Many compilers now include an editor, debugger, linker, profiler, and many other useful programming tools.

C has grown from rather modest beginnings in the late 1970s to the dominant development language of today.

How To Use This Book

It is best if you read everything from start to finish so we are communicating on the same topics at the same level.

I urge you to read this text while sitting in front of your computer. The sample programs have been kept simple and as short as possible so you can type in the programs without much effort. When it comes to learning a new language, there is no substitute for actually using the language. Even something as simple as a typing mistake will give you debugging experience. Typing in and running the sample programs will show how your particular compiler copes with different errors and the error messages they generate. This experience will prove invaluable when you start your own programming projects.

This book not only teaches you how to program in C, it should also be useful after you have finished reading it. Once you've mastered the concepts by working through each chapter, keep this book handy as you work with C—you can use it as a reference, or as a refresher when you need to brush up on a C topic.

Book Style Conventions

As you read this book, keep in mind a few stylistic conventions that have been used to make it easier for you to learn C.

When words used in C programming could be confused with standard English words, we have shown the C words in boldface. This convention is used for functions, keywords, and variables (you'll learn what these terms mean as you progress through the book).

Additionally, a function is shown with a set of opening and closing parentheses, as in **main()**, and a variable that is part of an array is shown with opening and closing brackets, as in **address[]**.

With all the preliminaries taken care of, let's get started learning C.

Some Assumptions about You

The first assumption I have made about you is that you have little or no programming experience. If you have previous programming experience, great! However, this book will teach you what you need to know about C programming "from the ground up."

A second assumption is that you have access to a computer and an ANSI C compiler or interpreter and that you will try out the concepts for yourself. Talking to your children about payroll taxes has no impact on them ... until they get their first jobs. Programming is much the same. It's one thing to read and discuss a program; it's quite another to sit down at the computer and get a program working.

I'm also assuming that you will take the time to experiment with the sample programs. Once you can modify a program and get it to do something else, you can be sure you are making solid progress in your understanding of C. Also, experimentation helps identify those areas that you may not thoroughly understand. The old adage "There's no substitute for practice" applies to programming, too.

Finally, let's quell the assumption that you have to be some kind of math genius to program a computer. Not so. If you can organize a programming task in a logical manner, you can program a computer. I will show you some techniques that will help you to break a programming problem into smaller, more manageable parts. You will also discover that C is perfectly suited to such a programming approach.

1

Compilers, Interpreters, and Other Programming Tools

How Interpreters Work

How to Write a Program for a Compiler

Differences between Compilers and Interpreters

Other Program Development Tools

THIS CHAPTER EXPLORES SOME OF THE TOOLS YOU MIGHT USE WHEN WRITing a C program. We will discuss how writing a program with an interpreter is different from writing a program with a compiler. If you use a C interpreter, most of the tools you need are bundled into the interpreter itself. If you use a C compiler, the tools are likely separate programs.

There are two important reasons to discuss the differences between compilers and interpreters. First, if you understand how each works, the error messages you get will make more sense. And when you understand the error messages, correcting program errors becomes easier.

Second, if you can train yourself to think like a compiler, the rules of the C language make more sense. If your previous programming experience is with BASIC, some of C's rules are going to seem pretty strange. Understanding what the compiler is doing will help demystify some aspects of C programming.

In the next two sections, we explore how interpreters and compilers work and how they differ from one another. Although we have simplified how each component actually works, the basic concepts should help you understand what each one does. Although we use MS-DOS for purposes of discussion, the concepts are equally true for a Macintosh, a UNIX machine, or a mainframe computer.

How Interpreters Work

Some of you may have experience with Microsoft's GWBasic (normally supplied with MS-DOS) or some other interpreter. There are some excellent C interpreters available and they provide a good platform for learning C. Regardless of the language, interpreters all work pretty much the same. Programming with an interpreter involves three layers of software on top of the computer system, as shown in Figure 1.1.

Figure 1.1
Layers of software used by an interpreter

If you were writing a program named GAME.BAS with GWBasic on an MS-DOS computer, the layers of software that sit on top of the hardware would appear as shown on the right edge of Figure 1.1. The top three layers are software (programs) that enable the hardware (the computer) to do something useful.

Notice that the software is loaded into the computer "from the bottom up." That is, when you turn on your computer, it first loads the operating system (MS-DOS in our example) from disk automatically. If you want to write a BASIC program, you load the interpreter (GWBasic) into memory. Once the interpreter is running, you can begin writing your program (GAME.BAS).

How an Interpreter Runs a Program

When you want to run a BASIC program, you save the source file (for example, GAME.BAS) and then issue a RUN command to the interpreter. It's important to notice that *the interpreter must be in memory when you run the program*. The reason is that the interpreter is responsible for communicating between your program and the operating system. This simple BASIC program shows how this works.

```
10 FOR J=1 TO 10
20   PRINT J;
30 NEXT J
```

After you type the program in, you can execute it by issuing the RUN command. It's at this point that things get interesting.

The interpreter knows that a BASIC program starts execution with the lowest line number. Therefore, the interpreter begins execution at line 10. The first thing the interpreter sees is the word FOR. In BASIC, FOR is called a keyword. A *keyword* is any word that has special meaning in the language being used.

In our example, FOR is a keyword used to create program loops. (We will discuss program loops in a later chapter.) Whenever the BASIC interpreter finds a keyword, it searches its list of keywords to see if FOR is in the list.

If the interpreter does not find the keyword FOR, it issues a syntax error. A *syntax error* arises because a program statement did not follow the rules of the language.

If you had typed in FRO instead of FOR, a syntax error would result because FRO is not a keyword in BASIC (and the rest of the line follows the FOR syntax rules).

The interpreter will, of course, find the keyword FOR in its list of valid keywords. Tied to the FOR keyword is a list of rules that must be followed when the FOR keyword is used. Because a variable assignment should come next on the line, the interpreter checks line 10 to see if a variable name follows FOR. The interpreter finds the expression J=1 and determines that it follows the syntax rules.

The interpreter then checks to see if a variable named J already exists in the program. It does this by scanning a chunk of memory that the interpreter has set aside for something called a symbol table. A *symbol table* is a piece of memory used by an interpreter or compiler to store information about the variables and other data used in the program.

At this point in the program, the symbol table is empty because no other variables have been used. Upon seeing that this is a new variable, the interpreter places the name of the new variable (J) in the symbol table.

Next, the interpreter must find a place in memory to store the new variable. The interpreter finds some free (unused) memory for J and places that memory address along with the variable name in the symbol table. In a simplified way, the symbol table might look like Figure 1.2.

Figure 1.2

A hypothetical symbol table entry

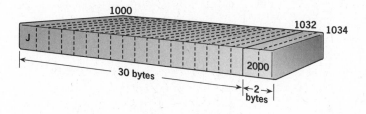

If the BASIC we are using allows variable names of up to 32 characters each, each symbol table entry has (at least) enough space to hold the variable name and its associated address in memory. In Figure 1.2, we have assumed that:

- The symbol table starts at memory address 1000.

- Each variable name can be up to 32 characters in length.

- The interpreter has set aside some memory where J is stored (at memory address 2000).

We also assume that only two bytes of memory are needed in the symbol table to hold the memory address where J is stored. Therefore, any new variable in the program would be entered beginning at memory address 1034 in the symbol table. (Note that the name is 32 bytes long, so the name runs from memory address 1000 *through* 1031. Because we have assumed that J's memory address requires two bytes of storage, the two memory addresses at locations 1032 and 1033 in the symbol table hold J's memory location.)

Thus far, we have checked part of the syntax of the first line, made a new entry in the symbol table, and found a memory location where the value of J is stored.

Next, the interpreter assigns the value of 1 into J. First, the interpreter must check the symbol table to find the memory address for variable J. The interpreter then goes to memory address 2000 and stores the value of 1 at those memory locations. (In BASIC, default variables usually require four bytes of memory.)

The interpreter then finds the BASIC keyword TO and searches its list of keywords for a match. Because TO is a keyword in BASIC, the interpreter then reads the next token "10" and reserves some memory to hold that value. This completes the interpreter's work for the first line of the program.

In line 20 of our example, the interpreter finds the keyword PRINT followed by the variable J. That is, the value of variable J is used by PRINT to display the current value of J on the screen. We often refer to J as an argument of PRINT. An *argument* is a data item that is made available to a program for use by a keyword, function, procedure, or subroutine.

Because PRINT is a BASIC keyword and J is in the symbol table, the interpreter knows that the syntax for line 20 is correct. The interpreter now sends control to the part of the interpreter that handles the code necessary to PRINT the value of a variable (variable J in our example).

When the interpreter sees line 30, it scans its list of keywords to see if NEXT is in the list. Because NEXT is a BASIC keyword, the interpreter then checks to see if J is in the symbol table. Because both checks are valid, the syntax for line 30 is accepted.

The interpreter then checks to see if J is greater than 10. (The value 10 was saved away when line 10 was processed. The interpreter keeps track of where this value is stored.) If J is less than 10, the interpreter finds the data stored at memory location 2000 (that is, variable J), increments it by 1, and performs the next iteration of the FOR loop. It performs the next iteration by repeating line 20 in the program. If J is greater than 10, the program ends.

As you can see, the interpreter spends most of its time:

■ Scanning each line of the program code.

■ Searching its internal list of keywords.

■ Checking the symbol table for the presence and location of variables.

A relatively small amount of time is actually spent processing the task for which the program was written. As a consequence, interpreted programs are relatively slow to execute.

How to Write a Program for a Compiler

Writing a program for a compiler is different from writing for an interpreter. Figure 1.3 helps to explain the difference.

Figure 1.3

Layers of software used with a compiler

Notice how we have replaced the GWBasic interpreter shown in Figure 1.1 with the layer "Step ?" in Figure 1.3. The reason for the question mark is because a compiled program does not use a single piece of software to produce the executable program. Rather, the programmer must follow a sequence of steps to produce the program.

Step 1, Writing the Program Source Code

The first step involves writing the source code for the program. The term *source code* refers to a text file that contains program statements that conform to the syntax rules of the language being used.

The file that contains the source code is usually written with either a text editor or word processor. As such, the file contains plain old ASCII (American Standard Code for Information Interchange) text data. You can find the ASCII codes in Appendix A.

In "the old days" (the late 1970s), programmers provided their own text editor to create the source code file. Today, most popular compilers provide a text editor with the compiler. In fact, many provide an Integrated Development Environment (IDE) that makes each step accessible from a single program. (We will have more to say about IDEs in later chapters.)

To make things more concrete, suppose you want to write a C program named TEST. A common naming convention in C is to use the letter C for the secondary file name (also known as the extension) of the source code file, for example, TEST.C.

Therefore, you would load your text editor, write the source code for the program named TEST, and then save the source code in a file named TEST.C. TEST.C is the output of your work from step 1.

Note that the source code creation step works for any compiled language. That is, if we wanted to compile the short example program shown earlier, we would probably save the file as TEST.BAS. If you were using a Pascal compiler, it would be TEST.PAS. If you advanced to the C++ language, the source file would be TEST.CPP. Regardless of the language, the result of step 1 is a source code file, usually stored in ASCII.

Step 2, The Compiler

The first difference between this step and step 1 is that the text editor used in step 1 (see Figure 1.3) is replaced with the compiler in step 2. Another difference is that step 1 did not require any input data to complete that step. That is, we didn't need to supply the text editor with any information before we began step 1. Not so in step 2.

In step 2, the compiler needs access to the C source code file that was created in step 1. When you run a compiler, one of the first things it needs to know is the name of the file that contains the source code to be compiled. If the compiler uses an IDE, you probably provide the source code file name—TEST.C, TEST.BAS, or whatever the compiler expects—via a dialog box. For non-IDE compilers, the source file is probably the second argument supplied on the command line. If the compiler is named XYZ, the command line might be:

```
XYZ TEST.C
```

After you press the Enter key, the compiler opens the input file (TEST.C) and begins reading and compiling the source code found in the file. Although the compiler may complete its task in a few seconds, what goes on during compilation is incredibly complex. Still, with a little simplification, we can understand what the compiler does.

How a Compiler Works

To remain consistent with our previous example, we assume that you are using a BASIC compiler to compile the source code shown earlier. Because it is a BASIC compiler, we assume the source code file is named TEST.BAS. (TEST.BAS was written with a text editor, too.)

The compiler begins by opening the source code file (TEST.BAS) and reading the first line of the program. The compiler first checks to see if the source code line obeys the syntax rules of the language. The compiler will also create and use a symbol table in much the same way shown in Figure 1.2.

If the compiler finds a syntax error, the compiler issues an error message. If the compiler thinks you're doing something that bends the rules of the language, but doesn't break them, it may issue a warning message.

An *error message* usually means you have broken a syntax rule of the language. A *warning message* means that you are doing something that may cause problems, but the error doesn't break any specific rules of the language.

Assuming that the source line passes all syntax checks, the compiler then generates intermediate code, or object code, for the line. *Object code* is an intermediate code that contains machine language instructions plus other information needed to produce an executable program.

For example, line 10 of our program generates object code that initializes variable J to 1. To do this, the compiler needs to know where variable J resides in memory. However, because the compiler itself is using the computer's available memory, it cannot determine the specific memory address where J will ultimately reside in the final (executable) program. Instead of fixing a memory address for variable J, the compiler leaves a message in the object code file for the next step in the compilation process. In essence, this message says: "I can't determine the exact place where J will reside in memory, so you fix up the memory address yourself when it's your turn to process the object code file." (We'll see in a moment for whom this message is written.)

In line 20 of the program, the compiler takes the code necessary to process a PRINT statement and places that code into the object code file. When line 30 is processed, the compiler places code in the object code file that checks the value of J to see if it's greater than 10. If J is less than 10, the compiler generates more code to increment the value of J by 1 and then jump back to the code associated with line 20. If the value of J is greater than 10, the compiler places code in the object file to end the program.

When the compiler finishes its job, it writes the object code file to disk. In simplified terms, the object file contains two types of code. The first type of code is machine code. *Machine code* consists of instructions that can be directly executed by the computer. (Nothing executes faster than machine code.)

The second type of code consists of messages that pass information on to the linker. (The linker is discussed in the next section of this chapter.) These two types of code combine to form object code.

In most PC environments, the object code file ends in .OBJ, although it could be almost any other secondary file name the compiler vendor chooses. In our example, the object code file might become TEST.OBJ. This file is the output from step 2 and the input file for step 3.

Step 3, The Linker

The purpose of the linker is to resolve all of the messages that the compiler left in the object code file and produce an executable program. For example, we already saw that the compiler may not be able to resolve the actual memory addresses for all of the variables in the program. Also, where our program used PRINT to display the values of J, the compiler might simply leave the message:

```
CALL PRINT, J
```

This is an example where the compiler is telling the linker to grab a pre-written chunk of code called PRINT and insert it at this point in the program. The compiler may also pass the linker information about the variable (J) that is to be printed. Depending upon the language, these chunks of code may be called subroutines, functions, or procedures.

Library Files

So where does the linker find these prewritten pieces of code? Often they are stored in library files. A *library* is nothing more than a collection of precompiled subroutines, functions, or procedures. Each of these precompiled library modules is designed to fulfill some small programming task.

For most MS-DOS compilers, library files end in .LIB. If a library file contains a collection of math subroutines, it might be stored on disk as MATH.LIB. If we extracted the cosine subroutine from the library file, it might be called COSINE.OBJ. Somewhere in our BASIC library file is a subroutine called PRINT. If we extracted it from the library, it might be called PRINT.OBJ. It is the linker's responsibility to fit the code extracted from the library into our program.

Notice that LIB files are usually nothing more than a collection of (precompiled) OBJ files. As such, the linker simply has to find the routine it needs from the library file (for example, PRINT.OBJ), and stuff it into the program file at the proper place.

Some linkers also supply the missing memory addresses for the variables used in the program. More complex linkers may leave instructions to resolve all memory addresses when the program is actually run. Regardless of the type of linker used, when it finishes its job, the result is an executable program. For an MS-DOS compiler, the name of the executable program ends in .EXE or .COM. For our sample program, the executable file is stored on disk as TEST.EXE.

We can summarize the steps for writing a compiled program in Figure 1.4. The result of the steps shown in Figure 1.4 is an executable program named TEST.EXE.

Differences between Compilers and Interpreters

It's important to notice the differences between an interpreter and a compiler (they're summarized in Table 1.1). With an interpreter, the program being run uses the code and other resources that are built into the interpreter to execute the program. This means that *both* the interpreter and the program being run must reside in memory at the same time.

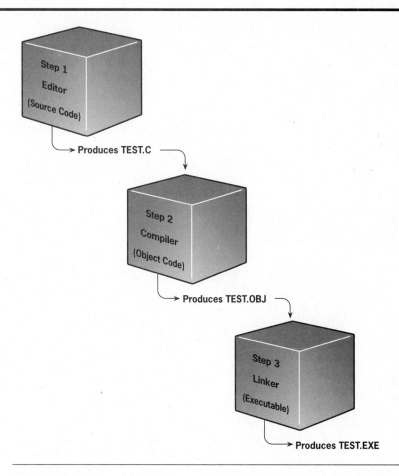

Figure 1.4
Steps in writing a
compiled program

A compiler, however, places the necessary code to process each line of the program in the object file. The linker "links" the pieces of code in the object file with the other pieces drawn from any required library files. The output of the linker is a stand-alone executable program.

With a compiler, the resulting program uses only the resources provided by the operating system. That is, we do not need another program (an interpreter) other than the operating system in memory to run a compiled program.

Because a compiled program contains all of the code it needs to run, no time is lost scanning, searching, and checking the program as it runs. As a result, compiled programs typically run much faster than interpreted programs. The downside of this increased speed is that compiled programs often take more disk space simply because they do contain all of the code necessary to execute.

Table 1.1 **Compiler versus Interpreter**

	Compiler	Interpreter
Source Code	Create an ASCII text file with your own editor	Create with editor built into the interpreter
Execute	Compile and link the program and then run from the command line	Type RUN from within the interpreter
Debug	Run a debugger as a separate program	Place debug statements in the program and type RUN
Overhead	Program file is directly executable from command line	Must load interpreter in memory and run the program as part of the interpreter

Another disadvantage of compiled programs is the time it takes to test and make changes to the program. It takes time to edit, recompile, and relink a program. With an interpreter, you simply make the change to the source code and type RUN.

Most dialects of BASIC have STOP and CONTINUE commands that let you pause a program, examine the data, and then continue its execution. This makes debugging an interpreted program fairly quick. Compiled programs require a separate debugger program to perform similar tasks.

So which is best? Some programmers use an interpreter during the design and testing stages of program development. When the code is stable and fully debugged, they compile it to produce an executable program. Other programmers use either an interpreter or a compiler. However, my guess is that the majority of all C program development is done with a compiler. For that reason, we will assume that you will be using a compiler while you read this text. If a situation arises where it makes a difference whether you are using a compiler or an interpreter, we will explain the difference.

Other Program Development Tools

If you purchased your compiler in the last few years, you probably received a number of other development tools that may prove useful. The most common tools are a debugger, a Make utility, a profiler, and a librarian.

Debuggers

A *debugger* is used to isolate program bugs. A program *bug* is an error that causes a program to behave in an unexpected manner. (Someone once called a bug an "undocumented feature" of the program.) Note that a bug is *not* a syntax error; the compiler should catch all syntax errors. In most cases, a bug is a flaw in the design of the program. This can result from faulty design, using a certain data type incorrectly, or a host of other mistakes.

Most bugs are of the "flat forehead" type. That is, when you discover the cause of the bug, you slap yourself in the forehead for making such a dumb mistake. (Personally, we haven't had a flat forehead bug for several hours now.) Still, everyone makes them and you should expect your fair share. It's part of the learning process.

The hardest part of debugging a program is finding the bug. Once you find the bug, fixing it often takes only a few minutes. Finding a bug, however, can take days. A debugger helps isolate a bug. A debugger lets you execute the program one line at a time (a process called *single-stepping*) and examine the data as the program executes. This can be very useful for tracing the flow of a complex program.

Debuggers also let you set breakpoints in the program. You would set the breakpoint at the line you think is causing the bug. When set at a particular program line, a *breakpoint* causes the program to run at full speed until it reaches that line. When the program reaches the breakpoint, it pauses so you can examine variables or perform other tests. (Single-stepping through several thousand lines of code is a real pain. Breakpoints let you get to the suspected problem area in a program at full speed, and then single-step from that point.)

Single-stepping and breakpoints are only two features found in most modern debuggers. They are powerful allies and well worth learning how to use.

The Make Utility

Most compilers come with a Make program. A *Make* program provides an intelligent way to compile a program. It is intelligent because it provides a means to avoid unnecessary compilation.

Suppose you are writing a very large program. As you will learn later in the book, it makes sense to break large programs into several smaller source code files. Let's assume that you have five source code files that make up the program. Everything seems to be working, but there is one last bug somewhere in source code file number 4. (Linkers can combine more than one OBJ file to create a single program.)

If you use a simple method to compile the program (for example, a batch file), you probably would recompile all five files and link them together. A Make program is smarter than that. By looking at the date and time of the source code and object code files, Make can tell which files need to be recompiled. If, for example, the source code file has a more current date and time than its object code file, the source code file needs to be recompiled to update the object code file.

In our example, if you are only changing file number 4, Make knows this and recompiles only that file. After all, the other source files have not changed, so there is no reason to recompile those files.

By avoiding unnecessary recompilation, the turn-around time for the edit-compile-link cycle can be reduced considerably. If your compiler supports Make files (sometimes called project files), you should learn how to use them. They can save you a bunch of time.

PROGRAMMING TIP. *Many compilers provide a Make facility with the compiler. For many of these compilers,* project files *are used to drive the Make program. The exact use of project files varies among compilers, so it's difficult to generalize about them. However, when you start writing large programs that use multiple source code files, project files are wonderful tools. While you may not need project files right now, keep them in mind. They can make life much simpler when you write large, complex programs.*

Profilers

Profilers are great for defining bottlenecks or "hot spots" in a program. A *profiler* is a program that times how long it takes for each part of a program to execute. There's an old saying that states "Ninety percent of a program's time is spent executing only ten percent of the code." A profiler is useful for determining where that ten percent is in the program.

Often program bottlenecks are in loop structures that are executed many times. If the bottleneck is bad enough, the program should be redesigned to eliminate it.

Profilers and Algorithms

The design and structure of a program is based on an alogrithm. An *algorithm* is the blueprint for a program. It details the sequence of steps necessary to achieve a desired goal or solve a particular task. The selection and implementation of an algorithm can have a tremendous impact on the performance of the program. (In Chapter 2, we mention one situation where an algorithm change reduced the run time for a program from years to hours!)

Using a profiler to detect bottlenecks in a program is often the first step in redesigning an algorithm. If you are concerned about the performance of a program, a profiler can be a real help in showing you where the changes need to be made.

Librarians

Another useful tool is called a librarian. A *librarian* is a tool that takes different object code files and converts them into library (for example, .LIB) files. These library files can then be used by the linker to link in previously written functions.

For example, suppose you've written 20 or 30 subroutines that you want to use in your latest (and future) programs. You could list all 30 routines as part of the command to the linker. This gets old in a hurry.

The alternative is to use a librarian to collect all 30 object files into a single library file. Now all you have to do is tell the linker to search the one library file rather than listing all 30 object code files individually. As you gain experience with C, you will be writing new functions of your own that you will want to place into a library file for use in other programs. Although you don't "need" a librarian, it sure makes writing programs simpler.

There are other program development tools available to you. A quick pass through any of the programming magazines and journals will show you the vast array of tools that are available.

For now, we will assume that none of these tools is available to you. We will ferret out program bugs without a debugger, detect hot spots without a profiler, and link in our object code files without the aid of a librarian. These are not serious limitations for the small example programs we will be using.

Conclusion

This introductory material on interpreters and compilers may not seem too important now. However, as we progress through the book, often we step back and discuss what the compiler does with each program statement. Such digressions may be just what you need to crystalize a new concept in your mind. Understanding what the compiler is doing can also be a great help when it comes time to debug a program.

Take the time to think about what is going on when the compiler is executing. It will make you a better programmer.

Checking Your Progress

1. What does the term keyword mean?

   A keyword is a word that has a special meaning in the language being used to write a program. For example, the word FOR in BASIC and **for** in C both tell the language that the program is about to create some form of looping task.

2. Why does an interpreted program usually run slower than a compiled program?

When an interpreted program is run, the interpreter must scan each program line and then decide what to do with that line. Once it determines what must be done, it executes the code for that line and then returns to the next line in the program and repeats the process over again. As a result, the interpreter spends a lot of time jumping back and forth between your program and its own internal code.

A compiler, on the other hand, also scans each source code line in the program. However, the compiler then generates executable code to accomplish the action embodied in the program line. When the compiler finishes its task, the result is a program file that contains all of the program's code. Because a compiled program does not need the aid or overhead of an interpreter, it executes machine code directly and runs significantly faster.

3. What are the basic steps required to write a compiled program?

The steps are:

1. Writing the source code for the program (for example, TEST.C).

2. Compiling the program source code to generate an object code file (TEST.OBJ).

3. Linking the program's object code files together to produce an executable program (TEST.EXE).

   If a compiler does not use external modules, subroutines, or functions, the compiler may be able to generate an executable program without a linker step. For most PC compilers, however, the linker step is required.

4. What is a symbol table?

A symbol table is a table (usually stored in memory) that contains information about each variable used in a program. In some languages, such as C, you must cause the compiler to make an entry in the symbol table for each variable *before* you can use it in the program. (You will see how to do this in the next chapter.)

5. What's the best language to use to write programs?

C. We hope to convince you of this fact, starting with the next chapter.

CHAPTER

2

Writing a Simple
C Program

N THIS CHAPTER YOU WILL LEARN THE FIVE BASIC STEPS THAT COMPRISE almost all computer programs. You will also learn the importance that program design plays in writing a program. Finally, you will write your first C program. The concepts discussed in this chapter lay the groundwork for writing all C programs.

The Five Program Steps

In all but the most trivial cases, a computer program involves five basic steps:

1. Initialization

2. Input

3. Processing

4. Output

5. Shutdown

Each of these five steps is discussed in detail in the following sections.

Initialization

Many programs require certain events to take place before the program actually begins execution. The *initialization step* of a program is responsible for taking any preliminary actions that may be required by a program.

For example, the program may need certain variables initialized to specific values before it can begin its task. In other cases, it may be necessary to open and read the contents of a data file before the program can begin.

It is possible that a program may not even require an initialization step. In fact, our first C program (presented later in this chapter) does not require an initialization step. Programs that do not have an initialization step, however, tend to be extremely simple and not terribly useful. In the real world of C programs, an initialization step is usually required. As you progress through this book, you will see many programs that require some form of program initialization.

Input

Most programs are designed to transform information. Obviously, the program needs to have access to the information before it can fulfill its task. The *input step* is responsible for collecting the data that is used by the program to accomplish its task.

In most cases, the information is either given by the user (usually from the keyboard or mouse) or read from a disk data file. At the beginning stages of your C programming experience, we will concentrate on getting input data from the keyboard.

There are other means of acquiring input from a program, however. Just a few of the alternatives include modem input, data acquisition equipment, and even fiber optic cables. Regardless of the source of the information, its purpose is to provide the raw information upon which the program acts.

Processing

Most programs are designed to gather data in one form and transform it into some other form of data (or information). The *processing step* is responsible for transforming the data from one form into a different form. For example, the data might be an unordered list of names and the desired form is a sorted list of names. In this example, the processing step is responsible for sorting the list of names.

The performance or efficiency of a program is greatly affected by the type of processing used. There are dozens of ways to sort a list of data, but they are not all equally efficient. The simple bubble sort, for example, often takes five to ten times as long as a shell or quick sort on a random list of names. However, if the list is almost in sorted order, the bubble sort can outperform many other sorting methods. Selecting the proper method for the task at hand requires an understanding of the problem and knowledge of the alternative means for solving it.

In short, the type of processing you do in the processing step of a program often determines how well the program performs. If you want to be a good programmer, you should think this step out very carefully *before* you start writing the program.

Output

After the data is transformed, the user needs to have access to the new information. The *output step* is simply responsible for presenting the processed input.

In our sorting example, this step is responsible for displaying the sorted list of names. Keep in mind that the sorted list might be displayed on the computer's monitor, a printer, written to a disk data file, or sent via a modem to some other part of the world.

Regardless of the output device, though, organizing the output so it is presented in some usable fashion is the ultimate goal of a program. In all but the most trivial cases, different programmers display the same information in different ways. The actual displaying of program information is the easy part; presenting the information in a usable manner takes a little more thought.

Shutdown

Trivial programs simply "end," but complex programs may require additional processing. The *shutdown step* is anything the program requires after the output step. For example, if your program reads a disk data file to get its input or save the output to the disk, you should close the disk file before the program ends. Other programs may require you to release memory that was being used by the program or, perhaps, turn off a machine that was supplying data to the program.

Some programs do not require any specific action after the output is displayed. You should, however, keep the shutdown step in mind; it may help prevent you from forgetting to do something important in the program!

The five program steps presented in this section serve as a general outline for almost any programming task. Too often, however, beginning programmers leap into a programming assignment without thinking about how each step relates to the others. Thinking about a program before you start writing it almost always results in code that is easier to write, easier to debug, and easier to maintain. Think before you write.

Sideways Refinement

The five programming steps mentioned earlier are nothing more than a guideline to help you organize a programming task. Each step needs to be refined before you can actually start writing the source code for a program.

A *sideways refinement* starts with the five major programming steps and continues to break each step down into smaller tasks. This process continues until each refinement is a single task. For example, let's suppose that your computer system contains a disk file with monthly sales figures. Let's further assume that your task is to write a program to present the sales figures as a bar chart. How would you write the program?

First, resist the urge to start writing program source code without a formal program design. A good starting point is a sideways refinement of the five program steps presented earlier in the chapter, shown in Table 2.1.

Notice how each of the five program steps is refined in a "sideways" manner. The purpose of this refinement is to provide more detail how each (smaller) task is to be resolved for each program step. The advantage is that a sideways refinement gives you some idea of the smaller tasks that need to be addressed to complete the overall goal of the program. As we shall see later in this chapter, the C programming language uses functions to accomplish each small programming task.

Note that you need to refine what is presented in Table 2.1 even further to end up with a working program. For example, we already know there are dozens of ways to sort data and you must decide which sorting method to use. In other words, you need to select a sorting algorithm.

Table 2.1 **Sideways Refinement of the Five Program Steps: Bar Chart of Monthly Sales**

Program Step	Task	Function Name
Initialization	-> clear the screen	cls()
	open the data file	open_database()
Input	-> how many months?	get_months()
	get memory for data	get_memory()
	read the data file	read_data()
Process	-> sort the data?	sort_data()
	find min-max values	do_min_max()
	determine the scale	do_scaling()
Output	-> draw axes	do_axes()
	label axes	do_labels()
	draw the bars	do_bars()
	do graph title	do_title()
Shutdown	-> close data file	close_data()
	free data memory	free()
	terminate program	exit()

The Algorithm

We introduced the algorithm in Chapter 1. An *algorithm* is nothing more than a formal statement of how a specific programming task is to be done. It's a recipe, or blueprint, for solving a programming task. In deciding how to sort the data, you could investigate a shell sort, heap sort, bubble sort, quick sort, insertion sort, and so on. Each of these sorting methods has an algorithm associated with it that tells you how to write the code necessary to do the sort. The bubble sort uses a fairly simple algorithm and, hence, is fairly easy to code. Other sorting algorithms are quite complex and are fairly difficult to code, but are faster in sorting most lists.

How much impact can an algorithm have on a program? In Jon Bentley's book *Programming Pearls*, he relates a story about his attempts to design an algorithm for a complex numerical processing problem. His first algorithm to solve the problem would have required 95 *years* on a Cray-1 supercomputer. His fourth (and final) algorithm took 5.4 *hours* on a TRS-80 (eight-bit) microcomputer. This equates to less than 10 *minutes* on a modern PC. Clearly, selecting the proper algorithm can have an important impact on the performance of a program.

The sideways refinement of the five programming steps forces you to think about how an algorithm must work to accomplish the task at hand. It also helps to make clear how each step can be subdivided into smaller, more manageable tasks. Finally, sideways refinement also helps show how each small task relates to the other tasks in the program.

Regardless of the amount of time it takes to actually write the program steps and their refinements, it will save you time in the long run. Try to develop the habit of writing the design of a program on paper *before* you write any program source code.

The Elements of a C Program

Let's write a simple program that displays a message on the monitor's screen. The program is so short that only two programming steps are involved: the input step and the output step. The source code for the program appears in Program 2.1.

Program 2.1   A Simple C Program

```
/*
    A simple C program
*/
#include <stdio.h>
main()
{
  printf("This is my first C program");
}
```

You should type this program into your computer and then compile it. It may generate several warning messages, but it should compile. (We will ignore these warning messages for now, and correct them as we proceed through the book.) As short as this program is, we can learn a lot about C from it. Let's examine Program 2.1 line by line.

Learning about Program Comments

The first thing you see in Program 2.1 is:

```
/*
     A simple C program
*/
```

The characters **/*** and ***/** mark the start and end of a program comment in C. Everything between the start of the comment (/*) and the end of the comment (*/) is ignored by the compiler. Program comments allow you to leave comments, program clarifications, and other information directly in the program source code.

PROGRAMMING TIP. *Some C compilers now support both the C and C++ languages. If your compiler supports C++, that language supports the double forward slash (//) comment characters. A comment in C++ might be:*

```
//   A C++ program comment
```

The major difference is that a C++ comment extends from the double slash characters to the end of the line. There is no closing comment character required. We will not use the C++ comment characters in this book because some C compilers do not support C++ comments.

It is important to remember that program comments have no effect on the code size or execution speed of a program. Comments are stripped out by the compiler before any program code is generated. Therefore, you should feel free to use them as often as you wish.

If you do something especially clever with a section of C code, you should use the comment characters to surround a comment that details what the code does. It can make life a lot easier when you return to that piece of code several months later. (If you're like most of us, you aren't equally clever on all days and a simple comment can make a "fuzzy" piece of code understandable.)

Nested Comments

In old (pre-ANSI) C programs, you often find comments within comments. For example, you might see something like this:

```
/*
     This is the first comment
/*
     This is a second comment and its end.
*/
     This is the end of the first comment.
*/
```

In this example, we have a comment "nested" within another comment. That is, a second comment starts before the first comment ends. According to the ANSI standard for the C language, nested comments are *not* allowed in C and you should avoid using them.

PROGRAMMING TIP.   *Some C compilers adhere strictly to nonnested comments, but may give misleading error messages. For example, when compiling a program with nested comments, the Quick C compiler for Windows gives the error message:*

```
'*/' found outside comment
```

followed by:

```
syntax error: '/'
```

The Borland compiler for Windows says:

```
Expression syntax
```

followed by:

```
Compound statement missing }
```

In both cases the first error message details the error; the second message should be ignored. It takes time to learn which error messages truly identify the error and which are spurious messages caused by the actual error. You may wish to write a program with nested comments in it so you can see how your compiler handles the error. As you gain experience with your compiler, these small nuisances disappear.

Most ANSI compilers will flag nested comments as errors, or issue a warning message. If you have inherited some old C code that has nested comments, there are two ways for you to handle them. First, you can convert the nested comments into "unnested" comments. Changing nested to unnested comments is simple to do, as shown here:

```
/*
    This is the first comment
*/
/*
    This is a second comment and its end.
*/
/*
    This is the end of the first comment.
*/
```

Notice that we could also write this code in either of the ways shown below:

```
/* This is the first comment          */
/* This is a second comment and its end. */
/* This is the end of the first comment. */
/*
   This is the first comment
   This is a second comment and its end.
   This is the end of the first comment.
*/
```

Any of the three comment forms shown above may be used.

A second way to cope with nested comments is to see if your compiler has a switch that allows them. Many compilers that adhere to the ANSI standard do have a switch setting that allows you to "bend the rules" for nested comments. This allows you to compile code that uses nested comments with an ANSI compiler. It is a better idea, however, not to write code that uses nested comments. That way, if you need to switch compilers at some later time, you won't need to worry about nested comments.

We will find other uses for the comment characters in later chapters. For now, however, let's continue to examine the rest of Program 2.1.

Header Files

The next line in Program 2.1 is:

```
#include <stdio.h>
```

This line contains a preprocessor directive that tells the compiler to read a disk file named stdio.h into this point in the program. A *preprocessor directive* is a command to the preprocessor pass of the compiler to perform some particular task. The *preprocessor pass* is simply a phase, or part, of the compiler that processes preprocessor directives.

There are many preprocessor directives, of which **#include** is just one. An example will help explain what the #include preprocessor directive does. Suppose you have created an ASCII text file named title.h, the content of which is:

```
/*
   This is my first C program
   JJP
   Jan. 16, 1993
*/
```

Now further suppose that we rewrite Program 2.1 so it appears like that found in Program 2.2.

Program 2.2   **A C Program with Two Include Files**

```
#include "title.h"
#include <stdio.h>

main()
{
   printf("This is my first C program");
}
```

The first thing the compiler does is invoke a preprocessor pass to examine the program source code. The preprocessor pass causes the compiler to look for certain preprocessor directives in the program's source code. One of the preprocessor's responsibilities is to process any #include preprocessor directives. After the preprocessor pass has finished processing the first line of the program, the actual code "left behind" is shown in Program 2.3.

Program 2.3   **Program 2.2 after the Preprocessor Pass**

```
/*
      This is my first C program
      JJP
      Sept. 16, 1991
*/

#include <stdio.h>

main()
{
   printf("This is my first C program");
}
```

As you can see from the code in Program 2.3, the #include preprocessor directive causes the contents of a header file (for example, title.h) to be read into the program at the point where the #include preprocessor directive appears in the program.

Your C compiler has a number of files that are often used with the #include preprocessor directive. These files are called *header files* and contain information that assists the compiler in checking the code being compiled for syntax and other errors. By convention, programmers use .h for the secondary file name of header files.

If you look in the subdirectory where you store your compiler, you will probably find another subdirectory named INCLUDE (or HEADERS). The INCLUDE subdirectory may have several dozen header files in it. Each of these header files fulfills a particular purpose in a program. We will discuss these header files as we need them throughout this book.

PROGRAMMING TIP. *Although we are not ready to discuss the topic of header files in detail now, we can tell you that header files should not contain executable program code. Header files are used to provide support information used by the compiler, not program statements needed to solve the programming task at hand. In later chapters you will see examples of when to create your own header files and how they are used. For now, we will use a few of the standard header files that come with your compiler in our examples, but defer a complete discussion until later.*

Storing Your #include Files

We mentioned that the header files often are found in a subdirectory named INCLUDE, although other names are possible. If you are compiling your program in a different subdirectory, how does the compiler find a specific header file?

The #include preprocessor directive may take one of two forms:

```
#include <filename>
```

or

```
#include "filename"
```

One form uses the angle brackets (<>) to surround the file name, while the second form uses double quotes (""). When angle brackets are used, the compiler looks in the environment space for a path variable that tells where the header files can be found.

Most MS-DOS compilers have an *environment variable* named IN-CLUDE that tells the compiler where to find the header files. If you are using an MS-DOS compiler, chances are pretty good that there is an environment variable named INCLUDE used by your compiler. For example, if you type the word SET at the MS-DOS command line prompt, you might see something similar to the line:

```
INCLUDE=C:\COMPILER\INCLUDE
```

This means that there is an environment variable named INCLUDE and it has been set to the subdirectory COMPILER\INCLUDE on drive C. The INCLUDE environment variable causes the compiler to look in the COMPILER\INCLUDE subdirectory on drive C for any header files whenever the angle brackets are used with a #include preprocessor directive.

When double quotes are used, the preprocessor first looks in the current working directory for the header file to be included before looking anywhere else. Therefore, if you are working in a subdirectory named C:\PROJECT and use double quotes for a **#include**, the preprocessor looks in the C:\PROJECT subdirectory before it looks in the C:\COMPILER\INCLUDE directory for any included files.

Why two different ways to find header files? Primarily, the two different methods allow you to keep the generic header files provided with your compiler separate from whatever project-specific header files you may write yourself. This allows you to use your own project-specific header files without cluttering up the subdirectory used for the compiler's generic header files.

What's in stdio.h?

Our example includes the stdio.h header file in the program. The stdio.h header file is important for all programs that do any program input or output (which is virtually all programs). All C programs should include the stdio.h header file.

Every C compiler provides this header file because it provides some necessary overhead information to perform basic program input and output functions. In fact, the file derives its name from "standard (std) input-output (io) header (h)" file—stdio.h. (Again, it is a common programming convention for all C header files to end with the letter h.)

Finally, because the compiler often needs the information in the header file to accomplish its task, the #include preprocessor directives should appear near the beginning, or top, of the program. (If you think about it, it wouldn't make much sense to include a header file at the end, would it?)

We will cover the details contained in the stdio.h (and other) header files later, especially in the chapters that use disk files. For now, just remember to **#include** stdio.h near the top of your programs.

The main() Function

To make things easier for you, we will repeat the next four lines of Program 2.3:

```
main()
{
    printf("This is my first C program");
}
```

Notice that the word main is followed by an opening and closing set of parentheses. Because main is not a keyword in C, the presence of the parentheses tells the compiler that **main()** is a C function. We mentioned earlier in this chapter that functions are used to solve a particular programming task. The main() function, however, is a very special C function.

There are a number of things that make the main() function special. First, program execution begins with the function named **main()**. The first thing that the user sees happen on the screen is whatever happens first in **main()**. That is, those executable program statements that appear first in **main()** dictate what the program does first.

Also note that C is a case-sensitive language. That is, **MAIN()**, **Main()**, and **main()** are not the same things in C. If you try to use **MAIN()** or **Main()**, your compiler (or linker) will complain because it cannot find the main() function in your program. Make sure you use **main()** with lowercase letters.

Second, every C program must have a main() function. Because **main()** marks the spot where program execution begins, it makes sense that every C program needs to have a main() function in it.

Finally, the main() function also marks the spot where the program ends. That is, when the program reaches the closing brace of the main() function, the program ends. This also means that everything a C program does is traceable to the main() function.

Now that we understand how important the main() function is, let's examine some of the parts that are common to all C functions.

The Parts of a C Function

All C functions have certain things in common. Figure 2.1 shows these common elements for a hypothetical function named **func()**.

Figure 2.1

A hypothetical C function

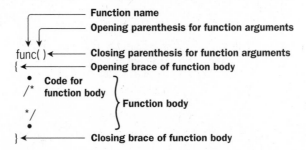

Function Names

For now, we can state that a function definition starts with a function name followed by an opening and closing set of parentheses. Function names can contain letters, digit characters, and an underscore.

They cannot start with a digit character such as 1, a math symbol such as a minus sign, or punctuation characters. Several other special characters (for example, &) are not permitted. The general rules for valid function names are as follows:

1. Function names may start with a letter or the underscore character.

2. A function name cannot begin with a digit character.

3. A function name cannot contain punctuation marks, math, or other special symbols.

4. ANSI guarantees the first 31 characters to be significant.

5. Function names that already exist in the standard library of C functions should not be used.

The fourth rule means that if two functions or variables have identical characters for the first 31 positions in the name but the 32nd character is different, the compiler is not required to differentiate between the two function or variable names. In most practical situations, this is not a severe limitation.

The fifth rule is not actually a rule; just some good advice. You will see why in the next section. By the way, the rules for function names listed above apply to variables, too. We will cover the details on variables in Chapter 4.

Table 2.2 shows some examples of valid and invalid function names.

The Function Body

On the next line in the program is an opening brace ({). The opening brace marks the beginning of the code that forms the body of the function. At the bottom of Figure 2.1 is a closing brace (}), which marks the end of the function body. Any code associated with the function must appear between the opening and closing braces of the function body. Anything that appears between the opening and closing braces is referred to as the *function body*.

In our program example, the function body of **main()** contains only one line of code:

```
printf("This is my first C program");
```

If we remove everything between the opening and closing parentheses for **printf()**, we get:

```
printf()
```

Table 2.2   **Valid and Invalid Function Names**

Valid Names

StateTaxRate()	OK to mix upper- and lowercase
federal_tax_rate()	Underscore is OK
_special()	Leading underscore OK
port125()	Numbers OK here
Section12_4()	A little of everything is OK

Invalid Names

1stPort()	No leading digit characters
!Myfault()	No punctuation marks
%TaxRate()	No special characters
+Discount()	No math symbols
write()	Not invalid, but replaces the standard library function with the same name

which looks like it could have something to do with a function. If you think this looks like another function, you're exactly right. Our main() function does only one thing: call another function named **printf()**.

Without getting into too much detail at this point, **printf()** (that is, **print formatted**) is a standard C function that is used to display data on the computer screen. Every commercial C compiler comes with a printf() function. In our program example, **printf()** simply displays the words:

```
This is my first C program
```

on the screen.

Function Arguments

Notice how we passed the information we wanted displayed to the **printf()** function. We simply placed double quotes around the message we wished to display and placed that information between the opening and closing parentheses of **printf()**. Anything that appears between the parentheses of a function when it is called by the program is called a function argument. As we mentioned earlier, function arguments are used to pass to the function any information it might need to complete its task. A function can have zero or more function arguments.

In Program 2.3, **main()** has no function arguments while **printf()** has one argument—the string of characters surrounded by double quotes. It's not uncommon for functions to have three or four arguments, but more than six or seven is unusual.

After **printf()** displays the message on the screen, the closing brace of **main()** tells the computer that there's nothing more for this program to do, so the program ends. (The closing brace of **main()** marks the end of the program, remember?)

If the program ends with the closing brace of **main()**, where does the code for the printf() function come from? The answer to that question is the topic of the next chapter.

Does Program Style Matter?

C does not care how you write a program. You could, for example, write Program 2.1, which we saw earlier, as:

```
/*A simple C program*/
#include <stdio.h>main(){printf("This is my first C program");}
```

A C compiler doesn't know or care about programming style. *Programming style* refers to the way you place the C statements in the C source code file. There are, however, some style conventions that almost all C programmers follow.

Aligning Function Names

First, the function name and its associated parentheses appear on one line. In Program 2.1, the first line for the main() function is

```
main()
```

Nothing else appears on the line, even though we could put other parts of the function on the first line.

Placing Function Body Braces

Second, the opening brace ({) for a function body is placed at the extreme left edge of the screen. In Program 2.1, the opening brace appears immediately below the m in **main()**.

The closing brace (}) for a function aligns to the extreme left edge of the screen. This means that it, too, aligns with the opening brace for the function body and the first letter in the function's name. This alignment of the opening and closing braces makes it easy to see the code that belongs to the function.

Indenting Program Source Code

Third, any code that appears between the opening and closing braces is indented from the left side of the screen by one tab stop. Most text editors expand the tab key to eight blank spaces. For most programmers, this is too much wasted space. If your editor lets you set the number of spaces for the tab character (most editors do allow you to change this), try setting the number of spaces to three spaces. This is enough space to see the program indentation, but not enough to push longer code lines off the screen to the right.

Again, these are style conventions, not rules that are etched in stone. However, a lot of programmers use these style conventions and you should expect to see a lot of C code that follows them. You may want to consider adopting them for your own use, too.

Conclusion

In this chapter you learned how to create a broad design for a program (the five program steps), how to refine that design (with sideways refinement), what **main()** is and why it is important, and the basic parts of a C function. You also wrote your first C program. That is quite a bit to absorb in one chapter, so take the time to get comfortable with the concepts presented here. If you can get the sample program in Program 2.1 up and running properly, you've made a good start at understanding how to use your compiler properly and C programming in general.

Checking Your Progress

1. What are the five program steps?

The five program steps are:

1. Initialization
2. Input
3. Processing
4. Output
5. Shutdown

2. What is meant by sideways refinement?

The five program steps are broad guidelines for program development. In all but the most trivial cases, each of these steps needs to have greater detail to be useful. Sideways refinement is the process of adding greater detail to each of the five program steps.

3. What is an algorithm?

An algorithm is a recipe for a program task. An algorithm contains the details necessary to write the code to accomplish a given programming task. Any given program task (for example, sorting a list) probably has many different algorithms that will solve the task at hand. However, different algorithms have differing performance effects. One algorithm may be very fast but require large amounts of memory. Another algorithm may be slower, but use less memory. The programmer must balance these tradeoffs for the task at hand.

4. Why is **main()** a special function in C?

The main() function marks the starting and ending point for a C program. Every C program must have a main() function.

5. What is a function argument?

A function argument is a piece of information that is passed to the function so the function can complete its task. Some functions do not require function arguments, while others may have a half-dozen or more arguments. The number of function arguments depends upon the amount of external information the function needs to accomplish its task.

CHAPTER

3

The C Standard Library

HIS CHAPTER EXPLORES THE C STANDARD LIBRARY. YOU WILL LEARN what a standard library is, why it came about, and what its advantages are. Finally, you will discover some of the standard library's features, and learn how to use them in your own programs.

What Is the C Standard Library?

Simply stated, the *C standard library* is a collection of functions available for use in your programs. To appreciate what the C standard library (library from now on) is, you first need a little background information.

When C was developed in the early 1970s, its designers specifically omitted all *input and output (I/O)* facilities from the language. Virtually all other languages have specific keywords to handle program I/O. BASIC, for example, has PRINT, PUT, GET, READ, and WRITE for specific I/O operations. In C, there are no keywords for program I/O. For this reason, program input and output are not restricted by the syntax rules of the language. This enabled each compiler vendor to implement all I/O operations as they saw fit. A good-news-bad-news situation arose.

The good news was that compiler vendors could write I/O functions in a manner that was efficient for the hardware and operating system being used. This freedom from language restrictions permitted vendors to pull off some very creative tricks to get I/O operations accomplished. The bad news was that function names and function arguments varied from one vendor to the next. There was no consistency in the I/O functions. Changing compilers could mean a major editing job, plus having to learn a whole new set of I/O functions.

Part of the inconsistency in the I/O functions was based on legal issues. Early vendors feared that AT&T would sue them if they used the same I/O function names. As a result, one vendor might call the printf() function **putfmt()** while another called it **pformat()**. The same problems cropped up with other commonly used functions.

This lack of consistency became less of a problem when AT&T made it clear they had no intention of suing anyone that used the same function names or function arguments. Still, there were minor differences between the way vendors performed such important tasks as screen and file I/O, string processing, and data manipulation.

The ANSI Standard Library

When ANSI created the standard for the C language, it also had the foresight to define a standard library of C functions. Any compiler vendor claiming to have an ANSI-compliant compiler must supply about 150 standard library functions that are detailed in the ANSI standard for the C language. Each of these functions uses the same function name, the same function arguments, and produces the same results regardless of the compiler vendor or the hardware setup. In other words, 150 small programming tasks are already solved for you. As you will learn shortly, the ANSI standard C library provides a consistent solution for all of your basic I/O needs, plus solutions to many other common programming tasks.

The Rest of Your Library

In addition to the ANSI standard library, most vendors supply 300 to 400 functions with their compilers. For example, many vendors provide a library of graphics functions even though no graphics functions are standard in the ANSI standard library. Therefore, the ANSI standard C library is only the core of library functions available to you.

Since your compiler supplies most (if not all) of the ANSI standard library plus several hundred more functions, several hundred programming tasks are solved for you. Can you imagine trying to cope with a language that had keywords for that many language facilities?

From now on, this book refers to the ANSI standard library functions plus the functions provided with your compiler as the *standard library*. This collection of functions is a valuable programming resource designed to simplify your programming tasks.

Using Standard Library Functions

Most compiler vendors supply the standard library functions in several different library files. For MS-DOS machines, these library functions have the extension .LIB. For example, your compiler may have library files named CORE.LIB, MATH.LIB, and GRAPHICS.LIB. CORE.LIB might contain the ANSI standard library functions (**printf()** and so on) while MATH.LIB includes all of the math functions (square root, trigonometric functions, and so on). The GRAPHICS.LIB file probably contains the graphics functions (plot a point, draw a line, and so forth) provided with the compiler.

The functions could fit in one large file, but in most cases that's not too efficient. It's faster to load a 50k file than one that's 300k. Also, it's faster to find a specific function in a small file. Finally, with separate libraries you don't waste time loading and searching library entries that you don't need. After all, why wade through all the graphics library routines if your program doesn't use graphics?

Most compilers are set up to search one or more specific default LIB files. The default LIB files contain the functions that are used most often in a program. In most cases, the default LIB files contain the ANSI standard C library functions, plus some additional functions that might be used frequently.

Program 2.1 of Chapter 2 used the printf() function to display a simple message on the screen. The code for **printf()** did not appear in the program. You know that the code for the printf() function comes from the standard library, but you don't yet know how the compiler finds and uses the printf() code.

Object Code Files and Libraries

Chapter 1 explained that the compilation process begins when the compiler reads the C source code (for example, TEST.C written in ASCII). Upon completion, the compiler produces an intermediate code file called an object file. (These object code files have the extension .OBJ for MS-DOS machines.)

Just as you can compile a complete program, you can compile a single function. Suppose you write ten functions and then compile them. The result is ten object files. You can then use a librarian to combine these ten object (OBJ) files into a single library (LIB) file. (You learned what a librarian is in Chapter 1.) Note that the compiler can produce object code files for use in executable programs (EXE files). In addition, you can place the object code in a library for reuse in other programs.

How the Linker Uses Library Files

Recall that it is the linker's job to combine all intermediate code files into an executable program. In Program 2.1 it was the linker's responsibility to find the code for **printf()** in the standard library file and combine it with the rest of the compiled program.

Remember, the compiler leaves messages for the linker to resolve any code that does not appear in the program itself. In Program 2.1, the code for **printf()** was missing. This meant that the compiler had to leave a message in the object file telling the linker to supply the missing code. In other words, the linker had to search a library for the printf() code.

Linkers are notoriously slow, mainly because they have a lot of work to do. For example, with a standard library file that is 50k in size, the linker must open the library file, scan the file for the missing functions, calculate the proper addresses for the code, close the library file, and then write the program's executable file. (Most linkers must scan the object file twice, once to find the necessary functions and a second time to fill in the missing addresses.)

Figure 3.1 gives a simplified view of how a library file might be constructed. The first piece of information in this file is the number 115, the number of functions in the library. We will assume that this number takes up two bytes of file space. (The numbers on the right edge in Figure 3.1 indicate how many bytes are used for a given entry in the file.) Let's also assume that 21 characters can be used for the function name and four bytes for a number that tells the linker the byte-position of that function in the library file.

Figure 3.1

Constructing a
hypothetical library
file

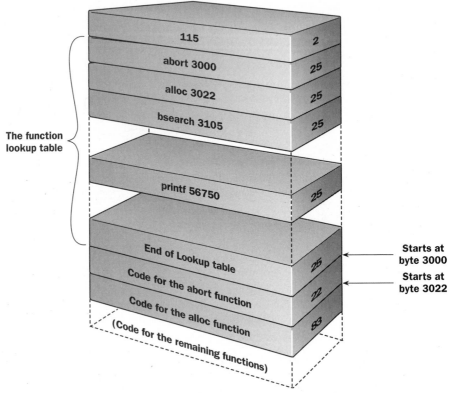

Using these numbers, the table that holds the function names and their
location in the file occupies 2,875 bytes (115 * 25 = 2,875). This section of the
file stores the library's *function table,* or dictionary. Adding the two bytes for
the first number in the table, the end of the function table is at byte position
2877. We will assume that the bytes between locations 2877 and 3000 in the library file store other information used by the linker.

Now suppose that the linker wants to find the alloc() function in the file.
The linker opens the file and reads the first two bytes to determine how
many functions are in the file. Because the linker knows that each entry
takes 25 bytes (the compiler and linker must be compatible), it knows how
many bytes it needs to read from the file for the function table.

The linker then searches the function table for a match on the missing
function. In our example, it eventually finds **alloc()** and the number 3022.
The number represents a byte index indicating the location of the code for

the alloc() function relative to the beginning of the library file. That is, the alloc() code is 3,022 bytes from the start of the library file.

In this simple scheme, you might use the next library entry to determine how many bytes to read for the function. For example, if you wanted to use the abort() function, the alloc() starting address tells you that the abort() function only uses 22 bytes of code (3,022 - 3,000 = 22). Once the linker has retrieved the missing code from the library file, it "links" the code to the program's object file. After the linker resolves all of the internal memory references, it writes out the executable program file. This becomes the program the user runs.

The actual process is considerably more complex than that described in this hypothetical example. However, the basic concepts are valid. You can consult your compiler's documentation if you want more specific details.

What Can Go Wrong?

What happens if the linker doesn't find a function in the library file's function table? Some linkers may search only one additional library file while others search every library file they can find. What your compiler does is something between these two extremes.

If the compiler cannot find a specific function, the linker needs to tell you about it. For example, suppose the linker cannot find a function named **myfunction()**. Usually, the linker issues an error message something like this:

```
Unresolved external: myfunction
```

This is the linker's way of saying: "I've tried to find **myfunction()**, but it's not where you told me to look." There are many ways that such an error can occur.

PROGRAMMING TIP. *Don't be confused if the error message does not reflect the exact function name. Many linkers place an underscore character in front of all variable and function names. If the linker cannot find **myfunction()** in either the library or source code object file, the error message will probably appear as **_myfunction()**. (Note the leading underscore character.) Don't be misled by this message; the linker is actually referring to **myfunction()**.*

Misspelling the function name is the most common cause of a linker error. For example, if you type **prontf()** instead of **printf()** in the source code, you will get an "unresolved external" error message. The same thing happens when you use **Printf()** instead of **printf()**. (Remember, C is case-sensitive; upper- and lowercase letters are distinct.)

COMMON TRAP. *Some compilers set a switch for the linker that turns case sensitivity either on or off. If the case-sensitivity switch is on and you use the wrong case, you will get "unresolved external" errors. This case-sensitivity switch is often set to some default state, especially for compilers with integrated development environments. If you have problems finding functions that are available in the standard library, try resetting the case-sensitivity switch.*

Another common mistake is forgetting to tell the linker to search the correct libraries. For example, if you are using some of the standard library math functions (**log()**, **sin()**, and so on) but forget to tell the linker to search the MATH.LIB library, you will get an "unresolved external" message. If you're like most of us, you'll get tripped up on both MATH.LIB and GRAPHICS.LIB.

It is always possible that the function does not exist in any of the library files. This often happens when you try to compile a C program from a magazine article. You type in the code only to discover that your library doesn't supply one of the functions used in the article.

In many such cases, both compilers have similar functions but the names are slightly different. Classic examples are Borland's findfirst() and findnext() functions versus Microsoft's _dos_findfirst() and _dos_findnext(). The functions are almost identical; only the names have been changed to confuse the innocent. A little digging around in your library documentation should help you find what you're looking for.

PROGRAMMING TIP. *Many compilers include a librarian as part of the compiler package. Most librarians have a switch that allows you to get a "table of contents" of the library. If you set the table of contents switch, the librarian lists all of the functions in the library. If you get an "unresolved external" error message, the function you need may be in another library. If your documentation doesn't tell you the library name for each function, use the librarian and the table of contents switch to inspect the library contents. The function may not be where you think it is.*

Keep in mind that your source code has precedence over library functions. If you write functions for your program that use function names from the standard library, the linker will *not* use those standard library functions. For example, if you write a function named **printf()**, the linker will use your code, not the code from the standard library. For this reason, you should not use standard library function names for your own function unless you are trying to replace standard library functions.

Linkers can issue many other error messages, but "unresolved external" errors are the most common ones. (By the way, compiler vendors are stingy with information about linker errors. The next time you're having cocktails with the president of one of these firms, you might request that they better document the linker errors.)

Table 3.1   **ANSI Standard Library Functions**

Character-processing Functions

isalnum	isalpha	iscntrl	isdigit
isgraph	islower	isprint	ispunct
isspace	isupper	isxdigit	tolower
toupper			

Date and Time Functions

asctime	clock	ctime	difftime
gmtime	localtime	mktime	time
strftime			

Input/Output Functions

clearerr	fclose	feof	ferror
fflush	fgetc	fgetpos	fgets
fopen	fprintf	fputc	fputs
fread	fseek	fsetpos	ftell
fwrite	getc	getchar	gets
freopen	fscanf	perror	printf
putc	putchar	puts	remove
rename	rewind	scanf	setbuf
setvbuf	sprintf	sscanf	tmpfile
tmpname	ungetc	vfprintf	vprintf
vsprintf			

Table 3.1   **continued**

String-processing Functions

atof	atoi	memchr	memcmp
memcpy	memmove	strchr	strcmp
strncmp	strcoll	strpbrk	strcspn
strcpy	strerror	strlen	strncpy
strcat	strncat	strrchr	strspn
strstr	strtod	strtok	strtol
strtoul	strxfrm		

Locale Functions

setlocale	localeconv

Math Functions

acos	asin	atan	atan2
ceil	cos	cosh	exp
fabs	floor	fmod	frexp
ldexp	log	log10	modf
pow	sin	sinh	sqrt
tan	tahn		

Memory-Management Functions

calloc	free	malloc	realloc

Miscellaneous Functions

abort	abs	atexit	bsearch
div	exit	genenv	labs
ldiv	longjump	memset	raise
rand	qsort	setjump	signal
srand	system	va_arg	va_start
va_end			

What's in the Standard Library?

You already know that the standard library consists of C functions: some ANSI standard functions plus others supplied by the compiler vendor. Table 3.1 lists some of the functions you can expect to find in the standard library.

Table 3.1 lists most of the ANSI standard library functions. When you first start programming in C, you will use many of the character- and string-processing functions. Notice that most of the character-processing functions begin with the letters "is" while most of the string-processing functions begin with "str."

You should take a few moments to review the library documentation that came with your compiler. Don't worry that you don't understand everything you see in the library manuals. That understanding will come in due time. For now, just look up some of the functions to get an idea of how they are described in your documentation.

Conclusion

The ANSI standard library forms the core of library routines supplied with your compiler. To that core your compiler vendor has probably added several hundred more functions. This book will help you to become aware of the wealth of programming resources available in the standard library. As you proceed through subsequent chapters, you will use many, but not all, of the functions presented in Table 3.1. While it's unlikely that any programmer has memorized every function in the standard library, the good programmers are familiar with most of them.

Before you start writing a new function, spend a few moments checking your standard library documentation. If you want to accomplish a commonly performed task, there's probably a library function to handle the job. Look before you write; you'll save time in the long run.

Checking Your Progress

1. What is a library?

   A library is a collection of functions that are supplied with a C compiler. Each function is written to solve a particular programming task. You can use these functions in your C programs; this saves you the time of writing them yourself.

2. What is the ANSI standard library?

The ANSI standard library is a collection of library functions that should be supplied with your compiler. These core library functions handle the basic programming tasks of data manipulation, I/O processing, and similar tasks.

3. What is the purpose of a linker?

A linker extracts precompiled code from a library and places that code into a program. When the linker is finished, the result is an executable program.

4. What does an "unresolved external" error message from the linker mean?

This error message occurs when the linker cannot find a function or variable that is used in your program. The two most common reasons for receiving this error message are misspelling the function or variable name and not telling the linker the correct library to search.

5. How many functions are in the standard library?

There is no fixed number of functions in the standard library. In the early days of C, some compilers only supplied a few dozen library functions. Today, most of the ANSI standard functions are supported in your library. In addition, competition has induced vendors to supply several hundred functions in their libraries. Even MS-DOS C compilers costing less than $100 supply several hundred library functions.

6. Why can't I use a **#include** for the library files?

The preprocessor is designed to read ASCII text files only; library files are object files. Also, even if the preprocessor could make sense of the object file, it would not know which functions should be kept in the program and which could be ignored. Simply stated, the preprocessor is not terribly clever and extracting library functions must be left to the linker.

CHAPTER

4

C Data Types

THIS CHAPTER DESCRIBES THE DIFFERENT TYPES OF DATA AVAILABLE IN C. (Although this chapter covers array variables, other complex data types are discussed later in the book.) You will also learn how to define a variable. Finally, you will write several short programs for obtaining data from the user.

Basic Data Types

There are four basic C data types identified by their associated keywords: **char**, **int**, **float**, and **double**. More formally, these four keywords are called type specifiers. A *type specifier* is one or more C keywords that describe the attribute list for a data type. The *attribute list* defines the characteristics of a data item.

For example, **int** is a C keyword and can be used as a type specifier for a data item, or variable. The attribute list for an **int** contains further information about what an **int** is on a particular machine. For example, for most MS-DOS compilers an **int** is a signed integer requiring two bytes of storage with specific minimum and maximum values. Therefore, an int attribute list for MS-DOS is a signed integer requiring two bytes.

However, an **int** on the Macintosh and most Unix machines is also a signed integer, but requires four bytes of storage and has different minimum and maximum values. That is, while an **int** is a type specifier in C, *its attribute list may vary from machine to machine.*

Even though the compiler needs a data item's full attribute list, this book simply refers to data items as data types. When the attribute list is relevant, it is mentioned in the text.

Four basic data types do not make a very impressive list. However, as you shall see shortly, you can modify the basic data types to create just about any data type you wish. Before you do that, however, you need to learn about the four basic types.

The char Data Type

A **char** is defined as a data type that is large enough to hold one character of the host character set. Most C compilers use the ASCII character set, which has defined characters from 0 through 127. Note that we can represent the entire ASCII character set in seven data bits (see Appendix A). Because eight bits is the normal unit of storage for small computers, a char data type is allocated one byte of storage. In a strict sense, the ASCII character set does not use the eighth bit. If you wish to use a single character as a constant in a program, it must be enclosed within single quotes. For example, suppose you have a variable named **exam** and you wish to assign the letter *A* into it. The assignment statement is:

```
char exam;
exam = 'A';
```

All character constants must appear within single quotes. In the previous example, if you didn't place the quotes around the letter *A,* the compiler would think you were trying to assign the value from a *variable* named **A** into **exam**.

Some programmers pronounce the word **char** as "care" while others pronounce it as "char," as in charcoal. I prefer the warm-fuzzy sound of "care" to the cold-prickly sound of "char." You should use whichever sounds best to you.

The double Data Type

A double data type is used to store floating-point numbers—that is, numbers that can have a decimal (3.14, for example), or fractional value. While ANSI does have a definition for floating-point numbers, most compiler vendors follow the IEEE Standard for these numbers. This means that you can represent a number within the approximate range of 2.2E-308 to 1.7E+308 using the double data type.

If you wish to see the defined range for your compiler's double data type, you can examine the float.h header file. The minimum floating-point value is associated with the constant DBL_MIN and the maximum value is associated with the constant DBL_MAX.

As you might guess, representing such large numbers requires more storage than a **char**. Most C compilers use eight bytes to store a double data type. The ANSI standard guarantees that a double data type will have ten digits of precision. However, in most cases, you can expect about 15 digits of precision. The precision of a floating-point number is associated with the constant DBL_DIG in the float.h header file.

Epsilon Error

You must exercise care when performing certain types of operations on floating-point numbers. Because most compilers use binary arithmetic to represent floating-point numbers, it is impossible to represent some numbers precisely (for instance, infinitely repeating fractions such as one-third). Because of this potential for imprecisely representing a floating-point number, ANSI specifies the magnitude of this error as DBL_EPSILON.

An *epsilon error* is a number such that 1.0 plus the epsilon error is detectable as not being equal to 1.0. (Some compilers offer Binary Coded Decimal, or BCD, floating-point options. BCD is useful in accounting and other packages where rounding error may be a serious problem.)

For example, suppose that DBL_EPSILON is equal to .000001. If you add the epsilon error to 1.0 (that is, 1.0 + .000001 = 1.000001), the compiler *can* detect that the resulting value is not equal to 1.0. However, if you add .00000099 to 1.0, the compiler may not be able to detect the difference between 1.00000099 and 1.0. Keep the epsilon error in mind if your program tests for very small floating-point numbers.

For the double data type, the epsilon error is quite small; approximately 1.0E-15 for compilers that use the IEEE floating-point standard. (The actual epsilon value is defined as DBL_EPSILON in the float.h header file.)

The float Data Type

The float data type is also used to store floating-point numbers. However, most compilers only use four bytes of storage for a **float**. Because of its reduced size, the range, precision, and epsilon error are all different. You can find the range (FLT_MIN and FLT_MAX), precision (FLT_DIG), and epsilon error (FLT_EPSILON) in the float.h header file. Note especially that the precision drops to as few as six digits and the range is approximately plus or minus 1.0E37.

Because of their lower precision and range, you normally wouldn't use the float data type. However, if you have a large array of floating-point numbers and memory is tight, you may have to use a float data type to fit the array in memory. Also, if you don't need the additional precision, it takes less room on disk to store files using the float data type. If you don't face memory or disk storage limitations, always use the double data type.

Some older C compilers are not very clever about sensing that a numeric constant is a floating-point number. For example, consider the code fragment

```
double x;
x = 5;
```

The default type specifier for constants is an integer (**int**). Some older compilers would create the numeric constant 5 as an **int** and try to force it into **x** as an **int**. This almost never works the way you want it to.

The solution is to write the assignment as

```
x = 5.0;
```

Because of the decimal point and zero following the 5, the compiler will recognize the data as a floating-point number and will create a floating-point data type. Even though modern compilers do not require the decimal point and zero after the numeric constant, you should use them with all floating-point constants. This will increase the portability of your code to older compilers, and will also make the code more readable.

The int Data Type

The int data type is used to store integer (whole) numbers. Integer data cannot have fractional values or a decimal point. The size of an **int** is often equal to the largest data register on the host machine. For the Intel family of processors (8086, 80286, and so on), the largest register pair is 16 bits. Because the high bit is used for the sign of the integer, the range is plus or minus 2^{15}, or -32,767 through 32,767.

On many machines, like the Macintosh (with the Motorola 680?0 processor family), the largest register holds 32 bits. Allowing for a sign bit, the numeric range is 2^{31}, or -2,147,483,647 to 2,147,483,647. In other words, even though the type specifier may be the same, the attribute lists for an **int** may vary substantially among machines.

Clearly, the range of an integer can differ a great deal from one processor to another. This means you should give some consideration to the range of the int data type if you expect to process large amounts of data. You can find the range for your integer data type by looking in the limits.h header file.

Data Modifiers

If C had just the four basic data types, it would be rather limited. Fortunately, you can use four modifiers with the basic data types to change their characteristics (attribute lists). These data modifiers—**long**, **short**, **signed**, and **unsigned**—may be applied to the four data types discussed earlier to modify the characteristics of a data item.

The long Modifier

You can apply the long modifier to the int and double data types. The ANSI standard guarantees that a long data type has a minimum value of -2,147,483,647 and a maximum value of 2,147,483,647. Using binary arithmetic with one sign bit, a **long** requires four bytes of storage. Note that an **int** and a **long** may have the same range of values on some machines. The limits.h header file can tell you the ranges of the int and long data types for your compiler.

The short Modifier

The short modifier is used to modify the int data type. The ANSI standard specifies that a **short int** has a range from -32,767 to 32,767. Therefore, a **short int** on the Macintosh is the same as an **int** on IBM-compatible machines.

Why would ANSI make this modified data type available? For one, it's faster to move two bytes of data around inside the processor than four bytes. Even though a machine may be capable of 32-bit data manipulation, it may be more efficient to move only 16 bits of data. By creating the short modifier, ANSI lets you pick which one is best for your particular situation. Also the data modifier makes it possible to use the same amount of storage for an **int** even though the processors are quite different.

The signed Modifier

The signed data modifier makes it explicit that the basic data type uses a sign bit. That is, the data type can accommodate both positive and negative numbers. If a variable is a **signed int**, it has the same positive and negative range as a regular **int**. (By default, an **int** is a signed data type.)

Why would ANSI create a new keyword for something that exists by default? Part of the reason is traceable to pre-ANSI compilers. Some vendors made the char data type a signed quantity while others made it an unsigned quantity (the data could not have a negative value). ANSI lets the vendor decide whether it is more efficient to use signed or unsigned characters. Using the signed keyword, you can adjust the attribute list of the data if needed.

The unsigned Modifier

The unsigned modifier specifies that no sign bit is used. Although an unsigned data type cannot have a negative value, the upper limit of its range of values is twice as high. For example, a 16-bit **unsigned int** can have a maximum value of 65,535 and a 32-bit **unsigned long int** can assume a maximum value of 4,294,967,295. An **unsigned char** can have a maximum value of 255. The unsigned modifier is a simple means of extending the range of positive numbers without using more storage. The unsigned keyword is used only with integral data types (**char** or **int**, not **float** or **double**).

Combining Data Types and Modifiers

This section examines how the data modifiers can be combined with the basic data types to alter the characteristics of the data. The valid combinations are shown in Table 4.1.

The first thing to notice is that the modifiers allow you to alter the range of values of the basic data types. The second thing to notice is that many of the modifiers duplicate other modified data types. For example, the data types **short**, **short int**, **signed**, **signed short**, and **signed short int** all have the same attribute lists for a given compiler. Each of the five alternatives behaves the same. However, the last one in the list documents itself better than the others. That is, defining a data item as a **signed short int** is more descriptive than using **signed** or **short**. Also, source code that uses the signed short int modified data type may prove easier to move from one machine to another.

Table 4.1 **Modified Data Types**

Modified Data Type	Description
char	Usually an eight-bit quantity capable of storing one character of the host character set. Normally it defaults to a signed quantity with a range of -127 to 127.
signed char	The same as char.
unsigned char	An unsigned char. The range is 0 to 255.
int	An integer data type. If the host machine has a 16-bit register set, the range is -32,767 to 32,767. If the host machine uses 32-bit registers, the range is the same as a long.
signed int	The same as int.
long	A signed integer with a range of -2,147,483,647 to 2,147,483,647.
long int	The same as long.
signed long int	The same as long.
unsigned long	An unsigned integer with the range 0 to 4,294,967,295.
unsigned long int	The same as unsigned long.
short	A signed integer with the range -32,767 to 32,767.
short int	The same as short.
signed	The same as short.
signed short	The same as short.
signed short int	The same as short.
unsigned	An unsigned integer. For 16-bit machines, the range is 0 to 65,535. For 32-bit machines, the range is the same as unsigned long.
unsigned int	The same as unsigned.
long double	Usually an 80-bit floating-point number. Consult your documentation for its properties.

Creating Program Variables

In this section you will learn how to use type specifiers to define a variable in C. In C you must define all variables before you can use them in a program. In order to define a variable, you need to learn how to create a variable name and you need to know the syntax rules for defining the variable.

Creating Variable Names

The rules for variable names are almost the same as those for function names presented in Chapter 3. They are

- Variable names may start with a letter or the underscore character (A-Z, a-z, _).

- Variable names cannot begin with a digit.

- Variable names cannot contain punctuation marks, math symbols, or other special symbols.

- ANSI only guarantees the first 32 characters to be significant.

- Do not use variable names that are the same as function names in the standard library.

By convention, C programmers write variable and function names in lowercase letters. (All of the standard library functions and **main()** must be lowercase.) Two alternative styles have emerged to help make variable names more readable.

One style uses the underscore character to break apart the variable name, as in video_memory_address. The other style uses initial capital letters, as in VideoMemoryAddress. (This form is particularly common in programming for Microsoft Windows.) Both forms are valid; use whichever you prefer. C doesn't care as long as the variable names conform to the rules. (If you plan to program under Microsoft Windows, the second form is preferred.)

Understanding C Expressions and Statements

Now that you know how to name variables, you need to know the syntax rules for defining variables. However, before defining variables, you must understand the basic elements of a C program statement.

The smallest syntactical unit in C is an *expression*. For example

```
a = c
```

is an expression. Expressions are comprised of operators and operands. An *operator* is a symbol (for example, the equal sign) that has special meaning in the language. In our example, the operator in the preceding expression is the equal sign, which is called the assignment operator. The assignment operator says to take the value of the right-hand operand (variable **c**) and assign it into the left-hand operand (**a**).

An *operand* is usually a variable name upon which the operator acts. In this case, variables **a** and **c** are operands. Because the assignment operator requires two operands, it is called a *binary* operator. C includes unary (one operand), binary (two operands), and ternary (three operands) operators.

C cannot act upon expressions alone, however; it needs a complete statement. A *statement* is simply one or more expressions terminated with a semicolon. For example

```
a = c;
```

is a statement that assigns the contents of variable **c** into variable **a**. The semicolon tells the compiler that the expression is complete and that it can now process and generate code for the statement. (Without the semicolon, the compiler wouldn't know when a complex expression was complete.)

Defining Variables in a Program

You are now ready to write the following simple program, which defines a variable, changes it, and displays the result.

Program 4.1   Square a Number

```
#include <stdio.h>

main()
{
    int number;
    number = 10;
    printf("The square of %d is %d", number, number * number);
}
```

Program 4.1 starts with the stdio.h header file, which all programs should include. First **main()** defines a variable named **number**. Let's see what happens when this line is compiled.

Defining a Variable

The compiler reads the line **int number;** into memory and then begins to examine it. First the compiler sees the int keyword. Then it sees the word

number followed by a semicolon. The semicolon tells the compiler it has a complete C statement that it can safely process.

By checking the syntax rules, the compiler also knows that you wish to define a variable named **number**. The int type specifier tells the compiler how much storage it takes to store **number** in memory. Because you have formed the statement properly, the compiler finds no syntax errors and proceeds to the next step.

Because you are defining a variable, the compiler next makes sure you don't have a variable named **number** already defined in the program. Although you and I know there are no other variables defined in the program, the compiler still needs to check. The compiler scans the list of variables in its symbol table and, upon finding no other variable named **number**, proceeds to the next step.

If the compiler does find another variable named **number**, it issues an error message something like "Multiple data definition" or "Duplicate declaration." (The precise error message varies from compiler to compiler.) You should find out why you have duplicate variable names, remove or change the name of one of the variables, and recompile the program. If the compiler does not find another number variable, it proceeds to the next step.

Storing a Variable

The compiler now asks the operating system for two bytes of storage (four bytes for 32-bit machines) for the **int**. If there is free memory available, the operating system passes back an address where the **int** can be stored. The compiler records this memory address in the symbol table along with the type specifier (**int**) and the variable name (**number**). Although this is a simplified view of how things work, the concept is correct.

The compiler now has all of the information it needs to find the variable in memory and use it when asked. The memory address tells the compiler where the variable is stored and the type specifier tells the compiler how many bytes are associated with the variable. That is, the type specifier tells the compiler how many bytes of memory must be accessed to retrieve the information in the variable. (Notice how the information in the data definition statement allows the compiler to construct an attribute list for the variable.)

Visualizing How number Looks in Memory

You can visualize the memory locations used by **number** with the help of Figure 4.1. This figure assumes that the operating system told the compiler that memory address 350,000 was available to store **number**. If you look at memory addresses 350,000 and 350,001 after executing the statement that defines **number**, the values found there contain whatever random bit pattern happens to be stored there. In other words, *C does not automatically initialize a* *variable to any particular value.* This means that after a variable is defined, it contains garbage. (This is why we show question marks for memory locations 350,000 and 350,001; we don't know what is stored there.)

Figure 4.1
Visualizing **number**

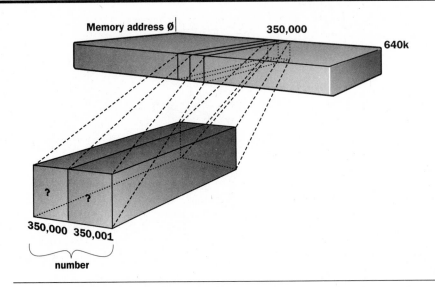

COMMON TRAP. *Unlike some programming languages, C does not often rely on defaults. In BASIC, for example, variables are defined when they are used and most dialects initialize variables to zero prior to using them. In contrast, C forces you to define a variable before you use it and only under special circumstances does the compiler initialize the variable to zero. Therefore, if you want to count something or perform some other operation that assumes the initial value of the variable is zero, you should explicitly set the initial value to zero before actual processing begins. Because C has so few data defaults, it's best to assume no default behavior. Otherwise, you may get unpredictable results.*

Understanding lvalues and rvalues

The *lvalue* of a variable is the address of where the variable is stored in memory. The *rvalue* of a variable is what is stored at that memory address. Notice that the lvalue (left value) is the memory address while the rvalue (right value) is what is stored at the lvalue memory address. Using lvalue and rvalue we can represent the information in Figure 4.1 in another, more convenient way, as shown in Figure 4.2. In this figure, the name of the variable (**number**) appears at the top of the two "legs" of the diagram. The lvalue forms the left leg and the rvalue forms the right leg.

Figure 4.2

lvalue and rvalue of
number
immediately after
definition

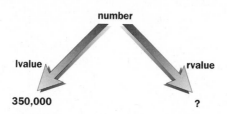

From the compiler's point of view, the lvalue of a variable is etched in
stone. After all, the compiler places the lvalue of the variable in the symbol
table. The lvalue is the only way the compiler can find where the variable is
stored in memory. The rvalue, on the other hand, is the value that the variable contains. You can change the rvalue of a variable whenever you need to.

Notice that Figure 4.2 conveys the same information as Figure 4.1: **number** is stored at memory location 350,000 (lvalue) and its content (rvalue) is
whatever happens to be stored there. (The question mark denotes that we
don't know what's stored there right now.)

Assignment Statement

The next statement in the program is

```
number = 10;
```

We already know this is an assignment statement using the assignment operator and two operands (**number** and the constant 10). The value of 10 is assigned into **number**. This seems simple enough, but consider what the
compiler does to generate the code to perform the assignment.

First, the compiler searches its symbol table to see if there is a defined
variable named **number**. If it cannot find the variable, the compiler must
issue an "Undefined variable" error message. Assuming that it does find
number, the compiler reads **number**'s type specifier (**int**) and its memory address (lvalue of 350,000). It then moves the value 10 into the two bytes starting at memory address 350,000. In other words, the assignment statement
places 10 into the rvalue of **number** at its lvalue of 350,000.

Figure 4.3 shows how **number** looks after the assignment statement is
processed. Notice that the rvalue of **number** is now 10. (The memory address
must remain fixed, otherwise the compiler couldn't find **number**.) The rvalue,
which reflects what **number** holds, has been changed by the assignment statement to 10.

Figure 4.3
lvalue and rvalue of
number after
assignment
statement

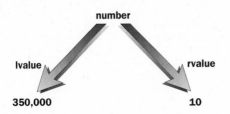

Using printf() with Multiple Arguments

The final statement in Program 4.1 uses **printf()** to display the original value of **number** and its square. The statement

```
printf("The square of %d is %d", number, number * number);
```

shows how **printf()** can be used to display the value of an integer. Notice the %d characters in the double-quoted character sequence. The %d characters have a special meaning to **printf()** and cause an integer value to be printed at that point in the double-quoted character sequence.

A percent sign (%) in a double-quoted character sequence is the first character of a *conversion character sequence*. That is, whenever **printf()** sees a percent sign within double quotes, it knows that the *next* character tells it how to convert the data associated with the conversion character. The letter *d* says to convert an integer variable to a decimal number. Therefore, the percent sign is saying: "Get ready to convert something" and the next letter tells **printf()** what conversion to perform. Table 4.2 shows some of the common conversion characters.

As you can see, **printf()** handles virtually any data you might wish to display.

Figure 4.4 shows how **printf()** uses its conversion characters and arguments to display the variables. Note how the first conversion character is used to convert the first argument after the double quotes. The %d causes **number** to be displayed as the decimal number 10. The second conversion pair is the second %d, which is used to display **number** multiplied by itself. (The asterisk in this example is the multiplication operator.) The output of the program looks like

```
The square of 10 is 100
```

Because there are no further statements in Program 4.1, the program ends upon reaching the closing curly brace of **main()**.

Table 4.2 **printf() Conversion Characters**

Character	Description
c	Converts **int** to an **unsigned char** and displays it.
d, i	Converts **int** to a signed decimal number.
o	Converts **int** to unsigned octal number.
u	Converts **int** to unsigned decimal number.
x, X	Converts **int** to unsigned hexadecimal number. If uppercase *X* is used, the hex letters are uppercase.
f	Converts **double** to decimal notation.
e,E	Converts **double** to scientific notation.
g, G	Converts **double** to the f or e style, whichever is shorter.
ld	Converts **long** to a signed decimal number.
lu	Converts **long** to an unsigned decimal number.
s	Displays an array of characters as a string.
p	Displays an lvalue as a memory address.
%	Displays a percent (%% displays %).

Figure 4.4
Relationship between **printf()**'s conversion characters and arguments

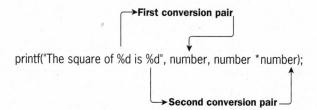

```
printf("The square of %d is %d", number, number *number);
```

Using the Comma Operator

In Figure 4.4, the arguments to **printf()** are separated by commas. You use the *comma operator* to separate expressions in C, but not to separate statements. You can use the comma operator to tell the compiler when one expression starts and another ends or to give two expressions the same attribute.

For example, suppose you wish to define two floating-point numbers. One way to define them is

```
double x;
double y;
```

However, you can use the comma operator to combine the two expressions like this:

```
double x, y;
```

This statement allows the compiler to distinguish between **x** and **y** and yet still define them with the attributes of a **double**. You will see many other uses for the comma operator as you progress through this book.

More on lvalues and rvalues

In this section you will modify Program 4.1 so you can see where **number** is actually stored in memory. Add the following new statement after the printf() function call in Program 4.1:

```
printf("\nThe lvalue = %p and the rvalue = %d", &number,
number);
```

Now run the program on your machine; the output should look something like this:

```
The square of 10 is 100
The lvalue = 8FF7:1000 and the rvalue = 10
```

You can learn several things from this new statement line.

Escape Sequences, the Newline Character, and printf()

The first character within the quotation marks is the backslash (\). When the compiler sees this character, it tells **printf()**: "Get ready, something special is coming up." Next you see the letter 'n'. These two characters taken together ('\n') are called the *newline escape sequence*. An *escape sequence* causes **printf()** and other functions to perform a specific action. As you might guess, a newline escape sequence causes whatever follows to be printed on the next (new) line. If you leave the newline sequence out of the printf() statement, the output will be one long line rather than two lines.

Note that the compiler views '\n' as a single character. The backslash simply draws the attention of the compiler; it is the letter 'n' that tells **printf()** and the compiler what to do next.

Actually, **printf()** must translate the newline character into two characters. Code must be generated to perform a line feed (ASCII character 10) followed by a carriage return (ASCII character 13). Chapter 21 covers the newline character in more depth.

Table 4.3 shows the available escape sequences.

Table 4.3 **Escape Sequences**

Escape Sequence	Description
\a	Alert. Causes an audible or visual alert.
\b	Backspace. Moves the active position on the display to the previous character.
\f	Form feed. Advances active position to the next logical page.
\n	Newline. Advances active position to the first position of the next line.
\r	Carriage return. Changes the active position to the first position of the current line.
\t	Tab. Advances active position to the next tab position.
\v	Vertical tab. Advances active position to next vertical tab position.
\\	Backslash. Displays a backslash.
\'	Single quote. Displays a single quote.
\"	Double quote. Displays a double quote.
??X	Trigraph. Advanced sequence for keyboards that are missing certain special characters in C.

Most of the escape sequences are fairly obvious. Technically, the double question mark does not belong in the table. However, it can be extremely useful.

Trigraphs

Some computers—especially European and Asian ones, and some U.S. computers with older keyboards—lack certain characters used in C. For example, some keyboards are missing the sharp sign (#). You can create such characters with a trigraph. For example, when the compiler sees the character sequence

```
??=    is the trigraph sequence for    #
```

it knows to interpret these three letters as the sharp sign. You will probably never have to use a trigraph, but you should be aware of them, just in case you accidentally string together a sequence of question marks and another character that happens to hit a trigraph sequence. Table 4.4 presents the trigraphs.

Table 4.4   **Trigraph Sequences**

Trigraph	Equivalent Character
??=	#
??(	[
??/	\
??)	]
??'	^
??<	{
??!	|
??>	}
??-	~

Printing Memory Addresses

You saw that the new output line for the modified program was

```
The lvalue = 8FF7:1000 and the rvalue = 10
```

(The numbers you see when you run the sample program most likely will be different.) Note that the %p causes the value 8FF7:1000 to be displayed. The %p conversion character causes most compilers to display memory addresses in hexadecimal (base 16) numbers. From this simple program modification, you now know exactly where the **int** named **number** is stored in memory. That is, you know its lvalue.

Using the Address-Of Operator

Take another look at the **printf()** you added to Program 4.1.

```
printf("\nThe lvalue = %p and the rvalue = %d", &number,
number);
```

Notice that the argument to the %p conversion character is **&number**. The ampersand (&) is called the *address-of* operator. You use this operator to obtain the lvalue rather than the rvalue of a variable. As you can see from the printf() statement, & is a unary operator: It only has one operand.

Normally you use **printf()** to display the rvalue of a variable. However, when you use the %p conversion character, you want to display the lvalue instead of the rvalue of the variable. Therefore, you need to pass the lvalue (the memory address) of **number** to **printf()**. To get the lvalue of a variable, simply place the address-of operator immediately before the name of the variable. The compiler then generates code to extract the lvalue rather than the rvalue of the variable.

Two Common printf() Mistakes

There are two common mistakes that people make when using **printf()**. The first is not to have a variable for each conversion character. For example, the expression

```
printf("the value of %d is %d", i);
```

has two conversion characters but only one variable. Most compilers do not catch this type of error. Because most C compilers use a stack mechanism for passing arguments to a function, *something* will be printed. However, it probably won't be the value you expect.

The second common mistake is to use the wrong conversion character for the variable to be displayed. Consider the following code fragment:

```
char c;
int i;

c = 65;
i = 1000;

printf("c is %c and i is %d", i, c);
```

This example uses the %c conversion character on **i** instead of **c**. Because **i** is an **int** (two bytes), the %c causes "half an **int**" to be displayed. We then try to use %d to print variable **c**. In this case, we will display the "other half" of **i** plus the character held in **c** as a single **int**. Clearly, the output won't look right.

The rules are simple; use the right conversion character for each variable and make sure that the number of conversion characters is equal to the number of variables.

Character Constants

As you saw earlier in this chapter, character constants must be enclosed within single quotes. A *character constant* is any symbol or value that is part of the host machine's character set.

The statements

```
char c;
c = 65;
```

use the numeric constant 65, which is the defined value for the letter 'A' in the ASCII character set. After the assignment statement, variable **c** holds the value 65, which is the ASCII value for the letter 'A'.

Likewise, the statements

```
char c;
c = 'A';
```

place the value 65 into **c**, but the intent of the assignment into **c** is much clearer than the previous example. Both forms, however, place the value of the character constant 'A' into **c**.

Obviously, life would grow tedious if you had to alter a program each time you wanted to display a different character constant. Program 4.2 allows you to enter a character from the keyboard.

Program 4.2   Get and Display a Character

```
#include <stdio.h>

main()
{
    char c;
    printf("Enter a character: ");

    c = getchar();

    printf("\nThe character is %c.", c);

}
```

When you run the program, press a letter and then press the Enter key. The getchar() function then gets the character entered by the user and assigns it into **c**. **getchar()** is a standard library function that gets a single character

from the keyboard. **getchar()** does not accept the input until after you press the Enter key.

In some situations, however, you may want the program to do something immediately when the user presses a key. Many programs that use menus react the instant you press a given key; they don't wait for you to press Enter. Let's modify Program 4.2 to do away with the Enter key.

Program 4.3 **Get and Display a Character (No Waiting Version)**

```
#include <stdio.h>

main()
{
    char c;
    printf("Enter a character: ");
    c = getch();
    printf("\nThe character is %c.", c);
}
```

We simply replaced the old input function **getchar()** with **getch()**. The getch() function is not part of the ANSI standard library and may not exist for all programming environments. However, all MS-DOS compilers have the getch() function and your library probably has an equivalent function.

When you press a key, **getch()** immediately assigns the letter into **c**. If you run the program, you will notice one other difference between **getchar()** and **getch()**: getch() does not display the letter you pressed. This could potentially be useful for entering passwords into a program.

If you need to display the letter that was pressed, you can use **printf()**. Many compilers have a function named **getche()** (get char with echo) that displays the letter that was pressed. Select whichever form suits your needs.

Conclusion

This chapter covered a lot of important material. Obviously, you can't do much with a program if you don't have any variables defined. Still, the most important concept is the relationship lvalues and rvalues have with variables. Remember, an lvalue is the (fixed) memory address of a variable. The rvalue is what a variable contains. You can change the rvalue of a variable, but not its lvalue. If you can understand this relationship, some of the more advanced C topics are going to be very easy.

Checking Your Progress

1. What is a type specifier?

A type specifier is one or more C keywords that describe a data type. In this chapter, you learned about the char, double, float, and int type specifiers.

2. What is a data type modifier?

A data type modifier is a C keyword that allows you to alter a basic type specifier. For example, the type specifier **int** has defined attributes for a given machine. On a 16-bit machine, the attributes for an int type specifier normally means a signed two-byte integer with the range -32,767 to 32,767. If you use the unsigned modifier to create an **unsigned int**, most of the attributes remain the same, but the range changes to 0 through 65,535.

3. What is an expression?

An expression is a combination of operators and operands. An operator causes the compiler to generate code that uses the operands in some specific way. Operands are the arguments that the operator acts upon. Operands are normally variables or constants. C has unary, binary, and ternary operators.

4. What is a statement in C?

A statement in C is one or more expressions terminated by a semicolon. A statement is a complete syntactic unit designed to accomplish some specific action or task.

5. What are lvalues and rvalues?

The lvalue of a data item is its address space in memory. The rvalue is what is stored at that lvalue.

6. Do constants have lvalues?

Constants to do not have associated lvalues. It is syntactically incorrect to take the lvalue of a constant, as in

```
i = &10;/* wrong */
```

7. What does the address-of operator do?

The address-of operator is a unary operator designed to find the lvalue of a variable.

8. Is the following statement valid?

```
&i = &i + 1;
```

No. The statement attempts to increase the lvalue of **i** by 1. If the compiler allowed this, it would no longer know where **i** was stored in memory.

9. Compare the following two statements.

```
i = j;     /* Statement 1 */
i = &j;    /* Statement 2 */
```

Statement 1 is a "default" form of assignment statement. The rvalue of one variable (**j**) is copied into the rvalue of a second variable (**i**). Statement 2 is a nondefault assignment statement. The lvalue of **j** is assigned into variable **i**. The address-of operator is used to override the default assignment form.

CHAPTER

5

Data Arrays

T HIS CHAPTER EXPLORES HOW TO USE DATA ARRAYS IN C, ALONG WITH some of the standard library functions that use data arrays. Most of these library functions are used either to process character data or to convert data from one form to another.

Aggregate Data Types

Thus far, we have only discussed simple variables. Programming projects, however, often require you to use more complex data types. In any programming language, an *array* is a group of identical data types that can be referenced as a single unit. Each unit of the array group is called an *element* of the array. Arrays are one example of an *aggregate data type*.

Suppose you wish to create an array of ten integer numbers, using the word "grades" for the array name. To define a ten-element integer array named **grades[ ]**, use the statement

```
int grades[10];
```

This statement causes the compiler to generate code for ten consecutive integers that can be referenced via the variable named **grades[ ]**. (We always follow an array name with empty brackets throughout this book. This makes it easy for you to tell we are discussing an array rather than a simple variable or a function.)

The general form for an array is

```
type_specifier variable_name[elements];
```

where:

type specifier	=	a C keyword for the array type (for example, **char**, **int**, **double**, etc.)
variable_name	=	the name of the array variable
elements	=	the number of data units in the array

When you define an array variable, you must supply the number of elements you want the array to have. There is no default array size in C like there is in some other languages.

Starting Array Elements with 0

All arrays in C start with element 0 of the array. This can cause some trouble if you are used to programming in a language that has element 1 as the first element. For example, suppose you define a character array

```
char name[10];
```

and then you try something like

```
name[10] = 65;    /* 65 is the letter A in ASCII */
```

The compiler does not complain about this assignment even though it is an error. Although **name[ ]** is defined for 10 elements, array elements start with 0, so only elements 0 through 9 are valid array elements for **name[ ]**. Therefore, the last valid array element is **name[9]**.

The N – 1 Rule

C does not check array boundaries. That is, a C compiler lets you access an element of an array that does not exist. Therefore, you should keep the N – 1 rule in mind when working with arrays in C: *For any array definition of size N, the valid elements for the array extend from 0 to N – 1.*

The most troublesome problem with the N – 1 rule is that you may not know you violated it. If nothing useful is stored after the array in memory, you might just overwrite an "unused" piece of memory. The program even appears to run correctly. Inevitably, however, as soon as someone else tries to use the program, something "useful" in memory gets stomped on and the system crashes.

So remember the N – 1 rule: it may save you some hair-pulling down the road.

Using an Array

Let's look at Program 5.1, which uses a character array.

We begin by including the stdio.h header file, as usual. (From now on, we won't mention including stdio.h. All programs should include this file, anyway.) Next we define a ten-element character array. We then print a prompt on the screen to tell the user to type in his or her first name.

Program 5.1 **Using a Character Array**

```
#include <stdio.h>

main()
{
    char name[10];
    printf("Enter your first name: ");
    gets(name);

    printf("\nWelcome to C, %s", name);
}
```

The gets() Function

The program then calls the gets() function using **name[]** as its argument. The gets() function is part of the standard library and is used to get a sequence of characters from the keyboard. As the user types in letters at the keyboard, **gets()** places those letters into the character array. **gets()** also allows the user to use the Backspace key to correct any errors as he or she enters the letters.

The user must press the Enter key to indicate he has finished typing. Pressing the Enter key causes the keyboard to send a newline character to the program. When **gets()** sees the newline character, it knows the input is complete and *substitutes* a null termination character for the newline character entered by the user.

The Null Termination Character

The null termination character is created by a backslash-0 character sequence:

```
'\0'          /* the null termination character */
```

Although this looks like it would take two bytes to store it, the compiler knows about the null termination character and converts the backslash-0 character pair into a single-byte null termination character. (For most compilers, the null termination character has an ASCII value of 0. However, the ANSI standard only standardizes the *interpretation* of the null termination character, not the actual value of the character itself.)

If I type my first name into the program and press the Enter key, the name[] array in memory looks like that shown in Figure 5.1.

Figure 5.1
Memory image of
name[]

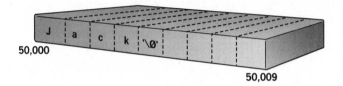

Notice that my name ends with the null termination character. Because we have assumed that the array was placed at memory location 50,000, the memory space allocated to the name[] array extends from memory location 50,000 to 50,009. (Looks like the old N - 1 rule, right?) In Figure 5.1, however, we are using only elements 50,000 through 50,004, including the null termination character. (The remaining bytes in the array are allocated to **name[]**, but not used in this example.) As we shall see in the next section, the null termination character can be very useful.

The Character String

One of the most common arrays used in C is an array of characters. An array of character data that ends with a null termination character is called a *character string*.

We can display a character string by using the %s conversion character in a call to **printf()**. Figuring out how **printf()** displays a character string (just string from now on) isn't too difficult. **printf()** simply looks at each element of the string and displays it on the screen. When **printf()** sees the null termination character, however, it knows there are no more characters to display. This is exactly what is done in Program 5.1.

The gets() function provides a simple way to get string data from the user and the %s conversion character of **printf()** provides the means to display the string. Simple.

Something Special about Array Names

If you look at Program 5.1 closely, you can see that we used the array name as an argument in both function calls. Also note that we did not use anything else with the array name—for example, there are no array brackets, element size, operators, or anything else. This happens in both function calls in the program:

```
gets(name);
printf("\nWelcome to C, %s", name);
```

So what is being passed to the two functions?

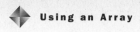

When an array name is an argument of a function call and it is not fully stated, it is the lvalue of the array that is being passed to the function. A *fully stated* array reference is one where the array name is followed by its full complement of brackets. In this case, a fully stated form for **name[]** would be **name** followed by a set of brackets. In other words, if we omit any of the brackets that were present in the data definition, it is not a fully stated array reference.

If the array that is passed to a function is like that shown in Figure 5.1, it is the value 50,000 that is passed to **gets()** and **printf()**. In other words, it is the lvalue of the array that is passed to the function. This makes sense, if you think about it.

Consider the gets() function for a moment. Inside **gets()**, the code is written in such a way that **gets()** expects an lvalue to be sent to it. There is no way that **gets()** (or any other function) can check—or even cares about—the name or size of an array. **gets()** simply assumes that it has been passed the starting address (lvalue) of a character array.

When the user presses a key, **gets()** shoves the character into the memory address passed to it. **gets()** then moves to the next memory address and waits for the user to press the next key. When the next key is pressed, it places that character into the new memory location (the lvalue plus 1, or 50,001 in Figure 5.1). This process continues until the user presses the Enter key.

In Program 5.1, what happens if the user types in a name with more than ten characters? **gets()** could care less; it keeps stuffing characters into memory until the user presses the Enter key. You might even get the first chapter of *Gone with the Wind* typed in before the system crashed.

What if you pass something other than an array name? For example, what would happen if you passed the lvalue of an **int**? If an **int** uses two bytes of storage, the lvalue of the **int** is a valid memory address only for those two bytes. However, **gets()** doesn't know that only two bytes of storage are valid. If you start typing in your name, **gets()** doesn't care. It will place the first two characters in the **int** and then start trashing whatever comes next in memory.

The rule is simple: *there is no array boundary checking in C*. Make your character arrays large enough to hold a reasonable amount of input that might be typed by the user plus the null termination character. You must also make sure you are passing a proper lvalue to **gets()**.

Let's check to see what you've learned about array names. What would happen if you called **gets()** using the following statement?

```
gets(&name[0]);
```

We need to determine what this statement sends to **gets()**. Let's break things down a bit. First, the argument to **gets()** is more than just the array name by itself. The address-of operator is present and there are brackets and an array element index following the array name. Therefore, we should not assume that we have sent the starting address to the function.

Next, let's figure out where element **name[0]** is in memory. If you look at Figure 5.1, you can see that **name[0]** starts at memory location 50,000 (the lvalue of **name[0]**). You can also see that the array contains the letter 'J' at that address. However, because we placed the address-of operator in front of **name[0]**, we are telling the compiler to generate code to send an lvalue of **name[0]**, *not* its rvalue. Therefore, we must end up passing the lvalue of **name[0]** to **gets()**. In this case, we end up passing the same lvalue (50,000) as before. **gets()** will function exactly as it did before.

Note what this means: An array name by itself as an argument in a function call is the same as the memory address of the starting element of the array. That is, the two statements

```
gets(name);

gets(&name[0]);
```

are equivalent statements and cause the compiler to generate identical code.

Let's try another example. What happens if we called **gets()** using the following statement?

```
gets(name[0]);
```

In this case, there is no address-of operator before the array name. Also, because we have the brackets following the array name, this is a fully stated array reference. This means that we are sending the rvalue of **name[0]** to the gets() function. Using Figure 5.1 as an example, the letter 'J' is passed to **gets()**. (After all, if we don't explicitly use the address-of operator and it is a fully stated array reference, it is the rvalue of **name[0]** that is used.)

What does **gets()** do with the value it receives? Remember, **gets()** and all other library functions are very trusting. The function trusts that you passed it a valid memory address where it can store safely all characters entered from the keyboard. Therefore, what **gets()** sees is what it *thinks* is the address of a character array starting at memory location 74. (The letter 'J' has an ASCII value of 74.) Whatever the user types in gets stored in memory starting at memory address 74. Not good.

Chances are that a low memory address like 74 is near the start of the operating system software. You may end up writing your name into the middle of the operating system! Don't feel bad if you didn't figure out what would happen. I doubt if there is a C programmer alive who hasn't customized his or her operating system at least once by passing an rvalue rather than an lvalue.

Now that we're on a roll, let's try one more example. Suppose we add the following two statements to Program 5.1. Let's also assume that we typed my first name in response to the first call to **gets()**.

```
printf("Enter a second name: ");
gets(&name[3]);
```

Place these two statements after the original call to the printf() function. What would the contents of the character array look like?

Because of the N - 1 rule, element number 3 is actually the fourth element of the string. Because we placed the address-of operator in front of the array name, we are passing the lvalue of the fourth element of the name[] array. Therefore, the lvalue value passed to **gets()** is 50,003. If I enter my name again, the altered memory image is that shown in Figure 5.2.

Figure 5.2
Altered memory
image of **name[]**

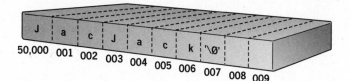

Notice that we have overwritten the original letter 'k' in my name. Because **gets()** started placing the new characters at location 50,003, printing the string with **printf()** now shows the name "JacJack".

String data is used a lot in C. Make sure you understand how character arrays, the null termination character, array names, lvalues, and rvalues all relate to string processing before you continue reading.

Remember that it is the lvalue of a variable that allows the compiler to keep track of where the variable is stored in memory. If you try to change the lvalue of a variable, the compiler must issue an error message. The exact wording of the error message varies among compilers, but it will be something like "lvalue required" or "different levels of indirection".

For example, consider the following code fragment:

```
char name[30];
name = 'J';          /* WRONG! */
```

If you try to compile code like this, an "lvalue required" error message should be given. The problem is that we are trying to make the letter 'J' (ASCII 74) the lvalue of **name[]**. The compiler knows that if it allowed this, it would not be able to find **name[]** again.

Another example of the same error is

```
int i;
&i = 'J';                /* WRONG...again! */
```

This code fragment should generate exactly the same type of error message. Again, we are trying to change the address of where **i** is stored in memory. That is, we are trying to change where **i** actually is stored in memory to memory address 74. Not a good thing to do.

Assignment statements result in an rvalue of a variable being assigned into the rvalue of another variable. Any attempt to change the lvalue of a variable should generate an error message.

Defining Other Arrays

The syntax rules for defining array data types do not change regardless of the data type used. The following code shows how we might define several different types of arrays:

```
#include <stdio.h>

main()
{
    char    name[30];
    int     grades[10];
    long    index[100];
    double  averages[4];

    /* The rest of the program */

}
```

In this code, we define four arrays, each with a different type of data. As you can see, the syntax rules for each data definition are the same. Each definition has a type specifier (**char**, **int**, **long**, and **double**), the name of the array (for example, **grades**), and an array size (**[30]**).

How Big Is an Array?

Let's take the code we saw above and turn it into a program. See Program 5.2.

Program 5.2   Sizes of Different Arrays

```c
#include <stdio.h>

main()
{
    char    name[30];
    int     grades[10];
    long    index[100];
    double  ave[4];

    printf("\nBytes allocated for name[] = %d", sizeof name);
    printf("\nBytes allocated for grades[]  = %d", sizeof
        grades);
    printf("\nBytes allocated for index = %d", sizeof index);
    printf("\nBytes allocated for averages[] = %d", sizeof
        ave);
}
```

If your compiler runs on a 16-bit processor, the output from the program looks like this:

```
Bytes allocated for name[] = 30
Bytes allocated for grades[] = 20
Bytes allocated for index[] = 400
Bytes allocated for averages[] = 32
```

The numeric values tell you how much memory has been defined for each of the arrays in the program.

The sizeof Operator

Notice the arguments to the various printf() function calls in Program 5.2. The sizeof operator determines the number of bytes of storage allocated to a variable. The general form is:

```
sizeof variable_name
```

Because **sizeof** has only one operand, it is a unary operator. If you want to use the sizeof operator with a type specifier, you *must* place parentheses around the operand. For example,

```
sizeof (int)
```

determines the amount of storage allocated for an **int** data type.

PROGRAMMING TIP. *Using sizeof can be a little confusing. You must use parentheses when the operand for sizeof is a type specifier. However, parentheses are not required with sizeof when it is used with variable names. To avoid this confusion, most C programmers always parenthesize the operand for the sizeof operator. The parentheses allow you to use type specifiers or variable names as the operand for sizeof.*

What would you get if you divided the size of the data item by the size of each element in the array? To find out, try Program 5.3.

Program 5.3   **Using the sizeof Operator**

```
#include <stdio.h>

main()
{
    char    name[30];
    int     grades[10];
    long    index[100];
    double  ave[4];

    printf("\nElements in name[] = %d",
            sizeof name / sizeof (name[0]) );
    printf("\nElements in grades[]  = %d",
            sizeof grades / sizeof (grades[0]) );
    printf("\nElements in index = %d",
            sizeof index / sizeof (index[0]) );
    printf("\nElements in  averages[] = %d",
            sizeof ave / sizeof (ave[0]) );
}
```

When I ran the program, the output was

```
Elements in name[] = 30
Elements in grades[] = 10
```

```
Elements in index[] = 100
Elements in aver[] = 4
```

Hmmm. Seems that I get the number of elements in each array. This is because we took the total storage space allocated to the array (for example, **sizeof index**) and divided it by the storage space required for one element of the array (**sizeof index[0]**). Because **sizeof index** yields a value of 400 and **sizeof index[0]** gives a value of 4, the result is 100. This is, of course, equal to the number of elements in the array.

In Program 5.3 we purposely mixed the two forms of **sizeof** (with and without parentheses) to show you that either form works in this example. For the rest of this book, however, we will always place parentheses around the operand for the sizeof operator.

Two-Dimensional Arrays

While simple arrays are great for lists of data items, many programming tasks involve manipulating tables of data. Data tables require a row-column format, or a two-dimensional array. The general form for defining a two-dimensional array is

```
type_specifier   variable_name[element1][element2]
```

The information is the same, except we have added another element size specification. For example,

```
double students_t[100][50];
```

defines an array of **double**s named **students_t[][]** that is 100 x 50 in size. In terms of a table, the **students_t[][]** array can have 100 rows and 50 columns. How many bytes of storage are allocated to **students_t[][]**? Program 5.4 can give us the answer.

On my computer, the answer displayed was 40,000. This seems to be correct because there are 5,000 elements (100 x 50) and each **double** takes eight bytes on my machine, or 40,000 bytes of storage (40,000 = 5,000 x 8).

If you typed the program in and didn't pay close attention to it, you might have typed in the %d conversion character in **printf()** instead of %u. If you did, the answer would be shown as a negative number. Why? Because %d is used to show signed integer numbers. On my machine, a signed integer has a range from -32,767 to 32,767. Because 40,000 exceeds the upper limit for a signed integer, the sign bit is turned on. (You cannot represent the value 40,000 in binary without using the 16th bit.) This is why it appeared as a negative number.

Program 5.4   **Using a Double-Dimensioned Array**

```c
#include <stdio.h>

main()
{
    double students_t[100][50];

    printf("\nByte allocated to students_t = %u",
        sizeof (students_t));
}
```

To properly display the storage size of the array, we must use the %u conversion character. Also, because **sizeof** cannot return a negative value, %u is the proper conversion character to use whenever you display a value using the sizeof operator.

Storing Two-Dimensional Arrays in Memory

It will help you better understand arrays if you can picture how the compiler places them in memory. We probably envision a two-dimensional array as shown in Figure 5.3.

Figure 5.3

A human view of a two-dimensional array

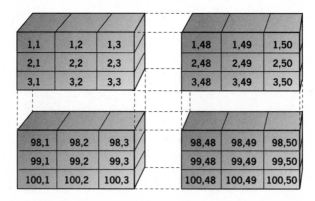

We tend to view our sample array as a matrix with 50 columns across and 100 rows deep. Even if we adjust our thinking for the zero-based arrays used in C, we still would think of the array as running from 0 through 49 across and 0 through 99 down.

To a computer, however, the array is simply one long vector of storage. The computer's view of the array is shown in Figure 5.4.

Figure 5.4

A computer's view of a two-dimensional array

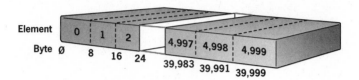

In Figure 5.4, the compiler stores the array in memory as one long sequence of bytes. Because the array is 100 x 50, the compiler knows that there are 5,000 total elements in the array. The type specifier **double** tells the compiler how big each element of the array is. Therefore, it knows that element 0 in the array starts at memory location 0 and extends through location 7. The second element of the array starts at memory location 8 and extends through location 16, and so on.

In other words, double-dimensioned arrays are stored as one continuous vector of memory. It is the compiler's responsibility to create the proper indexes into the vector from your program code.

Arrays and Scalars

The question is, how does the compiler find the value at **students_t[1][0]**? It finds the memory address by using the type specifier for the array and the scalar of the matrix. All data types have scalars. The *scalar* for a double-dimensioned array is the second array dimension times the size of the data type (**double**).

For the matrix in our example, the scalar is

```
scalar = second dimension x size of the data type
       =        50          x         double
       =        50          x            8
       =       400
```

You can think of the scalar size for an array as the point where the compiler "folds" the memory vector. That is, if we took the memory vector shown in Figure 5.4 and "folded" it every 400 bytes, it would look very similar to Figure 5.3. Figure 5.5 shows how this folding looks assuming the array starts at memory location 0.

Figure 5.5

Memory image of
array vector after
"scalar folding"

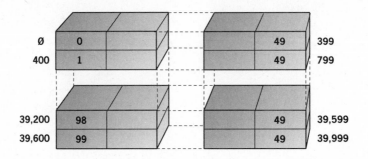

From Figure 5.5, you can see that element **students_t[1][0]** starts at memory location 400. (The numbers on the left and right sides of Figure 5.5 show the byte count for the first and last elements of each row of the array.) You should be able to convince yourself that element **students_t[1][1]** is stored at memory location 408. Hmmm. There seems to be a pattern here. To find the memory location for an individual element in the array, the formula is

```
address = [scalar * row] + [type specifier * col]
```

Therefore, to find the address of element **students_t[98][0]**, the address is

```
[scalar * row] + [type specifier * col]
  [400 * 98]   +     [double * 0]
  [400 * 98]   +     [8 * 0]
  [39,200]     +     [0]
   39,200
```

Therefore, element **students_t[98][0]** is stored at memory location 39,200. (We have assumed that the array starts at memory location 0. If it started at memory location 10,000, we would need to add that value to the result to find the proper spot in memory.)

Fortunately, you don't have to calculate the memory addresses to access the array. The compiler, however, does have to perform these calculations when you reference an array. If you understand how scalars work, it can make some of the more advanced C programming techniques much easier to master and may prove useful in program debugging.

Initializing Character Arrays

Frequently you need to create an array to hold a list or table of data. Just as often, the list or table needs to be filled in with a set of values. Establishing a set of values as part of the data definition is called *initialization* of the array. In this section, you will learn how to initialize an array.

Suppose you want to create an array that contains a list of names. Obviously, this list will be a list of character strings. Program 5.5 shows how to initialize a character array.

Program 5.5   Initializing a Character Array

```
#include <stdio.h>

main()
{
    char names[3][30] = {
        "Dave Cooper",
        "Don Dudine",
        "Chuck Lieski"
    };

    printf("\nThe first name is %s", names[0]);
    printf("\nThe second name is %s", names[1]);
    printf("\nThe third name is %s", names[2]);

}
```

In Program 5.5, we defined **names[ ][ ]** so it can hold three names of up to 30 characters each. We then initialized the three names using double-quoted strings. Program 5.5 shows you several things that you need to remember when initializing character arrays.

First, each string is surrounded by double quotes. Doing this causes the compiler to generate code for character string data and place it in the proper array elements. Because the compiler places a null termination character at the end of each name during initialization, we can use the elements in the arrays as character string data.

Second, the values used to initialize the array comprise what is called an initializer list. An *initializer list* contains the values that the data item will hold immediately after the data item has been defined.

An opening brace must appear before the first item in the initializer list. A closing brace must appear after the last item in the initializer list. Finally, the closing brace must be followed by a semicolon.

Third, a comma operator appears *between* each double-quoted string in the initializer list. Note that there is no comma operator before the first or following the last item in the initializer list.

When you run the program, it displays the names in the initializer list. But how does the printf() statement work? How does the compiler process the printf() argument **names[0]**? It's all done using scalars.

Earlier, we saw an equation that stated that a scalar for a two-dimensional array is defined as

```
scalar = second dimension x size of the data type
```

When the compiler saw the definition of **names[][]**, it took the second element size (30) and multiplied it by the size of a **char** to create a scalar size of 30. All the compiler has to pass to **printf()** is the names[] element times the scalar size. For example, even though "Dave Cooper" uses only 12 bytes (one for the null termination character, remember?), 30 bytes have been allocated to it. Therefore, using the N - 1 rule, Dave's name extends from byte 0 through 29 even though we don't fill in all of the space allocated to his name.

Let's assume that the compiler placed the names[][] array starting at memory location 40,000. The call

```
printf("\nThe first name is %s", names[0]);
```

is treated by the compiler as though it were

```
printf("\nThe first name is %s", 40,000 + (0 * scalar));
```

which reduces to

```
printf("\nThe first name is %s", 40,000 + 0);
```

Therefore, the first call to **printf()** sends the lvalue of **names[0][0]**. Let's look at the second call to **printf()**. Dave's names runs from 40,000 through 40,029, so we should expect Don's name to start at memory location 40,030. The next three lines show how the compiler calculates what to send to **printf()**:

```
printf("\nThe first name is %s", names[1]);
printf("\nThe first name is %s", 40,000 + (1 * scalar));
printf("\nThe first name is %s", 40,000 + (1 * 30));
printf("\nThe first name is %s", 40,030;
```

which is exactly where Don's name starts in the initializer list. You should also be able to convince yourself that the last name in the list becomes

```
printf("\nThe first name is %s", names[2]);
printf("\nThe first name is %s", 40,000 + (2 * scalar));
```

```
printf("\nThe first name is %s", 40,000 + (2 * 30));
printf("\nThe first name is %s", 40,060);
```

Because Don's name extends from memory address 40,030 through 40,059, Chuck's name should begin at memory address 40,060. It looks like all the array calculations work out correctly.

You sharpies out there are probably asking: "I thought you said that the lvalue is sent to a function when the only array name is used. In this program, we have an array name plus an element index." True, but the array name is not fully stated. To be fully stated, the argument must have both dimensions present (**names[1][0]**). Because the argument is not fully stated (that is, both dimensions are not given in the function call), it is the lvalue that is sent to **printf()**.

If you want to convince yourself that the above is true, try changing a **printf()** in Program 5.5 so that it is fully stated, such as

```
printf("\nThe second name is %s", names[1][0]);
```

and see what happens.

The Importance of Scalars

We have shown how the compiler uses the scalar to find the proper lvalue to send to **printf()** in Program 5.5. Our equation suggests that it is the second dimension in a two-dimensional array that plays the most important part in determining the scalar value. In fact, if you change the first part of the array definition in Program 5.5 to

```
char names[][30] = {
    /* The rest of the initializer list */
```

the compiler can still generate the code correctly. (Notice that we have omitted the first element size.) In this case, the compiler can determine the first element's size by counting the number of items in the initializer list. It cannot, however, create the data properly without the second element size. The second element size is crucial for calculating the scalar size for two-dimensional arrays.

Another variation in Program 5.5 might be

```
char names[4][30] = {
    "Dave Cooper",
    "Don Dudine",
    "Chuck Lieski"
};
```

In this case, the compiler allocates enough memory for four names, but only initializes the first three. The compiler, however, still allocates enough memory to hold four names. You could use **gets()** to get a fourth name from the user.

Initializing Numeric Arrays

Initializing numeric arrays is similar to initializing character arrays, except numeric rather than character data is used in the initializer list. An example is presented in Program 5.6.

Program 5.6 **Squaring a Table of Numbers**

```
#include <stdio.h>

main()
{
    double squares[5][2] = {
        1, 1,
        2, 4,
        3, 9,
        4, 16,
        5, 25
    };
    printf("\n%g squared is %g", squares[0][0],squares[0][1]);
    printf("\n%g squared is %g", squares[1][0],squares[1][1]);
    printf("\n%g squared is %g", squares[2][0],squares[2][1]);
    printf("\n%g squared is %g", squares[3][0], squares[3][1]);

}
```

Notice the similarities between the initializer lists in Program 5.6 and Program 5.5. The equal sign is followed by an opening brace, the comma operator separates elements in the list, a closing brace marks the end of the list, and a semicolon terminates the statement. The most noticeable difference is that numeric constants do not need to have a delimiter (strings use double quotation mark delimiters) surrounding the element values.

You can use delimiters with numeric data if you wish. For example, you could define the squares[][] array with the statement

```
double squares[6][2] = {
    {1, 1},
```

```
        {2, 4},
        {3, 9},
        {4, 16},
        {5, 25}
    };
```

The noticeable difference above is that the elements in the list are grouped together using braces as a delimiter rather than double quotes, as was the case in Program 5.5. However, the purpose of the delimiter is the same. Just as the double quotes told the compiler how many characters to place in each element of the array, the braces serve to delineate the numeric pairs in the array. You can initialize a numeric array with or without delimiters.

The only remaining difference between Programs 5.5 and 5.6 is the way we pass the data to **printf()**. Because we wish to display the values in the array (the rvalues), we use the fully stated array name. The fully stated array name causes **printf()** to use and display the rvalues held in the array.

Three-Dimensional Arrays

If you need to, you can create arrays with three or more dimensions. The syntax rules are the same. For example, to create a three-dimensional array, the statement is

```
double x_y_z[10][20][30];
```

which creates a "cube" of data that has 10 rows, 20 columns, and is 30 units deep. Although three-dimensional arrays are not used that often, they can be handy in some situations, such as graphics programming.

How do you determine the scalar size for a three-dimensional array? The scalar is the product of the number of elements in all but the first dimension times the size of the data type. In this example, the scalar is

```
scalar = element2 * element3 * sizeof(data_type)
       =    20     *    30    * sizeof(double)
       =    20     *    30    *     8
       =    600    *    8
       =    4800
```

Therefore, moving from element **x_y_z[0][0][0]** to **x_y_z[1][0][0]** means moving over 4,800 bytes of data. It also means that this array occupies 48,000 bytes of memory.

How Big Can an Array Get?

Arrays can eat up a lot of memory in a hurry, especially when the data type is a **long**, **float**, or **double**. The IBM-PC family of computers are based on the Intel 80x86 chip and use a segmented memory architecture. A segment for these chips is 64k in size, or 65,536 bytes of memory.

A PC C compiler's default setting specifies one segment for code space (the program code itself) and one segment for data (space for the variables used in the program). This default setup is called the *small memory model*. By setting certain compiler switches, you can increase this to one megabyte of code and one megabyte of data space. This is called the *large memory model*. However, no single variable can be larger than one segment in size. Some compilers have what is called the *huge memory model*, which allows you to have an array larger than one segment in size, but not all compilers provide the huge memory model.

Compilers that use the Motorola 680x0 chip family, like the Macintoshes', use a linear address space; there is no segmented memory architecture used. Every memory address requires four bytes. Creating arrays over 64k in size is not much different from creating smaller arrays. These compilers do not need memory models like the PC C compilers do. Still, arrays smaller than 32k can have some optimizations done to improve program speed.

The moral is: Don't create arrays that are either smaller or larger than you need. Making an array too small might mean overflowing it and stomping on some other data. Making one too large wastes memory that might be needed later in the program. As much as possible, try to determine the exact size of the array needed.

Conclusion

The concepts presented in this chapter extend to all of the basic data types available in C. You might experiment with some of the data types not explicitly used in this chapter to verify that they follow the same rules presented here.

There is one potential problem area: If you own a compiler that does not adhere to the ANSI standard, you may not be able to initialize an array using the methods discussed here. Without explaining why, just move the definition statement for the array so it appears after the **#include stdio.h** directive but before **main()**. (We will explain why this problem exists for older compilers later in this book.)

Checking Your Progress

1. What is an array?

   An array is a grouping of an identical data type that can be accessed by a single variable name.

2. If you define an array:

   ```
   int table[10][100];
   ```

   what are the valid element numbers you can use in your program?

   The valid subscript numbers for the array are 0 through 9 for the first subscript and 0 through 99 for the second subscript. These are the valid subscript ranges because arrays in C begin with element 0 (the N - 1 rule).

3. Using the array defined in question 2 and assuming that **table[][]** exists in memory starting at address 30,000, what is the lvalue of **table[2][0]**?

   First, calculate the size of the scalar for the array. The scalar is always the second element size times the size of the data type. Assuming an **int** takes two bytes for storage:

   ```
   scalar = 100 * sizeof(int)
   scalar = 100 * 2
   scalar = 200
   ```

   Because we want **table[2][0]**, the address becomes:

   ```
   address = table[2][0]
           = 30,000 + 2 * scalar + sizeof(int) * second
                element
           = 30,000 + 2 * 200 + 2 * 0
           = 30,000 + 400 + 0
           = 30,400
   ```

   Therefore, the lvalue of **table[2][0]** is memory address 30,400.

4. What is the null termination character and how is it used in C?

   The null termination character is a backslash-0 character sequence and is written as '\0'. It is useful because it is placed at the end of character sequences to create character strings. Many string library functions rely on the fact that character strings end with the null termination character.

5. If we define a character array as in Program 5.5, but with one empty element:

```
char names[4][30] = {
  "Dave Cooper",
  "Don Dudine",
  "Chuck Lieski"
};
```

what would the call to **gets()** look like to fill in the empty name? The call would be:

```
gets(name[3]);
```

This would send the lvalue of the fourth element in the array to **gets()** for input from the user. (It's not a fully qualified array reference, so the lvalue is sent to the function.)

6. What is the difference between the following three print() statements?

```
char day[7][10] = {
"Mon.", "Tues", "Wed", "Thurs",
"Fri.", "Sat.", "Sun"};

printf("%s", day);
printf("%s", day[1]);
printf("%s", day[0][0]);
```

The first example uses just **day** as the argument. Anytime a less than fully stated array name is passed to a function, it is the lvalue that is passed. In this case, the starting address of the array is passed. Therefore, "Mon." is displayed.

The second example is not a fully stated array reference, so the lvalue of **day[1][0]** is passed to **printf()**. This means that "Tues" is displayed.

The last example is a fully stated array reference. Therefore, it is the rvalue that is sent to **printf()**, *not* the lvalue. Therefore, the value 77 (the letter 'M' in "Mon.") is sent to **printf()**. Not knowing any differently, **printf()** goes to memory address 77 (probably in the middle of the operating system), and tries to display whatever code happens to be there. In most cases, the program will either print garbage on the screen, or it might hang the system.

6

Handling User Input

N THIS CHAPTER YOU WILL LEARN VARIOUS WAYS TO OBTAIN INPUT FOR USE in a program. Although input can come from a variety of different sources, including disk data files, modems, and light pens, this chapter concentrates on acquiring user input via the keyboard. You will also learn how to convert the input into a variety of different data types.

In Chapter 5 you used the gets() function, which is one of the most efficient ways to obtain user input from the keyboard. This function uses very little code space and executes much faster than a user can type characters at the keyboard. This chapter will continue to use **gets()**, and we will investigate other input functions.

Getting a Single Character

You have undoubtedly used programs that present a menu and ask you to press a key to make your selection from the menu. Figure 6.1 shows a hypothetical menu.

Figure 6.1

A hypothetical menu

Do you wish to:
 A. **Copy a file**
 B. **Delete a file**
 C. **Print a file**
 D. **Exit the program**

Enter your choice (A-D):

Most programs that use single-letter menu choices simply want you to press a letter that matches the menu option. Program 6.1 obtains a single keystroke from the user, without requiring him or her to then press the Enter key.

First the program defines a variable named **key** to hold the keystroke that is entered. The call to **clrscr()** just clears the display screen. Although **clrscr()** is not an ANSI standard function, all compilers provide a function that clears the display screen. (You can leave the call to **clrscr()** out of the program. The program won't look as nice, but it will work the same.) The series of printf() functions simply displays the menu options on the screen.

Getting a Character with getch()

The call to **getch()** is designed to obtain a single keystroke from the user. Although **getch()** is not part of the ANSI library, you can expect to find this function in your standard library. Notice the **printf()** call to display the character. **getch()** does not display the keystroke entered by the user. (Some compilers also supply **getche()**, which echoes the character entered at the keyboard.)

Program 6.1   Obtaining a Single Keystroke from the User

```
#include <stdio.h>

main()
{
    char key;
    clrscr();

    printf("\n\n          Do you wish to:\n\n");
    printf("\n          A. Copy a file");
    printf("\n          B. Delete a file");
    printf("\n          C. Print a file");
    printf("\n          D. Exit the program");
    printf("\n        Enter your choice (A - D): ");

    key = getch();
    printf("%c", key);
    key = toupper(key);
    printf("You selected %c, choice %d", key, key - '@');
}
```

Because the user may have entered a lowercase letter, the call to the standard library function **toupper()** checks whether **key** is uppercase. If **key** is uppercase, **toupper()** simply returns the letter. If key is lowercase, **toupper()** converts it to an uppercase letter and returns an ASCII value equal to the uppercase letter.

Converting a Character to a Number

The last statement in Program 6.1 simply displays the selected option. The expression

```
key - '@'
```

takes the uppercase letter held in **key** and subtracts the '@' character from it. (Remember, single character constants are enclosed within single quotes; string constants use double quotes.) For example, suppose the user pressed the letter *C*. An uppercase *C* has an ASCII value of 67. (Refer to Appendix

A for a list of ASCII codes.) The '@' character has an ASCII value of 64. Therefore, the expression resolves to

```
key - '@'
67  -  64
3
```

which says the user selected the third option. Note that the result of the expression is a numeric value, so we use the %d conversion character in **printf()** to display the value.

Forcing the User to Press Enter

Sometimes you may want to force users to press Enter after they press a letter. For example, some users are accustomed to pressing Enter to invoke commands. When they run a program using **getch()**, they press the appropriate letter and then press Enter by force of habit. If the next menu also uses **getch()**, they may have unintentionally answered the second question with the Enter key before reading the second menu on the screen.

You can use the getchar() function to force the user to press Enter after each single keystroke. In Program 6.1, simply replace the statement

```
key = getch();
```

with

```
key = getchar();
```

This change forces the user to press Enter before advancing to the next part of the program. It is a good idea to use **getchar()** for any option that might destroy data (deleting a file, for example).

Getting Numbers into a Program

In Chapter 5 you learned how to use **gets()** to collect string data from the user. As you will see in this section, you can also use **gets()** to get numeric data. Program 6.2 shows how you can create integer data from keyboard input.

This program defines two working variables **buff[]** and **value**. Next it calls **gets()** to get the input from the user. After the user enters a sequence of one or more digits and presses the Enter key, the number is stored in **buff[]** as a string.

Because the digit '1' has an ASCII value of 49, you cannot directly use the ASCII value for '1' (with a numeric value of 49) as the numeric value 1. After all, 1 times 1 should be 1, not 2401. It's important to understand the difference between a numeric value and its ASCII representation.

Program 6.2 **Getting an Integer Value into a Program**

```
#include <stdio.h>
#include <stdlib.h>

main()
{
   char buff[10];
   int value;

   printf("Enter a value: ");
   gets(buff);
   value = atoi(buff);
   printf("\nThe number is %d", value);
}
```

After the call to **gets()**, the content of **buff[]** is a string, not an integer. Therefore, you must convert the string representation of the number into an **int** before attempting to use **value**. The standard library function for converting a string to an integer value is **atoi()** (ASCII to integer).

In brief, **buff[]** is passed as the argument of **atoi()**. The atoi() function examines every ASCII character in the string and adjusts them by powers of ten to create a numeric value equal to the value held in the string. This value is then returned to the calling function.

If **atoi()** is passed data that cannot be formed into an integer, it returns the value 0. If only part of the input data is incorrect, **atoi()** attempts to make a partial number. For example, if you passed **atoi()** the string "Sam", the return value would be 0. If you passed it the string "123Sam", it would return the value 123. **atoi()** quits processing as soon as it sees a character that is not a valid numeric character. (Plus or minus signs are allowed.) For now, assume that the user types in a valid number.

As in most programming languages, the right-hand expression in an assignment is evaluated before the assignment takes place. In the call to **atoi()**, the function returns a numeric value. Visually, the sequencing would look something like this if you type in the digits "5343":

```
value = atoi(buff);         /* 1. The actual code  */
value = atoi("5343");       /* 2. with an argument */
value = 5343;               /* 3. What's produced  */
```

The argument to **atoi()** holds the character string "5343". This string is processed by **atoi()** so the numeric value is created.

After the number is created, **atoi()** is responsible for returning that value to the point in the program where **atoi()** was called. In essence, after processing, the value produced by **atoi()** takes the place of **atoi()** in the expression. Now the assignment occurs and the value 5343 is assigned into the rvalue of **value**.

In Chapter 13 you'll learn how arguments are passed to functions and how functions return values. For now, you just need to understand that **atoi()** can convert an ASCII digit string into a numeric value.

PROGRAMMING TIP. *Some people have accused C of being cryptic. They may be intimidated because C is so concise. For example, the previous program used the statements*

```
gets(buff);
```

and

```
value = atoi(buff);
```

Experienced C programmers would instead use the shorter version

```
value = atoi(gets(buff));
```

*which collapses the two statements into one. The call to **gets()** occurs first. When **gets()** finishes its task, it returns the lvalue of **buff[]**. Because **gets()** is where the argument for **atoi()** would normally be, the returned lvalue for **buff[]** "replaces" **gets(buff)**. This is no different than writing **atoi(buff)**. When the atoi() function call is finished, the numeric value returned from **atoi()** is assigned into **value**.*

Converting Strings to Other Data Types

Clearly, not all programming tasks use string or integer data. However, you can convert a digit string into other data types. Program 6.3 converts a digit string into a long and a double data type.

In this example, **gets()** acquires the digits from the user and stores them in **buff[]**. The call to **atol()** (ASCII to long) converts the digits in **buff[]** and returns a long integer data type. The call to **atof()** does the same thing, but converts the string to a **double**. (Like **atoi()**, these functions assume that valid input was passed to them. They return 0 if a numeric value cannot be formed.)

The printf() call first displays the value entered as a **long** using the %ld conversion character. Next, **printf()** displays the square root of the number using the double representation (x) in the call to **sqrt()**. The sqrt() function returns the square root as a **double**, hence we use the %f conversion character in **printf()** to display the square root.

Program 6.3   Converting a Digit String to a long and a double

```
#include <stdio.h>
#include <stdlib.h>
#include <math.h>

main()
{
    char buff[20];
    long long_integer;
    double x;

    clrscr();
    printf("Enter a number: ");
    gets(buff);

    long_integer = atol(buff);
    x = atof(buff);

    printf("\nThe value is %ld and its square root is %f",
            long_integer, sqrt(x));
}
```

Using the math.h Header File

Program 6.3 included a header file named math.h. This header file contains information about the math functions that helps the compiler detect certain types of programming errors. If you are ever in doubt about whether to include a header file, go ahead and include it. Standard library header files contain no code, so they don't make your program any larger. Header files simply contain information that makes the compiler a little smarter when compiling your code. You should include the math.h header file whenever you use **sqrt()** or any trigonometric library function.

Most compiler manuals tell you which header file is associated with each library function. If the manual does not mention a header file, chances are that the information is in stdio.h. If the function is unique in some way, or rarely used, its associated header file will probably be something other than stdio.h. If your manual lists a header file with the function, you should include it in your program.

With the conversion functions in the standard library, **gets()** should enable you to create just about any data type. There is, however, another function that can accept keyboard input from the user: the **scanf()** function.

Accepting General Input with the scanf() Function

The scanf() function is a general keyboard input routine that can accept input for a variety of different data types. The general format for **scanf()** is

```
scanf("conversion_character", lvalue_variable_list);
```

scanf() uses most of the same conversion characters as **printf()**, but there are some differences. The appropriate conversion character appears within double quotes in the first argument. The second argument *must* be the lvalue of the variable to name an array variable (without any brackets). You can place the address-of operator before the variable name if it is not an array.

Program 6.4 illustrates how to use **scanf()**.

Program 6.4 **Using the scanf() Function**

```
#include <stdio.h>

main()
{
    int i;
    long big;
    double x;

    printf("\nEnter an integer: ");
    scanf("%d", &i);

    printf("Enter a long integer: ");
    scanf("%ld", &big);

    printf("Enter a double: ");
    scanf("%lf", &x);

    printf("\n\nThe integer is %d", i);
    printf("\nThe long is %ld", big);
    printf("\nThe double is %f", x);
}
```

This program is asking for three different data types to be entered: **int**, **long**, and **double**. Because none of the variables is an array, the address-of operator must appear before the variable name in the second argument to **scanf()**.

The address-of operator must be used because, after **scanf()** converts the keyboard input to the requested data type, it stores the result directly into the variable in memory. That is, **scanf()** stores the results in the memory address (lvalue) of the variable. **scanf()** can only do this if you supply it with the lvalue of the variable. If you want to input data to a string, however, only the name of the character array is needed. (Remember, in Chapter 5 you learned that an array name by itself is a form of shorthand for the lvalue of the array.)

In Program 6.4 the conversion characters for the first two data types are identical to those used with **printf()**. To input a double value, however, you must use "%lf". The "%f" conversion character is used to input a float (four-byte) floating-point number. The remaining three statements display the results of the scanf() calls.

One of the advantages of **scanf()** is that it has many options that give you control over the data being entered from the keyboard. Most of these options are *input filters* that limit what is accepted as valid input from the keyboard. Consult the standard library documentation that came with your compiler for a list of scanf() options.

Combining scanf() Calls

If you wish, you can combine calls to **scanf()**, as shown in Program 6.5. Notice the call to **scanf()**. In this example, all three variables are in a single call to **scanf()**. When you run this program, be sure to press Enter after entering each variable type. This is explained in the next section.

Avoiding scanf() Pitfalls

There are many ways to misuse **scanf()**. For example, Program 6.6 asks you to enter your street address. The program seems simple, but try running it and typing your address. If you type "**123 Main Street**", the output shown by **printf()** is "123". What happened to "Main Street"?

The problem is in the way **scanf()** senses the end of input. While we are used to pressing Enter to signal the end of input, **scanf()** interprets any whitespace character as an end of input signal. The list of whitespace characters includes the blank (or space), newline, vertical tab, form feed, and horizontal tab characters. **scanf()** interprets the blank space between "123" and "Main" as the end of input for the variable.

Program 6.5   Multiple Inputs with One scanf() Call

```c
#include <stdio.h>

main()
{
    char buff[50];
    int i;
    double x;

    printf("\nEnter your name, an int, and a double: ");
    scanf("%s %d %lf", buff, &i, &x);

    printf("\nYour name is %s, i = %d, x = %f", buff, i, x);
}
```

Program 6.6   A scanf() Quirk

```c
#include <stdio.h>

main()
{
    char buff[50];

    printf("\nEnter your address: ");
    scanf("%s", buff);
    printf("\nYour address is %s", buff);
}
```

There are ways to overcome scanf()'s default behavior in this area. However, **gets()** accomplishes the same task, is easier to use, and generates less code. Even if you throw in conversion functions like those used in Programs 6.2 and 6.3, you will undoubtedly generate less code with **gets()** than with scanf(). The moral is, use the right tool for the job at hand. In most cases, using **scanf()** is like using nuclear weapons to settle a domestic dispute.

Still, it's worth reading your standard library documentation to explore scanf()'s options. You may encounter a situation in which **scanf()** offers the best solution. After all, the more you know about the available resources, the easier it is to solve your programming problems.

Conclusion

This chapter has demonstrated how to convert keyboard input into a variety of data types. As you learn more about C, you will discover more advanced ways to convert input. For now, however, you have enough conversion alternatives to create almost any data type you need.

Checking Your Progress

1. What is the difference between **getch()**, **getche()**, and **getchar()**?

   Both **getch()** and **getche()** return the keystroke immediately after the key is pressed. They do not require any other input from the user. **getch()** does not echo the returned key to the screen, but **getche()** does. **getchar()** also returns a single key, but requires that the user press Enter after pressing the key. **getchar()** also echoes the character to the screen.

2. What does the following code do?

   ```
   int key;
   key = toupper(getch()) - 'A';
   ```

   The right-hand expression is evaluated first. The call to **getch()** is made first because it is an argument to **toupper()**. When the keystroke is returned from the call to **getch()**, it immediately becomes the argument to **toupper()**, which converts the key to an uppercase letter. That uppercase letter then has the letter *A* subtracted from it, producing a numeric value which is assigned into **key**.

   For example, suppose the user presses *d*. The processing of the statement looks like the following sequence of events:

   ```
   key = toupper(getch()) - 'A';
   key = toupper('d') - 'A';        /* User presses 'd' */
   key = 'D' - 'A';            /* toupper -> uppercase */
   key = 68 - 65;                  /* ASCII numbers    */
   key = 3;                        /* Result           */
   ```

   This example assumes that a choice of 0 is valid.

3. Write a program that uses **scanf()** to get a **char**, an **unsigned int**, and a **double**. Note the size of the executable program. Then write the equivalent program using **gets()** and the conversion functions. What is the difference between the two program sizes?

This answer will vary greatly among compilers. One compiler produced a difference of only 1.5k while for another compiler the result was almost 8k. In all cases, the scanf() version was larger.

Arithmetic, Increment, and Decrement Operators

Five Basic Arithmetic Operators

Shorthand Assignment Operators

Preincrement and Postincrement Operators

Predecrement and Postdecrement Operators

Choosing an Increment Method

ALL PROGRAMMING LANGUAGES HAVE THREE TYPES OF OPERATORS available: arithmetic operators, logical operators, and relational operators. An operator is usually a word or symbol that causes a specific action to take place. This chapter discusses the arithmetic operators. C gives you a greater number of arithmetic operators than most languages, because it offers a number of "shortcut versions" of commonly used arithmetic operations.

Five Basic Arithmetic Operators

C provides five basic arithmetic operators: add, subtract, multiply, divide, and modulus. The operators are shown in Table 7.1.

Table 7.1   **Add, Subtract, Multiply, Divide, and Modulus Operators**

+	Addition (plus sign)
-	Subtraction (hyphen)
*	Multiplication (asterisk)
/	Division (forward slash)
%	Modulus (percent sign)

All five arithmetic operators are binary operators and are used according to the general form shown in Table 7.2.

Table 7.2   **General Form of the Arithmetic Operators**

expression1 + expression2	(addition)
expression1 - expression2	(subtraction)
*expression1 * expression2*	(multiplication)
expression1 / expression2	(division)
expression1 % expression2	(modulus)

The form of the first four operators shown in Table 7.2 needs little explanation. An arithmetic operation is performed on the operands (*expression1* and *expression2*) and a new expression results. The modulus arithmetic operator, however, may be new to you.

The Modulus Operator

Not all languages provide a modulus operator, but it can be very handy in a variety of ways. The *modulus* operator yields the remainder of two expressions. For example, consider the following code fragment:

```
int a, b;
a = 5;
b = 2;
printf("%d", a % b);
```

The output of the expression **a % b** is 1. Given the general form shown in Table 7.2, the modulus operator gives the remainder of *expression1* divided by *expression2*. More formally, the modulus operator is defined with the properties

```
(i / j) * j + i % j = i                    (j != 0)
```

where **j** is not equal to 0. From this equation, it follows that the *modulus operator can be used only with integer data*, not with floating-point numbers. If you attempt to use floating-point operands with the modulus operator, the compiler should issue an error message.

The modulus operator is perfect for ensuring that a sequence of numbers falls within certain limits. For example, suppose you want the computer to simulate shuffling a deck of cards, and you have assigned a number to each card from 0 through 51. With those assumptions, what does the following statement do?

```
deck[0] = abs(rand() % 52);
```

First of all, **rand()** is an ANSI standard library routine that generates random numbers between -32,767 and 32,767. Let's suppose the first time we call it, the return value is -2,043. Next we find the modulus 52 of -2,043. Because -2,043 / 52 = -39 with a remainder of -15, the result of the expression (-2,043 % 52) is -15. However, because **rand()** can return negative values, we use the abs() function to get the absolute value of the expression. Now we assign the value 15 into the first element of the deck[] array. In other words, the first card in the deck is card 15.

You should be able to convince yourself that only the values 0 through 51 (that is, 52 card values) can be produced with the statement above. In a real program, the statement would be used in a loop to fill in the values in the deck. You will see a complete example of this in Chapter 10.

Any time you need a random integer number that must fall within certain limits, the modulus operator will likely fit the bill.

Operator Precedence

Sometimes it is difficult to determine the result of an arithmetic expression. For example, suppose you have the following information:

```
int i, j, result;
i = 10;
j = 5;
result = i + j * 2;
```

Does **result** equal 30 or 20? The reason the answer is uncertain is because we don't know which arithmetic operation to perform first. Do we add **i** and **j** together and then multiply by 2 to get 30, or do we multiply **j** by 2 and then add **i** to get 20? The correct answer depends upon the precedence of the arithmetic operators.

Precedence is the term used to express the hierarchy, or order of processing, of arithmetic operators. In C, multiplication, division, and modulus operators have higher precedence than addition and subtraction operators. Given an arithmetic expression that uses operators with different precedence, those with the highest precedence are performed first. Therefore, our sample statement

```
result = i + j * 2;
```

means that the multiplication operator evaluates its two expressions (**j** and **2**) before the addition operator evaluates its two expressions (**i** and **10**). Therefore, the sequencing of the evaluation of the sample statement is

```
result = i + j * 2;
result = i + 5 * 2;
result = i + 10;
result = 10 + 10;
result = 20;
```

which shows that **result** is equal to 20. Another thing to notice in this example is that some operators must "wait" for their operands until some other expression is resolved. For example, in the statement above, **i** must wait until the **j** * **2** expression is resolved before **i** can access its second operand, the product of **j** times 2.

Parentheses

In some situations, you need to override the default operator precedence. Using our previous example, suppose you want the correct answer to be 30, not 20. You can use parentheses to force an expression to take place before other expressions. If you want **i** and **j** to be added before multiplying by 2, the statement would be

```
result = (i + j) * 2;
```

The parentheses force the resolution of the expression **i + j** before multiplying by 2. In this case, the multiplication operator must "wait" for its first operand to be resolved before it can perform its operation. In this instance,

```
result = (i + j) * 2;
result = (10 + 5) * 2;
result = 15 * 2;
result = 30;
```

the parentheses change the normal processing sequence and force the addition of variables **i** and **j** before multiplication takes place. Therefore, parentheses can be used to override the default precedence of any arithmetic operator.

Associativity

C lets you do some pretty strange stuff, if you want to. Indeed, that's one of C's strengths. You never feel handcuffed by the language. However, with this power comes a certain amount of responsibility. Consider Program 7.1.

Program 7.1   Associativity

```
#include <stdio.h>

main()
{
    int i, j, k;
    i = 10;
    j = 20;
    k = (j = j / 10) + (j + i) - (j * 2);
    printf("\nk = %d", k);
}
```

Does **k** equal -8 or 10? The problem is we don't know the order in which the subexpressions in the statements are evaluated. Because only the addition and subtraction operators are outside of a parenthesized expression and those two operators have the same precedence, the precedence rules alone cannot determine the correct answer.

For example, if the expression is evaluated from right to left, the processing sequence would be

```
k = (j = j / 10) + (j + i) - (j * 2);
k = (j = j / 10) + (j + i) - (20 * 2);
k = (j = j / 10) + (j + i) - 40;
k = (j = j / 10) + (20 + 10) - 40;
k = (j = j / 10) + 30 - 40;
k = (j = j / 10) - 10;
k = (j = 20 / 10) - 10;
k = (j = 2) - 10;
k = 2 - 10;
k = -8;
```

However, if we assume that processing is from left to right, the sequence becomes

```
k = (j = j / 10) + (j + i) - (j * 2);
k = (j = 20 / 10) + (j + i) - (j * 2);
k = (j = 2) + (j + i) - (j * 2);
k = 2 + (2 + 10) - (j * 2);
k = 2 + 12 - (j * 2);
k = 2 + 12 - (2 * 2);
k = 2 + 12 - 4;
k = 2 + 8;
k = 10;
```

Admittedly, this is a trumped-up example, but it does serve to point out some potential problem areas. If two or more operators have the same precedence level, we need a rule that tells us how the expressions are processed.

The order in which expressions of equal precedence are evaluated is determined by the *associativity* of the operator. In complex expressions with operators of equal precedence, their associativity is the tie breaker that determines how the expression is evaluated.

The add and subtract operators are called *left-associative*. That is, the expressions are evaluated from the left to right. Because of the left-associativity rules, the simple expression

```
i + j - k
```

is viewed as though the expression is written

```
(i + j) - k
```

The multiply, divide, and modulus operators also are left-associative operators. For example, the expression

```
j * k / i
```

also is processed as though it is

```
(j * k) / i
```

There are, however, some operators that are *right-associative*. This simply means that the order of processing is from right to left for operators of equal precedence. The associativity rules for all operators appear in Appendix B.

When the associativity rules and the precedence of operator rules are taken together, the result of an expression is unambiguous. (A complete list of the associativity and precedence rules appears in Appendix B.)

Shorthand Assignment Operators

If you have some programming experience, you know that there are certain expressions that are used over and over in a program. A common example is something like

```
a = a + b;
```

Adding one variable to another and then assigning it back into one of the variables is a very common programming statement.

To make things easier for you, C provides a variety of shorthand operators that condense these common programming expressions. For example, instead of writing

```
a = a + b;
```

the shorthand version of the same statement is

```
a += b;
```

The statement says: "Take the rvalues of variables **a** and **b**, add them together, and assign the result back into the rvalue of variable **a**."

All of the shorthand operators are a variation of the simple assignment operator (=). The compiler views the shorthand operators as a sequence of two tokens. The first token is the operation that is to be performed (for example, the + sign in the example above) followed by the assignment token. The two tokens taken together form the shorthand assignment operators.

There are several common guidelines that apply to the shorthand operators. Given the general statement form of:

```
expression1 shorthand_operator expression2
```

then:

1. The rvalue of *expression1* changes if *expression2* is not 0.

2. The rvalue of *expression2* does not change.

3. The operation performed on *expression1* is determined by the first token of the *shorthand_operator*.

Using these guidelines and applying them to our sample statement

```
a += b;
```

we conclude

1. The rvalue of variable **a** is changed if **b** is not 0.

2. The rvalue of **b** does not change.

3. Addition is performed because the first token (+) of the shorthand operator (+=) is the addition operator.

A complete list of the shorthand operators is presented in Table 7.3.

Although we have not examined the C bitwise operators, they also have shorthand assignment operators. (We will discuss the bitwise operators in Chapter 12.)

The precedence level is the same for all the shorthand operators and they are all right-associative.

Preincrement and Postincrement Operators

Another common program statement is something similar to

```
a = a + 1;
```

Although you now know that you can write the same statement using

```
a += 1;
```

there is a better way in C. Adding the constant 1 to a variable is the same as incrementing that variable by 1. C provides the ++ operator for incrementing a variable.

Program 7.2 shows how the increment operator is used.

Table 7.3 **Shorthand Assignment Operators**

Operator	Type	Replaces
Arithmetic:		
+=	Addition	a = a + b;
-=	Subtraction	a = a - b;
*=	Multiplication	a = a * b;
/=	Division	a = a / b;
%=	Modulus	a = a % b;
Bitwise:		
<<=	Shift left	a = a << b;
>>=	Shift right	a = a >> b;
&=	Bitwise AND	a = a & b;
|=	Bitwise OR	a = a | b;
^=	Complement	a = a ^ b;

Program 7.2 **Using the Increment Operator**

```
#include <stdio.h>

main()
{
    int i, j;

    i = 0;
    j = ++i;
    printf("\nThe value of i is %d and j = %d", i, j);
}
```

The increment operator is two adjacent plus signs (++) placed immediately before the name of the variable you wish to increment. Because the increment operator uses only one operand, it is a unary operator and is left-associative. The output of Program 7.2 is

```
The value of i is 1 and j = 1
```

In Program 7.2, we define two variables **i** and **j** and initialize **i** to 0. The statement

```
j = ++i;
```

looks simple enough, but the compiler must generate considerably more code than you might think. First, it must find the lvalue of **i**, load the rvalue of **i** into a register, increment the rvalue, and store the rvalue back into **i**'s lvalue. Only after these steps are done is the compiler ready to assign a value into **j**.

It is important to notice that the new (incremented) value of **i** is the rvalue of **i** after the increment operation has taken place.

The increment operator we used in Program 7.2 is formally called the pre-increment operator. As we descibed in the previous section, a *preincrement operation* increments a variable before anything else is done with the variable.

Now let's slightly modify Program 7.2 to get Program 7.3.

Program 7.3   Using the Postincrement Operator

```c
#include <stdio.h>

main()
{
    int i, j;

    i = 0;
    j = i++;
    printf("\nThe value of i is %d and j = %d", i, j);
}
```

Notice that the only change between Programs 7.2 and 7.3 is the statement

```
j = i++;
```

Instead of having the increment operator appear before its operand, now the operand is followed by the increment operator. The output of the program has changed to

```
The value of i is 1 and j = 0
```

Notice that **j** is assigned the value of **i** *before* the increment operation is performed. The reason is that we used the postincrement operator on **i**. The *postincrement* operator performs the increment on the variable only after the expression is evaluated fully.

In our example, this means that the increment on **i** is done after the rvalue of **i** is assigned into **j**. Therefore, the statement takes the rvalue of **i**, which is 0, assigns it into **j**, and *then* increments the value of **i** and stores the new (incremented) value back into the rvalue of **i**.

One final point: If there is no other expression in the statement that uses an increment operator, the pre- or postincrement operator yields the same results. That is, if the statement is

```
++i;
```

you can also use

```
i++;
```

and the value of **i** is the same in each case after the statement is executed. The reason the two statements are the same is because we are not using the rvalue of **i** as part of some other expression in the statement. However, any time there is another expression in the same statement, as was the case in Programs 7.2 and 7.3, the pre- and postincrement operators may affect any other expression that is part of the statement.

Predecrement and Postdecrement Operators

It is no less common to have a statement similar to

```
a = a - 1;
```

In this statement, we are decrementing the value of **a** by 1. As you might guess, we can use a decrement operator to accomplish the same task. A *predecrement operator* decrements the rvalue of the variable before using it in any other expression. In other words, its behavior is the same as a preincrement operator, except we are decreasing rather than increasing the value of the variable.

The *predecrement operator* is two minus signs (−−) placed before the name of the variable to be decremented. This statement

```
--a;
```

uses the predecrement operator to decrease the value of **a** by 1.

Obviously, if we have a predecrement operator, we should also have a postdecrement operator...and we do. A *postdecrement* of a variable places the decrement operator after the name of the variable, as shown here:

```
a--;
```

As with the predecrement operator, the postdecrement operator behaves like the postincrement operator. Program 7.4 provides an example of how the decrement operator works.

Program 7.4 **Pre- and Postdecrement Operators**

```
#include <stdio.h>

main()
{
    int i, j;

i = 5;
    j = --i;
    printf("\nPredecrement: i = %d, j = %d", i, j);
    i = 5;
    j = i--;
    printf("\nPostdecrement: i = %d, j = %d", i, j);
}
```

When you run Program 7.4, the output is

```
Predecrement: i = 4, j = 4
Postdecrement: i = 4, j = 5
```

The first line of output confirms that we decrement **i** before assigning the rvalue of **i** into **j**. The second line shows that we decrement the value of **i** *after* the assignment of **i** is made into **j**. A postdecrement operator decrements the rvalue of the variable after all other expressions are evaluated.

As was the case for the increment operators, if the decrement operator is the only expression in the statement, it doesn't matter whether you use the pre- or postdecrement operator. That is,

```
--i;
```

and

```
i--;
```

result in the same value for **i** and there is no other expression in the statement that uses **i**. It is only when some other expression appears in the same statement that the pre- and postdecrement operators may affect some other value.

The increment and decrement operators don't let you write statements you couldn't have written anyway; they simply let you write them more succinctly. For example, the postincrement operator lets us write the statements

```
j = i;
i += 1;
```

as the single statement

```
j = i++;
```

Likewise, the preincrement operator allows us to replace

```
i += 1;
j = i;
```

with

```
j = ++i;
```

The same can be said for the pre- and postdecrement operators. (You should be able to write the equivalent two statements for the operators yourself, right?)

Choosing an Increment Method

Now you have several choices available to you if you wish to increment a variable by 1. To increment variable **a**, you can use

```
a = a + 1;
```

or

```
a += 1;
```

or

```
a++;
```

All three statements accomplish the same task: add 1 to the current value of **a**. Which is best?

Actually, today's optimizing compilers probably generate the same code for all three statements. However, let's assume your compiler isn't all that smart. Now which statement is best?

The first two statements generate the same code—even using a really dumb compiler. The sequence involves finding the lvalue of **a**, moving its rvalue from memory to the accumulator of the CPU, adding 1 to it, and then moving the result from the accumulator back to the lvalue.

With the last variation, a++, once the value is in the accumulator, the compiler can use the assembly language INC (increment) instruction to increase the value by 1. INC is typically several clock cycles faster than a similar assembly language ADD instruction. The subtract statement is likewise slower than a DEC instruction. Therefore, a pre- or postincrement instruction is usually the most efficient of three alternative statements.

Conclusion

C has a very extensive set of operators. The list is long because C's designers wanted a language that gave them the power and flexibility to write systems software. Very few languages let you get as close to the hardware as C. Indeed, some of the operators are almost assembly language constructs. Yet, as you gain experience with the operators, you'll wonder how you ever got along without them.

Checking Your Progress

1. Write a statement that tests whether an integer number named **val** is odd or even.

   If the number is even, the number modulo 2 must be 0. If the number is odd, the number modulo 2 must be 1. Therefore, the statement

   ```
   result = val % 2;
   ```

   will see **result** equal to 0 if the number is even, and equal to 1 if it is odd.

2. What is operator precedence and why is it important?

   Operator precedence determines the order in which expressions are resolved. Precedence is important because statements in C are often compound expressions. That is, they contain multiple expressions. For example, in the statement

   ```
   a = b + (j * c) * d;
   ```

the expression (**j** * **c**) must be resolved before that product can be multiplied by **d**. Precedence ensures that arithmetic expressions are resolved in a known and orderly fashion.

3. What is associativity and why is it important?

   The associativity of an operator tells you how expressions of equal precedence are evaluated. Operators associate either from left to right or right to left. Knowing the associativity of an operator helps you to know how the compiler will resolve multiple expressions of the same precedence.

4. What are the equivalent statements for the pre- and postincrement and decrement operators? Use the general form

   ```
   j = ++i;
   ```

   for your answers.

   The equivalent statements are:

`j = ++i;`	is the same as	`i += 1;` `j = i;`
`j = i++;`	is the same as	`j = i;` `i += 1;`
`j = --i;`	is the same as	`i -= 1;` `j = i;`
`j = i--;`	is the same as	`j = i;` `i -= 1;`

5. Without looking at Appendix B, write the complete table of precedence and the associativity rules.

   Just kidding!

8

Relational and Logical Operators and the if Keyword

N THIS CHAPTER YOU WILL LEARN HOW THE IF STATEMENT IS USED TO MAKE decisions in a program. You will also learn how the if-else statement can be used to make either-or decisions. These two types of statements form the cornerstone of the process step in a program. You also learn about the relational and logical operators because they are often used in if statements.

Relational Operators

As their name suggests, *relational operators* are used to test the relationship between two expressions. Because they are used with two expressions, they are binary operators and are left associative. Table 8.1 lists the relational operators.

Table 8.1   **Relational Operators**

Operator	Meaning
<	Less than
<=	Less than or equal to
>	Greater than
>=	Greater than or equal to
==	Equal to
!=	Not equal to

In a technical sense, the tests for equality (==) and inequality (!=) are not relational operators. They are sometimes called the *equality operators* and their precedence level is one lower than that of the other four relational operators. However, these two operators behave and are used very much like the relational operators.

An expression that uses a relational operator has the general form

```
expression1   relational_operator   expression2
```

where *expression1* and *expression2* can be any valid C expression. Often the two expressions are variable names, as in

```
i < b
```

However, the expressions can also be constants or function names, as in

```
i < func()
i >= 20
i != MAXCHARS
```

The Result of a Relational Operation

A relational operation can yield only one of two possible outcomes: logical True or logical False. In C, a *logical False* result always evaluates to the value 0. A *logical True* result is always nonzero, but is not necessarily 1. Program 8.1 shows the results of several relational tests.

Program 8.1 **The Outcome of a Relational Operation**

```
#include <stdio.h>

main()
{
    int i, j;

    i = 10;
    j = 5;

    printf("\n 10 < 5: Logic = %d", i < j);
    printf("\n10 <= 5: Logic = %d", i <= j);
    printf("\n10 == 5: Logic = %d", i == j);
    printf("\n 10 > 5: Logic = %d", i > j);
    printf("\n10 >= 5: Logic = %d", i >= j);
    printf("\n10 != 5: Logic = %d", i != j);
}
```

The output of the program is

```
10 < 5: Logic = 0
10 <= 5: Logic = 0
10 == 5: Logic = 0
10 > 5: Logic = 1
10 >= 5: Logic = 1
10 != 5: Logic = 1
```

Program 8.1 shows that the result of a relational operation is either logical True or False. Although the logical True result in the program always resolves to the value 1, C does not require that the logical True value be 1. It can be any nonzero value, including negative values. Just remember that logical False is always 0 and logical True is any value *except* 0.

Because all relational operations return either logical True or logical False, the result of the expression is always an **int**. The result of a relational operation can be assigned into a variable, as in

```
a = i < k;
```

The value in **a** is either 0 or 1. Note, however, that the result is an intermediate value. The 0 or 1 is the result of the relational operation; it is not a variable with an lvalue. In other words, the statement

```
i < k;
```

is valid, but the result of the test is lost because there is no lvalue that can be used to store the result of the relational operation.

Using the if Keyword

The if keyword is used to make decisions in a program. It can test an expression and, based upon the outcome of that test, can decide which statements to execute next. The basic form for the if statement is

```
if (expression)
    statement;
```

The expression in the if statement must resolve to either logical True or logical False. If the expression is logical True (not 0), the statement *immediately* following the **if** is executed. If the expression is logical False, the statement is skipped. Program 8.2 shows how the if expression is used.

The program asks you to enter the letter *M* or *F* for male or female. The call to **getch()** gets the character from the user and **toupper()** converts it to an uppercase letter. The letter is then assigned into **you**. The if statement uses the test for equality to determine whether the value of **you** is the same as the character constant 'F'. If **you** does equal 'F', the expression within the parentheses following the if keyword is logical True.

A logical True result for the expression causes the program to execute the printf() statement immediately following the parenthetical if expression. This means **printf()** would display "You answered Female."

If **you** does not equal 'F', the first **if** has an expression that is logical False. Anytime the if expression is logical False, the statement immediately following the expression is bypassed. That is, the printf() statement saying "You answered Female" is skipped.

Program 8.2   Using the if Statement

```
#include <stdio.h>
#include <ctype.h>

main()
{
    int you;

    printf("\nAre you Male or Female (enter M or F): ");
    you = toupper(getch());

    if (you == 'F')
        printf("\nYou answered Female");

    if (you != 'F')
        printf("\nYou answered Male");
}
```

If the first expression is skipped, **you** is not equal to 'F' and the second if statement must have its expression return logical True. This displays the second printf() message.

Logical True Other Than 1

The next program (Program 8.3) tests whether the if statement requires either a 0 or 1 to function properly.

This program asks the user to enter an integer value from the keyboard. Then the modulus operator (%) finds the remainder of the integer. For example, if the user enters **19**, the modulus operator produces a result of 9. If the user entered 20, the modulus operation would produce a 0 (no remainder). Therefore, the if expression

```
if (val)
```

uses **val** to determine whether the associated **printf()** is called. Note that **val** can be any value from 0 (10 % 10) through 9 (19 % 10). The first if statement can only fail when **val** equals 0. In that case, the second if statement is logical True.

As you can see, any value from 1 through 9 creates an expression for the first if statement that is logical True. Logical False can only exist if **val** equals 0. In other words, logical True can be any nonzero value.

Program 8.3   Using Numeric Values with the if Keyword

```c
#include <stdio.h>

main()
{
    char buff[10];
    int val;

    printf("Enter an integer: ");
    val = atoi(gets(buff));

    val %= 10;                 /* Find the remainder */

    if (val)
        printf("\nThe integer is not a multiple of 10");

    if (val == 0)
        printf("\nThe integer is a multiple of 10");
}
```

Using if-else Statements

Program 8.3 is a clumsy way to solve the task at hand. You can streamline it using the if-else keywords. You can use the if-else construct any time you need to process an either-or programming task. The general form for the if-else statement is

```c
if (expression)
    statement1;   /* executed when expression = True  */
else
    statement2;   /* executed when expression = False */
```

Using this construct, if *expression* is logical True, *statement1* is executed. If *expression* is logical False, *statement2* is executed. Expanding upon the general form for the if-else construct, we can say

```c
if (result)
    do this statement if result is logical True (result != 0);
else
    do this statement if result is logical False (result == 0);
```

Notice that any time the if expression (that is, **result**) is True, the first statement after the **if** is executed. When **result** is 0, the statement following the **else** is executed. Now try rewriting Program 8.3 using the if-else construct, as shown in Program 8.4.

Program 8.4   **Improving Upon Program 8.3**

```
#include <stdio.h>
#include <stdlib.h>

main()
{
    char buff[10];
    int val;

    printf("Enter an integer: ");
    val = atoi(gets(buff));

    val %= 10;                      /* Find the remainder */

    printf("\nThe integer ");
    if (val)
        printf("is not");
    else
        printf("is");

    printf(" a multiple of 10");

}
```

Program 8.4 uses an if-else statement to determine how the message is displayed. If the integer is not evenly divisible by 10, **val** has a value between 1 and 9. Because these are nonzero values, the if expression is logical True and "is not" is displayed. If **val** is a multiple of 10, **val** is 0 (logical False) and "is" is displayed.

PROGRAMMING TIP. *Although Program 8.4 includes a third call to* ***printf()****, this call doesn't increase the program size by much. Once your program executes a single call to a function, the code for performing the function's task becomes part of the program. Calling this function a second time adds a few bytes of overhead to set up the function call, but the code for the function itself is already in the program. Never use two separate functions when one will do. For example, the puts() library function can display a string on the screen. However, if you already have* ***printf()*** *in the program, it is wasteful to use* ***puts()****.*

Using if-else with Multiple Statements

As you have learned, the if and if-else keywords can only control one program statement. Fortunately, by using statement blocks you can control multiple statements with the if or if-else keywords. A *statement block* is one or more statements within an opening and closing brace. The if statement can control a statement block using the following form

```
if (expression) {   /* opening brace = start of block */
    Tstatement1;
    Tstatement2;
        .
    Tstatementn;
}            /* closing brace = end of statement block */
```

The if keyword can now control *Tstatement1* through *Tstatementn*. (*Tstatement* indicates a statement associated with the logical True condition of the if expression.) Likewise, the if-else statement can control statement blocks:

```
if (expression) {
    Tstatement1;
    Tstatement2;
        .
    Tstatementn;
} else {
    Fstatement1;
    Fstatement2;
        .
    Fstatementn;
}
```

In this form, all of the Tstatements are controlled by a logical True result for the expression and Fstatements are controlled by a logical False result for the expression.

Programming Style with if and if-else

C doesn't care what style you use to write a program. In fact, you could write a program like this:

```
main(){printf("Hello.");}
```

However, this simple program is not very easy to read, and a less trivial program written in this manner would quickly become a nightmare to decipher. It's a chore to debug programs that use poor or inconsistent style. The next sections present several different C-style conventions.

Using Braces

One common style for the if statement is

```
if (expression)
{
    Tstatements;
}
```

Notice that the opening and closing braces align with the letter *i* in **if**. This helps you to see the code that is tied to the if statement. The if-else variation for this style is

```
if (expression)
{
    Tstatement;
}
else
{
    Fstatement;
}
```

However, this coding style tends to take up more lines than necessary. The following form occupies less space and permits you to see as many lines of code on the screen as possible:

```
if (expression) {
    Tstatement;
}
```

for simple if statements and

```
if (expression) {
    Tstatement;
} else {
    Fstatement;
}
```

for if-else statements.

Even though you only need to use braces with multiple statements, you might want to always use them with if and if-else statements. During debugging sessions, you may decide to include a printf() statement with the statement controlled by the **if**. However, since **printf()** itself is a statement, you would have to add the braces to the if statement.

For example, suppose you need to display the value of **sales_tax** in

```
if (totals > 0.0)
    sales_tax = totals * .05;
```

Now you decide to display **sales_tax** while the program runs. You must modify the code to

```
    if (totals > 0.0) {
        sales_tax = totals * .05;
printf("sales_tax = %g", sales_tax);   /* Debug statement */
    }
```

You must add the braces because the if statement can only control a single statement without the aid of statement block braces. It does no harm to use the statement block in the first place, so you may as well use

```
if (totals > 0.0) {
    sales_tax = totals * .05;
}
```

This style generates no more code and has no impact on execution speed. Also, the braces make it easier to see what the if statement controls, even if it is only one statement. Now when you need to look at **sales_tax**, you can simply insert the call to **printf()**. The braces are already there.

By the way, you should always leave debugging code flush with the left side of the screen. That way it's easy to find and remove when you are through debugging.

Using Code Indentation
Most C programmers indent the statements associated with an if or if-else statement one tab stop. The statements controlled by the **if** are placed one tab stop in from the *i* in **if**. This makes it easier to see the statements being controlled by **if**.

For most text and program editors, the Tab character expands to eight character spaces—too much blank space for program indentation. Long lines will get wrapped to the next line or you must scroll the screen to the right to see long program lines. Experiment with a Tab character of three spaces. This lets you see program indentation, but minimizes problems with long program lines.

There is no correct style for braces and tabs. Use the style you like best. Whatever your choice, stay with it. Consistency will make program debugging and maintenance much easier. If you are working in a programming team, make sure everyone agrees on the same style. It will make your work easier and the team more productive.

Using the Ternary Operator

The simple if-else statements are so common that there is an operator to replace them. This operator, called the *ternary operator*, is the only C operator that has three operands. Its general form is

```
expression1 ? expression2 : expression3
```

In most cases, *expression1* is a relational test just like the expression in an if statement. The second expression (*expression2*) is evaluated if *expression1* is logical True. *expression3* is evaluated if *expression1* is logical False. For example, an if-else statement might be

```
if (sex == MALE) {
    male++;
} else {
    female++;
}
```

Using the ternary operator, the same expression can be written as

```
(sex == MALE) ? male++ : female++;
```

If **sex** does equal MALE, **male** is incremented because *expression2* (that is, **male++**) is evaluated. In all other cases, *expression3* (**female++**) is evaluated.

You can also use the ternary operator in an assignment statement. For example

```
taxable = (do_tax == YES) ? 1 : 0;
```

In this situation, if **do_tax** equals YES, *expression2* is evaluated and 1 is assigned into **taxable**. In any other case, *expression3* is evaluated and 0 is assigned into **taxable**.

Using Nested if Statements

At times you may want to perform multiple tests before deciding which course of action to take. In such cases you can make use of *nested* if statements: if statements within if statements. C allows you to nest if statements as deeply as you wish (although some older C compilers limit you to 256 levels of nested if statements). Program 8.5 contains nested if statements.

Program 8.5   Nesting if-else Statements

```c
#include <stdio.h>

main()
{
    char buff[10];
    int sex, age;

    printf("\nEnter Male or Female (M, F): ");
    sex = toupper(getch()) - 'F';

    printf("\nEnter their age: ");
    age = atoi(gets(buff));

    if (sex) {
      if (age < 30) {
         printf("\nMale under 30");
      }
    } else {
      if (age < 30) {
         printf("\nFemale under 30");
      }
    }
}
```

The program begins by asking the user to enter M or F for the sex. The statement

```c
sex = toupper(getch()) - 'F';
```

gets the character from the user, converts it to uppercase, and then subtracts the ASCII value for 'F' from the (now uppercase) letter entered by the user. If she entered an *f*, **sex** equals 0. If he entered *m*, **sex** equals 7 ('M' - 'F' equals ASCII 77 - ASCII 70 = 7). The user then enters an age, which is converted via the gets() and atoi() calls and assigned into **age**.

The if test

```
if (sex) {
```

is actually testing whether **sex** is 0. If **sex** is not 0, the sex defaults to male. (You can type any letter other than *f* and the sex is assumed to be male.) If the sex is male, a second **if** is tested:

```
if (sex) {
   if (age < 30) {
```

This second test is only reached if the first test on **sex** is logical True. If **age** is less than 30, the appropriate message for a male under age 30 is displayed. Otherwise, this must be a male over age 30. If the sex is female, the same test on **age** is performed.

PROGRAMMING TIP. *Program 8.5 does not have closure. A piece of code is said to have* closure *if it can process all possible values or conditions. However, Program 8.5 does nothing if either the males or females are over age 29. Code that does not have closure is often a source of program bugs. Although closure is not always necessary, most programs should have closure. In numerical processing, boundary conditions (values of zero or infinity) make testing for closure easier than in other applications (for example, database design). Until CASE (Computer Aided Software Engineering) tools can test for complete closure, you'll have to test for it yourself.*

Using Braces with Nested if Statements

When you nest if statements, braces help you visualize which **if** controls which statements. Notice how the braces in Program 8.5 help you to see what each if and else statement controls.

```
if (sex) {                   /* start of if (sex)    */
   if (age < 30) {           /* start of if (age) */
      printf("\nMale under 30");
   }                         /* end of if (age)    */
} else {                     /* the else of if (sex)  */
   if (age < 30) {           /* start of if (age) */
      printf("\nFemale under 30");
   }                         /* end of if (age)    */
}                            /* end of if (sex) */
```

The outermost **if** uses the value of **sex** as its control variable. The two inner (nested) if statements are controlled by the value of **age**.

Suppose you remove the unnecessary braces and remove the tabs from the code, like this:

```
if (sex) {
if (age < 30)
printf("\nMale under 30");
} else {
if (age < 30)
printf("\nFemale under 30");}
```

It is more difficult to determine what controls what. For clarity, you should always use braces and an additional tab stop for each nested if statement.

Using Logical Operators

You can simplify Program 8.5 by using a logical operator. However, before you modify the program, you must learn about the available logical operators, which are listed here:

Operator	Meaning
&&	Logical AND
||	Logical OR

The logical operators are binary operators and are left associative. Their general form is

```
expression1 logical_operator expression2
```

where the expressions are the operands for the operators.

Understanding the Logical AND Operator

The logical AND operator (&&) is used to test whether two expressions are logical True or False. We can illustrate the relationship with the aid of a *truth table*. A truth table simply shows the possible combinations of expressions and their results. A truth table for the logical AND is shown in Table 8.2.

Table 8.2 shows that only when both expressions are logical True is the result a logical True. All other combinations are logical False.

Program 8.6 is a modified version of Program 8.5 using the logical AND operator.

Table 8.2   Truth Table for Logical AND

expression1 &&	expression2	Logical Result
True	True	True
False	True	False
True	False	False
False	False	False

Program 8.6   Using the Logical AND Operator

```
#include <stdio.h>
#include <stdlib.h>

main()
{
   char buff[10];
   int sex, age;

   printf("\nEnter Male or Female (M, F): ");
   sex = toupper(getch()) - 'F';

   printf("\nEnter their age: ");
   age = atoi(gets(buff));

   if (sex > 0 && age < 30) {
       printf("\nMale under 30");
     }
    if (age < 30 && sex == 0) {
       printf("\nFemale under 30");
     }
}
```

Notice how the logical AND operator tests both **sex** and **age** in the if expression. The first if statement

```
if (sex > 0 && age < 30) {
    printf("\nMale under 30");
}
```

says that only if **sex** is greater than 0 AND **age** is less than 30 is the resulting expression for the **if** logical True. Only if both expressions for the logical AND operator are True is "Male under 30" displayed.

Notice how the expressions are "stacked up." You know that the general form for an **if** statement is the keyword **if** followed by an expression enclosed within parentheses:

```
if (expression)
```

The expression in Program 8.6, however, consists of two subexpressions using the logical AND operator.

$$\text{if } (expression)$$
$$\downarrow$$
$$\text{if } (\text{sex} > 0 \quad \&\& \quad \text{age} < 30)$$
$$\downarrow \qquad\qquad \downarrow$$
$$\text{if } (expression1 \ \&\& \ expression2)$$

The compiler must generate code to resolve *expression1* (**sex > 0**) and then *expression2* (**age < 30**). Then the compiler decides if the logical AND expression is logical True or False. This means two relational expressions (**sex > 0** and **age < 30**) are tested before the logical AND expression is evaluated. Only after evaluating the logical AND expression can we determine whether the if statement is logical True or False. The steps for resolving the statement **if (sex > 0 && age < 30)** assuming **sex = 7; age = 20** are shown here:

1. **sex > 0**   Relational operators have higher precedence than logical operators

2. 1   Result is logical True because **sex** is greater than 0

3.   **age < 30**   Left associative, so we do this one next

4.   1   Result is logical True because **age** is less than 30

5. 1 &&   1   Obtain expressions for logical AND operator. The operands are the results of the previous relational operators

6. 1   Table 8.2 says if both expressions are logical True, the result is logical True

7. if (1)   The if statement is logical True

This shows how the compiler processes an if statement that uses a logical AND operator. Pay particular attention to the way that precedence of operators determines the order in which the subexpressions are resolved.

COMMON TRAP. *Can you catch the error in the following if statement from Program 8.6?*

```
if (age < 30 && sex = 0) {
    printf("\nFemale under 30");
}
```

*The second expression of the logical AND operator is written as **sex = 0** rather than **sex == 0**. This means that **sex** always equals 0, and the if test will always see a logical False as its expression value. The printf() call will never be executed. Instead write the if statement using the constant before the variable, as shown here*

```
if (age < 30 && 0 == sex) {
        printf("\nFemale under 30");
}
```

*This way the compiler can catch the error if you omit one of the equal signs because a constant doesn't have an lvalue. That is, the compiler has no memory address where it can store the value of **sex** because 0 is a constant, not a variable. Therefore, the compiler must issue an "lvalue required" error message. Although placing the constant before the variable in the expression may seem strange, it does work.*

Using the Logical OR Operator

The logical OR operator (||) is a binary left associative operator. With the OR operator, if either expression is logical True, the result is logical True. Table 8.3 shows the truth table for logical OR.

Three of the four possible states return logical True with the logical OR operator. The logical OR operator tests for the presence of *either* of two True conditions.

Table 8.3   **Truth Table for Logical OR**

expression1‖	*expression2*	**Logical Result**
True	True	True
False	True	True
True	False	True
False	False	False

Program 8.7 shows an example of the logical OR operator.

Program 8.7   **Using the Logical OR Operator**

```
#include <stdio.h>
#include <stdlib.h>

main()
{   char buff[10];
    int speed;
    printf("\nEnter a miles per hour number: ");
    speed = atoi(gets(buff));

    if (speed < 40 || speed > 65) {
        printf("\nYou're breaking the law!");
    } else {
        printf("\nHave a nice day...");
    }
}
```

The program requests a number for miles per hour. The keyboard input is converted in the usual manner and assigned into **speed**. The if statement uses the logical OR to see if the user passes both speed requirements for interstate driving. If **speed** is either too low *or* too high, the message "You're breaking the law!" is displayed. Otherwise, the "Have a nice day ..." message appears.

Notice that you can achieve the same results with the logical AND operator:

```
if (speed > 39 && speed < 66) {
   printf("\nHave a nice day...");
} else {
   printf("\nYou're breaking the law!");
}
```

Because we have reversed the test from a logical OR to a logical AND, we also have to reverse the printf() statements. However, the program remains essentially the same.

Conclusion

A study of over 10 million lines of public-domain source code showed that **if** is the most used C keyword and that the relational operators are the most used operators. The **if** forms the basic foundation of program decision making. The **if-else** simply gives you a more flexible way of making decisions. The AND and OR operators add even more versatility to the if and if-else statements.

Checking Your Progress

1. What is the value of **k** in the following statements?

```
int i, j, k;

i = 5;
j = 5;
k = j == i;
```

The test for equality comes first due to the order of precedence. Therefore, the first expression to be evaluated is

```
j == i
```

Because **i** and **j** are equal, the result is logical True. The logical True result yields an intermediate value of 1. We can now evaluate the rest of the statement

```
k = 1
```

The end result is that **k** equals 1, not 5.

2. Which message is displayed in the following code fragment?

```
int i;

i = 10;

if (++i == 10) {
   printf("Message 1");
} else {
   printf("Message 2");
}
```

Message 2 is displayed because we preincrement **i** before performing the relational test.

3. Why is this an example of poorly designed code?

```
if (i == 1) {
   printf("Monday");
}
if (i == 2) {
   printf("Tuesday");
}
if (i == 3) {
   printf("Wednesday");
}
if (i == 4) {
   printf("Thursday");
}
if (i == 5) {
   printf("Friday");
}
if (i == 6) {
   printf("Saturday");
}
if (i == 7) {
   printf("Sunday");
}
```

The code may execute six unnecessary tests if **i** equals 1 (the day is Monday). This is not efficient. It would be better to write

```
if (i == 1) {
   printf("Monday");
} else {
```

```
if (i == 2) {
   printf("Tuesday");
} else {
   if (i == 3) {
      printf("Wednesday");
   } else {
      if (i == 4) {
         printf("Thursday");
      } else {
         if (i == 5) {
            printf("Friday");
         } else {
            if (i == 6) {
               printf("Saturday");
            } else {
               printf("Sunday");
            }
         }
      }
   }
}
```

This code quits checking **i** as soon as a match is found. Chapter 9 describes a much more efficient way to write this type of code.

4. What is meant by the term "closure"?

A piece of code is said to have closure if all possible input values have known output values when the code is executed. Code that doesn't have closure is usually the source of program bugs.

5. What is a statement block and what is its purpose?

A statement block is formed by an opening and closing pair of braces. In C, many keywords are designed to control a single statement only. With statement blocks, you can use these keywords to control multiple statements.

6. Which programming style do you like to use with the if statement and why?

There is no one correct programming style for the if statement. However, once you have selected a style, use it consistently throughout your code. In addition, you should use this same style with the new keywords you encounter later in the book.

The switch Statement

THIS CHAPTER DISCUSSES THE **SWITCH** AND RELATED KEYWORDS. AS YOU will see, the **switch** offers a convenient way to handle what otherwise might be a rather clumsy series of if-else statements. Where the if-else statement is an "either-or" construct, the **switch** provides for complex decision making in a program. You will also find the **switch** useful with other C keywords, especially those that control program loops.

The Syntax of the switch Statement

The general form of the switch statement is

```
switch (expression) {
    case constant_expression1:
        .
    case constant_expression2:
        .
    case constant_expression3:
        .
    case constant_expressionN:
        .
}
```

The **switch** has three basic parts. The first part is the parenthesized expression that follows the switch keyword. The expression must be an integral data type; it cannot be a **float** or **double**. Typically, the expression is an **int** data type, but it can be a **char** or **long**.

The second part of the **switch** is the pair of opening and closing braces. *All statements controlled by the* ***switch*** *must appear between the opening and closing braces of the* ***switch***. The braces form the statement block of the switch statement. That is, everything between the braces is controlled by the switch statement. This can be seen in Figure 9.1.

Figure 9.1

Statement block for the switch statement

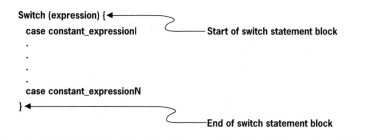

Any statements that appear within the switch statement block are controlled by the **switch**.

The third part of the **switch** is the keyword **case**. Note that all of the case keywords must appear within the opening and closing braces. Also note that *the case keyword must be followed by a constant expression and then a colon* (not a semicolon).

The term *constant expression* means that the value of the expression does not change at runtime. Further, the constant expression following the **case** must also be an integral data type. This means that the constant expression can be a **char**, **int**, **unsigned**, or **long** data type. You cannot use floating-point data types for the constant expression.

The keyword **case** cannot be used at any point in a C program other than within a switch statement block. With those rules behind us, let's see how we can use the **switch**.

Using the switch Statement

Program 9.1 shows how the switch might be used.

The program asks the user to enter a hypothetical test grade. The value entered by the user is converted to an **int** and stored in **grades**. Next we divide **grades** by 10 and use that value for the control expression in the **switch**.

The **switch** is much like the ON-GOTO statement in BASIC or a jump table in assembly language. The case keyword is actually nothing but a label, or memory address, in the program.

Depending upon the value of the expression controlling the **switch** (for example, **grades**), the program jumps to the **case** with the matching label value. For example, if you entered the value 75, the value in **grades** is 7. After the switch, the value of grades causes the program to jump to the program memory location associated with **case 7**. The actual code stored at that memory location is the code to process the printf() statement for **case 7**.

There's one small problem, however. If you run Program 9.1 and enter 75 for the grade, the output is

```
Grade is C. Not bad, but you can do better.
Grade is B. Very good!
Grade is A. Excellent!
Grade is 100. Did you cheat?
```

This probably is not what we intended. Remember that a **case** is nothing more than a memory label. Once we get to that location, there is nothing in the program to prevent us from "falling through" the rest of the case statements. Indeed, that's exactly how we handled grades between 0 and 59. Regardless of the exact value of **grades**, if its range is between 0 and 59, the same printf() statement is executed.

Program 9.1 The switch Statement

```c
#include <stdio.h>

main()
{
    char buff[10];
    int grades;
    printf("Enter your grade: ");
    grades = atoi(gets(buff));
    grades /= 10;       /* grades = grades / 10; */
    switch (grades) {
        case 0:
        case 1:
        case 2:
        case 3:
        case 4:
        case 5:
            printf("\nNot good! You flunked.");
        case 6:
            printf("\nGrade is D. Need work");
        case 7:
            printf("\nGrade is C. Not bad, but you can do
                better.");
        case 8:
            printf("\nGrade is B. Very good!");
        case 9:
            printf("\nGrade is A. Excellent!");
        case 10:
            printf("\nGrade is 100. Did you cheat?");
    }
}
```

Clearly, we need to find a way out of the **switch** when we are finished with the statement(s) associated with a given **case**.

Indenting a switch Statement

The style convention for the switch statement is to have each case label indented one tab stop. The statements controlled by the **case** should be tabbed in one additional tab stop. An example of this style was seen above in Program 9.1.

If the case label has an if statement in it, the statement controlled by the **if** is further indented one tab stop. For example,

```
case PASSED:
    if (val > 20) {
        val += 10;
    } else {
        val -= 10;
    }
    /* More code */
```

The levels of indentation makes it easy to see which statements are being controlled by which keywords. Get in the habit of using indentation to make your programs easier to read.

Using the break Statement

C provides the break keyword as a means by which we can solve the problems with Program 9.1 mentioned above. The break keyword is used to terminate a case statement block. When **break** is used within a switch statement, program control is sent to the first statement *after* the closing brace of the **switch**. This program control flow can be seen in Figure 9.2.

Figure 9.2
The switch-break program control flow

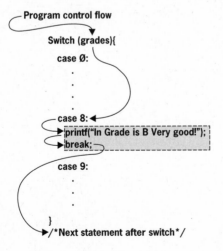

As you can see in Figure 9.2, program control starts at the switch keyword and its expression (**grades** in Figure 9.2) is evaluated. If we assume the

value of **grades** is 8, the compiler has generated machine language instructions that cause program control to jump to the memory address associated with **case 8:**. This causes the printf() call to display its message. The break statement is actually another jump instruction that sends program control to the first statement following the closing brace of the switch statement. In other words, we "jump around" all of the remaining case statements in the switch statement block.

　　If you place a break statement at the end of each **case** in Program 9.1, you will see that the program behaves as you would expect it to.

The Slightly Weird case Statement

The case statement is strange for several reasons. First, it is followed by a colon rather than a semicolon. This is probably a holdover from assembly language programming where labels are followed by a colon.

　　The second strange aspect of the case statement is that the colon following the **case** together with the break statement serve to form a statement block for the case statement. That is, every statement between the colon of the **case** and its break statement is considered part of the **case**. In this sense, it's as though the colon is like an opening parenthesis for the case statement block and the **break** is the closing brace of the statement block. All statements between are evaluated as part of the **case**. This relationship is illustrated in Figure 9.3.

Figure 9.3
The case-break
statement
relationship

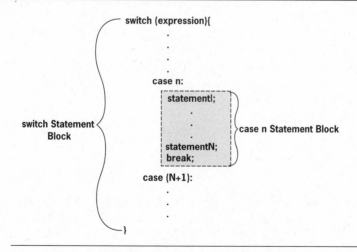

In Figure 9.3, *statement1* through *statementN* are controlled by **case n**. This is one of the few situations in C where multiple statements are controlled by a keyword without the use of braces. The break statement sends control to the first statement following the switch statement block.

The #define Preprocessor Directive

Although the code in Program 9.1 was fairly simple, you still need to spend a moment or two studying the code to figure out what it is doing. Anything we can do to lessen the time it takes to figure a program out, the better.

One technique is to use the #define preprocessor directive to create symbolic constants in the program. A *symbolic constant* is a symbolic name given to a data item. The general form for symbolic constants using the #define preprocessor directive is

```
#define symbolic_name    replacement_text
```

where *symbolic_name* is the name we wish to have associated with the text found in *replacement_text*. With this in mind, let's rewrite Program 9.1 as shown in Program 9.2.

When the C preprocessor sees a #define directive, it stores the symbolic name (for example, GRADE_IS_A) and its replacement text (9) in a symbol table. As the preprocessor scans the program source code, it replaces any symbolic names that it finds in the symbol table used in the program with the replacement text.

In Program 9.2, the first six lines cause each of the six symbolic constants (GRADE_IS_A, GRADE_IS_B, and so on) to be entered into the preprocessor's symbol table along with the text associated with each symbolic constant (9, 8, etc.). When the preprocessor sees the line

```
case GRADE_IS_A:
```

it checks its symbol table for the existence of GRADE_IS_A. Because we **#define**'d GRADE_IS_A to be a symbolic constant, the preprocessor takes the replacement text 9 and *substitutes* 9 in place of GRADE_IS_A. Therefore, when the preprocessor finishes with processing the line, the source code the *compiler* sees is

```
case 9:
```

Therefore, the #define preprocessor directive causes a *textual* replacement of the symbolic constant name (GRADE_IS_A) with its associated replacement text (9). It is important that you realize that '9' is the ASCII character for the character '9'—which is 49—not the binary number 9. All symbolic constants created with **#define** cause an ASCII character substitution in the program, not numeric substitution.

Program 9.2   A Better Way to Write Program 9.1

```c
#include <stdio.h>

#define GRADE_IS_100    10
#define GRADE_IS_A      9
#define GRADE_IS_B      8
#define GRADE_IS_C      7
#define GRADE_IS_D      6
#define GRADE_IS_F      5

main()
{
    char buff[10];
    int grades;
    printf("Enter your grade: ");
    grades = atoi(gets(buff));
    grades /= 10;
    if (grades < 6)
        grades = 5;
    switch (grades)
        case GRADE_IS_F:
            printf("\nNot good! You flunked.");
            break;
        case GRADE_IS_D:
            printf("\nGrade is D. Need work");
            break;
        case GRADE_IS_C:
            printf("\nGrade is C. Not bad, but you can do
                better.");
            break;
        case GRADE_IS_B:
            printf("\nGrade is B. Very good!");
            break;
        case GRADE_IS_A:
            printf("\nGrade is A. Excellent!");
            break;
        case GRADE_IS_100:
            printf("\nGrade is 100. Did you cheat?");
            break;
    }
}
```

As you can see in Program 9.2, symbolic constants make the code much easier to understand than if we use the "magic numbers" directly as we did in Program 9.1.

Keep in mind that the preprocessor must have the symbolic constant and its associated replacement value in the symbol table *before* the preprocessor sees the symbolic constant used in the program. That is, if the #define directives were at the bottom of the program, the preprocessor wouldn't know what GRADE_IS_A (any other symbolic constant) means because they won't be in the preprocessor's symbol table. Therefore, #define preprocessor directives are normally placed near the top of the program, just after the #include preprocessor directives.

PROGRAMMING TIP. *It is a common C programming convention to use uppercase letters for symbolic constants. First of all, uppercase constants stand out from the rest of the code. Second, because C programmers use lowercase letters for variable and function names, it makes it easier to see that the symbolic constant is a constant and not a program variable.*

Symbolic constants are commonly used for array sizes, hardware port addresses, ASCII codes, and any other constant value that won't change throughout the life of the program. Here are some examples of symbolic constants:

```
#define PI              3.1416

#define BAUD_BIT_MASK   0x01

#define SCREEN_WIDTH    80

#define SCREEN_LINES    24

#define MAX_STRING      30

#define ASCII_LETTER_A  65
```

Given these constants, you might see statements like these in the program:

```
char c, name[MAX_STRING];    /* Note array size */
int line_limit, max_cols, start_byte;
double x;

/* Some program code */

max_cols = SCREEN_WIDTH;
line_limit = SCREEN_LINES;
x = PI;
if (c < ASCII_LETTER_A)
```

Advantages of Using #define

We've already mentioned the first advantage of using **#define** to create symbolic constants. *Symbolic constants make the code more readable.* Moreover, they call your attention to the constants. If you have looked at a C program in a magazine, symbolic constants literally jump off the page.

The second reason for using symbolic constants is that *symbolic constants make your programs easier to maintain.* For example, suppose you are writing software for a company that produces a special piece of computer equipment that connects to computer port 0x3f. Let's further assume that you don't use a symbolic constant and that your program references port 0x3f at several hundred different places. You just finished the program, only to find out that the engineers decided to use port 0x4f. No problem. Just load up the source code and do several hundred search-and-replace commands with the text editor.

Now, what would happen if you had used a symbolic constant for the port address in the program? The **#define** might be

```
#define MAGIC_PORT_ADDRESS 0x3f
```

Now all you have to do is load up the source code, make *one* change to the **#define**, save the code, and you're done. When you recompile the program, the preprocessor automatically substitutes the new value of the symbolic constant throughout the program.

Symbolic constants make it simple to change magic numbers in a program. We will see other uses for the #define preprocessor directive as we proceed through this book. All of them are designed to make your work easier. They're worth using.

The default Keyword: Forming Closure on the switch

Programs 9.1 and 9.2 may seem to have closure, but they really don't. Have you ever shown your latest and greatest program to a friend and had him or her take delight in entering some screwball value that blows up your program? For example, Programs 9.1 and 9.2 don't do anything graceful if the user enters a value greater than 100. In other words, the programs don't have closure.

Closure on a switch statement using the keywords we have studied thus far could be pretty messy. Fortunately, we have a C keyword that we can use as a catch-all for input that we may wish to ignore.

The default keyword is similar to a **case**, except it has no constant expression associated with it. Let's modify the last few statements from the **switch** in Program 9.2.

```
case GRADE_IS_100:
   printf("\nGrade is 100. Did you cheat?");
   break;
default:
   printf("\nGrades must be 0 to 100");
}
```

Notice that there is no value following the **default**. This means that any value for **grades** in Program 9.2 that does not have a matching **case** equivalence is transferred to **default**. The **default** in a switch statement is the safety net for everything that doesn't fall into a case statement.

The default keyword can appear only once within a switch statement. C style conventions typically place the **default** at the bottom of the **switch** to reinforce the idea that it is a catch-all for invalid user input.

If **default** is the last statement in the **switch**, no break statement is needed. The program will process the default statements, and fall through to the first statement outside of the **switch**. If you place **default** at some place other than the end of the **switch**, you must use a **break**. Otherwise default values will "fall into" the first **case** following the **default**.

Using the default as a Debugging Safety Net

In many situations, the default case represents a program condition that should never be reached. I know of one very large program that placed a **printf()** in each default case with the message: "Should never reach this default."

The programmer's intentions were good, but the execution wasn't so good. The reason is because there were dozens of default cases in the program and the message gave no clue as to which one triggered the error condition.

If you use a similar approach to catch buggy conditions, you might use the following printf() statement:

```
default:
   printf("switch error: line %d, file %s",
__LINE__, __FILE__);
```

ANSI (and some non-ANSI) compilers define several preprocessor "macro variables" that can be used in your programs. The one named __LINE__ gives the line number (as a decimal integer number) in the source code file where the __LINE__ appears when the program was compiled. __FILE__ yields the name of the file being compiled as a string. Therefore, if this default case is ever executed, the printf() message tells you the line number and the source code file name where the offending **default** occurred.

Using the __LINE__ and __FILE__ macros in a **printf()** is a much more efficient approach to finding the error than wading through several dozen default cases.

Getting a Cursor Key from the Keyboard

Let's write another program using the **switch**, but this time let's try to capture a cursor key (Page Up, arrow keys, etc.) rather than a straight ASCII key. The code appears in Program 9.3.

The program begins with a series of **#define**'s to create symbolic constants for the cursor keys. What's a bit strange is that the symbolic constants for the cursor keys seem to equate to regular ASCII values. For example, the HOME constant has a value of 71, which is the same as the letter 'G' in ASCII. How can we tell them apart?

When a cursor key is touched, the keyboard actually sends out *two* keystroke messages. The first keystroke message is the ASCII null character (ASCII 0). The second message is the cursor key's scan code. Therefore, when you press the Home key, the messages are 0 followed by 71. The statements

```
if (key == CURSORKEY) {
   key = getch();
} else {
   key = ASCII;
}
```

test the first code to see if it was equal to CURSORKEY (which is a symbolic constant for 0). If **key** is zero, we need to read the keyboard again to retrieve the second keystroke message. This second keystroke message contains the cursor key scan code for the key pressed. It is that scan code that is assigned into **key**.

If the first keystroke message is not zero, we simply assume that it is an ASCII keystroke. Regardless of its actual ASCII value, we assign it the value of the symbolic constant ASCII (100). By making all ASCII keystrokes the same value, we can use the default statement for processing the input.

Assuming the **key** holds a cursor keystroke code, we use a switch statement to decide which string to create. We create the keystroke message string by using **strcpy()**. The strcpy() function copies the second argument (for example, the string "HOME") into the first argument (**keybuff[]**). As a result of **strcpy()**, **keybuff[]** holds the appropriate keystroke message. (Details of **strcpy()** and other standard library functions are provided with your compiler documentation.)

The break statements send control to the first statement outside of the **switch**. In Program 9.3, control is sent to the **printf()**, which simply displays a message identifying the key that was pressed.

Program 9.3   Capturing a Cursor Key from the Keyboard

```c
#include <stdio.h>

#define CURSORKEY     0
#define HOME          71
#define UPARROW       72
#define PAGEUP        73
#define LEFTARROW     75
#define RIGHTARROW    77
#define END           79
#define DOWNARROW     80
#define PAGEDOWN      81
#define ASCII         100

main()
{
    char keybuff[15];
    int key;

clrscr();
    printf("\nEnter a cursor control key: ");
    key = getch();
    if (key == CURSORKEY) {
        key = getch();
    } else {
        key = ASCII;
    }
    switch (key) {
        case HOME:
            strcpy(keybuff, "HOME");
            break;
        case UPARROW:
            strcpy(keybuff, "Up Arrow");
            break;
        case PAGEUP:
            strcpy(keybuff, "Page Up");
            break;
        case LEFTARROW:
            strcpy(keybuff, "Left Arrow");
            break;
```

Program 9.3   (Continued)

```
        case RIGHTARROW:
            strcpy(keybuff, "Right Arrow");
            break;
        case END:
            strcpy(keybuff, "End");
            break;
        case DOWNARROW:
            strcpy(keybuff, "Down Arrow");
            break;
        case PAGEDOWN:
            strcpy(keybuff, "Page Down");
            break;
        default:
            printf("\nMust be ASCII");
            break;
    }
    printf("\n\nThe key was a %s", keybuff);
}
```

Notice how the symbolic constants make it so much easier to interpret what the code is doing. It's much easier to understand **case PAGEDOWN** than **case 81**. You should use symbolic constants liberally in your code.

Conclusion

The **switch** provides a simple, yet powerful, way to handle statements that must cope with many possible alternatives. If you think about it, the **switch** is often a more direct way of making program control decisions than a series of complex if or if-else statements. The break and default keywords extend the power of the **switch** even more.

When you use the switch statement, keep the #define preprocessor directive in mind, too. Symbolic constants can add clarity to a program and make program maintenance much easier. If you go on to program under Microsoft's Windows operating system, you will see hundreds of symbolic constants and huge switch statements. (The switch statement in the main Windows processing function is often referred to as the "switch statement from hell"; it can be huge!)

Checking Your Progress

1. How does the compiler use the case keyword?

The case keyword is used by the compiler to create a label in a program. This label is actually nothing more than a memory address (an lvalue). An assembly language jump instruction is associated with each **case** of the switch statement. Based upon the outcome of the expression following the **switch**, the program "jumps" to the memory address for the statments controlled by the **case**.

2. What is the purpose of the default keyword?

In a switch statement, if there is no case label for an outcome of the switch expression, the program jumps to the memory address labeled **default**. If **default** is not used in the **switch**, the program jumps to the first statement following the closing brace of the **switch**. Therefore, the default keyword is used as a catch-all for expression values that do not have an associated case label.

3. Write a program that accepts a number from the user. Ask a second question that asks whether the number should be converted and displayed as a **char**, **int**, or **double** and then display the number.

There are, of course, many different ways you could write the program. One solution is

```c
#include <stdio.h>
#include <stdlib.h>          /* Needed for atof() function */

#define CHAR      'C'
#define INT       'I'
#define DOUBLE    'D'

main()
{
   char buff[20], c, format[5];
   int i;
   double x;

 clrscr();
   printf("Enter a number: ");
   gets(buff);
   printf("\nDisplay the number as a char, int, or double
      (c, i, d):");
   c = toupper(getch());
   switch (c) {
```

```
        case CHAR:
            printf("\nas a char is %c", c);
            break;
        case INT:
            i = atoi(buff);
            printf("\nas an int is %d", i);
            break;
        case DOUBLE:
            x = atof(buff);
            printf("\nas a double is %g", x);
            break;
        default:
            printf("\nis not in the list");
    }
}
```

4. When should you not use a switch?

Because a **switch** is actually a decision-making statement, it serves as a substitute for an if or if-else statement. However, if a **switch** would have only one or two possible outcomes, it is often easier to understand the logic of the program with an if or if-else statement. Only use the **switch** with three or more possible outcomes of the switch expression.

5. What advantage is there to using symbolic constants in a program?

First, symbolic constants help document what a program is doing, helping you understand the program. Second, symbolic constants make it easy to change constants in a program. All you have to do is change the symbolic constant, rather than editing all occurrences of the constant throughout the program.

6. Write a program that accepts a number from 0 through 6 where 0 represents Sunday. Display the day of the week associated with the number entered by the user.

```
#include <stdio.h>

main()
{
    char c;

clrscr();
    printf("Enter a digit 0 through 6: ");
    c = getch() - '0';
    switch (c) {
```

```
    case 0:
        printf("\nSunday");
        break;
    case 1:
        printf("\nMonday");
        break;
    case 2:
        printf("\nTuesday");
        break;
    case 3:
        printf("\nWednesday");
        break;
    case 4:
        printf("\nThursday");
        break;
    case 5:
        printf("\nFriday");
        break;
    case 6:
        printf("\nSaturday");
        break;
    default:
        printf("\nBetween 0 and 6, dummy.\n");
        break;
    }
}
```

(Although we didn't need to, we used a break statement as part of the default case. It does no harm to do this and is consistent with the way case statements are used.)

10

Program Loops:
The while and
do-while Statements

T HIS CHAPTER INTRODUCES YOU TO PROGRAM LOOPS. FIRST YOU LEARN what a program loop is and then you discover how to write a program loop using both the goto, while, and do-while statements.

Introducing Program Loops

Loop structures are one of the most powerful elements of a programming language. A *program loop* exists when the same set of program statements are executed multiple times. There are two types of loops: "well-behaved loops," and not so well-behaved loops.

Well-Behaved Loops

Well-behaved loops have certain common characteristics. First, these loops almost always have a control variable that is initialized to some starting value. Second, some form of test decides whether another pass through the loop is needed. Each pass through the set of statements that comprise the loop is called an *iteration* of the loop. Finally, a statement changes the control variable as the loop progresses. In other words, such loops include these three characteristics:

- Loop initialization

- Loop testing

- Loop control

As you will see in a moment, loops that are not well-behaved are missing one or more of these three characteristics.

Creating a Loop with the goto Statement

C provides a goto statement, even though **goto** has received some bad press in the past. The syntax for **goto** has two parts: the goto statement itself and a program label:

```
goto label;
    .
    .
    .
label:
```

Notice that the goto statement is followed by a label name and then a semicolon. The label name, however, is followed by a colon. The label can occur either before or after the goto statement. Program 10.1 shows a simple goto example.

Program 10.1 Using the goto Statement

```c
#include <stdio.h>

main()
{
    char buff[10];
    int i;

  start:

    printf("\nEnter a number between 1 and 5: ");
    i = atoi(gets(buff));
    if (i < 1 || i > 5) {
        printf("\n\n   I said between 1 and 5\n");
        goto start;
    }
    printf("\n\nThe number was %d\n\n", i);
}
```

First the program defines several variables. Next comes the label name used with the goto statement. In this program, the label name is **start**. Remember, a label name is nothing more than a label for a memory address and must be followed by a colon rather than a semicolon. This label is not a variable that can be used in the program. It is simply a placeholder for a memory address.

The program then requests a number between 1 and 5. The normal gets() - atoi() function calls convert the input into a number. The if statement uses a pair of relational operators (< and >) and one logical operator (||) to see if the number entered is within the required range of values. If the value of **i** is not within the required range, the program displays a message and then executes the goto start statement.

The goto start statement is just an unconditional jump instruction telling the computer to send program control back to the memory address labeled **start**. In other words, Program 10.1 creates a loop that can execute the same set of statements more than once.

If the user enters a value between 1 and 5, the **if** statement is logical False and the printf() and goto statements are ignored. In this case, the program simply displays the value that was entered.

Is this loop well-behaved? First see if a variable controls the loop. Check whether there is an initial starting value for the control variable. In this program, the variable that controls the loop is **i**, whose value is dependent upon

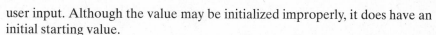

user input. Although the value may be initialized improperly, it does have an initial starting value.

Second, check whether there is a test of the loop-control variable. There is. The if statement checks the value of **i** to see whether another iteration of the loop is required.

Third, check whether the loop control variable changes within the loop. Perhaps. The user *could* keep entering any value outside of the desired range and the loop would repeat forever. In this sense, the loop is not ideal because it has the potential to run forever.

With some minor changes, we can make the loop perform better. Program 10.2 is an improved version of the loop.

This program is much like Program 10.1, but has a few additions. First, it includes another header file, stdlib.h, which contains information about functions not necessarily concerned with standard I/O. Next **#define** is used to define a symbolic constant MAXITERATIONS and set its value to 3. Finally, Program 10.2 includes this new set of statements:

```
++iterations;
if (iterations > MAXITERATIONS) {
    printf("\n\nI give up.");
    exit(EXIT_SUCCESS);
}
```

The variable named **iterations** keeps track of how many iterations of the loop have occurred. If **iterations** exceeds MAXITERATIONS, a message is displayed and the exit() function is called.

Using the exit() Function

The exit() function, part of the ANSI standard library, ends a program *without* reaching the closing brace of **main()**. Previous programs in this book ended simply because they ran out of program statements—that is, they reached the closing brace of **main()**. Program 10.2 uses the exit() function to quit executing without reaching the closing brace of **main()**.

Chapter 1 mentioned the five steps all programs have in common. The last step, the shutdown step, ensures that the program shuts itself down gracefully. That's what **exit()** does. If the program were more complex, **exit()** would automatically take care of some shutdown procedures. **exit()** is a good function to call when you want to terminate the program before the end of **main()**

The textual replacement for the symbolic constant EXIT_SUCCESS is found in the stdlib.h header file—one reason the header file was included in the program. EXIT_SUCCESS doesn't necessarily mean that the program went well, but that it is being shut down by choice. The EXIT_SUCCESS constant tells the operating system that it can shut down operations in the normal manner.

Program 10.2 Improving the goto Loop

```c
#include <stdio.h>
#include <stdlib.h>

#define MAXITERATIONS   3

main()
{
   char buff[10];
   int i, iterations;

   iterations = 0;

  start:

   printf("\nEnter a number between 1 and 5: ");
   i = atoi(gets(buff));

   ++iterations;
   if (iterations > MAXITERATIONS) {
      printf("\n\nI give up.");
      exit(EXIT_SUCCESS);
   }

   if (i < 1 || i > 5) {
      printf("\n\n   I said between 1 and 5");
      goto start;
   }
    printf("\n\nThe number was %d\n\n", i);
}
```

Under different circumstances, you might use another symbolic constant (EXIT_FAILURE) to tell the operating system that things did not close down properly. For example, maybe you tried to open a disk file and it wouldn't open. Under those circumstances, you might check for that possibility and use **exit(EXIT_FAILURE)**. (You can read about the atexit() function in the standard library documentation to see how to accomplish a "failure" shutdown gracefully.)

Program 10.2 simply ended at a point other than the end of **main()**, so it used EXIT_SUCCESS. There are more examples of the exit() function in later chapters, especially those dealing with disk data files and dynamic memory allocation.

The goto statement and its label are limited to the function body in which **goto** is used. That is, if you use a **goto** in the main() function, its label name must also appear in **main()**. You cannot have a goto statement in one function and its label name in a different function.

The loop in Program 10.2 is better behaved than the loop in Program 10.1 because the exit() function terminates the program after MAXITERA-TIONS passes through the loop. Still, using a goto statement doesn't produce the optimal loop structure.

Understanding while Loops

You can also use the while statement to create a loop structure. The general form for a while loop is

```
while (expression) {
    statement(s);
}
```

As long as *expression* is logical True, the statements are executed. Program 10.3 shows a sample while loop.

Program 10.3 uses a while loop to count the number of whitespace and punctuation characters that are entered. The while statement

```
while (c != ENTER) {
```

checks whether the user pressed Enter. A symbolic constant is used for the scan code associated with the Enter key. (Some older compilers may require that you check against the newline character instead of the carriage return.) As long as it is logical True that **c** is not the ENTER key, the statements within the while loop keep executing.

The call to **getch()** retrieves the characters and **printf()** displays them on the screen. The function **ispunct()** checks whether the character held in **c** is a punctuation character. If so, **ispunct()** returns a nonzero (logical True) value. This means the if statement is logical True, and the count of punctuation characters is incremented.

If **c** is not a punctuation character, the isspace() function is called to see whether it is a whitespace character. If so, the spaces variable is incremented. Any other input is not counted.

Program 10.3 A while Loop

```c
#include <stdio.h>
#include <ctype.h>

#define ENTER   '\r'

main()
{
    char c;
    int punctuation, spaces;

    clrscr();
    c = punctuation = spaces = 0;

    printf("\nType in what you want. Press Enter to end\n\n");

    while (c != ENTER) {
        c = getch();
        printf("%c", c);
        if (ispunct(c)) {
            ++punctuation;
        } else {
          if (isspace(c)) {
             ++spaces;
          }
        }
    }
    printf("\n\nwhitespace = %d\npunctuation =%d", spaces,
        punctuation);
}
```

When the user presses Enter, the while expression is no longer logical True and the loop ends. The final printf() call simply displays the two count variables.

PROGRAMMING TIP. *The is*() functions (**ispunct()**, **isalpha()**, **isspace()**, and so on) can check the properties of a character. They are perfect for logical tests. That is, they generally return 0 if they do not belong to the group being tested and nonzero if they do. If you use an is*() function, you should include the ctype.h (character type) header file. Also, including the header file means you don't have to link the is*() functions in from the standard library. The is*() functions are part of the ANSI C standard library and are also supported by the UNIX System V specification. They should be available with any commercial C compiler.*

Program Control Flow with a while Statement

As you saw in Program 10.3, the while expression determines whether there is another iteration of the loop. Figure 10.1 illustrates the program control flow for the while loop.

Figure 10.1
Program control flow for the **while** loop

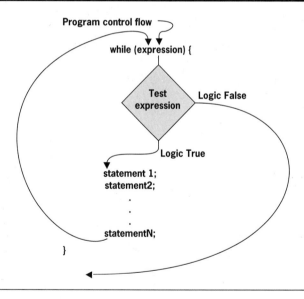

In Figure 10.1, program control enters the while loop and evaluates the expression that controls the loop. If the expression is logical False, all of the statements in the while loop are skipped. If the expression is logical True, the statements between the opening and closing brace are executed.

At the closing brace of the while loop, control is returned to the expression test. The expression is again evaluated to see if another iteration of the loop is necessary. Eventually, if the loop is well-behaved, the expression will evaluate logical False and control is sent to the statement following the closing brace of the while loop.

Note that the evaluation of the test expression is always performed *before* any of the statements in the while loop are executed. This makes it possible to skip the while loop completely if the initial evaluation of the while expression is logical False.

A More Complex Loop Program

So far the programs in this book have been fairly simple. Program 10.4 is a little more complex, but provides some interesting results. This program draws a distribution of numbers produced by the random number function **rand()**. The modulus operator limits the numbers to the values between 0 and 26, and the abs() function ensures that all numbers are positive values. A count of the numbers generated is stored in the totals[] array. Any time the running count of a specific number exceeds five, an asterisk is displayed in the column associated with that value. If **rand()** produces a sequence of random numbers, the result is a rectangular block of asterisks. That is, the probability of getting any one value is the same as the probability of getting any other number.

The program begins by defining several working variables, including the totals[] array, which is defined for MAXCOLUMNS elements. Next the user is asked for the number of iterations of the loop to perform; this is assigned into **limit**. (You might try 1000 when you run the program.) The program then uses a while loop to zero out each element of the totals[] array.

The program enters a second while loop, using **limit** as the maximum number of iterations to perform. The program calls **rand()** to generate a random number. The modulus operator ensures that the random number falls between -25 and +25. The abs() function takes the absolute value of the result so you can use **val** as an index into the totals[] array.

Next, the program ups the count in the totals[val] element of the array. The statement

```
gotoxy(val * 2 + 10, MAXROW - (totals[val] / 5));
```

is a bit strange, but allows you to plot the distribution of the random numbers. The function **gotoxy()** is the Borland cursor addressing function, which moves the cursor to the screen coordinates specified by its two arguments.

Program 10.4 Random Number while Loop

```c
#include <stdio.h>
#include <math.h>

#define MAXCOLUMNS    26
#define MAXROW        20

main()
{
    char buff[20];
    int count, limit, totals[MAXCOLUMNS], val;
    clrscr();
    printf("How many iterations: ");
    limit = atoi(gets(buff));

    count = 0;
    while (count < MAXCOLUMNS) {      /* Zero out the array */
        totals[count] = 0;
        count++;
    }

    count = 0;
    while (count < limit) {
        val = abs(rand()) % MAXCOLUMNS;
        totals[val] += 1;
        gotoxy(val * 2 + 10, MAXROW - (totals[val] / 5));
        printf("*");
        count++;
    }
    gotoxy(1, 24);
    getch();
}
```

(The arguments are in column-row, or X-Y, order for **gotoxy()**, but are re-versed for the Microsoft cursor addressing function.) Multiplying **val** by 2 produces a blank space between columns. Adding 10 to the result centers the display better.

The calculation for the row address takes MAXROW and subtracts the count in the **totals[val]** after that count is divided by 5. For example, if the rand() function has produced a count of 25 for **totals[val]**, the row position is

```
MAXROW - (totals[val] / 5)
20 - (25 / 5)
20 - 5
15
```

In the first pass through the while loop, **totals[val]** has a count of 0. The row coordinate in that case would be

```
MAXROW - (totals[val] / 5)
20 - (0 / 5)
20 - 0
20
```

Therefore, as the count increases in each element of the totals[] array, the row coordinate decreases. The result is that a column of asterisks rises from row 20 towards the top of the display as the count increases.

After the asterisk is printed, **count** is incremented and the program tests whether another iteration of the loop is needed. The while loop continues until **count** is no longer less than **limit**. At that point, the while loop ends, the cursor is placed near the bottom of the screen, and the program waits for the user to press a key. (This allows the user to pause the display before ending the program.) When the user presses a key, the program ends.

When I ran Program 10.4, the output looked like the Chicago skyline. This suggests that the random number generator is not completely random. However, this is not the fault of the compiler vendor. Generating a sequence of totally random numbers is not trivial. In fact, most rand() functions gener-ate a sequence of pseudorandom numbers where the sequence of the num-bers is repeatable. Consult your compiler documentation for details about your random number function.

If you are using an MS-DOS compiler that does not have a cursor ad-dressing function, you can use the gotoxy() function. Simply copy this code into your program after **main()** and add the line

```
void gotoxy(int x, int y);
```

before the main() function. Enter the code for the gotoxy() function just like this:

```
#include <dos.h>

void gotoxy(int x, int y)
{
    union REGS ireg;

    ireg.h.ah = 0x02;        /* Function    */
    ireg.h.bh = 0;           /* Video page  */
    ireg.h.dl = x;
    ireg.h.dh = y;
    int86(0x10, &ireg, &ireg);
}
```

You haven't yet learned about the union keyword, which is covered in Chapter 19. However, in the meantime this code will allow you to write programs that use cursor addressing.

Zeroing Out Arrays

The first while loop in Program 10.4 initializes the element values in the totals[] array to zero, often referred to as "zeroing out" the array. This process is needed because C does not necessarily set the values in an array to zero.

However, Program 10.4 doesn't zero out the array very efficiently. You can replace the first **while** in Program 10.4

```
while (count < MAXCOLUMNS) {     /* Zero out the array */
    totals[count] = 0;
    count++;
}
```

with the single line

```
memset(totals, 0, MAXCOLUMNS * sizeof(int));
```

The **memset()** sets a chunk of memory to a specified value. The arguments to **memset()** are

```
memset(address, value, bytes)
```

The function goes to the memory address held in **address** (which must be an lvalue) and sets the number of bytes held in **bytes** to the value held in

value. In the example, **memset()** goes to the lvalue of **totals[]** and sets MAX-COLUMNS * **sizeof(int)** bytes of memory to 0. Notice that the third argument is in bytes. This is why you must multiply MAXCOLUMNS by the size of an **int**. If you just used MAXCOLUMNS, you would only zero out half of the array.

memset() zeros out the array about twice as fast as a while loop, partly because it does no checking on the arguments supplied to it. **memset()** is very fast, but is as dumb as a box of rocks.

Using the break Statement in while Loops

In Chapter 9 you learned how to use the break statement to send control to the statement following a **switch**. You can also use the break statement in a while loop. In this section you'll modify Program 10.4 to trap a potential bug.

There are several potential bugs in Program 10.4. First, the user can enter a number larger than a signed **int** can hold. For example, if the user enters a number larger than approximately 32,800, the value of **limit** becomes negative (the sign bit gets turned on). Because **limit** is less than **count** in the program, nothing is displayed. As a way around this, you could write a while loop that forced the user to keep entering values until **limit** was less than INT_MAX as defined in the limits.h header file.

The second potential bug may occur if the user enters a very large number for **limit**, but a number that is less than INT_MAX (30,000, for example). If the count in an element of the totals[] array exceeds 105, the cursor positioning calculation can give a negative column value. For example, suppose **totals[0]** = 105. In our column calculation, we get

```
MAXROW - (totals[val] / 5)
20 - (105 / 5)
20 - 21
-1
```

What happens when this occurs depends upon how your vendor wrote the cursor addressing routine. Even if the routine handles this gracefully, it is still an error. Program 10.5 shows one way to address the problem.

Most of the program is the same as before. The string.h header file is included because the memset() function has been added to the program. This program also defines a new symbolic constant MAXCOUNT and sets it equal to 90, which produces two empty rows at the top of the display. That is, if a count of 105 could overflow the cursor addressing function, a count of 90 leaves two empty rows at the top of the screen.

Program 10.5 An Improved Random Number Program Using break

```c
#include <stdio.h>
#include <string.h>
#include <math.h>

#define MAXCOLUMNS    26
#define MAXROW        20
#define MAXCOUNT      90

main()
{
   char buff[20];
   int count, limit, totals[MAXCOLUMNS], val;

   clrscr();
   printf("How many iterations: ");
   limit = atoi(gets(buff));

   count = 0;
   memset(totals, 0, MAXCOLUMNS * sizeof(int));

   count = 0;
   while (count < limit) {
      val = abs(rand()) % MAXCOLUMNS;
      totals[val] += 1;
      if (totals[val] > MAXCOUNT) {
         gotoxy(25, 23);
         printf("overflow in column %d", val);
         break;
      }
      gotoxy(val * 2 + 10, MAXROW - (totals[val] / 5));
      printf("*");
      count++;
   }
   gotoxy(1, 24);
   getch();
}
```

The while loop now includes an if statement that compares the count in the totals[val] array to MAXCOUNT. If the count is greater than MAX-COUNT, the cursor is set near the middle of the screen and the word "overflow" is displayed. Next the break statement is executed. Much like the **break** in a switch statement, the break statement sends program control to the first line immediately after the while loop. In Program 10.5, program control is sent to the statement

```
gotoxy(1, 24);
```

near the bottom of **main()**. Figure 10.2 illustrates this program control flow.

Figure 10.2

Control flow with a **break** in a while loop

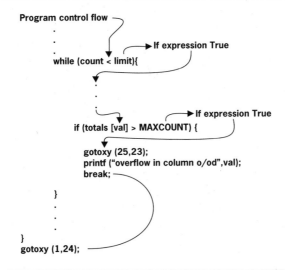

If **count** is less than **limit** and **totals[val]** is greater than MAXCOUNT, the gotoxy() and printf() statements controlled by the if statement are executed. Then the break statement is executed, transferring control out of the while loop. Therefore, the break statement always sends control to the first statement outside of the while loop that contains the break.

Nested while Loops and break Statements

Where does **break** send control if there is a while loop within a while loop? Consider the following code fragment.

```
while (i < MAXNUM) {
   while (j < MAXNUM) {

      /* some statements */

      if (j == goal) {
         printf("Bingo!");
         break;              /* Where do we go? */
      }
      /* More statements */
   }                         /* End while (j < MAXNUM */
   printf("Pass %d", i);

}                            /* End while (i < MAXNUM */
/* More program code */
```

If **j** equals **goal**, you've found what you're looking for and the if statement is logical True. The "Bingo" message is displayed and the break statement is executed. Now does program control go to the **printf("Pass %d", i)** statement or to the comment /* More program code */?

The break statement always sends control to the first statement following the while loop that contains the break statement. Because the break statement is within the second while loop, program control is sent to the **printf("Pass %d", i)** statement. If you wanted to break out of the while loop controlled by **i**, you would need to have another if test and a break statement where the **printf("Pass %d", i)** statement appeared. (Alternatively, you could use a goto statement.)

A single break statement, therefore, can only send control out of the the innermost loop that contains the break statement. If the loops are nested, you need to use multiple break statements.

Using the do-while Statement

The do-while statement is an important variation of the while statement. Its general form is

```
do {
   statement(s);
} while (expression);
```

The statements within the opening and closing braces are controlled by the do-while statements. The value of *expression* determines whether there is another iteration through the loop. Figure 10.3 shows how the program control flow works with a do-while statement.

Figure 10.3
Program control flow for a do-while statement

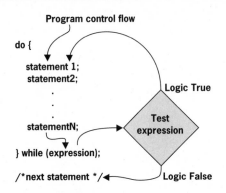

Program control first flows into the do-while statement and executes *statement1* through *statementN*. Next, the expression controlling the do-while statement is evaluated. If the result of the evaluation is logical True, the statements within the do-while loop are executed again. If the expression evaluates to logical False, program control is sent to the statement following the do-while loop.

Comparing the while and do-while Statements

In while loops, it's possible that the loop statements are not executed because the test on *expression* occurs at the top of the loop. In contrast, every **do-while** executes its loop statements at least once because the test on *expression* occurs at the bottom of the loop. In Program 10.4, for example, a negative value for **limit** means that nothing is printed. If Program 10.4 had used a **do-while**, it would have passed through the loop statements at least once.

Program 10.6 demonstrates how while and do-while loops differ.

The program requests a positive or negative value. Depending upon whether *P* or some other letter is entered, **i** is set to either 1 or -1 and the related message is displayed.

If the value is positive, the first while loop is not entered. Because the test is on **i** less than 0, a positive value returns a logical False for the test expression and all of the statements within the first while loop are skipped.

In the do-while statement, the same test expression is used. However, because the test expression is at the bottom of the loop, the loop statements are executed at least once, even if the test expression is logical False. Run Program 10.6 and note that this is exactly how it behaves.

Program 10.6 while versus do-while Loops

```c
#include <stdio.h>

main()
{
    int i, count;

    clrscr();
    printf("Select positive or negative (P or N): ");
    i = toupper(getch()) - 'P';

    if (i == 0) {
        printf("\nPositive\n");
        i = 1;
    } else {
        printf("\nNegative\n");
        i = -1;
    }

    while (i < 0) {
        printf("\nGoing through the while loop");
        i++;
    }

    do {
        printf("\nGoing through the do-while loop");
        i++;
    } while (i < 0);
}
```

Using the break Statement with a do-while Loop

The do-while loop can also include a break statement. As in the simple while statement, the break statement sends control to the first statement following the do-while loop. That is, it sends control to the first statement following the while (*expression*); component of the do-while loop. Therefore, you should only use a do-while loop when you want to be sure to execute the loop statements at least one time.

When Should You Use a do-while Loop?

At first, you might consider the do-while loop not terribly useful. Indeed, less than 5 percent of the loop structures in C use a do-while loop. However, the potential bugs in Program 10.4 presented a perfect situation for a **do-while**. Recall that if the number was greater than could be represented with a **signed int**, the variable could overflow, resulting in a negative number. Program 10.7 shows one solution for this problem using a do-while loop.

Program 10.7 Using a do-while Loop to Check Input

```c
#include <stdio.h>
#include <limits.h>

main()
{
   char buff[10];
   int limit;

   clrscr();

   printf("\n(Pssst. The maximum positive int is %d)\n\n\n",
      INT_MAX);
   do {
      printf("\nHow many iterations: ");
      limit = atoi(gets(buff));
   } while (limit < 0 || limit > INT_MAX);
   printf("\n\nThe number is %d\n", limit);

}
```

The program includes the limits.h header file so you have access to the symbolic constant INT_MAX, the largest value a **signed int** can have. The program begins by telling you what this maximum value is.

Next is the do-while loop. The user is prompted for the number of iterations to be performed, as in Program 10.4. The atoi() and gets() calls convert the input into a numeric value and assign it into **limit**. The test expression is

```c
(limit < 0 || limit > INT_MAX)
```

which says that if **limit** is negative or larger than INT_MAX, keep asking the user for input. Actually, the second expression of the logical OR test isn't really needed. (If the user enters any value greater than INT_MAX, the value will be negative.) However, the expression shows how you can use the test expression to bracket an input within two limits.

Obviously, it would be better to display an error message telling users what they did wrong. You should be able to add that embellishment yourself, if you wish.

Conclusion

The while and do-while statements are a simple means for creating loop structures. However, sometimes the **goto** provides the most direct solution to a problem. You can use a **goto** in a loop structure to jump over a large section of code that you do not want executed under certain conditions. However, there is otherwise little reason to use a goto statement to form a loop.

Checking Your Progress

1. What makes a "well-behaved" loop?

Well-behaved loops almost always include three elements: an initialization statement that sets a loop counter to a starting value, a test of the counter to see if another iteration of the loop is needed, and an increment or decrement operation on the loop counter on each pass through the loop.

2. What's wrong with this code?

```
start:
   /* Some code */
   start = 100;
```

In C, goto labels are followed by a colon. However, a goto label is not a variable in the program. It is simply a marker for the compiler; it contains a memory address and nothing else. Therefore, the compiler cannot let you assign anything into a label, which is what the code fragment above is attempting to do.

3. What purpose does the exit() function serve?

The exit() function enables you to terminate a program before reaching the closing brace of **main()**. Because **exit()** performs certain housekeeping chores before ending a program, it is a safe and graceful way to end a program.

4. What is the primary difference between a while and a do-while loop?

A while loop performs a test at the top of the loop to decide whether to execute the loop. If the test condition is False, the loop may not be executed. The test condition is also checked before each iteration of the loop. The do-while loop, on the other hand, has its iteration test at the bottom of the loop. Therefore, at least one iteration of the loop is always performed.

5. What function does the break statement have in while and do-while loops?

The break keyword allows you to send program control to the first statement following the while or do-while loop that contains the break statement. This allows you to exit from a loop before all iterations have been executed.

6. Why is the memset() function faster at zeroing out an array than a while loop?

The memset() function doesn't have the overhead of the loop structure. Most loops have a loop counter variable that decides whether another iteration of the loop is required, as well as a test condition that tests the loop counter. Because **memset()** does not use these loop elements directly, the CPU does not have to load, store, and compare them on each pass through the loop. The result is a very fast function.

7. Write a program that takes a string as input from the user, adds the values of the ASCII characters in the strings, and displays the total.

```c
#include <stdio.h>

main()
{

    char buff[200];
    int i, sum;

    clrscr();
    printf("Enter a string of characters: ");
    gets(buff);

    sum = i = 0;
```

```
while (buff[i]) {
    sum += buff[i++];
}
printf("\n\nThe total is %d\n\n", sum);
}
```

Notice that we rely on the null termination character in **buff[]** to terminate the while loop. Also notice the postincrement on **i** in the loop.

The for Loop

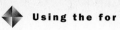

N THIS CHAPTER YOU WILL LEARN ABOUT THE FOR LOOP AND HOW IT IS used. We will also discuss the continue statement and how it can be used with different loop structures.

Using the for Loop

Of all of the loop structures that C offers, the for loop is the most often used. Although the **for** is not very different from the **while** or **do-while**, it has the advantage that all three conditions of a well-behaved loop—initialization, testing, and control—are visible on a single line of code.

The general form of the for loop is

```
for (expression1; expression2; expression3) {
    statement(s);
}
```

As you can see, there are three expressions in the for loop. The first expression (*expression1*) is normally used to initialize the variable that controls the loop. The second expression (*expression2*) is the test that determines whether another iteration of the loop is necessary. The third expression (*expression3*) is used to control the variable that governs the loop.

In most loops, the third expression either increments or decrements the variable that was initialized in the first expression. (It's not by accident that the three expressions coincide with the three elements necessary for a well-behaved loop.)

Program 11.1 presents an example of how the for loop is used.

The program simply uses a for loop to display MAXITERS random numbers. Our real interest is to see how the for loop controls the program.

The Initialization Expression (*expression1*)

In the for loop in Program 11.1, the first expression is

```
i = 0;
```

This expression initializes the starting value of the variable used to control the loop. In our example, **i** is the only variable used in the loop. You can, however, initialize more than one variable in *expression1*. For example, you could write

```
for (i = 0, j = 10; i < MAXITERS; i++)
```

(This assumes, of course, that **j** has been defined.) Simply separate each variable to be initialized with the comma operator.

Program 11.1   **A Sample for Loop**

```c
#include <stdio.h>
#include <stdlib.h>

#define MAXITERS   100

main()
{
    int i;

    clrscr();
    printf("The following is a list of random
        numbers:\n\n");
    for (i = 0; i < MAXITERS; i++) {
        if (i && i % 10 == 0) {
            printf("\n");
        }
        printf("%7d", rand());
    }
    printf("\n\n");
}
```

Note that the initialization of **i** (*expression1*) only occurs one time, when the program first enters the for loop. After the first expression is executed once, it is not executed a second time by the loop.

The Test Expression (*expression2*)

The second expression in the for loop is

```c
i < MAXITERS;
```

It is this expression that determines whether the loop executes another pass through the loop statements. As long as **i** is less than MAXITERS, the loop continues to process the statements contained within the braces that form the body of the loop. The loop body starts with the opening brace at the end of the for statement line and continues to the closing brace at the end of the statements within the loop.

COMMON TRAP. *If you write enough C code, you will eventually write a for loop similar to*

```
for (i = 0; i = MAXLOOP; i++) {
   /* Loop Body */
}
```

If MAXLOOP is a nonzero value, the loop never ends (an infinite *loop). The reason is because* expression2 *is always assigned the value represented by MAXLOOP. Unless MAXLOOP is zero (not very likely),* expression2 *is viewed as logic True and the loop executes forever. In most cases, you want to make sure* expression2 *at least has the potential to become logic False.*

The Control Expression (*expression3*)

The third expression in the for loop

```
i++
```

is used to increment the variable that controls the number of passes made through the loop. After each pass through the loop, **i** is incremented. You can also have multiple expressions for *expression3*. For example,

```
for (i = 0, j = 10; i < MAXITERS; i++, j++)
```

Notice how we increment both **i** and **j** in the third expression. Again, each subexpression must be separated by the comma operator.

In terms of the sequencing of the third expression, the behavior of the **for** is such that *expression3* appears as though it was in the program source code just before the closing brace of the for loop. That is, *expression3* is evaluated at the bottom of the loop. The program control flow for the for loop is shown in Figure 11.1.

As you can see in Figure 11.1, program control enters the for loop at *expression1*. In the figure, this expression initializes the loop control variable **i** to 0.

Program control immediately proceeds to *expression2*, which tests to see if **i** is less than MAXITERS. If **i** is not less than MAXITERS, the test evaluates to logic False and control proceeds to the first statement that follows the for loop.

If *expression2* is logic True, program control proceeds to execute the statements found in the body of the for loop. (The statements controlled by the loop, of course, must be within the opening and closing braces of the for loop.)

Figure 11.1

Program control
flow with a for loop

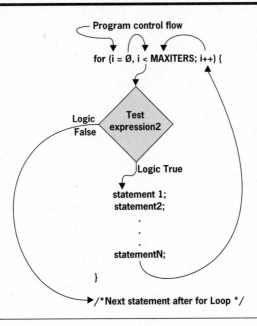

After the statements in the loop are processed, control is sent to *expression3*. Usually, the third expression is responsible for incrementing or decrementing the loop control variable (**i**), but any valid C expression can be used.

After *expression3* is processed, control is sent to *expression2* to determine if another pass through the loop is needed. In Figure 11.1, this process repeats until **i** equals MAXITERS. At that time, *expression2* is logic False and control is sent to the first statement following the for loop.

Visualizing a for Loop

It is important that you understand the sequence in which the three for loop expressions are processed. Figure 11.1 should help you visualize the sequencing of the for loop expressions. Program 11.2 shows you how the expressions are processed in an actual program.

The for loop in Program 11.2 looks strange because we have placed each loop expression on its own line. Also, we have added a printf() call as part of each expression. As you will recall, the comma operator is used to separate expressions. Placing a **printf()** as a subexpression in a for loop is perfectly legal in C (albeit a little harder to read).

Program 11.2

Sequencing of a for Loop

```c
#include <stdio.h>

main()
{
   int i;

   clrscr();
   for (i = 0, printf("\n        Expression1: i = %d\n", i);
     printf("\n Expression2: i = %d", i), i < 4;
     i++, printf("\n Expression3: i = %d\n\n", i)) {

     printf("\n        Pass number %d", i);
     getch();
   }
}
```

PROGRAMMING TIP. *Sometimes the error messages from the compiler are not terribly helpful. For example, you might be doing a function call with a function that has six or seven arguments, one of which the compiler isn't too happy about. Although debuggers are getting better, many can only pinpoint the line where the error is, not the exact argument causing the problem. To solve this problem, simply use your text editor to break up the arguments so each one appears on a new line. (Obviously, you should break them apart at the point where the comma operator appears between arguments.) Because C doesn't care about lines, spaces, or any other style considerations, the program will compile exactly as before. The only difference is that the compiler will tell you exactly which argument is causing the problem because it now appears on its own line.*

When you run Program 11.2, the output looks like

```
        Expression1: i = 0
Expression2: i = 0
      Pass number 0
Expression3: i = 1

Expression2: i = 1
      Pass number 1
Expression3: i = 2
```

and so on for each pass through the loop. First, note that *expression1* is only executed once. Its **printf()** is never called a second time while the loop executes.

Next, *expression2* is evaluated. Observe that the test criteria are evaluated *before* we execute the loop statements. In this sense, the for loop is similar to a while loop in that the test occurs before the loop is entered. It follows that a for loop may not make any iteration of the loop statements if the second expression evaluates to logic False upon entry into the loop. (In most programs, *expression2* is a relational test.)

Assuming that *expression2* is logic True, the statement(s) in the loop body are executed. In our example, we simply print out a message stating what the pass number is.

After all statements in the loop body have been processed, *expression3* is evaluated. This means that the loop behaves as though *expression3* is the last statement in the loop body.

After *expression3* is evaluated, control is sent back to *expression2*, not *expression1*. The purpose of *expression2* is to decide whether another pass through the loop is made. The sequence of *expression2*, loop statements, and *expression3* is repeated until *expression2* becomes logic False. When *expression2* becomes logic False, the loop ends and control is sent to the statement immediately following the closing brace of the loop body.

The behavior of the loop is the same as depicted in Figure 11.1.

Writing Infinite for Loops

Sometimes an infinite loop structure is desirable. For example, a computer system might be used to monitor a building's heating and cooling system. An infinite for loop could poll a series of sensors throughout the building, taking appropriate action based on the readings returned from the sensors.

To create an infinite for loop, simply omit all three expressions from the for loop. For example,

```
/* Some setup code */
for (; ;) {
    /* Loop statements */
}
```

Notice that we must still leave the semicolons in the parentheses of the for loop, but expressions 1 through 3 are omitted. A semicolon without an expression is called a *null program statement*. Null program statements are perfectly legal in C. When a for loop has null program statements for the three loop expressions, C creates an infinite for loop. (It views *expression2* as though it were logic True.)

In fact, you may run across code similar to this:

```
#define EVER    ;;

for (EVER) {
   /* Loop statements */
}
```

After the preprocessor is finished, the for statement becomes

```
for (;;) {
```

thus creating an infinite loop. The symbolic constant makes it clear that an infinite loop is desired. Kinda neat!

Style Considerations with for Loops

Because C doesn't care how the statements in a program are placed, you can use just about any style you wish with the for (or any other) loop. However, the two most prominent styles are the one shown in Programs 11.1 and 11.2 and the following:

```
for (expression1; expression2; expression2)
{
   /* statements */
}
```

The style above aligns the opening brace of the loop body with the "f" in the keyword **for**. The closing brace of the loop body aligns with the opening brace of the loop body. All statements controlled by the loop are indented one tab stop.

This style should look somewhat familiar to the alternative style used with the if statement. In fact, programmers are fairly consistent about the placing of braces and keywords. That is, if a programmer aligns the opening brace with the "f" of the keyword **for**, they also write the if statement with a similar style:

```
if (expression)
{
   /* statements */
}
```

Again, I prefer the form that places the opening brace on the same line as the keyword, as shown in Programs 11.1 and 11.2 and

```
for (expression1; expression2; expression3) {
   /* statements */
}
```

This allows me to get one more line on the screen, yet still retain the indentation to mark the statements controlled by the **for**.

Using the break Statement in for Loops

The break statement may be used in a for loop to transfer control out of the loop before it would otherwise terminate. We can modify Program 11.1 to show how the break statement works.

Program 11.3 is almost identical to Program 11.1, except we increased the number of iterations and provided a means of terminating the loop early. After PAUSE numbers are displayed, the **if** becomes logic True and we display a message telling the user how to continue or end the program. If the user touches the X key, the second if statement becomes True and we execute the break statement.

The behavior of the break statement in a for loop is the same as with the while and do-while loops. The **break** sends program control to the first statement immediately outside of the loop that contains the break statement. In Program 11.3, control is sent to the last printf() call near the bottom of the program.

PROGRAMMING TIP. *Over the past ten years, commercial programmers have begun to adopt certain* de facto *standards regarding how a program functions. The table below presents some of the keys that have become standards for certain program actions.*

Informal Standard Key Interpretations

Key	Action
Escape	Abort an operation
F1	Online help
F10	Continue to the next step or part of the program
Tab	Advance to next field. Also used to accept input for a field under Windows
Shift-Tab	Back up to previous field
Alt	Go to menu bar
Spacebar	Accept default input
X	End a program

*You don't have to use these keys as they're defined here, but it's smart to do so
because users are increasingly familiar with these definitions.*

Program 11.3   **Using the break Statement in a for Loop**

```c
#include <stdio.h>
#include <stdlib.h>
#include <ctype.h>

#define MAXITERS   10000
#define PAUSE      100

main()
{
    char c;
    int i;

    clrscr();
    printf("  The following is  a list of random
    numbers:\n");
    printf("          Press 'X' to end Program\n\n");

    for (i = 0; i < MAXITERS; i++) {
        if (i && i % PAUSE == 0) {
            printf("\n\n Press 'X' to end; any key to
                continue:\n");
            c = toupper(getch());
            if (c == 'X') {
                break;
            }
        }
        if (i && i % 10 == 0) {
            printf("\n");
        }
        printf("%7d", rand());
    }
    printf("\n\n\n");
}
```

The continue Statement

In some situations, you would like to skip over the code in a loop, but not exit from the loop. The continue statement allows you to continue with the next iteration of a loop, but skip over any remaining code in the loop. The program control flow of a for loop with a continue statement is shown in Figure 11.2.

Notice how the continue statement sends program control to the third expression in the for loop. All of the other statements in the for loop are skipped.

Program 11.4 shows an example of how the continue statement is used. The first thing to notice in Program 11.4 is *expression1* of the for loop:

```
flag = i = 0
```

This is a common C idiom that assigns the value of 0 into both **flag** and **i**. You can use a similar construct at any point in a C program. For example,

```
sum = squares = totals = 0.0;
```

sets all three values to 0.0. (This statement assumes that all three variables are **double** or **float** data types.)

If you wish, you can initialize variables to different values in *expression1* by separating them with a comma operator:

```
for (i = 10, j = 0; j < MAXLOOP; j++)
```

Just remember that a semicolon terminates a statement, not a comma.

Figure 11.2

Program control flow of continue statement in a for loop

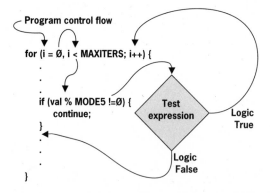

```
Program control flow

for (i = Ø, i < MAXITERS; i++) {
    .
    .
    .
    if (val % MODE5 !=Ø) {        Test
        continue;              expression      Logic
    }                                           True
    .
    .                          Logic
    .                          False
}
```

Returning to Program 11.4, we are simply using the program to display a series of random numbers, but *only* if the random number is evenly divisible by MOD5 (for example, 5). If the number is not evenly divisible by MOD5, we want to proceed immediately to the next iteration of the loop. In other words, we want to ignore the rest of the code in the loop.

Program 11.4   **Using the continue Statement**

```c
#include <stdio.h>
#include <stdlib.h>

#define MAXITERS  1000     /* Number of loop iterations  */
#define MAXVALS   101      /* Number shown before pause  */
#define MOD5      5        /* The modulus value          */
#define LINESIZE  6        /* Values shown per line      */

main()
{
   int flag, i, val;

   clrscr();
   printf("  The following is a list of mod-5 random
       numbers:\n\n");
   for (flag = i = 0; i < MAXITERS; i++) {
      val = rand();
      if (val % MOD5 != 0) {
         continue;
      }
      printf("%6d(%4d) ", val, i);
      flag++;
      if (flag % LINESIZE == 0) {
         printf("\n");
      }
      if (flag > MAXVALS) {
         printf("\n\n     Press any key to continue:\n");
         getch();
         flag = 0;
      }
   }
   printf("\n\n\n");
}
```

The continue statement is used with an if statement to see if the random value (**val**) is evenly divisible by MOD5. If it is not, the if statement is logic True and we execute the continue statement. The continue statement sends control to *expression3* of the loop. Because *expression3* behaves as though it were placed at the bottom of the loop, all the statements between the **continue** and the bottom of the loop are ignored.

Format Control with printf()

If you have paid close attention to the programs in this chapter, you've noticed that we have used some formatting features of **printf()** to form columns of numbers. The general form for a format control in **printf()** is shown in Figure 11.3.

Figure 11.3
printf() format controls

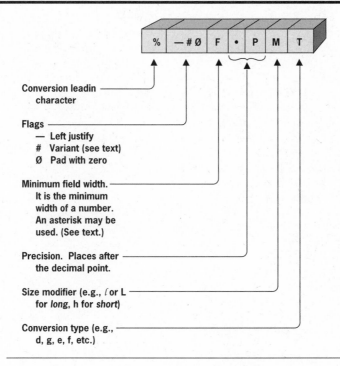

When using format control in a call to **printf()**, the first character must be the percent sign (%). In Figure 11.3, all of the conversion flags are options except the conversion leadin character (%) and the conversion letter (the T entry in Figure 11.3). In fact, until this chapter, we have not used any of the optional conversion specifications with **printf()**.

Let's examine the conversion specifications in a little more detail.

Conversion Flags

These flags modify the basic conversion in the following ways.

Minus Flag (–)

Causes the field to be left-justified. The default is right-justification. For example,

```
printf(">%-20s<", "Dog");
printf(">%20s<", "Dog");
```

displays

```
>Dog                 <
>                 Dog<
```

As you saw in this chapter, the minus sign can be used with numeric values, too.

Zero Flag (0)

Causes a field to be padded with zeros. The default padding character is a space. For example,

```
printf(">%5d<", 12);
printf(">%05d<", 12);
```

displays

```
>   12<
>00012<
```

The zero flag has an effect only when a minimum field width is specified and the number does not fill the field width.

The Sharp Flag (#)

Used only with the e, E, f, g, G, i, o, x, and X conversion types. The exact meaning depends upon the conversion type. For example,

```
printf("%#8x", 27);    /* Hexadecimal conversion */
printf("%8x", 27);
printf("%#8o", 27);    /* Octal conversion */
printf("%8o", 27);
```

displays

```
0x1b
1b
033
33
```

In these examples, the sharp sign causes the standard base numbering prefix to be placed before the number. Not all compilers support the sharp conversion flag. Consult your printf() documentation.

Field Width

The field width specifier tells the minimum number of spaces to use to display the output. If the data requires more spaces than this field width, the space required for the complete output is used. Therefore, if you are trying to format columns of data, make sure the minimum field width can hold the largest data item expected for the field.

The field width can be used with numeric or string data. For example

```
printf("%30s", "Don");
printf("%2s", "Don");
printf("%12f", 1.0 / 3.0);
printf("%f", 1.0 / 3.0);
```

displays

```
                             Don
Don
    0.333333
0.333333
```

First note that, even though we specified a width of 2 for the second **printf()**, the string needs three characters for display and, hence, the minimum field width is overridden. In the third **printf()**, the field width is larger than needed, thus the numbers are right-justified by default. In the last **printf()**, with no width specified, the number has no padding with blank spaces.

The asterisk provides one more interesting variation of the field specifier. The asterisk says that the field with is an argument in **printf()**. For example,

```
printf(">%*s<", 10, "DOG");
```

displays

```
>       DOG<
```

The first argument to **printf()** (10) becomes the field width specifier for the string. Because the argument can also be a variable, this provides a means of reformatting a string at runtime based on the value of a variable in the program.

Precision

If a decimal point is followed by an integer constant, **printf()** interprets the decimal and the integer constant together as a precision to use for display. For example,

```
printf("%12.8f", 1.0 / 3. 0);
```

is displayed as

```
0.33333333
```

The output is displayed in a field of 12 spaces with eight places following the decimal point.

Modifier

The modifier is only used with the l, L, or h modifier. The l and L are used with the **long** data type and the h is used with a **short int**. For example,

```
printf("%ld", 500000);
```

displays the value 500000 correctly. However, forgetting the modifier can cause some interesting problems. For example,

```
printf("%d", 500000);
```

is displayed as

```
-24288
```

on my PC. On some machines, the output will be shown correctly. However, my PC has a two-byte **int**, rather than four bytes on a true 32-bit machine. As a result, **printf()** displays "half a **long**," producing the negative number.

The final field is the conversion type. We have already covered these options in Table 4.5 of Chapter 4.

Different printf() Formats

Always keep in mind that the first argument to **printf()**, called the *control string*, is simply a string. Therefore, you can use different control strings by using a character string variable rather than a constant. Program 11.5 shows an example of how you can use a string for format control.

So why use a variable rather than a simple string constant? Several reasons. First, every time you use a string constant, the compiler must create data space for the string constant. By using a variable, the data space is only created once but may be used many times.

Program 11.5　　**Using a String for Format Control with printf()**

```c
#include <stdio.h>

main()
{
    char format[3][10] = {
            "\n%-12s\n",
            "%12d\n",
            "%12c\n"
            };

    printf(format[0], "Jack");
    printf(format[1], 12);
    printf(format[2], 'A');
    getch();
}
```

More important, if you decide to change the format used for a piece of data, by using a variable you need only change the definition of the format control string. If you use string constants, you have to use the program editor to search-and-replace all instances of the string constant. Using a variable simplifies changes in the format control string.

Using Nested for Loops

Obviously you can have a for loop within a for loop, forming what is called a *nested* loop. Program 11.6 illustrates a nested for loop.

The purpose of Program 11.6 is to present a number and its square and cube values. The program is a bit artificial because I wanted to use a switch statement within the for loops. First, we define a two-dimensional array of integers to hold the values. Symbolic constants are used for the subscript values so you can change them easily if you wish.

The two for loops are controlled by variables **i** and **j**. Variable **i** controls MAXLOOPS values, while **j** controls the three values that are placed in the array (TERMS). When we enter the **i for** loop, we immediately enter the **j for** loop. Therefore, on the first pass through both loops, we are looking at **array[0][0]** because **i** and **j** are both 0. The switch expression is **j**, so we immediately fall into **case 0:**. Because 0 times itself is not terribly interesting, we assign the value **i** plus 1 on each pass through the loops. Therefore, **array[0][0]** is assigned the value of 1. The break statement sends control to *expression3* of the **j** loop.

Program 11.6   **Nested for Loop**

```c
#include <stdio.h>

#define MAXLOOPS  10
#define TERMS      3

main()
{
    int array[MAXLOOPS][TERMS], i, j;

    for (i = 0; i < MAXLOOPS; i++) {
        for (j = 0; j < TERMS; j++) {
            switch (j) {
                case 0:
                    array[i][j] = i + 1;
                    break;
                case 1:
                    array[i][j] = array[i][0] * array[i][0];
                    break;
                case 2:
                    array[i][j] = array[i][0] * array[i][0] *
                                  array[i][0];
                    break;
                default:
                    printf("Should never get here.");
                    break;
            }                      /* End switch()  */
        }                          /* End for (j    */
    }                              /* End for (i    */
    clrscr();
    printf("    Number    Square    Cube\n\n");
    for (i = 0; i < MAXLOOPS; i++) {
        for (j = 0; j < TERMS; j++) {
            printf("%8d  ", array[i][j]);
        }
        printf("\n");
    }
}
```

Variable **j** is then incremented by *expression3* (that is, **j++**) and we proceed to the next iteration of the **j** loop. Because **j** now equals 1, **array[0][1]** is assigned the square of value **array[0][0]**. The break statement again sends control to *expression3* of the **j** loop.

Because **j** now equals 2, the switch statement sends control to case **2** where **array[0][2]** is assigned the cube of the value. The **break** again sends control to *expression3* which increments **j**.

Because **j** is now 3, which is equal to TERMS, *expression2* (**j < TERMS**) is logic False. Therefore, we are finished processing the **j** loop.

Control is now sent to *expression3* of the **i** loop, which increments **i**. Next, *expression2* (**i < MAXLOOPS**) of the **i** loop is evaluated. Because **i** is less than MAXLOOPS, we perform another iteration of the loop. Once again, we fall into the **j** loop and repeat its sequence over again. This process continues until **i** is equal to MAXLOOPS. At that time, we are finished with the **i** loop and control is sent to the clrscr() function call.

The screen is cleared by the clrscr() call and a column header is displayed. Next we enter an **i** - **j** nested loop to print out the values we just placed in the array. The **printf()** after the end of the **j** loop causes each value to be displayed on a new line.

Another aspect of Program 11.6 to notice is that the break statement *does not* send us out of the **j for** loop. It simply sends us to the bottom of the **j** loop. Recall that the break statement may be used with switch, while, do-while, and for statements and sends control to the first statement following the statement block that contains the **break**. In our example, the **break** sends control to the bottom of the **j for** loop, which is the same as sending it to *expression3* of the **j** loop.

You can nest **for** (and all other) loops as deeply as you wish.

Watching for Loop Inefficiencies

Program 11.6 contains a slightly inefficient piece of code. The statement in **case 2:**

```
array[i][j] =  array[i][0] *  array[i][0] * array[i][0];
```

has one more multiplication than is really necessary. We should use

```
array[i][j] = array[i][0] * array[i][1];
```

instead. Because **array[i][1]** contains the square of the number, all we need to do is multiply it by **array[i][0]** to get the cube. Although the time savings here is negligible, the modification could have a noticeable impact with a larger data set.

We could also have substituted the terms in the **switch** by using the pow() standard library function. (Be sure to include the math.h header file

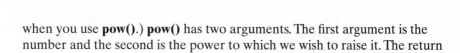

when you use **pow()**.) **pow()** has two arguments. The first argument is the number and the second is the power to which we wish to raise it. The return value is the first argument raised to the second argument. For example,

```
pow(4, 2);
```

returns the value 16 (that is, 4 squared) as a **double** data type. If we used **pow()**, we could do away with the switch statement altogether. The statement

```
array[i][j] = pow(i + 1, j + 1);
```

would take care of it.

The reason we didn't use it is because **pow()** is a very complex function capable of coping with very diverse set of values. As a result, it is also a very slow function. In most cases, if you are raising a value to a power less than 5, it is faster to use straight multiplication rather than **pow()**.

Conclusion

Of the loop structures we studied, the for loop is the most commonly used. Although you can use a while loop as a perfect replacement for a for loop, the substitution is rarely done.

The reason the for loop is so popular is probably because all the elements controlling the loop appear at one place in the program. The **do-while** has its loop initialization near the top, but the test appears at the bottom of the loop. The while loop must initialize its variables (for example, its equivalence of *expression1*) before the loop begins.

The for loop places everything in one place, warts and all, which is convenient and makes debugging easier. If you're like the rest of us, you will use the for loop a lot.

Checking Your Progress

1. What is the purpose of the three expressions in a for loop?

The first expression is used to initialize any variables that might be used in the loop. Normally, the variable used to control the loop is initialized in this expression. The *second* expression is evaluated and determines whether another iteration of the loop is made. Often this expression is a relational test, but any expression may be used. The third expression normally acts upon the variable that controls the loop. Typically, it is an increment or decrement operation.

2. Will the following for loop display the string held in **buff[]**?

```
for (i = 0; buff[i]; i++) {
   /* code to display the string */
}
```

Yes. The only tricky part is *expression2*. As long as there are characters in **buff[]** to display, the ASCII values stored there are nonzero, hence the expression is treated as logic True. At the end of the string is the null termination character. C guarantees that the null termination character is treated as logic False in any evaluation. Therefore, the loop stops upon sensing the null termination character—the end of the string.

3. Write a program that accepts a string from the user and then displays the characters on the screen using the putchar() standard library function.

```
#include <stdio.h>

main()
{
   char buff[31];
   int i;

   clrscr();
   printf("Enter up to 30 characters: ");
   gets(buff);

   printf("\n\nThe string was:\n\n");
   for (i = 0; buff[i]; i++) {
      putchar(buff[i]);
   }
}
```

You could also write the code using a while loop, as in

```
i = 0;
while (buff[i]) {
   putchar(buff[i++]);
}
```

For the most part, this is a matter of style. The code is probably identical for most compilers.

4. Quite by accident, I discovered that the sum of N odd integers, starting
with 1, equals the square of N. (I'm sure there's a formal proof for this,
but I haven't seen it yet.) For example, if N = 3,

$1 + 3 + 5 = 9$

Hence, the square of 3 is 9. Write a program that accepts N from the
user and uses this algorithm to display the square of the number.

```c
#include <stdio.h>
#include <stdlib.h>

main()
{
    char buff[10];
    int i, val, start, square;

    clrscr();
    printf("Enter a number: ");
    val = abs(atoi(gets(buff)));

    for (start = 1, i = square = 0; i < val; i++) {
        square += start;
        start += 2;
    }
    printf("\n\nThe square of %d is %d", val, square);
    getch();
}
```

The program contains no surprises. I did take the absolute value of the
number using **abs()** in case the user enters a negative number. This causes
the original value to be displayed as a positive number in the final **printf()**.
You might want to modify my solution to correct for this shortcoming.

5. Write a program that accepts a number between 0 and 255 (that is, an
eight-bit value) and displays the number in binary. Use Appendix A to
check your work.

A more elegant solution to this problem would use recursion, but the
brute force (some would say stupid) solution below works just fine:

```c
#include <stdio.h>
```

```
#define BITS   8

main()
{
    char buff[10];
    int i, val, remainder, times;
    int powers[] = {
        128, 64, 32, 16, 8, 4, 2, 1
        };

    clrscr();
    printf("\nEnter a number between 0 and 255: ");
    val = atoi(gets(buff));

    for (i = 0; i < BITS; i++) {
        times = val / powers[i];
        (times) ? printf("1") : printf("0");
        val %= powers[i];
    }
}
```

The program begins by defining several working variables, including the powers[] array. This array holds the powers of 2 that can be represented in an eight-bit number. In the for loop, if we divide **val** by **powers[i]** and **times** is not 0, that power of 2 is present in the number. We use the ternary operator to display a 1 if **times** is nonzero. Otherwise, we display a 0. The modulus operation gives us the remainder after factoring out the value in the **powers[]** array. Therefore, **val** keeps getting smaller as we progress through the array. After BITS iterations, the binary representation of the number has been displayed.

6. Write a program that plays a number guessing game. You think of a number between 0 and 100 and the computer tries to guess it. use 'H', 'L', and 'C' to tell the computer if the guess is too high, low, or correct.

```
#include <stdio.h>
#include <ctype.h>

#define EVER    ;;
#define TOP     101
#define GUESS   TOP / 2

main()
{
```

```
char c;
int bottom, guess, i, top;

printf("\nThink of a number between 0 and 100. Enter
    'H' if my");
printf("\nguess is too high, and 'L' if it is too low,
    and 'C'if");
printf("\nmy guess is correct.\n\n");
top = TOP;
guess = GUESS;
bottom = i = 0;
for (EVER) {
    printf("\n\nIs it %d", guess);
    i++;
    c = toupper(getch());
    switch (c) {
        case 'H':
            top = guess;
            guess = (top + bottom) >> 1;
            break;
        case 'L':
            bottom = guess;
            guess = (top + bottom) >> 1;
            break;
        case 'C':
            break;
    }
    if (c == 'C')
        break;
}
printf("\n\n\n   It took me %d tries to get it.", i);
}
```

12

The Bitwise, Shift, and Cast Operators

T HIS CHAPTER EXAMINES THE BITWISE OPERATORS, WHICH INCLUDE THE shift operators. The shift operators are often used to extract information from packed binary data. Not all languages provide these operators, but they can make some programming tasks much simpler. As you will learn, C allows you to get down to the bit level if necessary. Finally, this chapter discusses the cast operator. When you finish this chapter, you will have been introduced to all of C's operators.

Bitwise Operators

The bitwise operators let you "bit-fiddle" with a variable. You can only apply bitwise operators to an integral data type, not to floating-point data. There are three bitwise operators: bitwise AND, bitwise OR, and bitwise XOR (exclusive OR). Before you can learn about these operators, however, you need to understand how your computer works with numbers.

Binary Numbers

To use the bitwise operators properly, you need to know something about how binary numbers work. While people are used to working with decimal numbers, the computer only understands binary numbers. Binary numbers work in base 2 arithmetic: 1's and 0's.

Let's examine an eight-bit number. Figure 12.1 illustrates the bit layout for a single byte of storage, assuming that the bit positions run from left to right and the leftmost bit is the high bit.

Figure 12.1
Bit positions and
powers of 2 for a
data byte

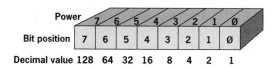

Each of the bit positions represents a power of 2. For example, if the bit in position 4 is turned on, its value is 2 to the fourth power, or 16 (2 * 2 * 2 * 2 = 16). Therefore, the binary representation for decimal 16 is

    00010000

What if you want the decimal value 17? You just need to add 1 to 16. Because any number to the zero power is 1, you need to turn on the bit in position 0. Therefore, the number 17 in binary is

    00010001

To determine the decimal value of the binary number, simply sum the bits that are turned on. For decimal 17, the binary representation is shown in Figure 12.2.

Figure 12.2

Binary representation for decimal 17

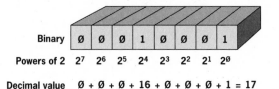

Binary   0   0   0   1   0   0   0   1

Powers of 2 2^7 2^6 2^5 2^4 2^3 2^2 2^1 2^0

Decimal value   0 + 0 + 0 + 16 + 0 + 0 + 0 + 1 = 17

Wherever a bit is turned on (1), you raise 2 to that bit position's power. In Figure 12.2, bits 4 and 0 are on, so the value is 2^4(16) plus 2^0 (1), which is 17. Therefore, binary 00010001 is decimal 17.

What about the value 65? Figure 12.1 shows that bits 6 and 0 must be turned on to form the value 65 (64 + 1). Therefore, the binary representation is

```
01000001
```

The numeric value 65 also happens to be the ASCII representation for the letter 'A'.

If you are unfamiliar with binary numbers, you may want to experiment a little before continuing. You can check your work using the binary and decimal values shown in Appendix A.

The Bitwise AND Operator

This section explains how you might use the bitwise AND operator (&) in your programs. The bitwise AND operator uses two operands (it's a binary operator). If the bit in both operands is on (that is, if it's logical True, or 1), the resulting bit is on. If either or both bits are off (logical False, or 0), the resulting bit is off.

The general form for the bitwise AND operator is

```
operand1 & operand2
```

The operator for a bitwise AND expression is a single ampersand (&) symbol. If you use the bitwise AND operator with the two integral values in *operand1* and *operand2*, only those matching bits that are turned on (have a value of 1) have a result of 1. For example, what is displayed on the screen if you have the following C statements?

```
int i, j, k;
j = 15;
i = 2;
k = j & i;
printf("k = %d", k);
```

First, the binary representation for 15 is

```
00001111        /* Decimal 15, j */
```

which is assigned into **j**. The binary representation for 2 is

```
00000010        /* Decimal 2, i */
```

and is the value of **i**. When you do a bitwise AND of two numbers, only those bit positions containing a 1 produce a result with a 1. Therefore

```
      00001111        /* variable j */
AND   00000010        /* variable i */
      -----------
      00000010        /* variable k */
```

Notice that only bit 1 is turned on in *both* **j** and **i**. This means that only bit 1 is turned on in the result of the bitwise AND operation. Therefore, **k** has a decimal value of 2.

PROGRAMMING TIP. *Enter the bitwise AND operator with some care. Because it uses the same ASCII character as logical AND (& for bitwise and && for logical AND), it is easy to type an extra & and unintentionally enter logical AND. The logical AND tests a relationship between its two operands, whereas the bitwise AND combines the operands to form a new value. Some programmers handle this problem using*

```
#define AND        &&
#define BITAND     &
```

and use the symbolic constants throughout their programs. Others don't like using symbolic constants for C operators or keywords. You can use whichever method you prefer.

So how can you use the bitwise AND operator? Suppose you need to determine whether an integer number is odd or even. In the previous chapter you used the modulus operator to solve this problem. However, you can also solve it using the bitwise AND operator, as shown in Program 12.1.

First, the program requests an integer number. The calls to **gets()** and **atoi()** convert the user's keystrokes into an **int** and assign it into **i**. Once the value is in **i**, a bitwise AND is performed on **i** and 1 with the result assigned into **i**. Depending upon whether or not **i** is zero, a message tells the user whether the number was odd or even.

Program 12.1   **Using Bitwise AND to Determine if a Number Is Odd or Even**

```c
#include <stdio.h>

main()
{
   char buff[20];
   int i;

   printf("Enter an integer: ");
   i = atoi(gets(buff));

   i = i & 1;

   printf("\nThe number is ");
   if (i)
      printf("odd");
   else
      printf("even");
   printf("\n\n   i = %d", i);

}
```

Let's see how the bitwise AND solves the odd-even task. Suppose the user enters the value 15. You already know that the binary representation for 15 is

```
00001111
```

Now use the bitwise AND operator with the two operands:

```
      00001111      /* variable i */
AND   00000001      /* 1          */
      ----------
      00000001      /* variable i */
```

Because both numbers have bit 0 turned on, the result of the bitwise AND is the value 1, which means the integer is odd.

Now try the value 127. The binary representation for 127 must have all eight bits turned on. Therefore, the AND statement becomes

```
        11111111        /* variable i */
AND     00000001        /* 1          */
        ----------
        00000001        /* variable i */
```

Again, the result is an odd number.

Now try an even number, like 62. The test result is

```
        00111110        /* variable i */
AND     00000001        /* 1          */
        ----------
        00000000        /* variable i */
```

Because variable **i** does not have the low bit turned on, the result is binary zero—the integer is an even number. Because all odd numbers must have the zero bit turned on, you can AND the integer value with 00000001 to find out if it is an odd or even number.

You can use the bitwise AND operator any time you need to test a given set of bits in an integral number.

Using Bitwise Operators to Get an MS-DOS File Date

MS-DOS uses a 16-bit integer to store the date when a disk file is created. Figure 12.3 shows this date format. This format is called a "packed date" because it stores the complete date in a single integer. Clearly, you can use the bitwise AND operator to extract a file date. (The notation 0x00 is used in C to represent a number using the hexadecimal numbering system.)

Figure 12.3
MS-DOS file date format

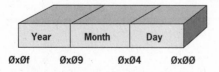

Figure 12.3 shows that bits 0 through 4 hold the day that the file was created. Bits 5 through 9 hold the month and the remaining bits hold the year. (The year is actually the number of years since 1980. Therefore, you must add **year** to 1980 to get the true year value.)

To get the day, take the packed date integer and use AND to combine it with 00000000 00011111. This binary value has a decimal value of 31 (0x1e in hexadecimal). Therefore, assuming that variable **packed_date** is the integer that holds the packed date, you can write

```
unsigned packed_date, day, month, year;

/* some code to get the packed date */

#define DAY      0x1f
#define MONTH    0x1e0
#define YEAR     0xfe00

day = packed_date & DAY;
```

To extract the month, the binary pattern is 00000001 11100000, or 480 (0x1e0 hexadecimal). The statement for retrieving the month becomes

```
month = packed_date & MONTH;
```

Finally, you can extract the year using binary 11111110 00000000, or 65,025 (0xfe00 hexadecimal). The final statement becomes

```
year = packed_date & YEAR;
```

Note that the data is defined as an **unsigned int** because the high bit in the packed date is not used for the sign of the value, but simply the year component of the date.

The values for **month** and **year** are *not* correct as they appear above. Because the month starts in bit position 4, you would need to use the right shift operator to obtain the correct date. (The shift operators are discussed near the end of this chapter.) For example, to get the correct month and year, you would need to add the following statements

```
month >>= 5;     /* Shift right 5 places */
year >>= 9;      /* Shift right 9 places */
year += 1980;
```

The **day** value does not need to be shifted since it occupies the lowest four bits.

The Bitwise OR Operator

The bitwise OR operator (|) allows you to manipulate bits in a different way. The bitwise OR operator is the vertical bar (usually found above the backslash key). Like bitwise AND, the bitwise OR operator is a binary operator requiring two operands. The general form for the bitwise OR operator is

```
operand1 | operand2
```

If the bit in either operand is on (logical True, or 1), the resulting bit is also on. Only if the bit in both operands is off (logical False, or 0) is the result also off.

For example, suppose you have the following two binary numbers:

```
00000101        /* decimal 5  */
00010100        /* decimal 20 */
```

A bitwise OR operation compares each bit and returns the value 1 if *either* bit of the two operands is 1. Given the two binary values for 5 and 20 as operands, a bitwise OR yields

```
         00000101        /* decimal 5  */
    OR   00010100        /* decimal 20 */
         ---------
result   00010101        /* decimal 21 */
```

Notice that if either bit is 1, the resulting bit is also 1. The C equivalent for the example is

```
unsigned a, b, result;
a = 5;
b = 20;
result = a | c;
```

The bitwise OR operator is most frequently used to turn on a bit in an integral value. This operator is used often in programs that manipulate devices such as I/O ports, modems, and printers.

The Exclusive OR Operator

The exclusive OR (abbreviated XOR) operator (^) is a binary operator that also performs a bit-by-bit comparison of two operands. If the bit in either operand is a 1, the result is a 1 for that bit. However, if the bit is 1 for both operands, the result is 0. The general form for the bitwise exclusive OR is

```
operand1 ^ operand2
```

Given the two binary values for 5 and 20, a bitwise XOR yields

```
         00000101        /* decimal 5  */
   XOR   00010100        /* decimal 20 */
         ---------
result   00010001        /* decimal 17 */
```

Notice that, because bit 2 is on (1) for both operands, the bit is off (0) as a result of the XOR operator. The equivalent test in C is

```
unsigned a, b, result;
a = 5;
b = 20;
result = a ^ c;
```

Using the XOR Operator

The XOR operator often is used in graphics programming. When you use XOR to compare a number with itself, the result is zero. However, when you use XOR to compare the same number with the result of the first operation, the result is the original number.

For example, suppose you have the following statements:

```
unsigned pixels, pattern;

pixels = 21;

pattern = pixels;
shows_pixels(pattern);          /* pattern = 00010101  */

pattern = pattern ^ pixels;
shows_pixels(pattern);          /* pattern = 00000000 */

pattern = pattern ^ pixels;
shows_pixels(pattern);          /* pattern = 00010101  */
```

The first statement

```
pattern = pattern ^ pixels;
```

has a binary equivalence of

```
        00010101      /* pixels  */
   XOR  00010101      /* pattern */
        ---------
pattern 00000000
```

The second time we execute the statement, the result is

```
        00010101      /* pixels  */
   XOR  00000000      /* pattern */
        ---------
pattern 00010101
```

which restores the original bit sequence. As you can see, using the XOR operator on a group of pixels allows you to turn the pixels on and off as a group. Because the bitwise operators use very few cycles, they execute very fast. In fact, XOR operations are important in graphics programming to achieve animation effects on objects.

The next example derives from the use of the XOR operator in assembly language programming. In assembly language, register space is often at a premium and programmers try to avoid using either a register or external memory to store intermediate results. Consider the following code fragment, which is used to swap two values:

```
int i, j, temp;

/* Statements */

temp = i;        /* swap i and j */
i = j;
j = temp;
```

An intermediate variable **temp** is used to swap the values in **i** and **j**. However, as you saw earlier, using the XOR operator with a number and itself a second time reproduces the original number. Program 12.2 uses this fact to get rid of **temp**.

Notice that only two integer variables are used; there is no **temp** equivalent in the program. When you run the program, enter two integer values. These values are displayed before the XOR operations are performed. After the three XOR statements, the values are again displayed, but their values are swapped. (Keep in mind, however, that the bitwise operators are limited to integral data.)

Although you probably won't use XOR very often, it can be very handy in specialized programming.

The One's Complement Operator

The one's complement operator (~) is a bit different from the other bitwise operators. It is a unary operator that simply flips the bits of the operand. That is, bits that were 1 become 0 and bits that were 0 become 1 after a one's complement operation.

The general form of the one's complement operator is

```
~operand
```

where *operand* must also be an integral data type. For example, if the number is 20

```
00010100      /* decimal 20 */
```

after a one's complement operation the binary value becomes

```
11101011      /* decimal 235 */
```

Program 12.2   A Swap with Two Variables

```c
#include <stdio.h>

main()
{
   char buff[10];
   int i, j;

   printf("\nEnter a number for i: ");
   i = atoi(gets(buff));
   printf("\nEnter a number for j: ");
   j = atoi(gets(buff));
   printf("\n\ni = %d  j = %d", i, j);

   j = i ^ j;       /* XOR with i and j */
   i ^= j;          /* XOR j into i     */
   j ^= i;          /* XOR i into j     */

   printf("\n\nAfter the swap:\n i = %d j = %d\n", i, j);
}
```

Like the XOR operator, the one's complement operator isn't often used in C programs. It's interesting to note that the maximum value of an 8-bit number is 255 and that the one's complement of 20 equals 235 (255 - 20).

Using the One's Complement Operator

While you may not use the one's complement operator frequently, it is used "behind the scenes" a lot. Negative numbers are often stored in a form known as two's complement. To find the two's complement of a number, you simply add 1 to its one's complement, as illustrated in Program 12.3.

Program 12.3 **Using the One's Complement Operator**

```c
#include <stdio.h>

main()
{
    char buff[10];
    int i, j;

    printf("\nEnter a number for i: ");
    i = atoi(gets(buff));
    j = ~i + 1;

    printf("\n\ni = %d   neg = %d\n", i, j);
}
```

The program requests a number, which is converted and assigned into **i**. Next the program takes the one'complement of **i**, adds 1 to it (to form the two's complement), and assigns it into **j**. Both values are then displayed. What happens if you enter a negative number to start with? Try this out for yourself.

The Shift Operators

The shift operators are binary operators whose operands must be integral data types. The shift operators cause the bit positions to shift either to the right (>>) or left (<<). The right shift operator has the angle brackets pointed to the right while the left shift operator points to the left. This makes it easy to remember which one is which.

Both shift operators have the general form

```
operand >> bits_to_shift      /* Right shift */
operand << bits_to_shift      /* Left shift  */
```

where *operand* is the variable to be shifted and *bits_to_shift* is the number of bit positions the operand is to be shifted.

For example, suppose the operand equals 10. The binary representation for 10 decimal is

```
00001010      /* 10 decimal */
```

If you shift this number one position to the right, the binary representation is

```
00000101      /* 5 decimal */
```

Notice that all bits have been shifted one place to the right. The high bit is automatically filled in with a 0. The low bit simply "falls off the end." Conversely, if you shift the original value (10) to the left instead of to the right, the binary value becomes

```
00010100      /* 20 decimal */
```

In this example, all bits are shifted one position to the left. The low bit is filled in with a 0 automatically and the high bit now "falls off the end."

Use this code to perform the same operations in C:

```
int i, j;

i = 10;
j = i >> 1;      /* Right shift, j equals 5  */
j = i << 1;      /* Left shift, j equals 20 */
```

You can experiment with the shift operators using Program 12.4.

Program 12.4   **Using the Shift Operators**

```
#include <stdio.h>

main()
{
    char buff[10];
    int i;

    printf("\nEnter a number: ");
    i = atoi(gets(buff));

    printf("\n%d >> 1 = %d", i, i >> 1);
    printf("\n%d << 1 = %d", i, i << 1);
}
```

The program requests a value to be shifted and the two **printf()** calls use the shift operator to display the resulting value.

Bit Shifting for Speed

The slowest math operation on a computer is division. The next slowest is multiplication. (Addition, subtraction, and modulus are fairly quick.) Often, however, you have to multiply or divide a value by 2. For example, many sorting and searching routines involve dividing the list in half on each pass through a loop.

Notice that when you shift a number to the right

```
00001010        /* 10 decimal */
```

becomes

```
00000101        /* 5 decimal */
```

In other words, *shifting a number one position to the right divides it by two.* In addition, when you shift decimal 5 to the left one position

```
00000101        /* 5 decimal */
```

it becomes

```
00001010        /* 10 decimal */
```

That is, *shifting a number one position to the left multiplies it by 2.* Because bit shifting is much faster than multiplying or dividing, the shift operators provide a very efficient way to double or halve an integral value.

If you use this technique in a program, you might want to include a comment explaining what you've done. Although most programmers are familiar with this technique, someone who is not might use your code.

The Cast Operator

The cast operator is not found in most languages. It consists of an opening parenthesis, a named data type specifier, and a closing parenthesis followed by an operand. The *cast operator converts the operand to the data type specified within the parentheses.* In other words, it forces the operand to have the same attribute list as the data type within parentheses.

Suppose you have an integer data type and you want to assign it into a double data type. The statements

```
int i;
double x;

i = 10;
x = i;
```

should draw an error or warning message from the compiler because you are trying to assign one data type (a two-byte **int**) into a different data type (an eight-byte **double**). Since this is a source of program bugs, C forces you to use a cast operator. The correct way to perform the assignment is

```
x = (double) i;
```

The cast operator tells the compiler to generate code to create an intermediate variable of size **double** and give it a value equal to **i**. Then it assigns the intermediate value into **x**. The cast operator tells the compiler exactly what you intend to do in the assignment. Indirectly, it also tells the compiler that you really do want to do this (data-mismatched) assignment because of the deliberate cast operation.

In the example, the cast operator is the parentheses and the data type specifier within them. This forces the compiler to take the two-byte integer value in **i** and "recast" it into an eight-byte value. Having done the conversion, the compiler can assign the value into **x**.

If the cast is done properly, the attribute list for the data type on the left side of the assignment statement matches that which appears within the parentheses of the cast statement. In other words, because **x** is a **double**, the cast should be **(double)**.

Understanding Your Compiler

Not all compilers are created equal. Consider Program 12.5.

Program 12.5   **A Fussy Test for Your Compiler**

```
#include <stdio.h>

main()
{
    char c;
    int i;
    double x;

    i = 10;
    c = i;          /* should be: c = (char) i;    */
    x = i;          /* should be: x = (double) i; */
    printf("%c %d %g", c, i, x);
}
```

On three different C compilers, this program produced no complaints whatsoever on the first compiler (no errors or warnings), one warning message that had nothing to do with the lack of cast statements in the second compiler, and a complaint about the lack of casts for **c** and **x** plus the same warning message as before in the third. However, all of the compilers displayed the correct values.

Clearly, the compilers that produced no error messages nevertheless generated the correct code to display the correct results. Some programmers think that the compiler should warn about the lack of cast operators, especially where potential bugs are concerned. Others think that correct results are what matter the most.

The code may work on one machine and not on another. While an **int** and a **short int** are the same on an MS-DOS machine, they are not the same for the Mac. Therefore, a program that works in MS-DOS might fail miserably on the Mac.

You should compile Program 12.5 and see how your compiler behaves under these circumstances. If it doesn't complain, you know that you're responsible for keeping the nonmatching data types straight.

Conclusion

The bitwise operators come in most handy when you are programming for external devices such as a modem, mouse, and graphics adaptor. However, the bitwise operators are also useful when programming software interrupts, sorting, searching, and other specialized routines. Remember, all of the bitwise operators except for the one's complement operator have associated shorthand operators: <<=, &=, |=, >>=, and so on.

The cast operator lets you safely use one data type where a different data type is expected. You will see more examples of the cast operator when you tackle more advanced topics like dynamic memory allocation.

Checking Your Progress

1. What does the bitwise AND operator do?

   The bitwise AND operator compares the bits in its two operands. If the same bit in each operand is 1, the result is a 1 for that bit. If either or both operands have a 0 for the bit, the result is 0 for that bit. The C statement for a bitwise AND operation is

   ```
   result = operand1 & operand2;
   ```

2. What does the bitwise OR operator do?

The bitwise OR operator compares matching bits in each of its operands. If either or both bits are equal to 1, the result is 1. Only when both bits are 0 is the result 0. The C statement for a bitwise OR operation is

```
result = operand1 | operand2;
```

3. What does the bitwise XOR operator do?

The bitwise XOR operator compares matching bits in each of its operands. If either bit, but not both, is a 1, the result is a 1. If both bits equal 0 or if both bits equal 1, the result is 0. The C statement for XOR is

```
result = operand1 ^ operand2;
```

4. Assume you've built and installed a home alarm system and are now writing the software to monitor it. You need to test the fire alarm sensor, which is bit 5 in a 16-bit integer (named **sensor_scan**). What would be the statement(s) to check for a fire?

```
#define FIRE_ALARM    32      /* bit 5 = 2^5th = 32 */
 .
 .
unsigned fire_status;
 .
 .
fire_status = sensor_scan & FIRE_ALARM;
```

Notice how the use of meaningful variable names and the symbolic constant FIRE_ALARM help document the code.

5. Program 12.3 doesn't use some of the operators you know. What is one possible change to the program?

You could simplify the statements

```
i = atoi(gets(buff));
j = ~i + 1;
```

in several ways. The easiest change is

```
i = atoi(gets(buff));
j++ = ~i;
```

which uses the increment operator to add 1 to **j**. You could also use

```
j++ = ~(atoi(gets(buff)));
```

which does away with variable **i** altogether. However, this code is much less readable than the previous version. In most cases where the statements are not in a loop, you're better off sacrificing a little efficiency for greater readability. In other words, don't use this last form in a program.

6. Modify Program 12.4 so you can shift the bits by any amount.

You just need to add a new variable to hold the shift value and get the value from the user.

```c
#include <stdio.h>

main()
{
    char buff[10];
    int i, shift;

    printf("\nEnter a number: ");
    i = atoi(gets(buff));

    printf("\nEnter a shift value: ");
    shift = atoi(gets(buff));

    printf("\n%d >> 1 = %d", i, i >> shift);
    printf("\n%d << 1 = %d", i, i << shift);

}
```

13

Functions

THUS FAR, YOU HAVE BEEN INTRODUCED TO THE MAJOR ELEMENTS OF THE C language and its operators. However, we have not said much about the cornerstone of C—its functions. In this chapter we will discuss the major components of functions. We will look at how function arguments are passed to a function, and introduce the concept of data privacy in C.

The Anatomy of a Function

Until now, the only function we have defined is **main()**. We have used functions from the standard library, but we've only written the code for **main()**. To begin our discussion, let's write a function that determines the area of a rectangle.

As we have said before, a function is designed to accomplish a small task. In this example, our function will determine the area of a rectangle. Therefore, we know that our function needs two pieces of information to accomplish its task: the length and width of the rectangle.

Without writing the actual code, let's look at a rough sketch of the sample function, which is presented in Figure 13.1.

Figure 13.1
The rectangle_area() function definition

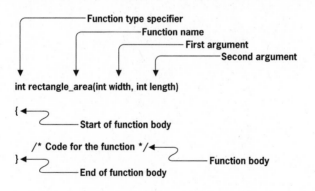

Let's examine each of these function parts in detail.

Function Type Specifier

The first part of a function definition is the function type specifier. The *function type specifier* states the data type that the function returns. In Figure 13.1, the function type specifier is an **int**. Therefore, the rectangle_area() function returns an **int** value. For example, if we call the rectangle_area() function from **main()**, we might see a statement similar to

```
w = 5;
l = 10;
area = rectangle_area(w, l);
```

In this case, **rectangle_area()** returns the value 50 as an integer value, which is then assigned into **area**.

In C parlance, if **rectangle_area()** is called from within the main() function, it is common to refer to **main()** as the *caller* of **rectangle_area()**. Caller is simply a term used to refer to whatever function happened to call **rectangle_area()**. It's easier to say caller than explicitly name **main()** each time. We will use caller from now on, unless it is important to know exactly which function performed the function call.

Varieties of Type Specifiers

The type specifier can be whatever data type you need the function to return. If you are returning a floating-point number, the type specifier would be either **float** or **double**. If the function needs to return a large integer number, the type specifier might be **unsigned** or **long.** As we will see in later chapters, we can create new, complex, data types in C. We can have type specifiers that return these complex data types.

In short, the type specifier can be whatever you need it to be. You can pick from the list of standard C keywords for data types (**char**, **int**, **double**, etc.), or you can create more complex data types and use those for the type specifier.

What happens if you omit the type specifier? The *default function type specifier for all functions is **int***. In all of our example programs thus far, we have defined the main() function without a type specifier. Therefore, **main()** has used a default type specifier of **int**. (Your compiler may have been warning you about this all along. We'll fix that little problem before this chapter ends.)

The void Function

You will write functions that do not return a value. For example, you might write a function that simply turns a pixel on in a graphics display. A different function might turn on a switch, or play a note on the speaker. Perhaps none of these functions requires a return value.

It seems we have a problem. If we don't want to return a value, we can simply omit the type specifier and solve the problem. However, we just stated if a function definition omits the type specifier, the function returns an **int** by default. This is confusing, because we say don't return a value but the compiler wants to return an **int**.

For this reason, the ANSI standard formalizes the keyword **void**. **void** is a "placeholder" data type created by the ANSI standard. The **void** data type is most often used as a type specifier for a missing or empty data type. When used as a function type specifier, it tells the compiler explicitly that we do not want the function to return a value. For example, if you define a function

```
void play_note(int note_to_play)
{
    /* The code goes here */
}
```

the keyword **void** tells the compiler that this function does not return a value to the caller. This is useful stuff to the compiler. Why? Suppose you try something like the following statement:

```
note = play_note(B_sharp);
```

The compiler can issue either an error or warning message for this statement. The reason the code above is an error is because **play_note()** does not return a value. Therefore, **note** cannot possibly have a valid value assigned into it by **play_note()**.

By using the keyword **void** for the type specifier for functions that do not return a value, the compiler can warn us if we try to do something stupid with the function, like assigning a value from the function when there is no value to assign.

Function Name

The *function name* comes after the type specifier in a function definition. The rules for creating a function name were discussed in Chapter 4, and are the same as those for naming variables. There are, however, a few things to keep in mind.

First, you should not select a function name that is the same as a standard library function. If you define a function in your code and use the same name as a function that already exists in the standard library, the code takes precedence. This means that the linker will never link in the code from the standard library for a function that shares the same name as one you have defined in your program.

Second, some older compilers and linkers have problems talking to each other. For example, in the old CP/M days, one compiler recognized function names with 32 characters of significance. The assembler and linker, however, could only recognize six characters of significance. Therefore, if one function is named **sales_tax_due()** and another is named **sales_tax_paid()**, the compiler knew they were different functions, but to the linker they both looked like **sales_()**.

The ANSI standard guarantees a minimum of 31 characters of significance in variable and function names. So, for most modern compilers, the uniqueness of function names won't be a problem.

Argument List

After the function name comes the function's argument list. The argument list begins immediately after the opening parenthesis of the function definition. The *argument list of a function lists the data type and identification of the arguments that are being passed into the function.* Each argument in the list is a type specifier (for example, **int**, **double**, etc.) followed by a name for the data item. If the function has more than one argument, the arguments are separated by the comma operator.

The end of the argument list is marked by the closing parenthesis of the function definition.

Functions with No Argument List

What if a function does not have an argument list? In all of our program examples, **main()** never had an argument list. If a function does not have an argument list, use the **void** type specifier in the parentheses of the function definition.

Therefore, if you happen to have a really fussy compiler, change the definition for **main()** that we have been using

```
main()
```

to

```
void main(void)
```

and the compiler should be a lot happier. We have now told the compiler that **main()** does not return a value, nor does it have any function arguments. These conditions for **main()** have applied to all of our program examples thus far. (Some compilers, such as Borland's, insist that **main()** returns an **int**. If you wish, change **main()**'s type specifier to **int** and place a **return 0** just before the end of **main()**.)

Functions with Unknown Argument Lists. . .

For some functions, we do not know how many arguments will be used until the function is called. For example, we have seen examples of **printf()** with one argument

```
printf("Print a string");
```

and we have seen other examples with multiple arguments

```
printf("\nc = %c i = %d  x = %g", c, i x);
```

If we were writing our own **printf()**, how could we cope with the variable number of arguments?

The ANSI standard created a new declaration type to cope with this very problem. It is called the ellipsis. *The ellipsis is simply three consecutive periods and means that the number and type of arguments is variable.* The ellipsis operator can only appear within the argument list of a function. With this in mind, our printf() function declaration becomes

```
int printf(char s[], ...);
```

which says that **printf()** returns an **int** data type, is named **printf()**, and has one or more arguments. The only thing we know for certain is that the first argument is a character string. Other arguments may follow, but we don't know how many there are or what data type they are. (The compiler figures the data types out by looking at the conversion characters in the control string.)

Start of Function Body

The opening brace in Figure 13.1 marks the beginning of the function body. It serves to tell the compiler: "Okay, you know everything you need to set up the function, now get ready for the code that makes the function perform its task".

The most common coding style is for the opening brace to be flush with the left side of the display screen. This means the brace aligns with the first character in the function's type specifier. Most programmers use this style and I suggest you follow their lead for your own style.

Function Body

The function body is the code that carries out the function's task. In all of our earlier examples, the function body was simply the code that appeared in the main() function. Starting with this chapter, we will be pushing the code out of **main()** and into functions where it really belongs.

End of Function

The closing brace marks the end of the function body and, upon seeing the closing brace for a function body, the compiler knows that it has seen all of the code associated with this function. The closing brace for the function marks the end of the function definition.

Writing a Function

Now that we understand the parts that make up a function, let's write our rectangle_area() function. Program 13.1 shows both the main() and rectangle_area() function definitions.

Program 13.1   **Finding the Area of a Rectangle**

```c
#include <stdio.h>
#include <stdlib.h>

void main(void)
{
    char buff[10];
    int area, length, width;

    clrscr();
    printf("Enter the width: ");
    width = atoi(gets(buff));

    printf("\nEnter the length: ");
    length = atoi(gets(buff));
    area = rectangle_area(width, length);
    printf("\n\nThe area is %d", area);
}

/*****
                  rectangle_area()

    This function finds the area of a rectangle.

    Argument list:   int width      width of the rectangle
                     int length     length       "
    Return value:    int            area of the rectangle

*****/

int rectangle_area(int width, int length)
{
    return (width * length);
}
```

The program begins by getting the width and length from the user. These two values are then passed to the rectangle_area() function as part of the function call. The program then executes the code for the rectangle_area() function.

The return Statement

There's not much to the function body for the rectangle_area() function. We simply multiply **width** times **length** and return the product to the caller via the return statement.

The return statement is required for several reasons. First, because the function's type specifier is **int**, there *must* be a return statement in the function. What's more, the return statement must be followed by an expression that has an **int** rvalue. The type specifier in the function definition demands that these two conditions be fulfilled. If these conditions are not met, the compiler should issue a warning or error message.

The second reason the return statement is required is because it provides the mechanism by which the value is sent back to the caller.

After the return statement is executed, control returns back to the caller. (The return statement always causes control to return to the caller.) In Program 13.1, control returns back to **main()**. More specifically, the program returns control back to the point where we are ready to assign the return value from **rectangle_area()** into **area**. The program then calls **printf()** to display the area and the program ends.

Now the question is how does **rectangle_area()** get the width and length information, and how does it pass the information back to the caller? This is the subject of the next section. Before we cover that area, however, let's look at the style used to write the rectangle_area() function.

Selecting a Function Header Style

In Program 13.1 we present one possible header style that might be used when you write a function definition. A *function header* is nothing more than the documentation that is placed in the source code to describe the function. The style shown in Program 13.1 is what my company uses for function definitions in all code for commercial applications. We adopted the style shown in Program 13.1 for several reasons.

First, centering the function's name within a comment makes it easy to find the function definition in the source code. Second, the comment provides a brief description of what the function does. The description doesn't need to be lengthy, just enough to describe the function's task.

Third, we always state what the function arguments are. It is very easy to forget what the arguments mean unless you document them in the function. If you don't document the arguments, you will find yourself looking at the code that calls the function and trying to figure out what the arguments mean. Defining the arguments as part of the function's documentation will save you a lot of time later on.

Finally, we always state what the return value is, even if it is a **void** function. This also helps us to remember exactly what the function's task is.

While this style is not for everyone, it does have the important elements present. That is, it tells the function's name, what it does, the "outside" data it needs to perform that task, and the return value generated by the function. You are free to create your own style, but I urge you to at least include the type of information shown in Program 13.1.

Passing Information to and from Functions

When **rectangle_area()** was called from **main()**, how did the values for **width** and **length** get passed to the function? Without getting too technical, the compiler uses a piece of memory called the stack. The *stack* is a section of memory that is used to pass information to and from functions. (The stack is also used for other things, which we will cover in detail in Chapter 15.)

Passing Data to a Function via the Stack

The most common analogy for the stack is a spring-loaded stack of plates that you often see at the salad bar in a restaurant. For a moment, pretend that a salad plate can hold one byte of data and that an **int** is two bytes in size.

When the compiler sees the call to **rectangle_area()** in **main()**, it looks at the function arguments and sees two variables; **width** and **length**. Because the compiler knows that both **width** and **length** are **int**s, it grabs four plates in preparation for the function call to **rectangle_area()**. The compiler now fills the first two plates with the value of **width** and sets them on the stack. The compiler then fills the remaining two plates with the value for **length** and places them on the stack. The compiler then calls the rectangle_area() function.

Remember that we can compile functions in files other than the one that contains **main()**. Therefore, the function has no idea what's going on in **main()**. It does know, however, that the stack is used for passing outside data to it.

When the code for **rectangle_area()** begins execution, the first thing it does is retrieve the data being sent to it. How does the function know there's data on the stack? The function's argument list tells it that there is data being passed to it on the stack. In fact, the number of arguments and their types tell the function everything it needs to know about the data that is being sent to it.

The type specifiers for each function argument tell it how many plates must be taken off the stack. Therefore, it pops off the top two plates and assigns their value into **length** and pops off the next two plates and assigns their value into **width**. The function has now retrieved all of the data sent to it from the stack.

(The compiler dictates the order in which arguments are pushed onto the stack by the caller and the order in which the arguments are popped off the stack in the function itself. The way in which the arguments are processed is, of course, synchronized so everything works correctly. It is important you understand how the process works, but you don't have to manage the process in your program; the compiler does it automatically for you.)

Passing Data Back to the Caller via the Stack

Now that the function has retrieved its arguments from the stack, it performs its calculation. The return statement in the function tells the function that it needs to send information back to the caller. The function's type specifier tells the function how many bytes to send back.

Because the function type specifier states that this returns an **int**, **rectangle_area()** grabs two plates, fills them with the product of **width** and **length**, and shoves them on the stack. It then sends program control back to the caller (main()).

Back in **main()**, the compiler sees that **rectangle_area()** has finished its job. It also knows that the result is sitting on the stack. Because all functions return an **int** by default, and nobody told the compiler anything different about **rectangle_area()**, the compiler grabs two plates from the stack. The value on the plates is the area of the rectangle. Therefore, the compiler can now assign the value into **area** in **main()**. Everything works out great...most of the time.

Messing Up the Stack

As you can see from the previous discussion, there is a lot of trust involved in passing information to and from a function. **rectangle_area()** must believe that the data passed to it from **main()** is correct and in the proper order. Likewise, **main()** must trust that **rectangle_area()** has placed the result from the function on the stack in the proper manner.

The problem is not going to be how the compiler coordinates the activities between **main()** and all other functions. The problem is that we programmers get careless from time to time and mess up the stack ourselves. An example will help you see how things can go wrong. Consider the following code fragment:

```
#include <stdio.h>

void main(void)
{
```

```
        int i, j, k;
        .

        .

        i = func1(j, k);
}

double func1(int j, int k)
{
        int result;

        .

        return result;
}
```

Now what happens when we try to compile the program? When the compiler sees the call to **func1()** in **main()**, it assumes that **func1()** returns an **int**. The compiler makes this assumption because it doesn't have any other information to the contrary about **func1()**. (Keep in mind that the compiler cannot "look ahead".) Therefore, the compiler generates code to pop an **int** off the stack after **func1()** is called and assigns the value into **i**.

However, **func1()** places the result on the stack as a **double**. (The function's type specifier tells us that, right?) Therefore, **func1()** grabs eight plates and places **result** on them and shoves them on the stack. Control returns to **main()** and **main()** pops *two* plates off the stack and shoves the value of the two plates into **i**. The code only grabs a quarter of the answer. (The result is eight bytes, but **main()** only pops off two bytes.) This probably won't work at all. We will see how to avoid this problem in Chapter 14.

Function Arguments Are Copies

When a function call is made in a program, the compiler places the rvalue on the stack and sends it to the function. For example,

```
int i, j, k;
/* Some code that sets i and j */
k = func1(i, j);
```

What the compiler does is to generate code that takes the rvalue of **i** and places it on the stack. Likewise the compiler generates code to place the rvalue of **j** on the stack. *Because the rvalue is sent to the function via the stack, it is a copy of the argument that is sent to the function, not the variable itself.*

This is a very important concept to understand. If the function receives only the rvalue as the function argument, the function has no way of knowing where the "real" variable is stored in memory. That is, the function does not know the lvalue of where the variable in **main()** is stored in memory; it only has the rvalue. Program 13.2 proves that a copy is in fact sent to the function.

Program 13.2   **Function Arguments Are Copies**

```
#include <stdio.h>

void main(void)
{
    int i;

    i = 10;
    printf("\nIn main: rvalue of i = %d lvalue of i = %p",
        i, &i);
    i = func1(i);
}

int func1(int i)
{
    printf("\nIn func1(): rvalue of i = %d lvalue of i =
        %p", i, &i);
    return i;
}
```

When I ran this program, the output of the program was

```
In main: rvalue of i = 10 lvalue of i = FFF4
In func1(): rvalue of i = 10 lvalue of i = FFF2
```

(The lvalues you get when you run the program will likely be different.) These numbers tell us two interesting facts. First, the **i** defined in **main()** is stored at a different memory address than the **i** in **func1()**. This also means that **func1()** doesn't really know where the **i** defined in **main()** is stored in memory.

The second interesting fact is that both memory addresses have relatively high lvalues, suggesting that the data is being stored in the program's stack area. After all, 0xfff4 is decimal 65,524, which is almost the top of a memory segment. (The stack mechanism is written to start at the top of memory and work back toward zero as data is placed on the stack.) If we are correct about using the stack, defining another variable in **main()** should alter the lvalue of **i** in **func1()**. Program 13.3 is the same as Program 13.2, but we have defined variable **j** in **main()** and displayed its values.

Program 13.3   **Checking Where Variables Are Stored**

```c
#include <stdio.h>

void main(void)
{
    int i, j;

    i = 10;
    printf("\nIn main: rvalue of i = %d lvalue of i = %p",
        i, &i);
    printf("\nIn main: rvalue of j = %d lvalue of j = %p",
        j, &j);
    j = func1(i);
}

int func1(int i)
{
    printf("\nIn func1(): rvalue of i = %d lvalue of i =
        %p", i, &i);
    return i;
}
```

This time the output of the program was

```
In main: rvalue of i = 10 lvalue of i = FFF4
In main: rvalue of j = 10 lvalue of j = FFF2
In func1(): rvalue of i = 10 lvalue of i = FFF0
```

It seems pretty clear that the stack is being used to store these variables. Note that **i** still has different lvalues in **main()** and **func1()**.

The conclusion of all this is:

- Because the lvalues of variables defined in one function and passed to another function are different, it is a *copy* of the variable that is sent to the function as an argument.

- Because a function argument is a copy of the variable, there is no way that the function can change the value of the *original* variable.

Think about what this means. The data defined in one function is private with respect to all other functions. That is, **func1()** cannot directly change the value of **i** in **main()**. Let's see if this assertion is true.

Program 13.4 is similar to Program 13.3, but this time we square the value of **i** in **func1()**.

Program 13.4 **Example of the Privacy of Data**

```
#include <stdio.h>

void main(void)
{
    int i, j;

    j = i = 10;
    printf("\nIn main:\n    rvalue of i = %d lvalue of i =
        %p", i, &i);
    printf("\n    rvalue of j = %d lvalue of j = %p\n", j,
        &j);
    j = func1(i);
    printf("\nIn main:\n    the value of j is %d and i is
        %d\n\n", j, i);
}

int func1(int i)
{
    printf("\nIn func1():\n    rvalue of i = %d lvalue of i
        = %p", i, &i);
    i = i * i;
    printf("\n    the value of i is now %d\n", i);
    return i;
}
```

When you run the program, it shows that **i** in **func1()** does in fact equal 100 after we square it. The **j** in **main()** also is 100 after the call to **func1()**. However, the original **i** defined in **main()** remains 10 in all cases.

This makes sense, if you think about it. If **func1()** does not have the lvalue of the **i** defined in **main()**, how can it change the rvalue of **i**? It can't. *A function cannot directly change the rvalue of a variable defined in another function.*

This is great stuff! This means that we can fiddle around with the code in one place in the program without worrying about affecting data defined in some other function. Data defined in a function is private to that function.

In some languages, like BASIC, the data is not private. If you've used BASIC, you've probably had a situation where a change in one part of the program caused a bug to crop up in another section. C allows you to squash these side-effect bugs by making the data private.

We will have a lot more to say about data privacy in Chapters 14 through 18.

Conclusion

In this chapter, we have discussed the major parts of a function and touched on some of the mechanisms used to pass data between functions. Although it may seem that we have explored the topic of data passing and privacy with greater detail than you think is necessary, understanding this detail makes some of the advanced C topics easier to grasp.

I urge you to spend enough time with this chapter to feel very comfortable with the topics covered. I also urge you to work through all of the exercises below. They will help you digest the material more easily.

Checking Your Progress

1. What are the major components of a function definition?

   1. Function type specifier

   2. Function name

   3. Function argument list

   4. Function body

2. The temperature at which water boils varies inversely with altitude. The approximate equation is

   boil = 212 − altitude / 550

   Write a function that gets the altitude as its argument and returns the new boiling point to the nearest degree.

```
#include <stdio.h>
#include <stdlib.h>

void main(void)
{
    char buff[10];
    int feet;
```

```
    clrscr();
    printf("Enter your elevation: ");
    feet = atoi(gets(buff));
    printf("Water at %d feet boils at %d", feet,
        new_boil(feet));
}
/*****
                        new_boil()
        Find the new boiling point of water relative to
altitude.
        Argument list:      int feet        altitude

        Return value:       int             new boiling point
*****/

int new_boil(int feet)
{
    return 212 - feet / 550;
}
```

Obviously, using integer data loses some accuracy, but for our purposes now, this is good enough.

3. The algorithm for finding a leap year is: If the year can be evenly divided by 4, but not by 100, it is a leap year. The exception occurs when the year is evenly divided by 400, which is a leap year. Write a function that returns 1 if a year is a leap year and 0 if it isn't.

```
#include <stdio.h>
#include <stdlib.h>

void main(void)
{
    char buff[10];
    int year;

    clrscr();
    printf("Enter the year: ");
    year= atoi(gets(buff));
    printf("\nIt ");
    (leap(year)) ? printf("is") : printf("is not");
    printf(" a leap year");
```

```
}
/*****
                                      leap()
        Function determines whether a year is a leap year or
not.
    Argument list:    int year       the year

    Return value:     int            0 = not leap year;
                                     1 = leap year
*****/

int leap(int year)
{
    if (year % 4 == 0 && year % 100 != 0 || year % 400 == 0)
        return 1;
    return 0;
}
```

4. Write a function that finds the maximum value in an array of integers that was produced by the rand() function.

```
#include <stdio.h>
#include <stdlib.h>
#include <math.h>
#include <limits.h>

#define MAXSIZE  100

void main(void)
{
    int array[MAXSIZE];
    int i;

    for (i = 0; i < MAXSIZE; i++) {
        array[i] = rand();
    }
    i = maxval(array, MAXSIZE);
    printf("The maximum value is %d", i);
}

int maxval(int a[], int num)
{
```

```
    int i, max;
    max = INT_MIN;
    for (i = 0; i < num; i++) {
        max = (a[i] > max) ? a[i] : max;
    }
    return max;
}
```

The key to solving this problem is knowing two things. First, C doesn't care about the size of an array other than when it is defined. Because the array is defined in **main()**, all we need to tell the function is that the first argument is an array. This is kind of a dirty trick, because we won't cover the topic of arrays as function arguments until the next chapter.

5. A function is passed three integers: the day, the month, and the year. Write a function that determines if the date is valid. The function should reject 6, 31, 1991 because June has only 30 days. The return value should be 1 if valid, 0 if not.

```
#include <stdio.h>
#include <stdlib.h>

void main(void)
{
    char buff[10];
    int day, month, year;

    clrscr();
    printf("Enter the day: ");
    day = atoi(gets(buff));
    printf("Enter the month: ");
    month = atoi(gets(buff));
    printf("Enter the year: ");
    year = atoi(gets(buff));

    printf("\nIt ");
    (valid_date(day, month, year)) ? printf("is") :
        printf("is not");
    printf(" a valid date");
}

/*****
```

```
                         valid_date()
              Function determines whether a date is valid.

         Argument list:    int day        the day
                           int month      the month
                           int year       the year

         Return value:     int            0 = not valid;
                                          1 = valid date

*****/

int valid_date(int day, int month, int year)
{
    int days[] = {0, 31, 28, 31, 30, 31, 30,
                     31, 31, 30, 31, 30, 31};

    if (month > 12 || month < 1 || day > 31 || day < 1)
        return 0;
    if (day > days[month]) {
        if (month == 2 && day == 29) {
            if (leap(year)) {
                return 1;
            }
        }
        return 0;
    }
    return 1;
}
```

The function uses the leap year function from question 3. This is only one example of how old functions can be used to build new ones. Note that the first element of the days[] array is 0 to make it easier to cope with January being month 1.

6. Write a function that passes the day, month, and year, and a character array to a function that returns the day of the week. Also have the function copy the day as a string into the character array passed to the function. (Use the strcpy() library function.) The equation is

```
day = ((13 * M - 1) / 5) + D + (Y % 100) + ((Y % 100) / 4)
      + ((Y / 100) / 4) - 2 * (Y / 100) + 77;
day = day - 7 * (day / 7);
```

where day 0 is Sunday, 1 is Monday, etc. Note that if the month is Jan. or Feb., they are viewed as being months 11 and 12 of the *preceding* year. Likewise, March through Dec. are viewed as months 1 through 10 of the current year.

```c
#include <stdio.h>
#include <std.lib.h>
#include <string.h>

#define MAXSIZE  100

void main(void)
{
    char buff[20];
    int day, month, year;

    clrscr();
    printf("Enter the day: ");
    day = atoi(gets(buff));
    printf("Enter the month: ");
    month = atoi(gets(buff));
    printf("Enter the year: ");
    year = atoi(gets(buff));

    day = weekday(day, month, year, buff);
    printf("\n\nThe day is %s\n", buff);
}


/*****

                        weekday()

    Function determines the day of the week for a given
date. The function also copies the day as a string into
s[].

    Argument list:    int day       the day
                      int month     the month
                      int year      the year
                      char s[]      character array for day

    Return value:     int           the day
```

```
*****/

int weekday(int day, int month, int year, char s[])
{
  char days[7][10] = {
    "Sunday", "Monday", "Tuesday", "Wednesday", "Thursday",
    "Friday", "Saturday"};
  int offset;

  if (year < 100) {        /* Make sure it's a full century */
    year += 1900;
  }
  if (month > 2) {         /* Adjust for Jan and Feb    */
    month -= 2;
  } else {
    month += 10;
    year--;
  }
  offset = ((13 * month - 1) / 5) + day + (year % 100) +
          ((year % 100) >> 2) + ((year / 100) >> 2) - 2 *
          (year / 100) + 77;

  offset = offset - 7 * (offset / 7);

  strcpy(s, days[offset]);
  return offset;
}
```

7. Using the day of the week function from questions 3 and 6, write a program that prints a calendar for a given month and year.

```
#include <stdio.h>
#include <stdlib.h>
#include <string.h>

#define MAXSIZE  100

void CALENDAR (int day, int month, int year);

void main(void)
{
```

```
    char buff[2Ø];
    int day, month, year;

    clrscr();
    printf("Enter the month: ");
    month = atoi(gets(buff));
    printf("Enter the year: ");
    year = atoi(gets(buff));

    day = weekday(1, month, year, buff);
    clrscr();
    calendar(day, month, year);
    printf("\n\n");
}

void calendar(int day, int month, int year)
{
    char days[8] = "SMTWTFS";
    char months[13][1Ø] = {" ", "January", "February",
                           "March", "April",
                           "May", "June", "July", "August",
                           "September",
                           "October", "November",
                           "December"};
    int day_count[] = {Ø, 31, 28, 31, 3Ø, 31, 3Ø,
                       31, 31, 3Ø, 31, 3Ø, 31};
    int all, i, j;
                                  /* Show days */
    printf("      %s %d\n\n  ", months[month], year);

    for (i = Ø; i < 7; i++) {
       printf(" %c ", days[i]);
    }

    all = day_count[month];

    if (month == 2)
       all += leap(year);   /* Correct for leap year */

    printf("\n");
    for (j = 1, i = Ø; j <= all; i++) {
```

```
      if (i % 7 == 0) {
         printf("\n ");
      }
      if (i < day) {
         printf("%3s", " ");
      } else {
         printf("%3d", j++);
      }
   }
}
```

The output is a small calendar that uses very little screen area. You could embellish it by using graphics characters. Or you could use this as the basis for an appointment calendar program.

14

Function Prototypes

Why You Need Function Declarations

Function Prototyping

Creating Your Own Function Declarations and Prototypes

This chapter discusses function declarations and function prototypes. It also explains the purpose of each, and describes how each is used in a program. Finally, it describes how to create your own function declarations with prototypes.

Why You Need Function Declarations

Chapter 13 gave an example of a function that returned a **double**. However, because **main()** didn't know that the function returned a **double**, it thought the function returned the default data type of **int**. Because of this assumption, **main()** retrieved only two bytes from the stack instead of the eight bytes actually returned from the function. Because of the confusion, **main()** leaves six extra bytes on the stack and constructs an incorrect return value from the function call. Function declarations can help you to avoid this kind of problem.

For example, assume that you need a function to calculate the sales tax on a purchase. The following code fragment shows what the program might look like:

```
#include <stdio.h>


#define TAXRATE   .05    /* 5 percent sales tax */

void main(void)
{
    double price, sales_tax;
    /* Some code that gets the price */
    sales_tax = find_tax(price);
    /* The rest of the code */
}


double find_tax(double p)
{
    return p * TAXRATE;
}
```

As the code is written, **main()** does not know that **find_tax()** returns a **double**. Therefore, **main()** *assumes* that the function returns the default data type of **int**. However, because **find_tax()** returns a **double**, the sales tax amount is an eight-byte value on the stack. Not knowing any differently, **main()** pops two bytes (that is, an **int**) from the stack and assigns them into **sales_tax**. Clearly, this isn't going to work right.

Most newer compilers will warn you about the preceding problem. Some older compilers, however, will not. You can use a function declaration to solve this kind of problem.

Make the following small change to the code:

```
#include <stdio.h>


#define TAXRATE   .05    /* 5 percent sales tax */

double find_tax(double p);    /* Function declaration */

void main(void)
{
    double price, sales_tax;
    /* Some code that gets the price */
    sales_tax = find_tax(price);
    /* The rest of the code */
}

double find_tax(double p)
{
    return p * TAXRATE;
}
```

In the preceding code, we simply copied the first line of the function definition at the bottom of the fragment and placed it before the main() function. Then we placed a semicolon at the end of the line. This entire line forms the function declaration.

A *function declaration* is a statement that contains the function type specifier, the function name and an opening parenthesis, the function's argument list, a closing parenthesis, and a final semicolon. The function declaration, therefore, is nothing more than the first line of a function definition with a semicolon at the end.

Function Definitions versus Function Declarations

Although some C programmers use the two terms "function definition" and "function declaration" interchangeably, they are *not* the same.

A *function declaration* contains only the function type specifier, the function name, and its argument list. Because the function body is missing, no code space is allocated for the function. The compiler uses the declaration for information only. In fact, a function declaration just causes the compiler to place the information about the function in its symbol table while the program is being compiled.

A *function definition*, in contrast, contains the information of a function declaration plus the function body with all of its source code. This means that the compiler must allocate code space for a function definition.

The distinction between a function declaration and definition is subtle, but important. Let's see how the compiler views this distinction.

How the Compiler Views a Function Declaration

After the compiler reads the #define for TAXRATE, it reads the statement

```
double find_tax(double p);
```

Not until it reads the closing parenthesis of the function does the compiler know whether it is reading the start of a function definition or a function declaration. However, when it reads the semicolon after the closing parenthesis rather than an opening brace for the function body, the compiler knows that it just read a function declaration.

Because the compiler now knows that it has read a function declaration, it readies itself to use the information in the function declaration. First, the compiler searches its symbol table to see if **find_tax()** is already in the table. Because it is not, the compiler makes an entry in the symbol table for **find_tax()**. Simplifying things a bit, the compiler enters the following information in the symbol table:

- The name of the function

- The return data type for the function (the function's type specifier)

- The data type of each argument in the function's argument list

- The number of arguments in the function

- A function declaration

These five pieces of information form the *attribute list* for the function. In other words, a function declaration simply causes the compiler to construct an attribute list for the function being declared in its symbol table. No program code space is allocated.

How the Compiler Views a Function Definition

Now let's see what the compiler does when it begins reading the definition for the function **find_tax()**.

When the compiler finishes reading the line

```
double find_tax(double p)
```

it does not find a semicolon. Therefore, it must continue to read the source code to find out what this line means. (The line isn't a function declaration because it doesn't end with a semicolon.) When the compiler reads the next character of the source code, it finds an opening brace, and now knows that it is about to read a function definition.

Once again, the compiler searches its symbol table for **find_tax()** and does find the previous entry. However, because the compiler marked the entry as a function declaration, the compiler says to itself: "I found the declaration for this function in the symbol table; the programmer now wants to define the function. Let's first check that the attribute list agrees."

The compiler then compares the attribute list in the symbol table with the information it just read at the start of the function definition. That is, the compiler checks that the function definition for **find_tax()** has a **double** as the function type specifier and that its argument is a **double**. If either one of these pieces of information does not match, the compiler issues an error message something like "type mismatch in redeclaration of find_tax." (The exact error message varies among compilers.)

Assuming that the attribute list for the function declaration matches the attribute list for the function definition, the compiler starts reading the source code for the function body. The compiler now creates storage to hold the code for the function body as it is compiled. When the compiler reads the closing brace for the function body, it knows that it has generated all of the code for this function.

As you can see from this example, function declarations provide information that the compiler places in the symbol table to construct an attribute list. No code space is allocated for a function declaration. Function definitions can place information in the symbol table, but they also cause storage to be allocated to hold the compiled code for the function body.

Therefore, function declarations provide information to the compiler about a function. Function definitions also provide information, but the compiler must generate executable code for the function and add it to the program. It follows that function definitions must also allocate code space for the code contained in the function body.

Function Prototyping

A function prototype is a special kind of function declaration. Prior to ANSI C, a function declaration consisted of the function type specifier, the function name, and an empty set of parentheses. That is, there were no type specifiers or names for the function arguments. For example, a pre-ANSI function declaration for the standard library function **strcpy()** was

```
int strcpy();
```

The primary purpose was to declare the function type specifier (**int**) and the function name.

With function prototyping, the same function declaration becomes

```
int strcpy(char d[], char s[]);
```

Note that the argument list now contains the data types for the parameters in the argument list. This form provides a lot more information to the compiler.

A *function prototype* is the list of type specifiers and optional argument names that appear within the opening and closing parentheses of a function declaration. In other words, the function prototype is what appears between the opening and closing parentheses following the function name. This is shown in Figure 14.1.

Figure 14.1
Function declaration with prototyping

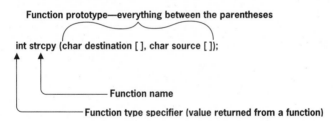

The function prototype provides the compiler with information about the type of the function arguments and the number of arguments to be sent to the function.

Two Varieties of Prototypes

In Chapter 13 we declared the function **rectangle_area()** as

```
int rectangle_area(int width, int length);
```

This form uses both the type specifier (for example, **int**) and argument names (for instance, **width**) in the function prototype. However, you can also write the function declaration using a different prototype form

```
int rectangle_area(int, int);
```

This example omits the names of the function arguments. You are free to use either form, but it makes a lot of sense to use the longer form, which includes argument names. Some programmers refer to the form that uses both the type specifier and name as the *documentation* form of prototyping. The form without the argument names is sometimes called the *short* form of prototyping.

PROGRAMMING TIP. *The longer prototype form, the one that includes the function argument names, is a better choice. Properly selected names help make it clear what the arguments are and the order in which they are passed. In the short form*

```
int rectangle_area(int, int);
```

*it's not obvious whether **width** or **length** comes first. Indeed, you must guess what the two **ints** are. When you include the names, it is clearer what the arguments are and the order in which they are used in the function call.*

The fact that you can use either prototyping form provides some clues as to the real purpose of function prototyping.

The Purpose of Function Prototypes

Given that you can use a function prototype with or without argument names, it follows that *the purpose of function prototyping is to allow the compiler to type-check the function arguments.* For example, assume that you are using the find_tax() function presented earlier. Furthermore, assume that you do something like this:

```
.
int value;
double tax;

/* Code to set things up */
tax = find_tax(value);

/* Rest of the program */
```

Because the compiler has already read the function declaration with prototyping

```
double find_tax(double p);
```

it knows that the function argument for **find_tax()** must be a double data type. However, because you try to use **value**, which is an **int**, the compiler can issue a warning message stating that you have tried to call **find_tax()** with an improper data type.

The addition of function prototyping allows the compiler to check the data types of arguments passed to functions. This type-checking of function arguments was one of the major enhancements that the ANSI standard made to the C language.

Unfortunately, not all compilers issue an error message when an improper data type is passed. However, if you do use a data type that is different than the data type in the function prototype, the compiler often converts the improper data type for you. In other words, if you call **find_tax()** as

```
tax = find_tax(value);
```

where **value** is an **int**, the compiler sees the call as though it were

```
tax = find_tax( (double) value);
```

The compiler automatically casts the improper data type to the data type used in the function prototype. It's best if the compiler warns you about such errors, but not all compilers do.

Testing Your Compiler's Prototype Checking

You should type in a program similar to the tax rate code fragment shown earlier in the chapter and see what your compiler does if you supply a function argument with a different data type. You can use Program 14.1 as a model for the test.

Program 14.1 contains several errors. First, it defines both **val** and **tax** to be an **int**. This means, of course, that the calculation of the sales tax due on the sale cannot include cents. This is an algorithm design error on our part. Second, it calls **find_tax()** with **val**, which is an integer, even though the prototype in the function declaration says the argument should be an **int**. Third, even though it declares that **find_tax()** returns a **double**, it assigns the return value into an **int**.

What's interesting is that both Borland's TurboC and Microsoft's QuickC compilers issued no error or warning messages. Ecosoft's Eco-C88 compiler complained about the mismatch on the argument and warned that **main()** always returns an **int** even though we defined **main()** to return nothing (**void**). (This is true, by the way; **main()** does return an **int** to the operating system when the program ends, regardless of how you define **main()**. If you run a program within the QuickC integrated development environment, it displays the return value in parentheses after the program ends.)

On the other hand, Microsoft's QuickC for Windows did catch the type mismatch error in the find_tax() function call. It also complained that it didn't know the function prototype for **atoi()**. (The Ecosoft compiler has the **atoi()** prototype in stdio.h, while QuickC for Windows places the prototype in stdlib.h.) Borland's C++ compiler still had no complaints.

Program 14.1   **Testing for Type-Checking Errors**

```c
#include <stdio.h>
#include <stdlib.h>

#define TAXRATE    .05

double find_tax(double v);

void main(void)
{
    char buff[10];
    int tax, val;

    printf("Enter the value: ");
    val = atoi(gets(buff));

    tax = find_tax(val);

    printf("Val = %d tax = %d", val, tax);

}

double find_tax(double v)
{
    return (v * .05);
}
```

Clearly, there are differences in the way the compilers view such errors in a program. The Borland TurboC and Microsoft QuickC compilers use the function declaration and prototype to force a cast of **val** to a **double** before calling **find_tax()**. Likewise, they force a cast of the return value from the function to an **int** prior to the assignment into **tax**. In other words, the compiler treats the code as though it were written as

```c
tax = (int) find_tax( (double) val);
```

Although this approach is convenient, it may result in bugs. It would be better if the compilers issued warning messages for the errors. That way, you would know that your program contained potential errors.

You should try using Program 14.1 to see how your compiler processes the errors it contains.

Creating Your Own Function Declarations and Prototypes

It is easy to create your own function declarations and prototypes. Simply use a text editor to copy the first line of the function definition to the top of the program file and place a semicolon at the end of the line. Voilá! The function is now declared with a prototype.

The "copy-and-paste" procedure works fine for small programs like those shown here, but you need a different approach when the program becomes fairly large. This is because large programs normally have multiple source code files, but each file may also need access to the function declarations and prototypes.

While you could copy the function declarations to each source code file, a better approach is to create your own header file for the function declarations.

Using Header Files for Function Declarations

To create your own header file, simply use your text editor to create a file to contain the function declarations. (Many programmers call the header file something like protos.h.) The layout for a hypothetical protos.h file is shown here:

```
/*****

Prototype Header File
Project TEXT.EXE
11/2/1992
*****/

int create_data(void);          /* init.c    */
int get_range(int max_val);      /* input.c   */
int min_max(int vals[]);         /* process.c */
int set_min(int vals[]);         /* input.c   */
int update_file(char name[]);    /* end.c     */

double commission(double amt);   /* process.c */

unsigned int get_date(void);     /* init.c    */

void show_data(int vals[]);      /* output.c  */
void print_data(int vals[]);     /* output.c  */
```

I prefer to list the function declarations by function type specifier in alphabetical order. However, other programmers that use a similar approach prefer to arrange the functions by name rather than type specifier. Unfortunately, not all programmers place the source code file name along with the function declaration. This is a mistake, because it can be so helpful during the debugging process.

PROGRAMMING TIP. *The comments in the hypothetical header file state the name of the file that contains the source code for the function definition. When you debug the program, you can usually trace a bug to a given function. However, with hundreds of functions, it can be a struggle to determine which source code file contains the function definition. Using a header file similar to the one just shown allows you to quickly find where a given function is defined using the "search" function of the text editor. Once you find the function declaration, the comment tells you the name of the source code module.*

After you have created your header file, you should include it in all of your source code files. Typically, the code will look like this:

```
#include <stdio.h>
#include "protos.h"

void main(void)
{
    /* The rest of the program. */
```

Notice that double quotes rather than angle brackets surround the header file name. Double quotes cause the compiler to look in the current working directory *before* looking anywhere else for the file. Angle brackets cause the compiler to first look everywhere *but* the current working directory. By using double quotes instead of angle brackets, we can have several different programming projects, each with its own protos.h header file, and never worry about reading the wrong project header file.

Note that header files should *never* contain source code for the program. That is, header files should never contain the source code for function definitions or other executable program code. You can have data definitions in a header file, but not function definitions.

You should not include source code in a header file because this often leads to linker errors. For example, if you define a function in a header file and include that header file in several program modules, there are multiple copies of the compiled function in each module. When the linker tries to pull all of the modules together, it finds multiple copies of the function definition code. Because the linker doesn't know which one to use, it issues a "multiply defined" error message for the offending function.

The message is simple: Keep function source code out of header files.

Conclusion

In this chapter you saw how function declarations with prototyping can help the compiler check your code for errors. You should also understand the difference between function declarations and function definitions. In this chapter and Chapter 13, you learned how the compiler passes information to and from functions. Finally, you learned how to create your own header files for function prototypes. You should get in the habit of using function declarations and prototypes for *all* functions, even when they use the (default) data type **int**. This will save you time in the long run.

Checking Your Progress

1. What is the difference between a function definition and a function declaration?

   A function definition causes the compiler to generate code for the source code contained in the function body. A function declaration simply causes the compiler to construct an attribute list for the function in the symbol table.

2. What might the attribute list in a symbol table for a function declaration contain?

   The actual attribute list will vary from compiler to compiler. However, all ANSI compilers are required to maintain the following items: the function type specifier (that is, its return value), the name of the function, the number of arguments for the function, and the type specifier for each function argument.

3. I once heard a programmer refer to "documented" and "undocumented" function prototypes. What do you think he meant by the two terms?

   I wasn't sure what he meant either, so I asked. To this programmer, if the function prototype contained argument names that conveyed the purpose of the function argument, it was a "documented" function prototype. If the argument names were missing or unclear, it was an "undocumented" function prototype. Clearly, you should strive to write "documented" function prototypes.

4. What three types of errors do function prototypes help prevent?

   First, function prototypes allow the compiler to see that you are passing the correct type of data to a function. That is, the compiler can check that the data type the function is expecting matches the data type you are sending it.

Second, function prototypes can check that you are passing the correct number of arguments to the function. If the function requires two or more different data types as function arguments, the compiler can also check that you are passing the arguments in the proper order.

Finally, the compiler can check the return value from the function. If you ignore the return value or assign it into a variable of a different data type, the compiler can let you know about it. (You would need to use a cast to assign the return value into a different data type.)

5. What is the advantage of using a header file for all function prototypes?

Placing the function prototypes in a header file allows different source code modes easy access to function prototypes for functions defined in other source code files. Also, if the prototype for a function changes, you only need to edit the prototype in the header file, not all of the source code files that are using it.

15

Scope and the auto and register Storage Classes

N THIS CHAPTER YOU WILL LEARN WHAT SCOPE IS AND WHY IT IS ONE OF C'S most important features. You will also learn about two of C's storage classes and how these storage classes can be used in your programs.

What Is Scope?

Simply stated, *scope refers to the visibility, availability, and life of a data item at various points in a program.* There are two broad classifications of scope: local scope and global scope. We will discuss these two scope classifications in the following sections.

Understanding Local Scope

Any data item that is defined within a statement block is said to have *local scope.* We can illustrate the concept of local scope with the help of Program 15.1.

Program 15.1 Local Scope

```
#include <stdio.h>

void func1(int val);

void main(void)
{
    int i;

    i = 20;
    printf("\n i in main() = %d at %p", i, &i);
    func1(i); }

void func1(int i)
{
    printf("\n i in func1() = %d at %p", i, &i);
}
```

The output of Program 15.1 was displayed as:

```
i in main() = 20 at FFF4
i in func1() = 20 at FFF2
```

Notice that the printf() function calls in **main()** and **func1()** both print the same information, but with different results. In both cases, the rvalues for **i** are the same. However, when we used the %p conversion character to display the lvalue of **i**, different lvalues are shown. Because the lvalue of **i** in **main()** is different from the lvalue in **func1()**, *the i in main() is not the same variable named i in func1()*.

Only when the lvalues for the two **i**'s are the same can they actually be the same variable. In more simple terms, there is an **i** variable that "lives" (that is, is available or visible) at memory address FFF4 in **main()**. Likewise, there is a different variable named **i** that lives at memory address FFF2 in **func1()**. Because they do not have the same lvalue, they cannot be the same variable.

The **i** in **main()** has local scope that is confined to the statement block in which it is defined. In our example, the statement block is actually a function block named **main()**. It begins "living" from the point of its data definition to the end of the main() function block. Because it has local scope, it is not visible outside of the function block named **main()**.

It is also true that a different variable named **i** is defined as the argument to **func1()**. It, too, has local scope. It exists (and is visible) from its definition in **func1()** to the end of the closing brace of **func1()**. Because it is defined within **func1()**, it cannot be used outside of **func1()**'s function body.

Figure 15.1 shows the scope for each of the different variables named **i**. Each variable has local scope because each is defined within the confines of a function body.

Figure 15.1

Local scope of two different variables named **i**

```
.
.
.
void main (void)
{
    int i;
    .                    scope of i is limited to main( )
    .
    .
}

void func1 (int i)
{
    .                    scope of i is limited to func1( )
    .
    .
}
```

Local Scope and Data Privacy

Scope has some very beneficial characteristics. Variables defined within a function have local scope, thus limiting their availability to the function in which they are defined. This means that you can use the variable name **i** in as many functions as you wish without conflicting with variables with the same name defined in other functions. That is, the data for each **i** is private to the function within which it is defined.

It is also safe to say that once you leave the scope in which the variable is defined, the variable is no longer visible. Simply stated, the variable dies and is no longer available for use in other parts of the program.

Figure 15.1 shows that the scope of **i** for **main()** extends from its definition to the end of the function. In similar fashion, the scope of **i** in **func1()** extends from its definition to the end of the function block in which it is defined. However, because the two scopes do not intersect, they are different variables. This is confirmed by the fact that they have different lvalues.

Now let's see how global scope differs from local scope.

Variables with Global Scope

Let's make a slight modification to Program 15.1 and call it Program 15.2.

Program 15.2 Global Scope

```
#include <stdio.h>

void func1(void);

int i;

void main(void)
{
    i = 20;
    printf("\n i in main() = %d at %p", i, &i);
    func1(i);
}

void func1(int i)
{
    printf("\n i in func1() = %d at %p", i, &i);
}
```

Notice that we have moved the definition of **i** outside of the main() function. *Because **i** is now defined outside of a statement block (or function), it has global scope.* This means **i** now lives from the point of its definition to the end of the source code file in which it is defined. Therefore, both **main()** and **func1()** have access to **i** because the scope of **i** now encompasses both **main()** and **func1()**. This can be seen in Figure 15.2.

Figure 15.2

Global scope of the variable named **i**

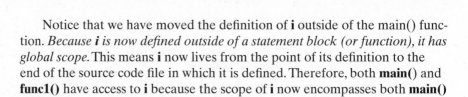

```
int i;

void main(void)
{
    .
    .
    .
}
void func1(void)
{
    .
    .
    .
}
```

Scope of **i** when defined outside of a function. Both **main( )** and **func1( )** have access to the same variable **i**.

Variables with global scope have several important consequences for your programs. First, because both functions now have access to **i**, there is no reason to pass **i** as an argument to **func1()**. After all, **i** is perfectly visible to **func1()** anyway. When I ran Program 15.2, the output changed to

```
i in main() = 20 at 0320
i in func1() = 20 at 0320
```

Note that both memory addresses are the same. Because the lvalues are the same, it *must* be the same **i** in both printf() function calls.

Another important implication is that the data of *variables with global scope is not private.* Any function in the source file can manipulate variables that have global scope.

Global Scope—Goods News, Bad News

Some will view the fact that we no longer have to pass **i** to **func1()** as good news. Indeed, it does simplify the call to **func1()** to a minor degree. That's the good news.

The bad news is the same: Any function can manipulate a variable with global scope. Variables with global scope are good candidates for "side effect bugs." That is, the global scope variable is changed by one function but can be inadvertently changed by a different function. *Variables with global scope do not have the data privacy that variables with local scope enjoy.* This often makes debugging much more difficult because you aren't sure which function is changing the variable.

As a result, most C programmers make a conscious effort to keep the number of variables with global scope to a minimum. The hard part is deciding which variables to make global. As a general rule of thumb, if more than 20 percent of your functions need access to a particular data item, you might consider making it a global variable. This is not a rule etched in stone but simply a guideline that might be used before you even consider defining a variable with global scope.

(Most programmers simply refer to variables with global scope as a global variable. We will use this terminology from now on.)

PROGRAMMING TIP. *If you need to make a variable global, make sure you give it a meaningful name. For example, suppose you're writing a sales-reporting system and you think gross sales and net sales should be global variables. Don't call them something like **s1** and **s2**. Use **gross_sales** and **net_sales**. Descriptive names will make it more clear which variable is being used in which function, so they will be less likely to "collide" with variables that have local scope. If a function has the ability to change the value of a global, it is also a good idea to state this fact in the function header documentation. (For an example of how you might write a function header document, see the rectangle_area() function header in Chapter 13, Program 13.1.) This will help you isolate those functions that change global variables during the debugging process.*

More Detail about Local Scope

We stated at the beginning of the chapter that the scope of a variable extends from its data definition to the end of the statement block in which it is defined. In Program 15.1, the **i** defined in **main()** has its scope extend from its data definition to the closing brace of **main()**. The scope "statement block" is the same as the function block for main(). However, C does not restrict you to a scope level that extends for an entire function block. Consider Program 15.3.

When I ran this program, the output shown was

```
i (scope level 1) = 500 at FFF4
i (scope level 2) = 777 at FFF2
i (scope level 1) = 500 at FFF4
```

If you examine Program 15.3 closely, you will notice that we have two variables named **i** defined within **main()**. However, because the second definition appears within the **if** statement block, it is defined at a different scope level than the first **i** defined in **main()**. Because they are defined at different scope levels, the compiler does not issue a "variable multiple definitions" error message.

Program 15.3 Multiple Local Scope Levels

```
#include <stdio.h>

void main(void)
{
   int i;          /* Call this i scope level 1 */

   i = 500;
   printf("\ni (scope level 1) = %d at %p", i, &i);
   if (i == 500) {
      int i;       /* Call this i scope level 2 */
      i = 777;
      printf("\ni (scope level 2) = %d at %p", i, &i);
   }
   printf("\ni (scope level 1) = %d at %p", i, &i);
}
```

This illustrates an important rule about local scope: *If two variables share the same name, the one with the most current scope takes precedence.* In Program 15.3, the **i** defined within the **if** statement block has precedence when the second **printf()** is called. Notice that its rvalue and lvalue are different from the first **i** defined in **main()**.

Also notice that the last **printf()** displays the original rvalue and lvalue for the first **i** defined in **main()**. Why? Because once we leave the statement block controlled by the if statement, its **i** variable "dies" and is no longer in scope. Figure 15.3 shows the scope levels for the two variables named **i**.

When program control is within the statement block controlled by the if statement, we are at scope level 2. The **i** defined at scope level 2 takes precedence over the **i** defined at scope level 1 when the assignment of 777 into **i** takes place. Therefore, it is the "second" **i** that receives the value 777 and is displayed by the second call to **printf()**.

When we reach the final **printf()** in Figure 15.3, the **i** at scope level 2 has died and is no longer in scope. The value 777 stored in **main()** is not available to any statements that lie outside of the if statement block.

Figure 15.3

Two different local scope levels

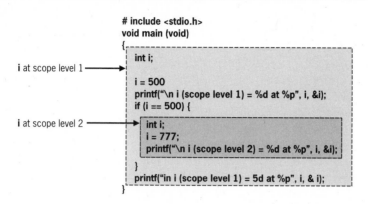

i at scope level 1 ⟶

i at scope level 2 ⟶

```
# include <stdio.h>
void main (void)
{
    int i;

    i = 500
    printf("\n i (scope level 1) = %d at %p", i, &i);
    if (i == 500) {
        int i;
        i = 777;
        printf("\n i (scope level 2) = %d at %p", i, &i);
    }
    printf("in i (scope level 1) = 5d at %p", i, & i);
}
```

If you are curious, define a variable named **j** at scope level 2 and then try to print its value out in the third **printf()**. What happens? Nothing, because the compiler won't compile the program. You will get an "undefined symbol" error during compilation because the **j** defined at scope level 2 is not available at scope level 1.

Why Have Different Local Scope Levels?

You might be asking: "I would never use the same variable name in a function the way you've shown it in Program 15.3. So why even worry about it?" I doubt if anyone would write a program using the constructs shown in Program 15.3. However, the program should drive home the point about data privacy. C uses the concept of scope to enable you to hide data even if it has local scope.

The benefits of data privacy can be appreciated only after you've tried to debug someone else's code in which they used nothing but global variables. It's a nightmare. The point is: use local scope whenever possible. Try to minimize the use of global variables and thereby avoid trouble when the various data items interact with each other.

The auto Storage Class

In almost all of our programs thus far, we have defined variables with local scope. (Except for Program 15.2, all of our variables have been defined within a function or keyword statement block.) With the exception of the variable **i** in Program 15.2, all of our variables have used the auto storage class. The reason is because *the auto storage class is the default storage class* *in* C. Unless you explicitly state otherwise, any variable defined with local scope uses the auto storage class. Consider the following code, which uses the default auto storage class:

```
void main(void)
{
    int i;
```

The definition of **i** looks like all of the other variables we defined in other programs. It uses the default auto storage class. Now see how the auto storage class is used:

```
void main(void)
{
    auto int i;
```

The second code fragment is exactly the same as the first code fragment, except it contains the C keyword **auto** before the definition of **i**. The compiler will generate exactly the same code as before and the program will execute exactly as it would without the keyword **auto**.

Most C programmers never place the keyword **auto** in front of a variable with local scope. Instead, they rely on the compiler to use the auto storage class by default. (I have never seen a piece of production code that contained the keyword **auto**.) Using the default form is perfectly acceptable—it is one of the few areas in which it is safe to use the default behavior of the language.

What auto Storage Means

It we can omit the keyword **auto** from our local variables, why do we even need to know about the auto storage class? Understanding the auto storage class can come in handy when debugging a program.

If you refer to Program 15.1, you will notice that the lvalue for the **i** in **main()** was FFF4 and the lvalue for **i** in **func1()** was FFF2. However, the lvalue for **i** in Program 15.2 was 0320. Notice that the variables with local scope were stored at a very high memory address while the variable with global scope was stored at very low memory address.

Because variables with the auto storage class have local scope, we would expect them to be stored in high memory and this is usually the case. The reason is because of the way compilers allocate memory for the auto storage class.

The auto Storage Class and the Stack

C compilers allocate storage for auto variables from something called the *local heap*. You can think of the local heap as a chunk of unused memory that the compiler sets aside for auto variables when the program first starts executing. When the compiler finds a definition statement for an auto variable, like variable **i** in Program 15.1, it grabs enough storage from the local heap to store the variable.

Although it's not mandatory, most popular C compilers use the stack for the local heap. If you recall our discussion in Chapter 13, the stack is like a spring-load plate dispenser at a salad bar. As auto variables are defined, plates are pushed onto the stack. Figure 15.4 shows how the stack might look when we define two integer variables.

Figure 15.4

Defining two auto variables

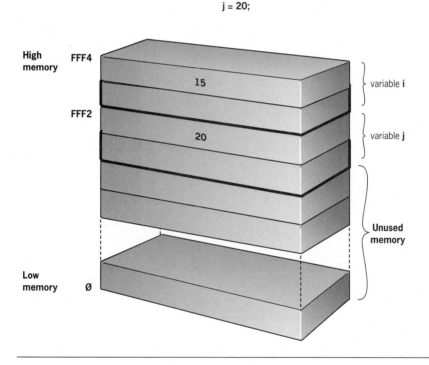

In Figure 15.4, we assume that the two variables are defined in a function and have the auto storage class. Because they are defined within a function block, they have local scope.

When the compiler sees the definition statement for **i** and **j**, it takes the value of **j** and places its two bytes on the stack and then takes the value of **i** and places its two bytes on the stack. As a result, the stack now looks similar to that shown in Figure 15.4.

When the function finishes its job, the compiler causes the four bytes of memory used by **i** and **j** to be freed. That is, because these variables are no longer in scope—program control just left the function in which they are defined—their storage is given back to the local heap. The memory is now free to be reused for storing new data.

This is one reason why values with local scope do not have known values when they are first defined. If we just left a function with local variables, a few nanoseconds earlier, an entirely different variable may have been using the same storage space the current function is using.

If a function defines a lot of local variables, the stack may dig deeply into the unused portion of the local heap. However, when control leaves the function, all of the storage used by the local variables is freed up for use by the next function that is called. As a result of this allocation and deallocation stack mechanism, the stack ebbs and flows throughout the execution of your program.

The Stack with a Function Call

Now let's see how the stack would look if we define a local variable in **main()** and two more variables in a different function. This is shown in Figure 15.5.

Figure 15.5

Stack with local variables in different functions

```
void main (void)
{
    int i; /* Picture 1 */

    funcl( );
    printf("i = %d", i); /*Picture 3 */
}
void funcl (void)
{
    int j, k; /* Picture 2 */
    .
    .
    .
}
```

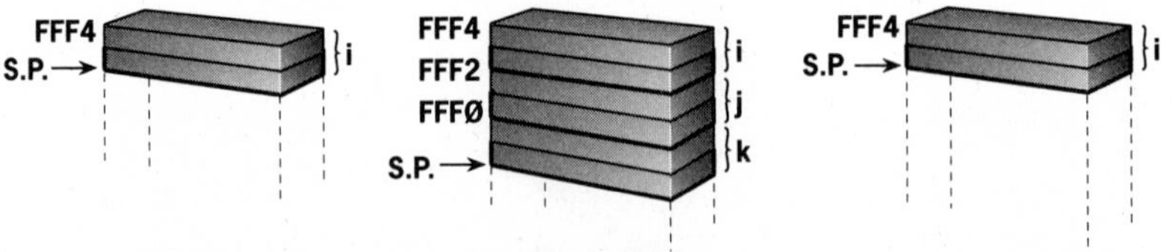

Stack picture 1   Stack picture 2   Stack picture 3

After (local variable) **i** in Figure 15.5 is defined, the stack looks like that shown in Stack Picture 1. As you can see in the figure, **i** uses two bytes of stack space starting at memory location FFF4. The S.P. arrow shown in Figure 15.5 is called the *stack pointer*, which points to the next free storage location on the stack. After variable **i** is defined, the stack pointer points to memory address FFF2.

After **i** is defined in **main()**, **func1()** is called. Because **func1()** has no function arguments, the first variables defined in **func1()** are **j** and **k**. After these two variables are defined, the stack picture looks like that shown in Stack Picture 2. Note that the stack pointer now points to memory location FFEE (that is, FFEE = FFF0 - 2).

When **func1()** finishes its task, variables **j** and **k** are no longer in scope. The compiler will generate code that simply moves the stack pointer back to memory location FFF2. Therefore, when control returns to **main()** in preparation for the call to **printf()**, the stack looks like Stack Picture 3 in Figure 15.5.

PROGRAMMING TIP. *Sometimes the stack gets messed up. This might happen because you forgot to call the function with the proper argument types or number of arguments. This shouldn't happen often with compilers that support function prototyping, but it is common with non-ANSI compilers. If you see a value appear in one function that looks very similar to a value in the function you just left, chances are the stack pointer got confused somewhere. The first thing to check are the arguments used to call the previous function. Was the proper number of arguments sent to the function and were they the proper data types? Also check to see that the proper data type was returned from the function; does the return type match the function's type specifier?*

Running Out of Memory

As you might guess from Figure 15.5, the depth of the stack pointer rises and falls as program control enters and then leaves a function. If you define large amounts of data, like arrays, the stack pointer slides down toward low memory accordingly. Some programming techniques (for example, recursion) can eat up stack space at an alarming rate.

If you recall our discussion of Program 15.2 when **i** had global scope, you will remember that **i** was stored at memory location 320. Most compilers store global data starting at low memory, and place each new data item at a higher memory address. If low memory is filled up with a lot of global data and the stack starts sliding down toward low memory, it is possible for the stack pointer to collide with the global data being stored in low memory. This can cause an "out-of-memory" error.

Actually, most modern compilers check for such data collisions. The compiler checks to see how close the stack pointer is coming to the global data area. Typically, the compiler will only allow the stack pointer to get within a few hundred bytes of the global data area. If the stack pointer does come close, an out-of-memory message is given.

What to Do When You Run Out of Memory

There is no set solution for solving an out-of-memory error. On an IBM-compatible computer, programs are typically given one segment (64k) for code space and one segment for data space . Keep in mind that global and local data must share the space in the data segment. Clearly, defining an array of 8,000 **double**s isn't going to work too well.

The first thing to check is whether you are actually using all of the auto variables you have defined in a function. Some compilers such as Borland's do an excellent job of catching defined variables that aren't being used. Other compilers may not check at all. Delete all unused variables.

The second step is to take a hard look at the data you've defined with global scope. Unlike variables with the auto storage class, which come and go as the various functions are called, global variables live throughout the life of the program. Strip out all global data that can easily be made into auto variables.

Third, you may have to redesign the algorithm. C allows you to write functions that call themselves in a process known as *recursion*. While recursion often provides an elegant solution to certain programming tasks, recursive functions chew up a lot of memory. The reason is because each time the function calls itself, a new set of the auto variables is created for the function. This causes the stack pointer to slide deeper and deeper down the stack. You may have to forego the elegant recursive solution for a different algorithm.

Fourth, it might help to break down very large functions into smaller ones. Calling three or four smaller functions that use the same number of variables as one large function will use less stack space. Think about it.

Finally, on IBM-compatible computers, you can use a different memory model for the compiler. The various memory models supported by most PC C compilers are shown in Table 15.1.

Table 15.1   **Memory Models for 80x86 C Compilers**

Model	Description
Tiny	A maximum of 64k for code, data, and stack area. Usually generates a COM program file.
Small	Up to 64k of code space and 64k of data space.
Medium	Code space can be up to 1 megabyte, but data space is limited to 64k.

Table 15.1   **(Continued)**

Model	Description
Compact	Code space is limited to 64k, but data space can be up to 1 megabyte.
Large	Both code and data space can be 1 megabyte, but no single data item (for example, an array) can exceed 64k.
Huge	Similar to Large model, but a data item can exceed 64k.

For example, the large memory model gives you up to one megabyte for code space and one megabyte for data. Clearly, this eases the chance of running out of memory. However, there is a slight performance penalty for this choice. (We will discuss this in more detail when we talk about pointers in Chapters 17 and 18.)

The out-of-memory problem does not have a single solution. More likely, you will use a combination of the suggestions presented here to solve the problem.

The register Storage Class

The register storage class is used to define a data item that you wish to store in a CPU register. For the Intel 80x86 family of CPUs, there are four 16-bit registers that might be used for data. The Motorola 680x0 family of CPUs, on the other hand, has up to eight data registers that can be used in eight-, 16-, or 32-bit configurations. Therefore, the actual data that can be used with the register storage class will vary somewhat depending on the CPU being used.

The syntax for the register storage class is

```
register type_specifier variable_name;
```

The type specifier needs to be sensible for the host CPU. For example, it wouldn't make sense to say

```
register double x;
```

because a **double** is too large to fit in a single register on most CPUs.

Likewise, it would be odd to define two dozen register variables in a single function when there are only four data registers available in the CPU. Most of the time, if you define one or two register variables, the compiler attempts to comply with the request. If the compiler cannot fulfill the request, the data items revert to the auto storage class.

You cannot use the register class for global data; all register data items must be defined within a function or statement block. Also, you cannot use the address-of (&) operator with a register variable. This makes sense if you think about it. The address-of is used to get the memory address (lvalue) of a variable. Because register variables are not stored in memory, it makes no sense to try and get their lvalue. A register variable does not have an lvalue.

Why Use a register Variable?

The whole idea behind the register storage class was to give the programmer some control over how the data items are used in a function. The idea was that variables that are used intensively in a function should be kept in a CPU register. This would be more efficient because the register variable wouldn't have to be loaded from memory each time it was used. Keeping the data item in a register prevents the fetch-and-store sequence of instructions and can improve performance.

Does the register storage class affect performance that much? Consider Program 15.4.

Program 15.4 simply times how long it takes to complete the program. Note that we **#include** the time.h header file because it contains the function prototype for **clock()** and the CLK_TCK symbolic constant.

Several unneeded variables are defined so the compiler's optimizers cannot place all of the variables in registers. The program simply loops though 65,000 iterations of the inner for loop 100 times. On my 80386, 33MHz machine, the program required 9.73 seconds to run.

Next, I modified Program 15.4 so that the line that defines **index** reads:

```
register unsigned int index;
```

The rest of the program is exactly as before. The new data definition causes the compiler to try and place **index** in a CPU register. When I ran the modified program, the time dropped to 8.46 seconds—about a 13 percent improvement. (Your results may vary substantially from mine, depending upon how your compiler generates the code.)

The reason for the speed improvement should be clear by now. Without the register storage class, the compiler must generate code to get **index** from the stack each time it is accessed. When the register storage class is used, **index** sits in the CPU register, thus eliminating several hundred thousand load-and-store instructions.

PROGRAMMING TIP. *In Program 15.4, we made **index** the register variable because it is the variable that is used most in the program. The way the program is written, it is accessed about 650,000 times. On the other hand, loop variable **j** is used only about 100 times in the program. Therefore, if you want to use the register storage class, look for the loop counter variable that is most used in the program. Typically, this is the loop counter for the innermost loop. (A profiler can help you determine where a program spends most of its time.)*

Program 15.4 Timing Test for the register Storage Class

```
#include <stdio.h>

#include <time.h>


#define MAXITERS 65000

void main(void)
{
   unsigned int index;
   unsigned int j, k, l, m;
   long count;
   long start, end;

   start = clock();        /* Start the timer */
   count = 0L;
   for (k = l = m = j = 0; j < 100; j++) {
       for (index = 0; index < MAXITERS; index++) {
           count++;
           k++;
           l = k;
           m = l;
       }
   }

   end = clock();
   printf("Elapsed time: %f\n", (end - start) / CLK_TCK);
}
```

Conclusion

In this chapter you learned about the auto storage class. You also learned that it is the default storage class for all local variables. It is important to keep in mind that auto variables "live" on the stack, and be aware of what happens if you crash the stack. It's much easier to fix a bug if you understand what the compiler is doing with your program data. You should also understand where global data is stored and how the two storage classes are different.

Finally, you learned how the register storage class is used. Most modern compilers do a pretty good job of selecting which variables would best be stored in registers. (This is part of the optimizing that compilers do automatically.) However, situations may arise when the register storage class can cause noticeable improvement in performance.

Checking Your Progress

1. What is the default storage class in C?

The default storage class is **auto**. Variables with the auto storage class are normally stored on the stack.

2. What is the stack?

The stack is the data segment in memory that is used to store auto variables. The stack begins at the high memory address in the data segment and grows downward as new auto variables are defined.

3. What does the term scope mean?

Scope refers to the visibility of a data item. In broad terms, variables may have either local or global scope. Variables with local scope are visible only in the statement block that contains their definition. Variables with local scope are stored on the stack in the data segment.

Variables with global scope are defined outside of any statement block. Their scope extends from their point of definition to the end of the file in which they are defined. Variables with global scope normally reside in low memory of the data segment.

4. What is a "stack collision"?

As functions are called in a program, new auto variables for those functions come into scope (that is, they are defined). Because auto variables reside on the stack, each new set of variables uses more and more of the stack's memory. If enough variables are defined on the stack, the depth of the stack may reach that section of the data segment where the global variables reside. When this happens, there is a stack collision.

5. What is the register storage class?

When a register keyword precedes the type specifier in a data definition, the programmer is making an explicit request that the variable being defined be placed in a CPU register. The compiler may or may not be able to fulfill the request.

6. What happens when a request for the register storage class for a data item cannot be fulfilled by the compiler?

Because the CPU has a very limited number of registers that can be used for data, not all register storage requests can be fulfilled. In that event, the data item is given the default auto storage class.

7. What are the distinguishing characteristics of a register variable?

First, the register variable resides in a CPU register rather than the data segment in conventional memory. Second, because a register variable does not exist in the data segment, you cannot obtain an lvalue for the data item. This means you cannot use the address-of operator with a register variable. In some situations, this can make debugging more difficult for register variables.

16

The static and extern Storage Classes

THIS CHAPTER DISCUSSES THE LAST TWO STORAGE CLASSES THAT C provides. When you finish this chapter, you should have a good idea of how the compiler allocates storage for all data types. You will also learn how multiple source code files have an impact on the storage classes that you use.

The Internal static Storage Class

There are two types of the static storage class. The first is the internal static storage class. (The second type of static variable is covered near the end of this chapter.) It has some properties that make it different than the other storage classes you've studied.

As you will recall, variables with the auto storage class are local variables that are defined within a function block. You also saw that once program control left the function, that function's auto variables were no longer in scope. In a real sense, when you left the function the auto variables "died." If you reentered the same function a second time, the values of the auto variables in that function contained garbage until you reinitialized them to some known value. Program 16.1 demonstrates this behavior.

In this program, each time **func1()** is called **count** is reinitialized to equal 0. Therefore, when you run the program, the output displayed is

```
count = 1
count = 1
count = 1
count = 1
count = 1
```

Because **count** is an auto variable, each time **func1()** is called in **main()**, **count** is re-created on the stack, initialized to 0, and its value displayed (which is always equal to 1). Because auto storage class variables die whenever you leave the function, you must re-create them each time you reenter the function.

Now make one small but important change to Program 16.1. The only line you will change is the definition statement for **count**. The new statement line is

```
static int count = 0;
```

Program 16.1   **Displaying an auto Variable in a Function**

```
#include <stdio.h>

#define MAXITERS  5

void func1(void);

void main(void)
{
    int i;

    for (i = 0; i < MAXITERS; i++) {
        func1();
    }
}

void func1(void)
{
    int count = 0;

    count++;
    printf("\ncount = %d", count);
}
```

Now run the program and see what happens. Instead of all the output lines being the same, **count** increases by 1 on each call to the function. Therefore, the output now looks like this:

```
count = 1
count = 2
count = 3
count = 4
count = 5
```

Clearly, the static storage class has an impact on the way **count** is now processed in the program.

Count behaves differently because it now has the internal static storage class. An *internal static storage class variable has its scope limited to the function in which it is defined, but it continues to live after the function is left*. What this means is that the last value that an internal **static** had when program control leaves the function is the same value it has the next time program control enters the function. This is an important deviation from the auto storage class.

How Does an Internal static Retain Its Value?

How can an internal **static** keep its previous value? After all, the definition of **count** is

```
static int count = 0;
```

Shouldn't this reset the value to 0 when you enter the function? Clearly, the answer must be no. Otherwise, the value would always be 1 as it was when it had the auto storage class.

The value retains its previous value because the definition statement of **count** is really never executed as part of the function call. So what happens to the definition statement?

When the compiler sees the definition of **count** with the static storage class, it handles the allocation for **count** differently than if it were an auto variable. The compiler stores **count** in such a way that *count is defined when the program is first loaded*. That is, memory is given to **count** and its value initialized before **main()** even starts executing. By the time **main()** starts executing, the code behaves as though the program has already executed the statement

```
static int count = 0;
```

in **func1()** and left a message saying: "**count** lives in this function, and I have already defined it. You can find count at lvalue *XXXX*." By the time you call **func1()** for the first time, all you find is code telling you where you can find **count**. Program 16.2 illustrates how an internal static variable might be used.

Most of the code in Program 16.2 should look familiar by now. The program clears the screen and displays a column of MAXITERS values. After each value is displayed, a call to **pause()** is performed to see if you need to stop the display so the user can view it.

In the pause() function, **line** was initialized to 0 before the code in **main()** began executing. On each call to **pause()**, **line** is incremented and then checked to see if you need to pause the display. The if statement

```
if (line % SHOWLINES == 0) {
```

checks whether **line** is equal to SHOWLINES (20). If it is not, there is no need to pause the display. Any value for **line** other than SHOWLINES causes the if test to evaluate to logical False and the compiler skips the statement block controlled by the if statement, returning control to **main()**.

Program 16.2   **Pausing a Program with an Internal static Variable**

```c
#include <stdio.h>

#define MAXITERS  50
#define SHOWLINES 20

void pause(void);


void main(void)
{
    int i;

    clrscr();                       /* Clear display screen */

    for (i = 0; i < MAXITERS; i++) {
        printf("\ni = %d", i);
        pause();
    }
}


void pause(void)
{
    static int line = 0;

    line++;
    if (line % SHOWLINES == 0) {
        gotoxy(20, 23);
        printf("Press any key to continue: ");
        getch();
        clrscr();
        line = 0;
    }

}
```

When **line** equals SHOWLINES, the modulus operation yields a result
of 0 and the if test is logical True. In that instance, the gotoxy() function
places the cursor at row 23, column 20, and displays a message. After the

user has viewed the display and pressed a key, the screen is cleared and **line** is set to 0.

It should be clear that **line** must be able to retain its previous value between calls. If instead **line** were always being reinitialized to 0, the display would never pause.

The internal static storage class allows you to have a variable with local scope, but which can retain its values between function calls. Therefore, the two distinguishing characteristics of variables with the internal static storage class are

- They have local scope.

- They retain their previous value between function calls.

You will use the internal static storage class often for variables that must maintain a running count of some kind. Internal **static**s are also useful for keeping track of the state of something. For example, you might use an internal **static** to keep track of a certain area of the screen. If the user selects a certain option, you highlight the option and set a static variable to 1. If they select the option again, you might set the static variable to 0 to show that they have deselected the option.

PROGRAMMING TIP. *Internal static variables are not stored on the stack, but are placed in low memory, near variables with global scope. If you're curious, place the following statements near the top of the pause() function in Program 16.2:*

```
gotoxy(15, 24);
printf("\nlvalue of line = %p, rvalue = %d", &line, line);
```

*If you place the statements outside the if statement in **pause()**, the information is updated on each call to **pause()**.*

The External Storage Class

Although you didn't know it, you used a variable with the external storage class in Chapter 16. When you moved variable **i** from inside of **main()** to just before **main()**, **i** changed from a variable with local scope to one with global scope. *Variables defined outside of a function are given the external storage class.* Therefore, variables with the external storage class have global scope. Such variables are visible from their point of definition to the end of the source code file in which they are defined.

Unlike the auto, register, and internal static storage classes, you don't use a C keyword to give a variable external storage class. Any variable defined outside a function body by definition has the external storage class. Indeed, variables with the external storage class are often simply called *global variables*.

Program 16.3 makes a few simple additions to Program 16.2 to illustrate some of the properties of the external storage class.

First, notice that **global** is defined outside of any function near the top of the program. Also note that the variable is not initialized to any particular value. When I ran the program, the first **printf()** in **main()** displayed

```
global = 0 lvalue = 0362
```

The lvalue you see may vary, but the rvalue should be 0 if you are using an ANSI compiler. This is because all variables with the external storage class are initialized to 0 before the program starts execution.

Initializing Variables Explicitly

Even though an ANSI compiler *should* initialize all external storage variables to 0, it's a good idea to set their starting values with code. First, some pre-ANSI compilers may not initialize external storage variables to 0. Second, your program may overwrite the initialized value of an external variable. This is almost always caused by a bug, but assuming a value for a variable can lead to days of fruitless debugging. (The next chapter shows how pointer variables can cause this kind of mischief.)

Finally, explicitly initializing a variable indicates what the assumed starting value for the variable is. Because external variables have global scope, their initial value can be changed anywhere in the program. When you see a global variable assigned a specific value, you know the programmer wanted it to have that value at that point in the program. If you rely on default initialization, you aren't sure whether its value is 0 by accident, by default initialization, or because it was set to 0 in some other function.

When you want a global to have a specific value at a given point in a program, do it yourself. It will make life a lot easier in the long run.

The Scope of the External Storage Class

The scope of the external storage class variable extends from its point of definition to the end of the file in which it is defined. To prove this to yourself, use your text editor and move the definition of **global** from its current position in Program 16.3 to the last line in the program (after **pause()**). Now compile the program and see what happens.

You should get a few error messages saying that **global** is undefined. Keep in mind that the compiler cannot look ahead in the program. Therefore, we try to use **global** in **main()** and in **pause()** before we have defined it.

This is why we are very careful to say that the scope extends *from its point of definition* to the end of the file in which it is defined.

Program 16.3 **Using the External Storage Class**

```c
#include <stdio.h>

#define MAXITERS  50

void pause(void);

int global;              /* external storage class */

void main(void)
{
    int i;

    clrscr();
    printf("global = %d lvalue = %p\n", global, &global);
    for (i = 0; i < MAXITERS; i++) {
        printf("\ni = %d", i);
        pause();
    }
}

void pause(void)
{
    static int line = 0;

    line++;
    if (line % 20 == 0) {
        gotoxy(20, 23);
        printf("Press any key to continue: ");
        gotoxy(21,24);
        printf("global = %d lvalue = %p\n", global, &global);
        getch();
        clrscr();
        line = 0;
    }
}
```

The Characteristics of the External Storage Class

These are the characteristics of the external storage class:

- External storage class variables have global scope.

- Their scope extends from their point of definition to the end of the file in which they are defined.

- ANSI compilers initialize external storage class variables to 0.

- External storage class variables typically reside in low memory (not on the stack).

There is a fifth feature in well-written C code. Most C programmers give global variables descriptive names. This is because global variables tend to be used in multiple functions. Indeed, one strong reason for having a global variable is because it is needed by so many different functions. (Because of their global scope, global variables reduce the number of arguments that must be sent to a function.) Giving global variables long and descriptive names makes it easier to understand their purpose.

PROGRAMMING TIP. *Beginning C programmers are often tempted to make everything a global variable. This is understandable, because the idea of function arguments, passing data back and forth on the stack, and many other elements of C are new. However, when you use global variables you sacrifice C's ability to give privacy to data. Because global data can be changed by any function, it makes tracking down bugs much more difficult. When data is instead passed from function to function as arguments, it's easier to trace where the data goes astray.*

The extern Keyword

As mentioned, your programs will eventually get so large that you will want to split the source code into multiple files. When you do this, it takes less time to compile and link a program. Your Make utility will not recompile files that have not changed since they were last compiled. After all, why recompile code that you haven't changed?

Using your Make facility can save you time. There are, however, some things you need to think about when the source code spans multiple files. Consider Figure 16.1, for example.

The first file defines variable **i** so that it has the external storage class and global scope. This also means that the **i** in **func1()** (file 1) can use **i**. So far, so good.

Now the compiler sets about compiling file 2. Note that **func3()** in file 2 wants to use the **i** defined in file 1. Now there's a problem. The **i** that **func3()**

wants to use is defined in file 1 and, hence, is not available in file 2. Remember that the scope of **i** in file 1 extends from its point of definition *to the end of the file in which it is defined.* Therefore, as the code is presently written, file 2 cannot have access to the **i** defined in file 1.

Figure 16.1

Compiling multiple source files for one program

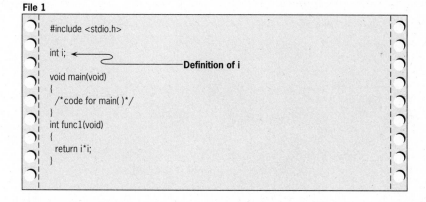

File 1

```
#include <stdio.h>

int i; ←                    ──────Definition of i

void main(void)
{
   /*code for main( )*/
}
int func1(void)
{
   return i*i;
}
```

File 2

```
int func2(void)
{
   /*code for func2( )*/
}
int func3(void)
{
   return i/100; ←         ──────Problem: i is not defined in File 2
}
```

Using the extern Keyword

You can solve the problem by using the keyword **extern** in file 2. You just need to add the following statement near the top of file 2:

```
extern int i;
```

The change is shown in Figure 16.2.

The keyword **extern** gets the attention of the compiler. In essence, it says to the compiler: "I realize that I haven't defined this variable in this file, but it is defined in another file. Let me use the variable in this file." The compiler responds with: "I'll assume the programmer knows what he or she is doing. However, I'll have to leave a message to the linker to provide the proper lvalue for this variable." The compiler then proceeds to compile the file as though **i** were defined in file 2.

Figure 16.2

Solving the undefined variable problem

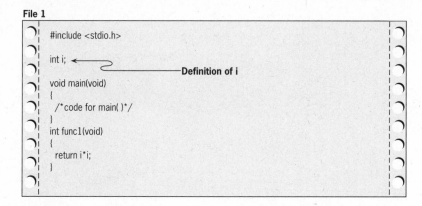

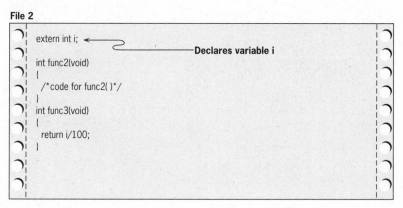

It's important to understand that the keyword **extern** is a declaration for a variable. That is, **i** is defined in file 1. It has storage with an lvalue and an rvalue. However, the **extern** keyword for **i** in file 2 causes **i** to be declared in file 2. This means the compiler does not allocate storage for **i** in file 2. The compiler simply constructs an attribute list for **i** and lets file 2 use it according to that attribute list.

Because we placed the statement

```
extern int i;
```

outside of any function block, the **i** in file 2 has global scope in file 2. Any function that needs **i** in file 2 now has access to it.

The Linker's Job with extern Variables

After the compiler has finished compiling the two source files in Figure 16.2, it is the linker's responsibility to join the two files to form an executable program.

The linker also constructs a symbol table during the linking process. When the linker examines the object code for file 2, it finds the message left by the compiler about the *declaration* of **i** in file 2. Now the linker knows that **i** must be defined in some other file. The linker then scans its symbol table for the missing variable **i**. If it does not find **i** in the symbol table, it issues an "unresolved external" error message and quits. (Linkers usually have to make two passes over the source code files to construct a complete symbol table. This is because the linker may not examine the files in the exact order needed to find all of the variables in one pass through the code.)

Because **i** was defined in file 1 of Figure 16.2, the linker will find **i** in its symbol table. The linker then takes the lvalue of **i** defined in file 1 and writes it into the appropriate places as required in file 2. It then combines the object code for the two files (plus any library code) to produce an executable program.

To summarize, any time you need to use a variable in a file in which the variable is not defined, simply place the keyword **extern** before the type specifier for the data item. This declares the variable for use in the file.

The External static Storage Class

In the discussion of the internal static storage class, the examples used the static keyword with variables that were defined within a function or statement block. The *external static storage class is used with variables defined outside of a function block*. Figure 16.3 shows how an external **static** might be defined.

Suppose that file 3 has several functions that need to keep a count of some data item. Near the top of the source code file in Figure 16.3 is the statement

```
static int counter;
```

Because this variable is defined outside of any function or statement block, it has the external static storage class. This means that any function in file 3, and *only* in file 3, has access to **counter**. The scope of an external static variable is from its point of definition to the end of the file in which it is defined. *No other file can have access to a data item with the external static storage* *class.* It is important to understand that the scope of an external static data item is restricted to the file in which it is defined. Simply stated, there is no way for the code in any another file to gain access to **counter**; it is totally private to file 3.

Figure 16.3

Defining a variable with the exernal static storage class

File 3

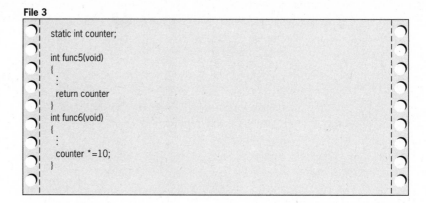

```
static int counter;

int func5(void)
{
    ⋮
  return counter
}
int func6(void)
{
    ⋮
  counter *=10;
}
```

When the compiler sees the definition of **counter** in Figure 16.3, it places it into its symbol table, but makes a special note to itself. The note reminds the compiler to remove **counter** from the symbol table when it finishes compiling file 3. Therefore, any subsequent files that might be compiled have no way they can even know about **counter** in file 3. For all other program files, **counter** might as well not exist.

You might wonder whether the linker will find the statement

```
extern int counter;
```

if you place it in another file. No, it will not. You will simply get an "unresolved external _counter" error. This is because the compiler knew that no other file should have access to **counter**. That is, all references to **counter** only occur in this file. Therefore, the compiler can generate all of the code necessary to reference **counter** in file 3. This also means that the compiler doesn't need to leave any messages for the linker about **counter**. By the time the linker sees the object code for file 3, it's as though **counter** doesn't exist.

The external static storage class gives you a way to have a global data item for one file, but make it totally invisible to any other file. It's like having a private global data item that's only visible in the file in which it was defined.

Why Use External static Data Items?

You use an external static data item any time you want to create a data item with global scope that you don't want any other file to know about. For example, suppose you are writing a database program and need to sort some integer data. As part of that sorting process, you need to write a compare() function. Assume that the sorting function and the compare() function are in file number 8. (It's a big program.) The file might look like this:

```c
#include <stdio.h>   /* sort integer data */

void MyIntSort(void)
{
    /* Some code that starts the sort */
    .
    index = compare(i, j);
    .
    /* More code to finish the sort */
}

int compare(int i, int j)
{
    /* The code that does the sort */
    .
    return val;
}
```

You place the **compare()** in this file because only **MyIntSort()** will ever call it. In these cases, it makes sense to keep such synergistic functions in the same source file. You compile the file and everything works fine.

Several months later, you need to sort some double data types from the database. You create a new file (perhaps file number 30) and, because you've forgotten about the old code, you write the file as follows:

```c
#include <stdio.h>   /* sort double data */

void MyDoubleSort(void)
{
    /* Some code that starts the sort */
    .
    index = compare(i, j);
    .
    /* More code to finish the sort */
}
```

```
int compare(double i, double j)
{
   /* The code that does the sort */
      .
   return val;
}
```

The linker will object to this compare() function because another function with the same name resides in file number 8. The linker must issue some form of "multiply defined" error message because it finds source code for two functions with the same name. To solve the problem, you simply define each compare() function with the external static storage class. For the first code fragment, the line becomes

```
static int compare(int i, int j)
```

and the second compare() function becomes

```
static int compare(double i, double j)
```

Because you've used the static keyword in each function definition, only those functions in the same file can call the compare() function. As far as the other source files are concerned, the compare() functions don't exist. However, because **MyIntSort()** is defined in the same file as the integer compare() function, **MyIntSort()** can call its compare() function.

Likewise, **MyDoubleSort()** can call its compare() function because both functions are defined in the same file. *All functions have global scope by default.* This means that all files can have access to a function. However, placing the keyword static in front of the function type specifier makes the function private to the file in which it is defined. An external static function cannot be called by any function outside its own source code file.

Any time you write a function that you only want called by one other function, you should consider defining it with the external static storage class. That way, you never have to worry about any other function calling the function; it is totally private to its own file. The external static storage class provides an effective way to hide data or functions that would otherwise have global scope.

Conclusion

In this chapter you have seen how the static keyword can define two different types of data. Internal **static**s retain their values between function calls. External **static**s are useful because they have global scope, but only for the file in which they are defined. The extern keyword lets you define a global variable in one file, but declare and use it in a different file.

Take some time to study the concepts presented in this chapter. They provide effective means for coping with a variety of programming problems, especially that of maintaining data privacy.

Checking Your Progress

1. What are the characteristics of the internal static storage class?

They are

- The keyword **static** precedes the type specifier for the data item being defined (for example, **static int count**;).

- The definition of the static data item must occur within a function or statement block.

- Internal static data items retain their value between function calls.

- If the definition includes an initializer (for example, **static int count = 100**;), the internal **static** is initialized at the start of program execution, not when the function is entered.

- The scope of an internal **static** is the function or statement block in which it is defined.

- Internal static data are not allocated on the stack.

2. Why do you think C includes the internal static storage class?

One of the most important reasons is the internal **static**'s ability to retain its value between function calls. Without this ability, you would need to use a global variable. However, internal **static**s have local scope, thus affording more data privacy than a global scoped variable.

3. What is the purpose of the extern keyword?

The extern keyword enables you to reference a global variable that is defined in a different file.

4. What does the following statement mean?

```
extern int i;
```

This statement tells the compiler that the variable named **i** is defined in some other source code file. Because **i** is defined elsewhere, the statement is a declaration of **i** and enables you to reference the variable in the current file.

5. What are the characteristics of an external static data item?

They are

- The keyword **static** precedes the type specifier for the data item being defined (for example, **static int count;**).

- The definition of the static data item must occur outside of a function or statement block.

- External static data items have global scope, but that scope is limited to the file in which the data item is defined.

6. What is the purpose of using an external static data item?

If a data item is defined outside of a function block and is preceded by the keyword **static**, its scope is restricted to the file in which the data item is defined. The data item—be it a variable or a function—cannot be referenced or called from outside of its own source file.

17

Introduction to Pointers

THIS CHAPTER WILL EXAMINE POINTERS, PERHAPS C'S MOST POWERFUL
data type. You will learn how to define, initialize, and use a pointer
variable. You will see why scalars are so important when using
pointer variables. You will also look at the null pointer and how it can
be used in logical tests. Finally, you will learn how to perform pointer arithmetic on pointers. In Chapter 18, we will explore some of the more advanced
topics concerning pointer variables.

What Is a Pointer Variable?

Stated simply, *a pointer variable is a variable that can be used to manipulate
another variable, and the rvalue of a pointer is the lvalue of a different variable.* The first thing you need to understand is how to define a pointer variable. In the previous chapters, you saw that the definition of a variable
required two parts: a type specifier and a variable name. For example,

```
int i;
```

defines a variable named **i** that has an **int** type specifier. This definition allows us to use **i** as an integer variable in a program.

A pointer variable, however, has three parts: a type specifier, an indirection operator, and the name of the pointer variable. These three parts are
shown in Figure 17.1.

Figure 17.1
The parts of a
pointer definition

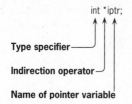

int *iptr;

Type specifier

Indirection operator

Name of pointer variable

A pointer variable's name follows the same naming conventions used for
all C variables.

PROGRAMMING TIP. *Although you are free to name a pointer whatever
you wish, many C programmers use **ptr** as part of a pointer variable's name.
This helps reinforce the idea that the variable is a pointer. In Figure 17.1, we
used **iptr** because we are defining an integer pointer. Using a variable name for
the pointer that begins with the letter of the object being pointed to keeps you
from using the pointer incorrectly.*

The first two parts of a pointer definition need further explanation. Let's begin our examination of a pointer definition with the unusual part of the definition: the asterisk.

The Pointer Definition's Asterisk

The pointer definition shown in Figure 17.1 represents the first time we have used an asterisk in a data definition. You have probably guessed why: an asterisk can only appear in a data definition when you are defining a pointer. In other words, *the asterisk in a data definition tells the compiler you wish to define a pointer variable.* The asterisk causes the compiler to give this variable a special attribute reserved only for pointer variables. This special attribute allows us to do some special things with this pointer variable, as you shall see.

It is unfortunate that the asterisk is used to give a variable its pointer attribute. You already know that an asterisk signifies multiplication. When used to indicate multiplication, the asterisk requires two operands (a * b). That is, the asterisk is a binary operator when it's used to indicate multiplication.

However, look at Figure 17.1 closely. Notice that the asterisk has only one operand—the variable's name. The asterisk in this context must be a unary operator. When the asterisk has only one operand, it is the indirection operator, not multiplication. *When used in a data definition, the asterisk is the indirection operator and simply tells the compiler that this variable is capable of performing indirection.* Because only pointers can perform indirection, the indirection operator causes the compiler to give the variable the special indirection attribute. (You will learn what indirection is all about later in this chapter.)

Because the asterisk can have more than one meaning (multiplication or indirection), it is called an *overloaded operator.* However, it is very easy to determine which meaning the asterisk has by its context (semantics) and rules (syntax). The rules are simple:

- An asterisk in a data definition is an indirection operator. It causes the compiler to mark the variable as a pointer variable.

- If the asterisk has only one operand, it is the indirection operator. That is, the indirection operator (*) is a unary operator.

- If either (or both) of these rules is true, the asterisk is the indirection operator.

Understanding How the Compiler Uses Memory

We stated that the code in Figure 17.1 defines an **int** pointer. You also know from previous chapters that a data definition means that the compiler must allocate storage for the data item being defined. The question is: How much memory is allocated for **iptr** in Figure 17.1? *Whenever a pointer is defined, the compiler must allocate enough storage to form a complete memory address (an lvalue).* The actual storage for a pointer variable, therefore, depends upon how much storage is required for the compiler to form a complete memory address from the information stored in the pointer.

Allocating Memory for Small Model Pointers

For example, if you are compiling a program on a PC using the small memory model, there is one memory segment used for the program code. There is also one memory segment used for the program's data. You can think of the data segment as a 64k chunk of memory beginning at some constant memory address. Because the segment address is fixed when the program is run, we only need to know the offset from the base of the data segment to the data item we wish to use. This is illustrated in Figure 17.2.

Figure 17.2

Memory usage for a typical PC (small memory model)

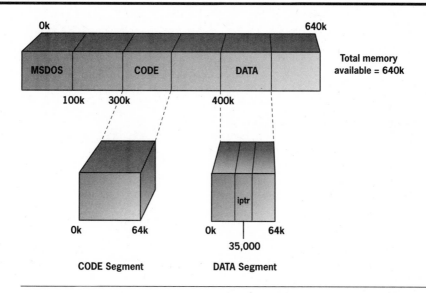

Most PCs today have at least 640k of memory available. Let's assume that the first 100k of memory is used by MS-DOS, the operating system. Perhaps we don't know what's stored in the next 200k of memory. Now let's assume that the compiler picks a code segment that starts at memory location 300,000 and places the data segment starting at memory address 400,000. Therefore, all of the program's code is limited to a 64k block of memory beginning at memory address 300,000. All of the data in the program must fit in a different 64k block of memory starting at 400,000.

The compiler keeps track of where the segment address starts for both the code (300k) and data (400k) segments. These two segment addresses will not change while the program runs; they are constants available to the compiler.

Now suppose the compiler places **iptr** starting at memory address 435,000. Does the compiler need to save the number 435,000? No. It already knows the data segment starts at memory address 400,000. To find **iptr**, all the compiler needs to do is add 35,000 to the segment address. This 35,000 value is called the *offset* portion of the memory address. In other words, we can find **iptr**'s unique memory address by taking the segment address and adding the offset to it. Because the data segment is fixed, the compiler only needs to keep track of the offset for **iptr**. Since it takes only two bytes (16 bits) to form all possible offset values within the range of the data segment (0 to 64k), the offset requires only two bytes of storage.

Now let's return to our original question: How much storage is allocated for **iptr** in Figure 17.1? We stated at the beginning of the chapter that a pointer variable has an rvalue that is the lvalue of a different variable. As we have just seen, we can locate any variable in the data segment simply by storing its offset. Therefore, we only need two bytes to store the offset of any data item in **iptr**. When the offset is added to the (fixed and known) segment address, we can locate any data item in the data segment.

Allocating Memory for Large Model Pointers

If you compile a program using the large memory model, you can have up to 1Mb of code space and 1Mb of data space. This means that there are multiple code and data segments. With the large memory model, the compiler now must store both the segment address and the offset to find a particular data item. Therefore, because a pointer must always hold enough information to find any data item, the storage required for a large memory model pointer is increased to four bytes.

Although it's a simplification, you can think of four-byte pointers as using two bytes for the segment address and the remaining two bytes for the offset component of the address. A four-byte pointer, therefore, allows the compiler to store the complete lvalue for any data item used in the program.

If you happen to be using a machine that doesn't use a segmented memory architecture (for example, the Motorola 680x0 CPU family), chances are pretty good that it uses four-byte pointers. Check your compiler documentation for details.

As we have seen, the storage needed by a pointer varies according to the memory model (or CPU) being used. Fortunately, the compiler keeps track of most of the details for us. Now let's see how we actually use a pointer.

Type Specifiers versus Scalars

So far we have discussed the name that can be used for a pointer variable and the meaning of the indirection operator. The only element of Figure 17.1 that we have not discussed is the meaning of the type specifier when used to define a pointer variable.

In a pointer definition, the type specifier tells the compiler what type of data the pointer will manipulate. As you learned in the previous section, the amount of storage required for a pointer is always the same regardless of the type specifier for the pointer. A small model pointer always requires two bytes of storage and a large model pointer always needs four bytes for storage.

Program 17.1 defines pointers to a **char**, **int**, and **double**.

Program 17.1   **Showing Pointer Sizes**

```
#include <stdio.h>

void main(void)
{
    char *cptr;
    int *iptr;
    double *dptr;

    printf("\nstorage for cptr = %d", sizeof(cptr) );
    printf("\nstorage for iptr = %d", sizeof(iptr) );
    printf("\nstorage for dptr = %d", sizeof(dptr) );
}
```

When I compiled and ran this program using the small memory model, the output was

```
storage for cptr = 2
storage for iptr = 2
storage for dptr = 2
```

I then recompiled the same program and used the large memory model. As you might expect, the output changed to

```
storage for cptr = 4
storage for iptr = 4
storage for dptr = 4
```

Notice that the type specifier for each pointer variable defined in Program 17.1 is different, but the amount of storage required for each pointer is constant. In earlier programs where we defined a **char**, an **int**, and a **double**, the storage requirements varied according to the type specifier of the variable (**char** equals one byte, **int** equals two bytes, and a **double** equals eight bytes). Clearly, the type specifier serves a different purpose when used with a pointer definition.

When you define a pointer variable, *the type specifier sets the scalar size of the object pointed to, not the size of the pointer itself.* Figure 17.3 might help you understand how the scalar is used.

Figure 17.3

Using a scalar to look at a data item

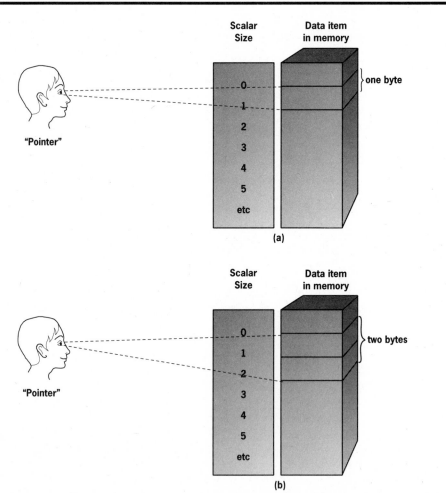

In Figure 17.3(a) we have assumed that the type specifier is a **char**. This means that the scalar for the pointer variable equals 1. When the scalar is 1, the "pointer" can see a data item that uses one byte of storage (a **char**). In Figure 17.3(b) we have assumed that the scalar size is 2. If, for example, the type specifier for the pointer were an **int** or an **unsigned**, the "pointer" can see two bytes of storage in memory.

To summarize, the type specifier in a pointer definition sets the scalar for the pointer variable. The scalar is like a set of glasses that limits the pointer to viewing objects that only match the scalar in size. Pushing the analogy further, a scalar of 1 is like a pair of glasses that only lets the pointer see one-byte objects in memory. Likewise, a scalar of 8 only lets the pointer see eight-byte objects in memory.

You can make the scalar any size you need by changing the type specifier of the pointer. You can use a pointer with a scalar of 1 to examine a two-byte object in memory. The only problem is the program won't work correctly (bugs!). The rules are simple:

■ The type specifier used in a pointer definition sets the scalar of the pointer.

■ The scalar determines the type of object a pointer can manipulate in memory.

■ The storage requirements of a pointer never change regardless of its scalar.

Keep these rules in mind when you define any type of pointer variable.

Using a Pointer

Now that we understand how to define a pointer and what the pointer can manipulate, we can write a simple program that uses a pointer. See Program 17.2.

In Program 17.2 we define an integer variable **j** and a pointer to **int** (**iptr**). We then assign the value 10 into **j**, but do nothing to the pointer. When I ran the program, the first part of the output was

```
Step 1: rvalue of    j = 10  lvalue of    j = FFF2
        rvalue of iptr = Ø  lvalue of iptr = FFF4
```

Notice how we used the %x conversion character to display the rvalue of **iptr**. As you know, this conversion character causes the rvalue of **iptr** to be displayed in hexadecimal. Although we could have used the %u, or even the %d, conversion characters, using hex values simplifies subsequent discussion.

Program 17.2   **Using a Pointer**

```
#include <stdio.h>

void main(void)
{
    int *iptr, j;

    j = 10;

    printf("\nStep 1: rvalue of   j = %d  lvalue of   j =
        %p", j, &j);
    printf("\n        rvalue of iptr = %x  lvalue of iptr =
        %p\n\n", iptr,
        &iptr);

    iptr = &j;

    printf("\nStep 2: rvalue of   j = %d  lvalue of   j =
        %p", j, &j);
    printf("\n        rvalue of iptr = %x  lvalue of iptr =
        %p\n\n", iptr,
        &iptr);

    *iptr = 20;

    printf("\nStep 3: rvalue of   j = %d  lvalue of   j =
        %p", j, &j);
    printf("\n        rvalue of iptr = %x  lvalue of iptr =
        %p\n\n", iptr,
        &iptr);
}
```

Figure 17.4 shows how the two variables look in memory after Step 1. Together with the program output, this figure tells us quite a bit about the two variables. First, the lvalues for both variables are quite high, suggesting that they both are allocated on the stack. This is consistent with what you learned about the auto storage class in Chapter 15.

The second thing to notice is that the rvalue of **iptr** is 0. However, just like any other auto variable, **iptr** contains whatever random bit pattern happened to be in memory at the time the first **printf()** is called. You should never rely on the rvalue of any variable having a known value unless it has been initialized first.

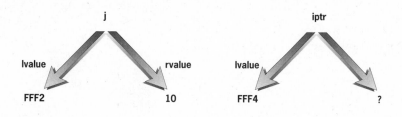

Initializing a Pointer Variable

The next statement in Program 17.2 is very important:

```
iptr = &j;
```

This statement assigns the lvalue of **j** into **iptr**. That is, instead of doing a normal rvalue-to-rvalue assigment (**a = b**), the address-of operator (**&**) causes the lvalue of **j** to be assigned into the rvalue of **iptr**. The output after this statement is

```
Step 2: rvalue of    j = 10  lvalue of    j = FFF2
        rvalue of iptr = FFF2  lvalue of iptr = FFF4
```

Figure 17.5 shows how our memory image looks after Step 2 is finished.

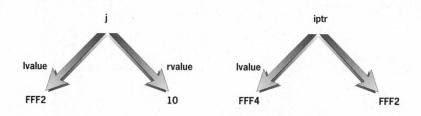

As shown in the output of Step 2 and Figure 17.5, the rvalue of **iptr** now contains the lvalue of **j**. This has some very important implications. First, **iptr** now knows where **j** is stored in memory. Second, because we defined **iptr** as a pointer to **int**, the scalar for **iptr** (which is 2 for an **int**) also tells **iptr** how many bytes are associated with **j**. In terms of Figure 17.3(b), **iptr** is the "pointer" on the left side of the figure, the scalar size is 2, and it is "looking" at the two bytes starting at memory offset FFF2.

It should be clear that the initialization of **iptr** to the lvalue of **j** allows **iptr** to determine where **j** is stored in memory. The scalar's job is to tell **iptr** how many bytes to examine starting at memory address FFF2: 2 in our example.

Using Indirection with a Pointer

Up to this point, we have simply set things up so we can use indirection. *Indirection is the process of using the rvalue of a pointer variable to change the rvalue of some other variable.* The statement

```
*iptr = 20;
```

illustrates the process of indirection. After this statement is executed, the output of the program becomes

```
Step 3: rvalue of     j = 20   lvalue of     j = FFF2
        rvalue of iptr = FFF2  lvalue of iptr = FFF4
```

Notice how the value of **j** has been changed to 20. Everything else remains the same. **j**'s value changed from 10 to 20 because of the process of indirection. Let's examine how indirection works in detail.

First, notice how the indirection operator (*) appears just in front of **iptr**. (Because there is only one operand for the asterisk, it must be the indirection operator.) Once the compiler sees the indirection operator, it knows it must generate code to perform indirection.

The compiler generates code to perform the following steps:

1. Get the scalar value for **iptr** (2).

2. Get the rvalue of **iptr** (FFF2).

3. Go to that memory address.

4. Get the value of whatever is on the righthand side of the assignment operator (20).

5. Now store that value (20) at the address pointed to by **iptr** (FFF2) using exactly scalar-bytes (2) of storage.

We used **iptr** to indirectly change the value of **j**. This is exactly what indirection is all about: using a pointer to a variable to change the value of some other variable.

Can you use indirection to read a value from one variable into a different variable? Consider Program 17.3.

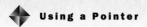

Program 17.3   **Another Pointer Program**

```c
#include <stdio.h>

void main(void)
{
    int *iptr, j, k;

    j = 10;        /* Initialize a value for j */

    printf("\nj = %d  k = %d  iptr = %x", j, k, iptr);

    iptr = &j;     /* Initialize iptr to point to j */

    printf("\nj = %d  k = %d  iptr = %x", j, k, iptr);

    k = *iptr;     /* Assign j into k via indirection */

    printf("\nj = %d  k = %d  iptr = %x", j, k, iptr);

}
```

In this program, we use **iptr** to copy the value of **j** into **k**. Let's see how this is done. First we initialize **j** to 10 and call **printf()** to display the rvalues of all of the variables. When I ran the program, the output was

```
j = 10  k = 6  iptr = 0
```

The rvalues for **k** and **iptr** are simply the random bit patterns that existed when I ran the program. (The values for **k** and **iptr** when you run the program will likely be different.)

The next statement

```
iptr = &j;
```

initializes **iptr** to hold the lvalue of **j**. The output for the second **printf()** was

```
j = 10  k = 6  iptr = FFF4
```

If you modified the **printf()** to also show the lvalue of **j**, you would find that it does equal the rvalue of **iptr** (FFF4).

The statement

```
k = *iptr;
```

uses indirection to change the value of **k**. In this example, the compiler generates code to get **iptr**'s rvalue (FFF4), get scalar (2) bytes of data from that memory address, and then assign those two bytes into **k**.

Note that the process of indirection is the same as before, only this time we retrieve the scalar bytes of data and assign them into a new variable (**k**).

It's important to remember that it is the **iptr**'s scalar that determines how many bytes of data to fetch from memory. The rvalue of **iptr** simply tells the compiler where to find those bytes in memory.

Program 17.2 shows that we can use a pointer to assign a value into the memory address pointed to by the rvalue of a pointer. Program 17.3 shows that we can read a value from the memory address stored in the rvalue of the pointer. In either case, the process of indirection is the same.

PROGRAMMING TIP. *It is easy to understand what the compiler is doing during the process of indirection by observing where the pointer is in the indirection statement. If the pointer is on the right side of the assignment operator, as in*

```
j = *iptr;
```

*indirection is being used to retrieve a value (**j**) from memory. If the pointer is on the left side of the assignment operator, as in*

```
*iptr = j;
```

*indirection is being used to store a value (**j**) in memory.*

The Three Rules for Using Pointers

The three rules you must follow when using pointers are:

- Define the pointer with the correct type specifier.

- Use the indirection operator in the pointer definition.

- Initialize the pointer to the proper lvalue.

The first rule is important because the type specifier sets the scalar size for the pointer. If you use the wrong type specifier, the compiler may not use the proper number of bytes during the indirection process.

The second rule is important because it tells the compiler that this variable is capable of indirection. The compiler makes a special note of this variable's capability in its symbol table. If you try to perform indirection on a nonpointer data type, the compiler will issue an error message.

The third rule is very important, yet is often forgotten by many beginning C programmers. You should always assume the rvalue of a pointer variable is garbage until you initialize it to the lvalue of some other variable. If you don't initialize the pointer, you could end up writing a value to some unknown memory location. This can cause all kinds of mysterious things to happen.

Using the Increment and Decrement Operators on Pointers

The increment and decrement operators that we studied earlier in the book behave exactly as they did before. That is, the rvalue of the variable may either be increased (++) or decreased (−−). The fact that we want to use these operators with a pointer variable does not change the way we use these two operators. The actual mechanics, however, are different.

When you use the increment and decrement operators with a pointer, each operation is adjusted for the scalar of the pointer. For example, if **iptr** points to **int** data, the statement

```
iptr++;
```

increments the rvalue of **iptr** by its scalar (2 for an **int**). If the pointer was a **char** pointer, the same statement would increment the rvalue by 1. If we increment a pointer to **double**, the rvalue of the pointer is incremented by 8.

The increment and decrement operators are always adjusted by the scalar of the pointer. If the pointer is incremented, adjusting the increment to the size of the scalar ensures we are pointing to the next item in the list. If the pointer is decremented, subtracting the scalar from the rvalue of the pointer ensures we are looking at the previous item in the list.

Using the Decrement Operator with a Pointer

Let's write a program that gets some input from the user and then displays that input in a different way. See Program 17.4.

The program begins by asking the user to enter his or her name. A for loop is used to fill in the buff[ ] character array. (We could have used **gets( )** instead.) When the user presses the Enter key, the if statement becomes logical True and we replace the carriage return (Enter or ASCII 13) with the null termination character. A call to **printf()** then displays the name.

The program then calls **strlen()** to determine the length of the string just entered. The next statement

```
cptr = &buff[length - 1];
```

is a bit strange, but not difficult to understand when you study it. Suppose the user entered the name "Jill". The value returned from **strlen()** would be

4. However, only elements buff[0] through buff[3] contain the letters for the name. (All arrays in C start with element 0.) Element buff[4] holds the null termination character. Therefore, we initialize **cptr** to point to the last letter in the user's name, not the null termination character.

Program 17.4   **Using the Decrement Operator on a Pointer**

```c
#include <stdio.h>
#include <string.h>

#define MAXSTRING 50
#define ENTER     13

void main(void)
{
    char buff[MAXSTRING], *cptr;
    int i, length;

    printf("Enter your name: ");

    for (i = 0; i < MAXSTRING; i++) {
        buff[i] = getch();
        printf("%c", buff[i]);
        if (buff[i] == (char) ENTER) {
            buff[i] = '\0';
            break;
        }
    }
    printf("\n\nHello, %s\n\n", buff);

    length = strlen(buff);

    cptr = &buff[length - 1];

    while (length) {
        printf("%c", *cptr);
        cptr--;
        length--;
    }
}
```

The while loop is then used to display the user's name, but the output is backwards. Figure 17.6 helps explain what the while loop is doing.

Figure 17.6

The relationship between **buff[]** and **cptr**

J	i	L	L	'\0'
buff[0]	buff[1]	buff[2]	buff[3]	buff[4]
1000	1001	1002	1003	1004

Let's assume that **buff[]** is stored in memory starting at memory location 1000. We already know that the length of the string is 4. Therefore the statement

```
cptr = &buff[length - 1];
```

can be expanded to reflect the information in Figure 17.6 as

```
cptr = &buff[4 - 1];

cptr = &buff[3];

cptr = 1003;
```

Therefore, the rvalue of **cptr** (1003) is the last l in Jill. Now let's look at the first statement in the body of the while loop.

```
printf("%c", *cptr);
```

Because the indirection operator is used in the **printf()**, the compiler gets the rvalue of **cptr** (1003), goes to that memory address, and grabs scalar bytes of data stored there. Because the type specifier for **cptr** is a **char**, **cptr**'s scalar is 1. The program grabs one byte of data at location 1003 (the letter 'l') and passes it along to **printf()** to be displayed.

The next statement in the while loop is

```
cptr--;
```

As we saw earlier, this is the decrement operator. It is a unary operator and decrements the rvalue of its operand. In this case, it means that the rvalue of **cptr** (1003) is decremented to 1002. This is because the scalar for a **char** is 1.

The last statement in the while loop is

```
length--;
```

This simply decrements the number of characters that remain to be displayed. Because its starting value was 4 and the program has already displayed one of those characters, **length** is decremented so that three more passes are made through the while loop. Because **length** is still nonzero, a second pass is made through the loop.

Why isn't **length** decremented by its scalar of 2? The reason is because it was defined as an **int**, not a pointer to **int**. The compiler marks variables with the pointer attribute differently in the symbol table. When an increment or decrement on a pointer is performed, the compiler looks for the scalar of the pointer and adjusts the increment or decrement by the scalar. Increment or decrement operations on a "normal" variable are not adjusted by the scalar.

PROGRAMMING TIP. *If increment or decrement operations seem to be skipping over data or you are getting strange values after these operations, chances are you have defined the pointer with the wrong type specifier. This causes the compiler to use the wrong scalar for the pointer. For example, if you define an **int** pointer and initialize it to point to a **char** array, an increment or decrement operation causes the pointer to skip over every other character in the array. When you see this type of behavior, check to see that the type specifier for the pointer is correct. Also, check that you have initialized the pointer to point to data with the same type specifier as the pointer. If the type specifiers don't match, strange results will occur.*

When **printf()** is called, the rvalue of **cptr** is now 1002. The indirection operator causes the compiler to fetch one byte from memory location 1002 and **printf()** pops another 'l' on the screen. Notice how the decrement operator works the same as before; it simply decreases the rvalue of the variable by 1.

You should be able to convince yourself that the rest of the user's name is displayed on the screen in reverse order. You should also understand why the while loop eventually terminates.

Using the Increment Operator with a Pointer

Let's modify Program 17.4 to use the increment operator with a pointer. See Program 17.5.

Several changes have been made to the program. First, we have done away with the for loop that indexed into the buff[] array. Instead, we initialize **cptr** to point to the beginning of **buff[]**. *If only an array name is used in* *an expression (that is, without the brackets following it), the array name re-solves to the lvalue of the array.* In other words, the statement

```
cptr = buff;
```

is the same as

```
cptr = &buff[0];
```

Program 17.5   **Using the Increment Operator on a Pointer**

```
#include <stdio.h>
#include <string.h>

#define MAXSTRING 50
#define ENTER     13

void main(void)
{
    char c, buff[MAXSTRING], *cptr;
    int i, length;

    cptr = buff;
    printf("Enter your name: ");
    while ( (c = getch()) != ENTER) {
        *cptr = c;
        printf("%c", *cptr);
        cptr++;
    }
    *cptr = '\0';
    printf("\n\nHello, %s\n\n", buff);

    length = strlen(buff);

    cptr = &buff[length - 1];

    while (length) {
        printf("%c", *cptr);
        cptr--;
        length--;
    }
}
```

Both statements initialize **cptr** to the lvalue of **buff[ ]**. After the statement is executed, **cptr** points to **buff[0]**. Therefore, we can use the array name as a shorthand for the lvalue of the array.

Next the program enters a while loop and calls **getch()** to get a character from the keyboard and assign it into **c**. As long as **c** does not equal ENTER, the code continues to process the loop. If a key other than Enter is pressed, the statement

```
*cptr = c;
```

assigns the key into **buff[ ]** by the process of indirection. (The printf() call displays the character because **getch()** does not echo characters to the screen.)

The statement

```
cptr++;
```

simply increments **cptr** by 1. Because **cptr** has a scalar of 1 (a **char**), **cptr** points to **buff[1]** after the increment statement is executed. We continue to get characters until the user presses the Enter key. The null termination character is added so we can use **buff[ ]** as a string. The remainder of the program is the same as Program 17.4.

Keep in mind that both the increment and decrement statements are set by the scalar of the pointer. With **cptr**, each increment increases the lvalue by 1. However, if we were using an **int** pointer, each increment would increase the lvalue by 2. The scalar keeps the pointer and the data item pointed to in alignment when the increment and decrement operators are used.

Using far Pointers

Many PC compilers have added the keyword **far** for use with pointers. Whenever the keyword **far** appears in a statement, it tells the compiler to use a four-byte pointer. For example, the characters that you see on your screen are actually stored in a chunk of memory called video memory that is not part of a PC's basic 640k address space. It follows that the video memory cannot be part of the data segment of your program. So how can we access that memory? Simple. We create a far pointer to it.

The keyword **far** is not part of the ANSI standard for the C language. Therefore, an ANSI-compliant compiler is not required to support the keyword **far**. However, most C compilers for the PC do support it. If your compiler does not support the far keyword, you will have to compile the example programs that follow with the large memory model. Also, some compilers such as Microsoft's and Borland's have a compiler option to switch between strict ANSI keywords (no far keyword) and "language extensions" that do support the far keyword. (You can usually turn the language extensions on using the compiler options in the integrated development environment. Consult your compiler manual for details.)

Program 17.6 shows you how to define and use a far pointer to access video memory.

Program 17.6   **Using a far Pointer to Access Video Memory**

```
#include <stdio.h>

#define VIDEO_BASE   0xb8000000L;   /* Start of video
                                        memory */

void main(void)
{
   char buff[50];
   unsigned int far *uptr;
int color = 0, i;

   printf("Enter a maximum of 49 characters: ");
   gets(buff);

   uptr = (unsigned int far *) VIDEO_BASE;
   uptr += 80 * 10;

   for (i = 0; buff[i]; i++) {
      color = (i + 1) % 16;
      color <<= 8;
      *uptr++ = color + buff[i];
   }

}
```

The statement

```
unsigned int far *uptr;
```

defines a far pointer that contains a complete memory address. Unlike the small memory model where a pointer only contains the offset portion of a memory address, a far pointer includes both the segment and offset components of a memory address. For that reason, far pointers typically use four bytes of storage.

The program begins by asking the user to enter up to 49 characters of text. The statement

```
uptr = (unsigned int far *) VIDEO_BASE;
```

initializes **uptr** to point to the video memory. The symbolic constant VIDEO_BASE is set to the constant 0xb8000000L, which is the start of the video memory for a color monitor. (If you do not have a color monitor, you will need to change this constant to 0xb0000000L.) The L at the end of the constant ensures that the compiler forces the constant into a four-byte (**long**) value. This constant represents the upper-left corner of your screen.

Notice that we must cast VIDEO_BASE to an **unsigned far** pointer to match the attribute list of **uptr**. After all, the compiler thinks VIDEO_BASE is simply a **long** data type. The cast makes sure that the assignment of VIDEO_BASE into **uptr** has a matching attribute list.

For purposes of illustration, we chose to display the text ten lines down from the top of the screen. The statement

```
uptr += 80 * 10;
```

increases the rvalue of **uptr** by 800. You should be able to convince yourself that, for an 80-column screen, this will place the text ten lines down from the top of the screen.

The for loop is used to write the text to video memory. However, because the video memory is what you see on your display, we end up writing the string to line 10 on your screen. To make things a bit more interesting, we change the foreground color of the letters as they are displayed. To understand what the for loop does requires that we understand a little more about how video memory works on a PC.

When your monitor is displaying text on the screen, it is said to be in *text mode*. In text mode, the screen can display 2,000 characters (25 lines times 80 characters per line). Each character takes one byte of storage in video memory. However, each character you see on the screen has a second byte associated with it. This second byte, called the *attribute byte*, determines the attribute of each character. For example, we can have white characters on a black background, or red letters on a white background. We can even cause the characters to blink if we wish.

Figure 17.7 shows how the character byte and the attribute byte appear in video memory.

The first byte of video memory is a character byte followed by its attribute byte. This sequence alternates throughout video memory. Even though you can only see 80 characters on each line, it takes 160 bytes of memory to display a single line because of the attribute byte.

Figure 17.7

The character and attribute bytes in video memory

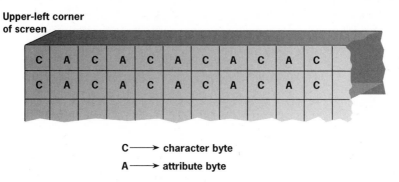

Upper-left corner of screen

C ⟶ character byte

A ⟶ attribute byte

We can do some interesting things with text by manipulating the attribute byte. Figure 17.8 presents the interpretation for each bit of the attribute byte.

Figure 17.8

Bit interpretation of the attribute byte

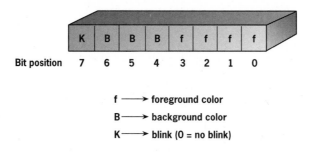

Bit position 7 6 5 4 3 2 1 0

f ⟶ foreground color

B ⟶ background color

K ⟶ blink (0 = no blink)

Figure 17.8 shows that the lowest four bits are used for the foreground color. The next three bits are used for the background color. The high bit is the blink bit. If the blink bit is 1, the character blinks. A little quick arithmetic tells us that there are 16 (2^4) foreground colors, but only eight (2^3) background colors available for each character. The values of these colors are presented in Table 17.1.

Table 17.1 shows that the first seven colors are the same for both the foreground and background colors. The fourth bit of the foreground color is sometimes called the *intensity bit* as it forms a lighter shade of the first eight colors.

Another thing to notice in Table 17.1 is that the numeric values for the background colors do not assume they are in the fourth through the sixth bit positions. The numbers in parentheses in Table 17.1 show their actual numeric values. For example, if you wanted a blue background, you would take the value of 1 and shift it five bit positions to the left. This yields the value of 16.

Table 17.1   **Attribute Byte Color Values**

Foreground		Background	
0	Black	0 Black	(0)
1	Blue	1 Blue	(16)
2	Green	2 Green	(32)
3	Cyan	3 Cyan	(48)
4	Red	4 Cyan	(64)
5	Magenta	5 Magenta	(80)
6	Brown	6 Brown	(96)
7	White	7 White	(112)
8	Gray		
9	Light blue		
10	Light green		
11	Light cyan		
12	Light red		
13	Light magenta		
14	Yellow		
15	Bright white		

Now that we understand the attribute byte in video memory, let's look at the rest of Program 17.6. The for loop statements are repeated here for convenience.

```
for (i = 0; buff[i]; i++) {
   color = (i + 1) % 16;
   color <<= 8;
   *uptr++ = color + buff[i];
}
```

The first statement in the for loop body takes the value of **i**, adds 1 to it, and then performs a modulo 16 on the result. This ensures that the color is always within the permissible range of values. We added 1 to **i** so the first color would not be a black character on a black background, which would be invisible.

Next we shift the value eight bit positions to the left. Why? The reason is because the 80x86 CPU chips store the data with the high byte followed by the low byte. That is, if we stored the letter 'A' and an attribute byte value of 15, the two bytes are stored as the sequence 15-A, not A-15. Because we wish to manipulate both the character and the attribute byte at the same time, we use an **unsigned int** as the scalar for **uptr**. If we had chosen to use a **char** pointer, we could manipulate the character and its attribute byte separately. (It is slightly faster, however, to manipulate both at the same time.)

After the color is shifted to the left eight bit positions, the lower eight bits are all zero. Therefore, we simply add the character to the color value with the statement

```
*uptr++ = color + buff[i];
```

We then use indirection to write the character and its attribute byte to the video display. Notice that we use a postincrement on **uptr**. This ensures that we write to the video memory before advancing to the next character position in video memory.

You might experiment with this program to learn how the video memory works. For example, you could try turning on the blink bit or changing the background color, too. If you try some timing tests, you will find that writing directly to video memory is much faster than using **printf()**.

The Advantages of Using a Pointer

Program 17.6 suggests two reasons for using a pointer. First, we can use pointers to access data that lies outside of our normal data segment. In Program 17.6 we used a far pointer to access a chunk of memory that isn't even part of our program.

A second reason is because pointers are a very efficient way to manipulate data. In Program 17.5, we used the statements

```
*cptr = c;
printf("%c", *cptr);
cptr++;
```

to access and display characters entered by the user. We could have used something like

```
buff[i] = c;
printf("%c", buff[i]);
i++;
```

but it is less efficient. The reason is because we must load the lvalue of **buff[0]**, load the value of **i**, add **i** to the lvalue of **buff[0]**, and then assign **c** to the resulting memory location. In the pointer version, we do away with **i** altogether. In fact, the compiler may simply place **cptr** in a register and never reload it during the entire loop.

We will say more about the relationship between arrays and pointers, and the real reason for using pointers, in the next chapter.

Using a Null Pointer

If you have read your compiler's standard library documentation, you have probably seen some functions that return a null pointer under certain conditions. For example, **strchr()** has the form

```
char *strchr(char *s, int find);
```

The purpose of **strchr()** is to search string **s** for the letter **find**. If **strchr()** locates the letter **find** in the string, it returns a pointer to that letter. However, if the search cannot locate a match on **find**, **strchr()** returns something called a null pointer. *A null pointer is guaranteed never to point to valid data.* As such, the null pointer is often used to indicate that a particular function or process failed to accomplish its task.

The following code fragment shows how **strchr()** might be used:

```
if ( (cptr = strchr(s, letter)) == NULL) {
    printf("No match on %c found", letter);
    return 0;
}
/* Code if a match was found */
```

The call to **strchr()** examines the string pointed to by **s** for the character held in **letter**. The function returns a character pointer and assigns it into **cptr**. Next, the program checks to see if **cptr** equals the symbolic constant NULL, which is used to define a null pointer. Most compiler vendors place the **#define** for NULL in the stdio.h header file.

If **cptr** does equal the null pointer, the program displays a message and returns 0 to the calling function. If a match on **letter** was found, the program continues with whatever code may be required next.

PROGRAMMING TIP. *In logical tests the null pointer is guaranteed to return a logical False condition. For example*

```
cptr = strchr(string, 'A');
if (cptr) {
   printf("Found a match");
} else {
   printf("No match found");
}
```

*This code fragment shows that if **cptr** is not a null pointer, a match was found on the letter 'A'. If no match had been found, **cptr** would equal a null pointer and the "no match" message is displayed. For PC compilers, the NULL is normally **#defin**ed as '\0'. However, you should not use '\0' in your code in place of NULL. The reason is because the ANSI standard does not fix the value to '\0'. ANSI only guarantees that a null pointer is viewed as logical False. Therefore, always use NULL instead of '\0' in your programs. It will help make them more portable to other machines.*

Using the Null Pointer in a Logical Test

Let's write a program that performs the same function as **strlen()**. The code is shown in Program 17.7.

Program 17.7 gets a string of characters from the user via the gets() function and stores them in **buff[]**. The program then calls **mystrlen()** with **buff[]** as its argument. In **mystrlen()** we initialize **count** to 0 and enter a while loop. Because we use a postincrement operator on **s** (the pointer to **buff[]**), the code first checks to see if the character pointed to by **s** is a nonzero character. Any character other than the null termination character returns a nonzero value. As long the null termination character is not read, the code continues to increment **count** in the while loop.

Eventually, the code reads the null termination character and the while loop ends. At that point, **count** has counted all of the characters in the string, the value of which is returned to the caller.

Note that we could have written the test for the null termination character as

```
while (*s++ != NULL) {
```

and the code would perform exactly as before. That is, the program continues to increment **count** as long as the code does not read a NULL pointer. The fact that we can use either form of the test on **s** confirms that we can use the NULL pointer to indicate a logical False condition in an expression.

Program 17.7   **Using the Null Termination Character as a Logical False Condition**

```c
#include <stdio.h>

#define MAXCHARS    50

int mystrlen(char *s);

void main(void)
{
    char buff[MAXCHARS + 1];
    int length;

    printf("Type in some characters (%d max): ", MAXCHARS);
    gets(buff);
    length = mystrlen(buff);
    printf("\nThe string length is %d", length);

}

int mystrlen(char *s)
{
    int count = 0;

    while (*s++) {
        count++;
    }
    return count;
}
```

Conclusion

The majority of C programmers agree that pointers are the most powerful feature in the language. Alas, with that power comes a lot of responsibility. For most beginning C programmers, pointers are less than intuitively obvious. You should spend as much time as it takes to feel comfortable with the material presented in this chapter. The next chapter (and several others) depend heavily on a good understanding of what pointers are and how they work.

Don't rush into the next chapter until you've mastered this one. Make a real effort to answer the review questions below. If you can answer the questions and get the programs working on your own, you're on your way to becoming a real C programmer!

Checking Your Progress

1. What is a pointer variable?

A pointer variable is a variable that is capable of manipulating another variable. The rvalue of the pointer must equal the lvalue of the data item to be manipulated.

2. What are the three required steps to use a pointer correctly?

First, you must define the pointer using the indirection operator in the definition. Second, you must initialize the pointer to the lvalue of the data item to be manipulated by the pointer. Third, you must use indirection to change the data item.

3. Why is the type specifier different for a pointer?

Unlike nonpointer definitions, the type specifier for a pointer does not specify the size of the pointer. A pointer's size is fixed for a given memory model. In a pointer definition, the type specifier tells the size of the object being pointed to; it sets the scalar for the pointer.

4. What is a scalar?

A scalar for a pointer reflects the size of the object that the pointer manipulates. The scalar affects how pointer arithmetic, incrementing, and decrementing work.

5. Why does the memory model used to compile a program affect the size of the pointer?

The default (small) memory model is limited to one code and data segment. Therefore, all memory addresses must fit within one data segment, or 64k. Because we can identify all addresses in 64k with a 16-bit number, pointers only need to store the offset to a specific data item (the segment address is fixed). The pointer requires only two bytes of storage.

If there are two or more data segments in a program (for example, when the large memory model is used), both the segment and offset must be maintained. This requires a four-byte pointer.

Other things being equal, two-byte pointers are faster than four-byte pointers.

6. What does the keyword **far** do?

The keyword **far** is not part of the ANSI standard, but has been added to many PC compilers. The purpose of **far** is to force the compiler to generate a four-byte pointer so both the segment and offset of a data item can be stored in the pointer. This allows you to use small pointers whenever possible, but large pointers when you must.

If your compiler does not support the far keyword and you need to address data outside a single code segment, you must compile the program using the large memory model.

7. Suppose you have just written a great piece of software for the PC and you would like to port the code to a Macintosh. The problem is that you've used the far keyword in hundreds of places in the PC source code. The Mac doesn't need the far keyword, because all pointers are the same size. What's the easiest way to remove the far keyword from your code?

The nuclear-weapons approach is to use the search-and-replace feature of your text editor to make the changes. The simpler way is to place the following preprocessor directive

```
#define far
```

in either the source files or a header file that is included in each source file. Because nothing follows the word **far** in the **#define**, the directive has the effect of removing the word **far** from the source code.

8. What is a null pointer?

The null pointer is defined as NULL for every compiler. The actual value may vary, but it is normally defined as the null termination character '\0'. However, because the exact value is not specified by the ANSI standard (only the behavior of NULL is defined in the standard), you should always test against NULL rather than '\0'. Doing this will make your code more portable across different computer systems.

9. What are the advantages to using a pointer?

There are three advantages. First, pointers are usually faster in certain processing tasks than nonpointer equivalents. Second, pointers allow us to access data that may not reside in our data segment. And third, pointers give us a way to modify data that has local scope even though control may be in another function. This topic is covered in Chapter 18.

18

Using Pointers Effectively

THIS CHAPTER CONTINUES THE DISCUSSION OF POINTERS. YOU WILL LEARN how to use pointers with function calls; pointers let you change data with local scope between functions. You will also see how to use pointers to reduce the memory requirements in a program. The memory savings can be significant for programs that use many string constants. Next you will learn which types of arithmetic pointer operations you can use and which you cannot. Finally, you will learn how to allocate memory dynamically as the program executes. With dynamic memory allocation, you can create variables whose storage requirements are unknown until the program is run. This allows you to create more flexible and efficient programs than you can create with static memory allocation methods.

Using Pointers with Function Calls

Chapter 13 explained that an argument passed to a function is a copy of the argument. Program 18.1 illustrates how the arguments passed to a function are stored in memory.

When I ran Program 18.1, the output displayed was

```
in main()  lvalue of i = FFF4 rvalue = 10
in func1()  lvalue of j = FFF2 rvalue = 10
now:  lvalue of j = FFF2 rvalue = 100
in main()  lvalue of i = FFF2 rvalue = 10
```

When the program begins execution, storage for **i** is allocated at offset FFF4. Next, the value of 10 is assigned into **i** and **printf()** is called to display **i**'s lvalue and rvalue. The program then calls **func1()**.

Before the code in **func1()** is called, the program pushes a copy of the rvalue of **i** on the stack. After that, the program calls **func1()**. Inside **func1()**, first a variable named **j** is defined. The **printf()** in **func1()** shows that **j** was given memory address FFF2. Once the storage for **j** is created, the program pops the int value on the stack into variable **j**. At this point in the program, the **i** in **main()** and the **j** in **func1()** look like Figure 18.1.

Figure 18.1
Representation of **i** and **j** from Program 18.1

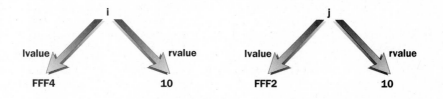

Program 18.1   **Passing an Argument to a Function**

```
#include <stdio.h>

void func1(int j);

void main(void)
{
    int i;

    i = 10;
    printf("\n in main()  lvalue of i = %p rvalue = %d",
        &i, i);
    func1(i);
    printf("\n in main()  lvalue of i = %p rvalue = %d",
        &i, i);
}
void func1(int j)
{
    printf("\n in func1()  lvalue of j = %p rvalue = %d",
        &j, j);
    j = j * j;
    printf("\n now:  lvalue of j = %p rvalue = %d", &j, j);
}
```

Notice that the rvalue rather than the lvalue of **i** (10) defined in **main()** is sent to **func1()**. In **func1()**, **j** is a newly defined variable with an lvalue of FFF2. The rvalue of **j**, however, does equal the rvalue of **i** in **main()**. In other words, a copy of **i** is sent to **func1()**. Programmers often refer to this phenomenon as *call by value*. Call by value means that, by default, function arguments in C send a copy of the argument to the function.

The second **printf()** in **func1()** shows that the value of **j** in **func1()** has been squared. Program control now returns to **main()** for the final **printf()**, which shows that the value of **i** has remained unchanged by the call to **func1()**.

As you learned in Chapter 13, in C call by value means that data defined in one function (**main()**) cannot be changed by another function (**func1()**). This is also consistent with what you learned about scope in Chapter 15: The data defined within a function has local scope and does not exist outside of the function in which it is defined.

There are situations, however, when you want a function to alter the value of a data item. In Program 18.1, suppose you want **func1()** to square the value of **i**. How can you have one function alter the data defined in another function? Simple: you use a pointer.

Using Functions and Pointers to Change Local Data

As you know, a pointer is a special kind of variable whose rvalue is the lvalue of some other variable. With this in mind, let's modify Program 18.1 so **func1()** can change the value of **i** in **main()**. See Program 18.2.

Program 18.2   **Passing a Pointer to a Function**

```
#include <stdio.h>

void func1(int *iptr);

void main(void)
{
    int i;

    i = 10;

    printf("\n in main()  lvalue of i = %p rvalue = %d",
        &i, i);
    func1(&i);
    printf("\n in main()  lvalue of i = %p rvalue = %d",
        &i, i);

}

void func1(int *iptr)
{
    printf("\n in func1()  lvalue of iptr = %p rvalue = %p",
        &iptr, iptr);
    *iptr = *iptr * *iptr;
    printf("\n now:  lvalue of iptr = %p rvalue = %p",
        &iptr, iptr);
}
```

When I ran the program, the output was

```
in main()  lvalue of i = FFF4 rvalue = 10
in func1()  lvalue of iptr = FFF2 rvalue = FFF4
now:  lvalue of iptr = FFF2 rvalue = FFF4
in main()  lvalue of i = FFF2 rvalue = 100
```

Notice that the value of **i** has indeed been squared. That is, data that was private to **main()** was changed by **func1()**. Let's see how this was done.

There are several changes in Program 18.2. First, the statement that calls **func1( )** has been changed to

```
func1(&i);
```

Because the program used the address-of operator with **i**, it is passing the lvalue of **i** to **func1()**. The program is no longer using call by value because it is passing the address of **i**, not its rvalue. (Program 18.1 passed the rvalue of **i** to **func1()**.) Passing an lvalue to a function is referred to as *call by reference.* Call by reference means that the reference address (lvalue) of the data item is passed instead of the rvalue. Program 18.2 uses a call by reference for variable **i** instead of call by value, as in Program 18.1. The call by reference in Program 18.2 causes the compiler to place the lvalue of **i** (FFF4) on the stack.

In **func1()**, the definition of the argument that is being passed to **func1()** has been changed. The argument in Program 18.1 was defined by the line

```
void func1(int j)
```

In Program 18.2 the line is

```
void func1(int *iptr)
```

The new version of the program tells the compiler to create a variable that is a pointer to **int**. (The earlier version simply defined the argument as an **int**.) The program creates enough storage to hold a pointer variable and calls it **iptr**.

The compiler knows that there is a value sitting on the stack that is to be placed into the variable named **iptr**. Therefore, immediately after **iptr** is defined, the compiler pops the value on the stack into the rvalue of **iptr**. Our representation is modified to look like that in Figure 18.2.

If you compare Figures 18.1 and 18.2, the rvalue and lvalue for variable **i** in **main()** are the same. (When I ran the program, even the lvalue for variable **iptr** was the same as it was for **j** in Program 18.1.) The important thing to notice, however, is the rvalue of **iptr**. Instead of being the rvalue of **i** in **main()**, it is the lvalue of **i** in **main()**.

Figure 18.2
Representation of **i** and **iptr** from Program 18.2

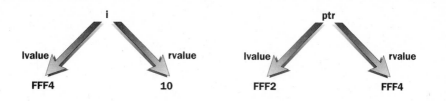

Chapter 17 described the three things you must do to use a pointer:

■ Define the pointer

■ Initialize the pointer

■ Use indirection

Let's see if we have fulfilled these rules for using a pointer in Program 18.2. First, the line

```
void func1(int *iptr)
```

does in fact define a pointer named **iptr**. Second, the pointer must be initialized to the lvalue of the data item being pointed to. Both Figure 18.2 and the output of Program 18.2 show that the program has initialized **iptr** to point to **i** in **main()**. **iptr** was initialized when the program popped the lvalue of **i** off the stack and stored it into the rvalue of **iptr**. Note that this initialization is done automatically. You just need to make sure that an lvalue is placed on the stack when the function is called. (The program did this when it executed the **func1(&i)** statement in **main()**.)

Because the first two steps have been done properly, we should be able to perform indirection on **iptr** to change **i** in **main()**. The statement

```
*iptr = *iptr * *iptr;
```

may seem like a mouthful, but it simply says to take the value pointed to by **iptr**, square it, and assign it back into the item pointed to by **iptr**. This might be more clear if we enclosed the indirection expressions within parentheses, as in

```
(*iptr) = (*iptr) * (*iptr);
```

or

```
exp1  =  exp2   *    exp3;
```

Because multiplication has higher precedence than assignment, *exp2* and *exp3* are the first expressions resolved in the statement. The expression **iptr* causes the program to get the rvalue of **iptr** (FFF4), go to that memory address, and get scalar (2) bytes of data. Because FFF4 is the address of **i** in **main()** and the scalar for **iptr** is 2 (it's an **int** pointer), the compiler gets the two bytes that form the rvalue of **i** in **main()**. This process is illustrated in Figure 18.3.

Figure 18.3

Using indirection on **iptr** in **func1()**

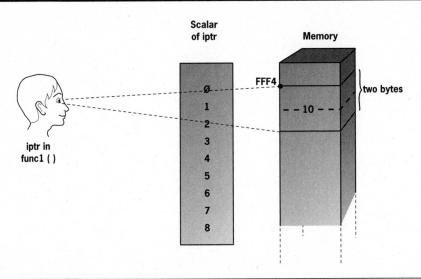

iptr looks at memory starting at FFF4. Because we defined **iptr** as an int pointer, its scalar is 2. Therefore, the indirection causes **iptr** to retrieve two bytes starting at memory address FFF4. This is exactly where **i** is stored in memory, so the indirection process retrieves the rvalue of **i** directly from memory. This process is performed for *exp2* and *exp3*. Therefore, the statement

```
(*iptr) = (*iptr) * (*iptr);
```

can be abbreviated as

```
exp1  =  exp2   *    exp3;
```

This statement may be viewed after indirection on *exp2* and *exp3* as

```
exp1  =  10   *    10;
exp1  =  100;
```

So far, we have resolved multiplication of *exp2* and *exp3* and produced an intermediate value of 100. We can also rewrite this last expression as

```
(*iptr) = 100;
```

As you learned in Chapter 17, when indirection is on the lefthand side of an assignment expression, the value being assigned is placed into the memory location pointed to by **iptr**. Therefore, the expression causes indirection to assign the value of 100 into the two bytes of memory starting at offset address FFF4. This causes the value in **i** in **main()** to change from its previous value of 10 to its new value of 100. The output of Program 18.2 confirms that the new value of **i** is 100 after returning from **func1()**.

This is pretty exciting stuff. Program 18.2 shows you how to change the value of a data item that is local to **main()** by a function call to **func1()**.

Maintaining Data Privacy with Pointers

You now know how to maintain data privacy within a function while still being able to change the data values by calls to other functions. If you define the data items for a program in one function, those data items have local scope and are not visible outside that function. That is, data are private to the function in which they are defined.

Generally, data privacy is an admirable goal, because other functions cannot inadvertently change the data values. This also makes it easier to debug a program because the data only live in one function.

The bad news about data privacy is that, because the data are private to their own function, there is no way for other functions to modify their values. However, when you use pointers you have the best of both worlds. You can keep the data private to a function, but allow other functions to have access to the data by using pointers. Only if you send the lvalue of a data item to a function can that function alter the data. In all other circumstances, data privacy is maintained.

PROGRAMMING TIP. *Before you learned about pointers, you may have thought that some data needed to have global scope so other functions could change its value. Now that you know how to use pointers, you can see that there is very little reason to use global data items. You can always use a pointer to pass the data to a function if the function needs to change its value. Using pointers to local data instead of using global data items will make debugging and program maintenance much easier.*

Using an Array as a Function Argument

Passing arrays to functions is a little different than passing other data types. Many programs in this book have used statements similar to

```
gets(buff);
```

Clearly, we are passing **buff[ ]** to the gets() function so the program can store the information typed by the user. The question is, "What is sent to **gets()** in the function call?"

Chapter 17 explained that using an array name in a function call causes the lvalue of the array to be passed to the function. Therefore, the statements

```
gets(buff);
```

and

```
gets(&buff[0]);
```

are the same. Both statements pass the lvalue of **buff[0]** to the gets() function. Because the statements are the same, passing an array name to a function is a call by reference rather than a call by value. Why would C make this exception to the call by value that occurs with nonarray data types?

For one, copying an array onto the stack could take quite a bit of time, especially for large arrays. Secondly, duplicating an array could also chew up a lot of stack space in a hurry. The original copy of the array would be on the stack from when the array was first defined (assuming the array has the auto storage class), and a second copy of the array would exist when the function call was made.

Suppose the function call were in a loop. You might have so many copies of the array on the stack that you would quickly run out of stack space. For these reasons, only the lvalue of the array is passed to the function.

To see how you might use an array in a function call, write your own version of **gets()**, using the code shown in Program 18.3.

First the program requests up to 50 characters. (We defined **buff[ ]** for MAX-CHARS plus 1 so we can also store the null termination character if the user enters 50 characters.) The program then calls **mygets()** with **buff[ ]** as its argument.

We have defined the mygets() function as

```
char *mygets(char *s)
```

The type specifier for the function states that **mygets()** returns a pointer to **char**. It also tells the compiler that the argument passed to the function is a pointer to **char**. Therefore, the compiler creates enough storage for **s** to hold a memory address. Next it pops the lvalue from the stack and assigns it into **s**.

Program 18.3   **Writing Your Own gets() Function**

```c
#include <stdio.h>

#define MAXCHARS     50
#define ENTER        '\r'
#define BACKSPACE    8

char *mygets(char *s);

void main(void)

{
    char buff[MAXCHARS + 1];

    printf("Type in some characters (%d max): ", MAXCHARS);
    mygets(buff);
    printf("\nYou entered: %s", buff);

}

char *mygets(char *s)
{
    char c, *cptr;

    cptr = s;

    while ( (c = getch()) != ENTER) {
       if (c == BACKSPACE && cptr != s) {
          printf("%c%c%c", BACKSPACE, ' ', BACKSPACE);
          cptr--;
          continue;
       }
       printf("%c", c);
       *cptr++ = c;
    }
    *cptr = '\0';
    return s;
}
```

The pointer **s** is now defined and holds the lvalue of **buff[]**, which was defined in **main()**.

The first statement in **mygets()** defines several working variables and then initializes a second pointer with the statement

```
cptr = s;
```

This statement copies the rvalue of **s** into the rvalue of **cptr**. Therefore, both **cptr** and **s** now point to **buff[]**. (You will see why in a moment.)

The while loop calls **getch()** and assigns the key pressed by the user into **c**. As long as the user does not press Enter, the function continues to retrieve characters from the keyboard. If the user presses Backspace, the function must move the cursor back one character position, erase the character, and then move back to the (now blank) position. However, because the function has deleted a character that used to be in the string, it must decrement the pointer so it points to the deleted character. This allows the user to use the Backspace key to delete any typing mistakes.

The second part of the **if** statement ensures that the function doesn't try to decrement the pointer past the first element of the character array. If the function didn't do this, it could decrement the pointer enough times so that **cptr** did not point to any element within **buff[]**. This could lock up the program because of other information that is stored on the stack.

If the user doesn't press Backspace, the function displays the character with a call to **printf()**. The statement

```
*cptr++ = c;
```

assigns the character just entered into **buff[]** via indirection and then increments the pointer. (We need to do the assignment first, which is why we use the postincrement operator.) **cptr** now points to the next empty element in **buff[]**. The loop continues until the user presses the Enter key.

The statement

```
*cptr = '\0';
```

adds the null termination character to the string. This allows the program to use the character array as a string.

The final statement

```
return s;
```

returns the original lvalue to the caller. We created **cptr** for two reasons. First, we needed to check that we did not decrement the array beyond its starting value. We checked this value as part of the if statement in the while loop. We also needed to return the original lvalue that was passed to the function. By creating **cptr** as a working variable, we can increment and decrement it all we want and not worry about its original lvalue. When it is time to return program control to the caller, we simply return the lvalue stored in rvalue of **s**.

This is an important point. The rvalue of **cptr** is changing as the user enters keystrokes at the keyboard. Because the program is incrementing and decrementing **cptr** all the while, **cptr** no longer points to the starting value of **buff[]** in **main()**. However, because we have not changed the rvalue of **s** in the function, we can return its value to the caller if it needs to know where the start of the array is in memory.

For example, the statements

```
mygets(buff);

printf("\nYou entered: %s", buff);
```

in **main()** could be replaced with

```
printf("\nYou entered: %s", mygets(buff));
```

and the program still works the same. This is because **mygets()** returns the lvalue of where **buff[]** is stored. (That is, **mygets()** returns a pointer to **char**, which points to **buff[0]**.) Therefore, **printf()** still would get the lvalue of **buff[0]** as it did when the two statements were used.

You now know how to pass a single data item or an array to a function in a way that allows the function to modify the content of the data item. Using pointers in functions is easy, but you must follow certain rules.

- If you are passing a data item that is not an array, you must use the address-of operator (**func1(&i)**).

- If you are passing an array to a function, simply use the array name (**func1(buff)**).

- If you need to pass something other than the starting address (**&buff[0]**) to a function, you must use the address-of operator (**func1(&buff[15])**).

The rules are fairly simple. The third rule shows how you would pass a character array if you wanted to have the function start placing data in element 16 of an array (**func1(&buff[15])**) instead of the first character of the array.

Using Pointer Arithmetic

Only two arithmetic operations, addition and subtraction, are allowed with pointers. These operations are valid provided the two pointers point to the same data item. Pointer arithmetic often provides the most efficient way to solve a given problem.

Pointer Subtraction

Suppose you want to find a certain character in a string and you wish to know the character position where the match occurred. Program 18.4 shows how you can use pointer subtraction to solve this problem.

Program 18.4   **Using Pointer Subtraction**

```
#include <stdio.h>
#include <string.h>

#define MAXCHAR    50

int findlocation(char *s, char c);
void main(void)

{
    char buff[MAXCHAR + 1], c;
    int length;

    printf("Type in some characters (%d max): ", MAXCHAR);
    gets(buff);
    printf("\nNow type in a letter to locate: ");
    c = getch();
    printf("%c", c);
    length = findlocation(buff, c);
    if (length) {
        printf("\nA match was found at position %d",
            length);
    } else {
        printf("\nNo match was found");
    }
}

int findlocation(char *s, char c)
{
    char *cptr;
    int location, length;

    cptr = s;
    length = strlen(s);
```

Program 18.4 **continued**

```
while (*s) {
    if (*s == c) {
        break;
    }
    s++;
}
location = s - cptr;
if (location == length) {
    return Ø;
}
location++;
return location;
}
```

This program asks the user to type in a group of characters and to then enter a character to locate in the string. If it finds a match, the program should report its position in the string. If no match is found, it lets the user know.

The code in **main()** should be familiar by now, so we will skip to the find-location() function. The function begins by initializing **cptr** to point to the start of the string. Variable **s**, of course, points to the start of the string entered by the user (**buff[0]**). The function then uses indirection

```
if (*s == c) {
```

to see if the character pointed to (***s**) matches the character being sought (**c**). If a match is not found, the pointer is incremented and the program continues to examine the rest of the characters in the string.

If a match is found, the statement

```
location = s - cptr;
```

subtracts the two pointers. **cptr** holds the original lvalue of the string while **s** holds the incremented lvalue. If a match is found, the difference is the array index where the match occurred. The statement

```
if (location == length) {
    return Ø;
}
```

checks whether the entire string was searched without a match being found. If no match was found, the return value is 0.

If a match is found, **location** is incremented and its value is returned. **location** is incremented because people are not used to thinking in terms of zero-based arrays. That is, if the match occurs at **buff[6]**, element **buff[6]** is the seventh character in the string.

You can safely subtract pointers provided they point to the same data item. This rule applies to all memory models. However, if two pointers do not point to the same data item, pointer subtraction is not guaranteed to work. One reason is that the two data items could be in different data segments. Subtracting different data segments could produce an answer in a segment that's not even used by the program.

Pointer Addition

Pointer addition is only valid for the offset portion of a data item. For example, suppose a character array named **buff[]** contains the characters shown in Figure 18.4.

Figure 18.4
An array of
character digits

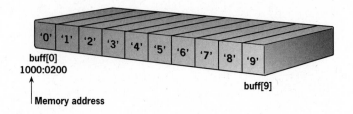

Figure 18.4 assumes that the compiler has allocated space for **buff[]** at segment address 1000, offset 0200. If you are compiling a program that uses the small memory model, the code fragment

```
char buff[] = "0123456789", *cptr;
cptr = buff;
```

causes the rvalue of **cptr** to equal 0200. If the same code were compiled under the large memory model, the rvalue of **cptr** would be changed to 1000:0200 because both the segment address and the offset are stored in the pointer. Keep in mind that the contents of an initialized pointer vary according to the memory model used, *even if the source code does not change.*

With this in mind, try modifying Program 18.4 so that you can display a certain element in a string. The modified code is shown in Program 18.5.

Program 18.5	**Using Pointer Addition**

```c
#include <stdio.h>
#include <stdlib.h>

#define MAXCHAR    50
#define END        99

int findlocation(char *s, char c);

void main(void)

{
    char buff[MAXCHAR + 1], val[20], *cptr;
    int position;

    printf("Type in some characters (%d max): ", MAXCHAR);
    gets(buff);
    position = 0;
    cptr = buff;

    while (position != END) {
        printf("\nNow type in the element to show (99 =
            END): ");
        position = atoi(gets(val));
        if (position == END) {
            break;
        }
        printf("\n%c", *(cptr + position));
    }
}
```

Program 18.5 asks the user to enter a string of text followed by an element number. The statement

```c
printf("\n%c", *(cptr + position));
```

causes the element number entered by the user to be displayed on the screen. Suppose, for example, that you entered the string shown in Figure 18.4 and then entered the value 5. (Because the address shown in Figure 18.4

has both the segment address and its offset, a four-byte pointer is being assumed.) If we assume that **buff[]** is stored at 1000:0200, the expression

```
*(cptr + position)
```

becomes

```
*(1000:0200 + 5)
*(1000:0205)
'5'
```

and the character digit 5 is displayed.

This expression illustrates the proper way to perform pointer addition. The only valid way to perform addition on a pointer is to add an offset to the pointer. Also notice that the parentheses in the expression are required for the indirection process to work properly. You'll learn more about this in a moment.

If the small memory model is used and the data segment address remains 1000, the arithmetic reduces to

```
*(0200 + 5)
*(0205)
'5'
```

The results are the same in either case. The addition works because only the offset is being used.

COMMON TRAP. *When adding offsets to pointers and using indirection, always enclose the expression within parentheses. For example, in the expression*

```
*(cptr + position)
```

*you must use parentheses to force the addition of **position** to **cptr** before indirection is performed. If position equals 5, the string is "fedcba", and you didn't use parentheses, the expression would resolve to*

```
*cptr + position
*cptr + 5
'f' + 5
'k'
```

which is not even in the string.

Although well-known C experts have said that you can add pointers in C, it is incorrect to do so. Consider the following code fragment:

```
char buff[50], *cptr;

cptr = buff;
```

```
printf("%c", *(cptr + buff));
```

If **buff[ ]** is stored at address 1000:0200, the expression

```
*(cptr + buff)
```

resolves to

```
*(1000:0200 + 1000:0200)
*(2000:0400);
???
```

Who knows what is stored in segment 2000? You cannot add pointers in C. You can only add offsets to pointers.

To summarize the rules for pointer arithmetic:

- You can only subtract pointers that point to the same data item.

- You cannot add pointers; you can only add offsets to pointers.

- If you wish to use indirection and offset addition to a pointer in the same statement, you must enclose the pointer and its offset within parentheses so addition occurs before indirection.

Finally, C allows you to perform just about any arithmetic operation you wish on a pointer. However, a good percentage of such operations may lock up the system. Only arithmetic operations that follow the rules listed above will work properly in all cases.

Saving Memory with Pointers

Programmers seem less concerned about memory limitations today than they were a few years ago. After all, new operating systems and program enhancements have increased the amount of memory available for use. Although newer machines provide more memory, multitasking operating systems like Microsoft's Windows still require that you use memory efficiently. You can use pointers to save memory.

Suppose that you want to store several peoples' names in a character array. You might write the code as shown in Program 18.6.

If you run Program 18.6, it simply prints the names in the initialized name[ ][ ] character array. Figure 18.5 shows how the compiler allocates space for the name[ ][ ] array.

The program initializes the name[ ][ ] array five names even though the array can hold a maximum of ten names. Each name can have a maximum length of 30 characters, including the null termination character. As a result, a block of memory similar to that shown in Figure 18.5 is allocated by the compiler for the name array. The memory requirement for the name[ ][ ] array is 300 bytes. When I compiled the program, the resulting EXE file size was 9,263 bytes.

Program 18.6 **Using Multidimensioned Character Arrays**

```
#include <stdio.h>

void main(void)
{
    char name[10][30] = {
        "Dave Cooper",
        "Dave Fenoglio",
        "Carl Landau",
        "Winsario Manichilouski",
        "David Schmitt"
        };

    int i;

    for (i = 0; name[i][0]; i++) {
        printf("\n%s", name[i]);
    }
}
```

Now let's modify Program 18.6 to use pointers, as shown in Program 18.7. There are only two changes in the program. First the definition of **name[ ]** begins with

```
char *name[10] = {
```

which is an array of pointers to **char**. The second change is in the second expression of the for loop, where only a single array subscript is used. Everything else is the same, including the program output. The real difference is that the program .EXE size dropped to 9,071 bytes. We just saved 192 bytes of memory with relatively minor changes to the program. How did the compiler save those 192 bytes?

Figure 18.5

Representation of
name[][]

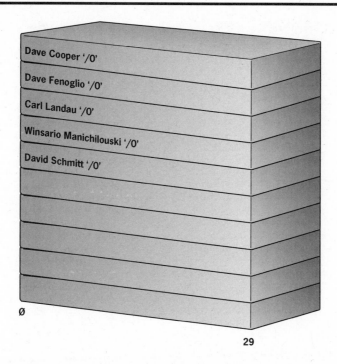

PROGRAMMING TIP. *Because of its flexibility,* ***printf()*** *uses a fairly large code space. Any time a program uses only one feature of* ***printf()*** *and you're concerned about memory limitations, look for an alternative to* ***printf()***. *Because Program 18.7 only uses the string display feature of* ***printf()***, *you could use* ***puts()*** *instead.* ***puts()*** *is a much simplier function for displaying strings and uses less code space. Substituting* ***puts()*** *for* ***printf()*** *in Program 18.7 dropped the code size from 9,071 bytes to 7,413 bytes, a savings of almost 18 percent.*

Saving Memory with Arrays of Pointers

Figure 18.6 illustrates how the compiler saved the memory in Program 18.7. The leftmost column in Figure 18.6 represents the lvalues for each element of the name[ ] array. Each element has an lvalue that is two greater than the previous lvalue. This sequence tells you two things. First, the program was compiled using a memory model that used two-byte pointers. Second, the name[ ] array is stored on the stack.

The second column in Figure 18.6 is simply a reference point. It tells you which element of the name[ ] array is being examined.

Program 18.7 **Using Pointers for a Multidimensioned Character Array**

```c
#include <stdio.h>


void main(void)
{
    char *name[10] = {
        "Dave Cooper",
        "Dave Fenoglio",
        "Carl Landau",
        "Winsario Manichilouski",
        "David Schmitt"
        };

    int i;

    for (i = 0; name[i]; i++) {
        printf("\n%s", name[i]);
    }
}
```

Figure 18.6
Representation of
*name[]

Address of name [i]	name [i]	name [i] rvalue	Contents at Address
FFE2	0	188	Dave Cooper
FFE4	1	200	Dave Fenoglio
FFE6	2	214	Carl Landau
FFE8	3	226	Winsario Manichilouski
FFEA	4	249	David Schmitt
FFEC	5	?	
FFEE	6	?	
FFF0	7	?	
FFF2	8	?	
FFF4	9	?	

The third column represents the rvalues that are stored in **name[]**. Because **name[]** is an array of pointers, these rvalues should represent the addresses of where the constants in the initializer list are stored. As you can see, the memory addresses stored in **name[]** have fairly small offset values, suggesting that the string constants (the names) are stored in low memory in the data segment.

The fourth column simply displays the names stored at the addresses shown in column three. However, notice the relationship between the rvalues in **name[]** and the length of the names. For example, Dave Cooper's name takes 11 bytes for the characters (including the blank space). However, because we initialized the list as double-quoted strings, the compiler must add a byte for the null termination character. Therefore, the total storage for "Dave Cooper" is 12 bytes. If we add 12 to the rvalue of **name[0]**, we get 200 (188 + 12). It's not by accident that the rvalue in **name[1]** is 200; it represents the address in memory where we can find "Dave Fenoglio".

There are question marks in the second half of column three because we have not initialized those pointers to point to anything useful.

Try the following experiment. Count the the length of each name in the list and add one for the null termination character (call it the total length). Get the rvalue of the name you just counted. Add the total length of the name to its rvalue and you should get the rvalue of the next item in the name[ ] array.

Now you can see that the pointer version of the program saves memory because the compiler only allocates enough space to hold each string; no more, no less. In the double-dimensioned array version, all of the elements had to be the same size. This means all elements had to be at least as big as the largest name in the array.

PROGRAMMING TIP. *As one example, you can use arrays of pointers to save space when your programs use frequent prompts. Large programming projects often use prompts repeatedly. The following code fragment shows how you might change your prompts to save space:*

```
char *prompts[] = {
    "Enter your ", "name", "phone number", "city",
    "state", "zip", "Invalid data. Re-enter",
    "Out of memory. Aborting program."
};
```

Keep in mind that string constants are allocated each time they appear in a program. That is, if your program uses

```
printf("Out of memory. Aborting program.");
```

several dozen times, each one uses 33 bytes of memory. However, if you use

```
printf("%s", prompt[7]);
```

the string constant is only stored once.

Using Dynamic Memory Allocation

You have already studied how the compiler allocates storage for a data item when it is defined. However, sometimes you need storage for a data item whose requirements are not known until the program starts executing or the user has answered one or more questions. The process of acquiring storage for a data item at runtime is called *dynamic memory allocation*. This section explains how to use dynamic memory allocation in C.

Writing a Magic Square Program

Figure 18.7 illustrates what is often called a *magic square*, in which all of the rows, columns, and main diagonals add up to the same value. Program 18.8 presents the code for creating a magic square. The user can select any size he or she wants, provided the size of the square is odd and has more than one element. This approach forces us to use dynamic memory allocation because we do not know how large the square will be until the program is run.

Figure 18.7

A magic square

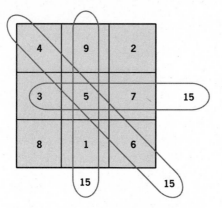

One obvious change in this program is that a more formal header is used for each function in the program. This style is used because you may actually use this program again. (Most of the other functions used in this book are fine for learning and experimenting, but are not terribly useful.)

There are several functions called from within **main()** to construct the magic square. The first one is **get_size()**. It finds out what size of square to construct, checking that the size is an odd number greater than one.

Program 18.8   **Magic Square Using Dynamic Memory Allocation**

```c
#include <stdio.h>
#include <stdlib.h>

int magic(int row, int col, int n),
    getsize(void)
    *get_room(int n);

void show_square(int *matrix, int n),
     do_magic(int *s, int n);

void main(void)
{
    int *matrix, size;

    size = get_size();
    matrix = get_room(size * size);
    do_magic(matrix, size);
    show_square(matrix, size);
    free( (void *) matrix);
}

/*****

                                do_magic()
     This function sets each element in the matrix.

    Argument list:    int *elements      pointer to matrix
                      int n              size of matrix
    Return value:     void

*****/

void do_magic(int *elements, int n)
{
    int i, j;

    for (i = 0; i < n; i++) {
        for (j = 0; j < n; j++, elements++) {
            *elements = magic(i + 1, j + 1, n);
        }
    }
}
```

Program 18.8 **continued**

```
/*****
                                        show_square()

        This function displays the matrix.

        Argument list:    int *elements        pointer to matrix
                          int n                size of matrix

        Return value:     void

*****/

void show_square(int *elements, int n)
{
    int i, j;

    for (i = 0; i < n; i++) {
        for (j = 0; j < n; j++, elements++) {
            printf("%4d", *elements);
        }
        printf("\n");
    }
}

/*****
                                        get_room()
        This function gets the required storage for the matrix.

        Argument list:    int n                size of matrix

        Return value:     int *                pointer to storage

*****/

int *get_room(int n)
{
    int *iptr;

    iptr = (int *) calloc( (unsigned) n, sizeof(int));
```

Program 18.8   **continued**

```
      if (iptr == NULL) {
      printf("\nNot enough memory");
      exit(EXIT_FAILURE);
      }
      return iptr;
}

/*****

                                    get_size()

      This function gets the size of the matrix.

    Argument list:    void

    Return value:    int  the size of the desired matrix

*****/

int get_size(void)
{
    char buff[20];
    int n;

    for (;;) {
       printf("\nEnter the size of matrix (must be odd and
          > 1): ");
       n = atoi(gets(buff));
       if (n % 2 == 1 && n > 1) {
          break;
          }
       }
    return n;
}

/*****

                                    magic()
```

Program 18.8   **continued**

This function calculates the values to fill in the
matrix.

Argument list: int row   row to fill in
                       int col   col to fill in
                       int n   size of matrix

Return value: int   the magic number for this

                                     row-col element of matrix

```c
*****/

int magic(int row, int col, int n)
{
   int term1, term2;

   term1 = col - row + (n - 1) / 2;
   term2 = col + col - row;
   if (term1 >= n) {
      term1 -= n;
   } else {
     if (term1 < 0) {
        term1 += n;
     }
   }
   if (term2 > n) {
      term2 -= n;
   } else {
     if (term2 <= 0) {
        term2 += n;
     }
   }
   return term1 * n + term2;
}
```

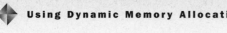

The next function called from **main()**, **get_room()**, is where the dynamic memory allocation takes place. For that reason, the code is repeated here:

```
int *get_room(int n)
{
    int *iptr;

    iptr = (int *) calloc( (unsigned) n, sizeof(int));
    if (iptr == NULL) {
        printf("\nNot enough memory");
        exit(EXIT_FAILURE);
    }
    return iptr;
}
```

First, notice how we defined **get_room()**. The function is designed to return a pointer to **int**. The statement

```
iptr = (int *) calloc( (unsigned) n, sizeof(int));
```

is a call to the standard library function named **calloc()**.

The first argument to **calloc()** is the number of items to be stored (**n**). The second argument tells the function how large each of the **n** items is in bytes. If the user wants a 3 x 3 magic square, nine integers are needed to store the data. (Notice that the program squared **size** when it called **get_room()** in **main()**.)

Because the program needs nine integers, each of which occupies two bytes, **calloc()** asks the operating system for 18 bytes of storage. If the call to **calloc()** is not successful, **calloc()** returns a NULL pointer. If that happens, the program displays an error message and ends the program.

If the storage request was successful, **calloc()** returns a (non-NULL) pointer to the storage. We must cast the pointer returned from **calloc()** to be a pointer to **int**. The cast is the

```
(int *)
```

part of the statement. This ensures that the attribute list of the pointer returned from **calloc()** is the same as **iptr**. On some pre-ANSI compilers, you might be able to leave out the cast. However, you should play it safe and always cast the pointer returned from **calloc()** to match the pointer on the left-hand side of the assignment. When the statement is finished, the rvalue of **iptr** is the memory address for the 18 bytes that will hold the magic square. This pointer is returned to **main()** and assigned into **matrix**. The remaining function calls simply fill in the magic square and display it on the screen. However, we need to examine the last statement in **main()**.

Releasing Dynamic Memory Allocations with free()

You can think of dynamic memory allocations as a loan from the operating system. When you borrow some memory, you should give it back when you're finished using it. The statement

```
free( (void *) matrix);
```

returns the storage for **matrix** to the operating system just before the program ends. The function prototype for **free()** states that the pointer argument is a pointer to **void**. This is why we cast **matrix** to a void pointer before calling **free()**.

If you do dynamic memory allocations and fail to free the memory, the operating system may or may not reclaim it when the program ends. (The exact behavior depends upon the operating system.) Rather than take a chance, always free all dynamic memory before the program ends.

PROGRAMMING TIP. *It can be disasterous to free a pointer that was not allocated any memory. Although you may get away with it, sometimes it can lock up the system. The following code fragment shows one way to avoid the problem:*

```
int *matrix;

matrix = NULL;

/* code to initialize the dynamic memory to matrix */
/* The rest of the program code */

if (matrix != NULL) {    /* Use before program ends */
    free( (void *) matrix);
}
```

*Using this scheme, you would not call **free()** unless **matrix** had been initialized.*

Using a Pointer to a Function

A friend of mine was writing a program to emulate a board game. The board included 64 squares, each of which was associated with a specific action. He wrote the program so each square was processed by its own function. The problem was, how should he invoke each function when he landed on a given square?

He could have written a large switch statement with 64 cases. However, that would not be the best solution. Instead, he created an array of 64 pointers and initialized each element to point to a specific function. That is, each array element held the lvalue of where the function was stored in memory. When a player "landed" on a specific square, the pointer was used to call the function.

Using Pointers to Functions

Program 18.9 illustrates how you can use a pointer to a function.

Program 18.9   **Invoking a Function with a Pointer**

```c
#include <stdio.h>

int square(int i);

void main(void)
{
    int i, val;
    int (*ifptr)(int i);

    ifptr = square;
    for (i = 0; i < 10; i++) {
        val = (*ifptr)(i);
        printf("\n%d * %d = %d ", i, i, val);
    }
}

int square(int i)
{
    return i * i;
}
```

Most of this code should look familiar by now. However, several statements need some explanation. First, the statement

```c
int (*ifptr)(int i);
```

defines a function pointer. Specifically, this definition states that **ifptr** (an integer function pointer) is a pointer to a function that has one integer argument (**i**) and the function returns an **int**. The first set of parentheses (**(*ifptr)**) tells the compiler that we are defining a pointer to a function. If we left them out, the statement would become

```c
int *ifptr(int i);
```

which looks like we are declaring a function named **ifptr()** that requires an int argument. *When you define a function pointer, you must enclose the pointer name and the indirection operator within parentheses.*

The statement

```
ifptr = square;
```

initializes **ifptr** to point to the square() function. Notice that there are no parentheses following **square**. Any time a function name appears without parentheses, the compiler knows that it should not generate code to call the function. Instead, *the compiler generates code to get the lvalue of where the function is stored in memory*. In this statement, the lvalue where **square()** is stored is assigned into **ifptr**. After this statement is executed, the rvalue of **ifptr** equals the lvalue where **square()** is stored in memory.

Inside the for loop, the statement

```
val = (*ifptr)(i);
```

uses **ifptr** to call **square()** using indirection. The second set of parentheses enclose any function arguments needed by **square()**. The answer produced by **square()** is returned to **main()** in the normal way (via the stack) and assigned into **val**. The program proceeds to display the square of the numbers 0 through 9.

There's nothing mysterious about pointers to functions. They simply represent another way to call a function. Remember, when indirection appears on the right side of an assignment statement, the compiler generates code to get the lvalue of the pointer, go to that address, and retrieve whatever was stored there. Function pointers work in much the same way, with one major difference.

The statement

```
val = (*ifptr)(i);
```

tells the compiler to get the rvalue of **ifptr**, push anything in the second set of parentheses (**i**) on the stack, go to the address pointed to by **ifptr**, and *execute* the code found there. Instead of going to a memory address and getting scalar-bytes of memory, we go to the address and start executing the code at that address.

Using Standard Library Functions that Use Pointers

Several library functions (for example **qsort()** and **bsearch()**) use pointers to functions. Program 18.10 shows how to use the qsort() standard library function.

This program creates MAXVALS random numbers that fall within the range 0 through 99. The first for loop displays the numbers produced by the random number generator. The program then calls **qsort()** to sort the list of random numbers. The general form for **qsort()** is

```
qsort( (void *) base, size_t num, size_t size,
(*comp)());
```

Program 18.10   **Using the qsort() Library Function**

```c
#include <stdio.h>
#include <stdlib.h>

#define MAXVALS    50

int compare(int *, int *);

void main(void)
{
    int i, val[MAXVALS];
    int (*comp)();

    comp = compare;
    for (i = 0; i < MAXVALS; i++) {
        val[i] = rand() % 100;
        if (i % 10 == 0) {
            printf("\n");
        }
        printf("%6d", val[i]);
    }
    qsort( (void *) val, MAXVALS, sizeof(int), comp);
    printf("\n\n");
    for (i = 0; i < MAXVALS; i++) {
        if (i % 10 == 0) {
            printf("\n");
        }
        printf("%6d", val[i]);
    }
}

int compare(int *i, int *j)
{
    if (*i < *j) {
        return -1;
    }
    if (*i > *j) {
        return 1;
    }
    return 0;
}
```

where *base* is the lvalue of the first element in the array. *num* is the number of elements in the array, *size* is the size in bytes of each element in the array, and *comp* is a pointer to function for the comparison function. (The size_t type specifier for *num* and *size* is a generic type specifier that is usually the same size as an **unsigned int** on the host machine.)

The advantage of using **qsort()** is that you only have to write the function that compares the elements in the array. The actual work of sorting the data is buried in the library function. Note that the arguments to the comparison function must be pointers.

Program 18.10 defines a pointer to function named **comp**. The statement

```
comp = compare;
```

initializes **comp** to the lvalue of where **compare()** resides in memory. **qsort()** is then called with the statement

```
qsort( (void *) val, MAXVALS, sizeof(int), comp);
```

As the qsort() function processes the data, it calls the compare() function many times. (Put a **printf()** and a **getch()** call at the top of the compare() function to see for yourself.) Eventually, **qsort()** finishes its task and the sorted list is displayed.

You can write any comparison function you wish. This allows you to use the qsort() function to sort any type of data. All you need to do is write the comparison function and initialize a pointer to it. **qsort()** takes care of everything else.

PROGRAMMING TIP. *Some compilers are very fussy about casting the pointer to the comparison function in **qsort()**. If you have problems, try the following form for the call to **qsort()**:*

```
qsort( (void *) val, MAXVALS, sizeof(int),
       (int(*)(const void *, const void *)) comp);
```

*This tells the compiler to cast the comparison pointer to match the pointer type that **qsort()** expects.*

The Right-Left Rule: Making Sense Out of Complex Data Definitions

We have had some fairly complex data definitions in this chapter. For example, you've seen

```
char *name[];
int (*ifptr)(int i);
```

and several other similar definitions. How can you decipher what these data types mean?

Let's start with a definition you already understand:

```
char *name[];
```

The Right-Left rule says that you start with the identifier of the data type (**name**) and look right for the first attribute. You then look left for the next attribute. You continue to spiral your way out of the data definition until no attributes are left. The Right-Left rule is illustrated in Figure 18.8.

Figure 18.8
Using the Right-Left rule

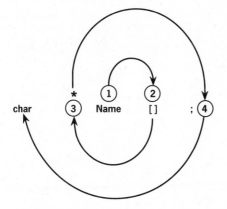

First you find the identifier, which is **name**. So far, you can say, "**name** is...." In step 2, you look to the right for the next attribute for **name**. You find a set of array brackets. After step 2, you can say, "**name** is an array...."

Next you spiral to the left to look for the next closest attribute to **name**. You see the asterisk. Because this is a definition statement, the asterisk is used to signify a pointer. After step 3 you can say, "**name** is an array of pointers to...."

You must look back to the right for the next attribute. At step 4, you find the semicolon for the data definition, so you must continue the spiral back to the left. The last attribute is **char**. You now have the full attribute list for the data item: "**name** is an array of pointers to **char**."

Try the other example definition.

```
int (*ifptr)(int i);
```

If you start with **ifptr** and spiral your way out, you should end up with "**ifptr** is a pointer to function taking one **int** argument which returns an **int**." (Notice that you must stay within the parentheses until all attributes within the parentheses are used.) If you understood this one on the first try, you really *do* understand C.

Conclusion

This chapter covered a lot of ground because much of the power of C comes from the use of pointers. You also learned how important scalars are in using pointers correctly. You can image how pointer arithmetic can get confused if the scalars are wrong. Chapter 17 explained how pointers can make a program faster. In this chapter you also saw how pointers can save memory. Many functions in the standard library use pointers and a few even use pointers to functions. These resources are just waiting for you to use them. Lastly, you saw how to verbalize a complex data definition. The Right-Left rule can spiral you out of the most complex data definitions. And you can't use the data unless you understand what it is.

Perhaps the greatest advantage of pointers is data privacy. You can hide the data in a function, but other functions can still manipulate the data through pointers. If you avoid using global data and use pointers to process the data, you will find program debugging much easier.

Pointers are not easy to understand. However, you should spend as much time as neccessary to feel comfortable with them; it is worth the effort.

Checking Your Progress

1. Functions can only return a single value from a function. Suppose you need a function to change two arguments that are passed to a function. How would you write the function call and the function prototype?

   The function call would be

   ```
   func1(&i, &j);
   ```

   This passes the lvalue of both of the variables that need to be changed. The function prototype might be written

   ```
   void func1(int *i, int *j)
   ```

   The function can now use indirection to change the values of **i** and **j** as needed.

2. What is the difference between the following two statements? (Assume **buff[]** contains the string "Program".)

   ```
   func1(&buff[3]);
   func2(buff[3]);
   ```

The first statement passes the address of the fourth element of the **buff[]** array. If **buff[]** is stored starting at address 1000, **func1()** receives an lvalue equal to 1003. In the second statement, the rvalue of **buff[3]** is sent to **func2()**. This means that the letter "g" is sent to **func2()**. Mixing these two types of statements is a fairly common mistake.

3. In what way is the type specifier for a pointer definition different from other data definitions?

   The type specifier for a pointer does not dictate the amount of storage allocated to the pointer. The storage for a pointer is fixed regardless of its type specifier. For a pointer, the type specifier sets the scalar that is used in all pointer operations. When used with indirection, the type specifier tells how many bytes of data to store or retrieve in memory. When used with the increment or decrement operators, the type specifier tells by how much the count stored in the pointer's rvalue is incremented or decremented.

4. Suppose you have an 81-element character array named **screen[]** and a second array named **buff[]** that contains a string of some unknown length (but less than 80 characters). You need to center the **buff[]** on the display screen. Because the output might go to the printer as well as the screen, you cannot use cursor addressing. How would you write the code?

   There are, of course, many ways to write this code. The first step is to calculate where to place the string to center it on the screen. You could enter a for loop and call **printf()** to display blank spaces until you reach the point where the string is to be displayed. This works, but it's not very efficient.

   The following code fragment shows another method.

   ```
   memset(screen, ' ', 81);
   col = (80 - strlen(buff)) / 2;
   strcpy(&screen[col], buff);
   printf("%s", screen);
   ```

   The **memset()** provides a fast way of setting all elements in the screen[] array to blank spaces. Using **memset()** is much more efficient than using a loop. Next we calculate where the string should be displayed so it is centered on the screen. For example, if the string is ten characters long, the string should start in column 35 of the screen (**col** equals 35).

   Once the column position is known, we need to copy **buff[]** into **screen[]** starting at element **col**. The call to **strcpy()** does exactly that by passing **&screen[col]** as the lvalue for the destination character array. We then call **printf()** to display the centered string. Try it.

5. Write a code fragment that sets up **qsort()** to sort a list of **double**s. Assume that **x[]** holds the **double**s and MAXVAL is the number of **double**s.

The fragment would be

```
int compare_double(double *x1, double *x2);
.

int (*dfptr)();

dfptr = compare_double;
qsort( (void *) x, MAXVAL, sizeof(double), dfptr);
```

First you need to present a function prototype for the comparison function. Next you define a function pointer (**dfptr**) and initialize it to point to the comparison function. We can now call **qsort()** with the proper arguments.

6. What's wrong with the following code fragment?

```
char buff[MAXCHAR];
int i, *ptr;
strcpy(buff, "This is a test of it.");
ptr = buff;
for (i = 0; *ptr; i++) {
    printf("%c", *ptr++);
}
```

The problem is that **ptr** is defined with a scalar of 2 but points to **buff[]**, which has a scalar of 1. The increment on **ptr** will not display the contents of **buff[]** correctly.

7. Verbalize the following data definitions.

   a. int *ptr[10];
   b. int (*ptr)[10];
   c. int (*ptr[10])(void);
   d. int (*(*ptr)(int))(void);

The attribute lists for the definitions are

   a. "**ptr** is an array of ten pointers to **int**."
   b. "**ptr** is a pointer to an array of ten **int**s."
   c. "**ptr** is an array of ten pointers to function that have no arguments that return **int**."
   d. "**ptr** is a pointer to function that takes an int argument that returns a pointer to function with no arguments that returns an **int**." (If you got this one right, send me your resume!)

Structures and Unions

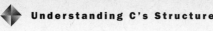

I
N THIS CHAPTER YOU WILL LEARN ABOUT TWO NEW DATA TYPES CALLED structures and unions. The **structure** data type provides a convenient way to organize dissimilar data items. You will see parallels between structures and the data type named records or fields in other languages. A union does not have a parallel with many other languages. You will learn, however, that unions provide an efficient way to store a variety of different data types.

Understanding C's Structures

You have probably encountered a programming task where you wanted to keep a group of dissimilar data items together. For example, suppose you are writing an invoicing program and you must track up to 20 items, each of which might have a different price. The items that belong to the group might be

```
char name[30];
char address[100];
int item[20];
double price[20];
```

Because the group is comprised of dissimilar data items, you cannot place all of the items in a single array. (Arrays require that each element be the same type of data.) The next best alternative is to give each item in the group a similar name. Faced with these restrictions, you rename the group to be

```
char billing_name[30];
char billing_address[100];
int billing_item[20];
double billing_price[20];
```

In many languages, this is as far as you can go toward grouping the items together. Not so in C.

The concept of a structure is similar to a record in some other languages and not too different from a FIELD statement in BASIC. A structure organizes different data items so they can be referenced as a single unit. Normally, a structure consists of two or more different data types (although nothing prevents you from using a single data item in a structure).

Declaring a Structure

The first thing you must do to create a structure is declare it. Let's use our billing example as a starting point. Figure 19.1 shows how you declare a structure.

Figure 19.1

Declaring a
structure

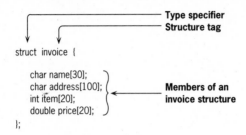

Type specifier
Structure tag

```
struct invoice {
    char name[30];
    char address[100];
    int item[20];
    double price[20];
};
```

Members of an
invoice structure

There are three important elements of a structure declaration. First, the keyword **struct** is the type specifier. When the compiler sees the keyword **struct**, it records several special attributes for the pending data item in the symbol table.

The second important element is the structure tag, which is the name, or identifier, of the particular structure. In Figure 19.1 the structure tag is **invoice**. The compiler must record the structure tag in the symbol table. The reason is because C allows you to use many different types of structures in the same program. The structure tag enables the compiler to distinguish one structure from the others in the program.

The third important element is the list of members in the structure. In Figure 19.1, **name[]**, **address[]**, **item[]**, and **price[]** are the members of the structure. These four variables together form the member list of the invoice structure. Notice that the member list is surrounded by an opening and closing set of braces. The closing braces tells the compiler that the list of members is complete for the invoice structure.

Notice how we have been very careful to say that we are *declaring* a structure. Because a data declaration does not allocate storage for a data item, you have not yet defined a variable that you can use as an invoice structure. So what do you have after declaring a structure like that shown in Figure 19.1? All you have is a structure declaration that describes what an invoice structure looks like. *A structure declaration creates a "mold" or "cookie cutter" that describes the contents of a structure.* It does not create a variable that you can use in your program.

The structure tag is not a variable, it is simply a label that lets the compiler locate a particular structure in its symbol table. It seems obvious, therefore, that next you need to know how to create an invoice structure variable.

Defining a Structure Variable

Figure 19.2 shows the statement that defines a variable that is an invoice structure.

Figure 19.2
Defining a variable
of type **struct
invoice**

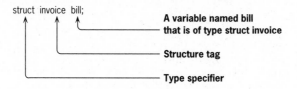

The statement in Figure 19.2 causes the compiler to search the symbol table for a structure named **invoice**. Once the compiler locates **invoice**, it allocates enough storage to create one structure of type **invoice** and records its name as **bill** in the symbol table. You now have a structure variable named **bill** that you can use in your program. Program 19.1 shows you how to define a structure of type **invoice**.

Program 19.1   **Defining a Structure of Type invoice**

```
#include <stdio.h>

struct invoice {
   char name[30];
   char address[100];
   int item[20];
   double price[20];
   };

void main(void)
{
   struct invoice bill;

   printf("The size of bill is %d", sizeof(bill));
}
```

Notice how we have declared the invoice structure outside of any function, thus giving it global scope. Because the declaration has global scope, any function can define a structure variable of type **invoice**. If we had placed the declaration inside of **main()**, only **main()** could define a variable of type **invoice**.

Once inside of **main()**, the program defines a type invoice variable named **bill**. The **printf()** simply displays the size of **bill**. When I ran the program, the output was

```
The size of bill is 330
```

Let's see if that's correct. Table 19.1 shows how the total storage requirements for **bill** are calculated.

Table 19.1   **Calculating the Number of Bytes Allocated to bill**

Structure Member	Data Type	Scalar	Total Bytes for Each Member
name[30]	**char**	1	30
address[100]	**char**	1	100
item[20]	**int**	2	40
price[20]	**double**	8	160
			——
Total bytes for **bill**			330

It appears that the output from Program 19.1 is correct.

Declaring and Defining a Structure with One Statement

You can also declare and define a structure at the same time. The statement that does this is shown in Figure 19.3.

The only difference between Figures 19.1 and 19.3 is that we placed the name of the structure variable to be defined (**bill**) between the closing brace of the structure declaration and the semicolon. This statement both declares a structure of type **invoice** and defines a variable named **bill** of this structure type.

Figure 19.3
Declaring and
defining a structure
with one statement

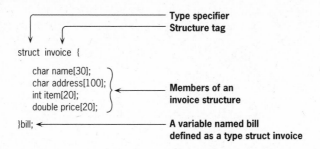

If you need two variables of type **invoice**, you can use either

```
struct invoice {          /* Form 1 */
    char name[30];
    char address[100];
    int item[20];
    double price[20];
    } bill, past_due;
```

or

```
struct invoice {          /* Form 2 */
    char name[30];
    char address[100];
    int item[20];
    double price[20];
    };
```

```
struct invoice bill, past_due;
```

Either of these two forms defines **bill** and **past_due** as variables of type **invoice**.

You might be wondering if one form of variable definition is preferable to another. There may be one disadvantage to the first form shown above, which declares and defines the variables in the same statement. Because structure definitions normally have global scope, the variables are also given global scope. Normally, you should try to minimize the number of global variables to maintain data privacy.

In the second form above, you could declare the invoice structure outside of any function giving it global scope, but move the definitions of **bill** and **past_due** inside of a function. Doing this keeps the two variables private to the function where they are defined, but still lets you define additional variables of type **invoice** as you need them. Unless you need global invoice variables, you might want to use the second form.

Defining a Structure Variable without a Structure Tag

Finally, you can define a structure variable without a structure tag. The statement

```
struct {
    char name[30];
    char address[100];
    int item[20];
    double price[20];
    } bill;
```

defines a structure named **bill** with **name[]**, **address[]**, **item[]**, and **price[]** as its members. Notice that there is no structure tag used to define **bill**. We can get away with this without confusing the compiler because the declaration and definition of the structure occur in the same statement.

There is a disadvantage to this type of structure definition. Because there is no structure tag, there is no "cookie cutter" for this structure in the symbol table. Therefore, if you need a second structure variable of this type, you would have to repeat the structure definition each time you need another variable of this structure type. Because of this limitation, it is rarely used in real programming situations.

Using an Initializer List with a Structure

You can also initialize a structure as part of its definition. The following code fragment shows how this is done:

```
struct invoice bill = {
    "Don Dudine",
    "CCI    Indianapolis, IN   46214",
    1000,0,0,0,0,0,0,0,0,0,0,0,0,0,0,0,0,0,0
    9999.95
    };
```

The only odd part is the initializer list for the item[] member of the structure. If you don't list all 20 elements of the item[] array, the compiler thinks that the value 9999.95 is the second element in the item[] member rather than the first element of the price[] member. The initializer list shown here sets the first element of item[] to 1000 and the remaining elements are initialized to 0. Only the first element of the price[] member is initialized to a known value. You should assume that the remaining 19 elements in the price[] member are garbage values.

The initializer list for structures is not much different from that used with common arrays. Each item in the list is separated by a comma, except the last item in the initializer list. The only major difference when initializing structures instead of arrays is that the items in the list can be different data types.

Referencing a Structure Member

Now that you know how to define a structure variable, let's see how to use a member. Program 19.2 shows you how to add information to each member of the structure.

Using the Dot Operator

When you reference a member of a structure, you must use the dot operator (.) between the name of the structure variable (**bill**) and the member you wish to reference (**name[]**). Once you have used the dot operator, you can use each structure member as though it was a nonstructure member. For example, the statement

```
gets(bill.name);
```

in Program 19.2 treats the name[] member of **bill** as though it were a "normal" character array. So how does the compiler view the statement? The compiler first sees the structure name **bill** followed by a dot operator. The compiler checks its symbol table to see if **bill** is in scope. Assuming it is, the compiler checks to see if there is a variable named **name[]** in the bill structure. When the compiler finds **name[]** in the structure, it will also see that **name[]** is a character array. Because we used **name** without any brackets after it, the compiler knows it must pass the lvalue of **name[0]** to **gets()**. The end result is the same as passing any other character array to **gets()**.

If you examine how the remaining structure members are used in Program 19.2, you will see they all use the dot operator in the same general way.

Program 19.2   **Placing Information in a Structure**

```c
#include <stdio.h>
#include <stdlib.h>

struct invoice {
    char name[30];
    char address[100];
    int item[20];
    double price[20];
    };

void main(void)
{
    char buff[20];
    struct invoice bill;

    printf("\nEnter your name: ");
    gets(bill.name);

    printf("Enter your street address: ");
    gets(bill.address);

    printf("Enter an item number: ");
    bill.item[0] = atoi(gets(buff));

    printf("Enter a price for the item: ");
    bill.price[0] = atof(gets(buff));

    printf("\n\nThe content of bill is:\n\n");
    printf("\n   name = %s", bill.name);
    printf("\naddress = %s", bill.address);
    printf("\n   item = %d", bill.item[0]);
    printf("\n  price = $%-10.2f\n\n", bill.price[0]);
}
```

Using Array Members of a Structure

Suppose you want to fill in ten items and prices in the **bill** structure. You could do that with something like the following code fragment.

```
for (i = 0; i < 10; i++) {

    printf("Enter item number %d: ", i + 1);
    bill.item[i] = atoi(gets(buff));

    printf("Enter the price for item %d: ", i + 1);
        bill.price[i] = atof(gets(buff));
    }
```

This code allows you to march through each of the first ten elements and fill in their values. The only change needed was to add a for loop and use **i** to index into the proper element of each array of items and prices.

Now let's see if we can figure out a way to stuff additional information in the address[] member of the structure. Program 19.3 shows one approach.

Program 19.3 is similar to Program 19.2, except we now ask for the user to enter the street, city, state, and zip code. Rather than define character arrays (and new structure members) for each piece of information, you simply divided the bill.address[] string into substrings for each item. For example, the statements

```
printf("Enter your city: ");
gets(bill.address + CITY);
```

get the city entry from the user and write it to character position address + CITY. We have **#define**d CITY to equal 32, so the entry is written starting with the 33rd character in the bill.address[] array. For example, if the lvalue of bill.address[] is 1000, then the lvalue passed to **gets()** is 1032.

What we are doing with the approach above is creating substrings within **bill.address[]**. Because **gets()** writes a null termination character upon sensing the Enter key, we can treat this substring within **bill.address[]** as a normal string. We make use of this fact when we display the string with **printf()**.

```
printf("\n   city = %s", bill.address + CITY);
```

Some programmers don't like using substrings; they would rather have a smaller bill.address[] character array and new members for the street, city, state, and zip character fields. Either form works so you are free to choose whatever best suits your needs.

Program 19.3   **Using Subfields in an Array of a Structure**

```c
#include <stdio.h>
#include <stdlib.h>

#define CITY        32
#define STATE       63
#define ZIP         90

struct invoice {
    char name[30];
    char address[100];
    int item[20];
    double price[20];
    };

void main(void)
{
    char buff[20];
    struct invoice bill;

    printf("\nEnter your name: ");
    gets(bill.name);

    printf("Enter your street address: ");
    gets(bill.address);
    printf("Enter your city: ");
    gets(bill.address + CITY);
    printf("Enter your state: ");
    gets(bill.address + STATE);
    printf("Enter your zip: ");
    gets(bill.address + ZIP);

    printf("Enter an item number: ");
    bill.item[0] = atoi(gets(buff));

    printf("Enter a price for the item: ");
    bill.price[0] = atof(gets(buff));

    printf("\n\nThe content of bill is:\n\n");
    printf("\n   name = %s", bill.name);
```

Program 19.3 **continued**

```
        printf("\naddress = %s", bill.address);
        printf("\n   city = %s", bill.address + CITY);
        printf("\n  state = %s", bill.address + STATE);
        printf("\n    Zip = %s", bill.address + ZIP);
        printf("\n   item = %d", bill.item[0]);
        printf("\n  price = $%-10.2f\n\n", bill.price[0]);
}
```

Using Structures with Function Calls

As with most programming tasks, you have a variety of ways to solve the same problem. ANSI C gives you more options than do compilers that don't support the ANSI standard, which allowed structures to be passed to functions. Some (pre-ANSI) compilers do not support structure passing. (If your compiler does not support structure passing and you want a function to have access to a structure, you must use a pointer to the structure. You will see how to do that later in this chapter.)

Assuming you have an ANSI-compliant compiler, there are several ways that you can use functions with structures. Let's examine the most direct approach first.

Using Return Values from Functions with Structures

The simplest way to use a function with a structure is to call the function and have the function return a value that can be assigned into a structure member. For example, suppose a function named **get_price()** determines the proper price to fill in for one of the values in the price[] array. The argument to get_price() might be the item number and the return value is the price. The following code fragment shows how we might write the code:

```
double get_price(int item_number);   /* Declare what it is
                                         */
void main(void)
{
      /* Code similar to Program 19.3 */

      bill.price[item_number] = get_price(item_number);

      /* The rest of the program */
```

First, the program calls **get_price()** with the proper item number (**item_number**) as its argument. The function determines the correct price and returns a **double** that we assign directly into the proper element of the price[] structure member. This is the easiest way to use a function to get a piece of data and assign it into a structure member. It's not the only way, however.

Passing a Structure to a Function

Now let's assume you want to pass the entire **bill** structure to a function. We will continue to use **get_price()** as the function doing the work and its purpose remains the same as it was before. We also assume that we only wish to fill in one element of the price[] structure member. Program 19.4 shows one way to accomplish the task.

Program 19.4 begins with the structure declaration followed by the function declaration for **get_price()**. In **main()** we ask the user to enter the item number. This will be used as the index into the price[] member of the bill structure. The input statements are enclosed in an infinite while loop that forces the user to enter an index between 0 and 19. Notice that a message is displayed to help the user if the input is incorrect. The systems bell (or buzzer) is also sounded to call attention to the screen. By checking that **item_number** is within the proper range before you use it, you ensure that you will not write outside the bounds of the price[] array.

Once you have a valid index, you pass **bill** and **item_number** to **get_price()**. The get_price() function simply generates a random number and, upon getting one that falls within the proper range, it is assigned into the proper element and the entire structure is returned.

It is important to note that we copied the entire bill structure onto the stack when we called **get_price()**. Likewise, we push the entire structure back on the stack with the **return bill** statement. Upon return from the call to **get_price()** in **main()**, we pop the structure off the stack and assign it into **bill**.

PROGRAMMING TIP. *Each time you call a function that passes a structure to the function, the entire structure is copied onto the stack. As your programs get more complex, so will your structures. If the call to a function that has a structure as one of its arguments is in a loop, you can eat up a lot of stack space in a hurry. If you must call a function in a loop that needs to work with a structure, you might want to consider using a pointer to the structure.*

The final statement in **main()** displays the value that was assigned into the price[] member. Although this approach works, it is not very efficient because the code must push and pop the entire structure (all 330 bytes) from the stack. There is a better way.

Program 19.4   **Passing a Structure to a Function**

```c
#include <stdio.h>
#include <string.h>
#include <stdlib.h>

#define TRUE       1
#define MAXITEMS   20
#define BELL       7

struct invoice {
    char name[30];
    char address[100];
    int item[MAXITEMS];
    double price[MAXITEMS];
    };

struct invoice get_price(struct invoice bill, int number);

int main(void)
{
    char buff[20];
    int item_number;
    struct invoice bill;

    while (TRUE) {
        printf("\nEnter the item number: ");
        item_number = atoi(gets(buff));
        if (item_number >= 0 && item_number < MAXITEMS) {
            break;
        } else {
            printf("\n *** Improper value. Must be between 0
                and %d %c***\n", MAXITEMS, BELL);
        }
    }
    bill = get_price(bill, item_number);
    printf("\n\n  price = $%-10.2f\n\n",
        bill.price[item_number]);

}
```

Program 19.4   **continued**

```
struct invoice get_price(struct invoice bill, int number)
{
   double val;

   val = 0.0;
   while (TRUE) {
     val = (double) rand();
     if (val > 0.0 && val < 100.0) {
        break;
     }
   }
   bill.price[number] = val;
   return bill;
}
```

Using Pointers with Structures

Before there was an ANSI standard, compilers did not allow passing structures to be passed to a function. Although the ANSI standard provides for
structure passing, you may be forced to use a pointer to the structure instead.
Structures provide a perfect solution for the complex data types often found
in database programming. It's not uncommon to have structures within structures, each of which might contain its own set of arrays and other members.
Structures requiring more than a thousand bytes are not uncommon.

If a function calls other functions with a structure as its argument or if
the function calls itself (using recursion), it is possible that the program could
run out of stack space. In these situations, you may have to use a pointer to
the structure as the function argument. Program 19.5 shows how to use a
pointer to a structure.

Program 19.5 draws from the previous examples in this chapter. The
function declaration for the get_item() function near the top of the program
indicates that two arguments are passed to the function. The first argument is
the lvalue of the bill structure and the second argument is the element you
wish to enter.

main() simply calls **get_item()** with the proper arguments. As with all pointers, you need to pass the lvalue of **bill** to the function. This is done using the address-of operator. The compiler generates code to place the address of where the
bill structure resides in memory on the stack. The second argument (ITEM-
NUM) is not a pointer, so a copy of its value is also placed on the stack.

Program 19.5   Using a Pointer to a Structure

```c
#include <stdio.h>
#include <stdlib.h>

#define ITEMNUM    10
struct invoice {
   char name[30];
   char address[100];
   int item[20];
   double price[20];
   };

void get_item(struct invoice *bill_ptr, int item_number);

void main(void)
{
   int i;
   struct invoice bill;

   get_item(&bill, ITEMNUM);

   printf("\n    item[%d] = %d", ITEMNUM,
      bill.item[ITEMNUM]);
}

void get_item(struct invoice *bill_ptr, int item_number)
{
   char buff[20];

   printf("Enter item number %d: ", item_number);
   (*bill_ptr).item[item_number] = atoi(gets(buff));
}
```

Think about the impact this change has on stack requirements. Before, when the entire structure and one **int** were placed on the stack, 332 bytes of stack space were used to call the function. By using a pointer to function, we have dropped the stack requirements to four bytes (assuming two-byte **int**s and pointers). Under tight memory conditions, the memory savings could mean the difference between a program that works and one that doesn't.

PROGRAMMING TIP. *Using pointers to structures in function calls not only saves memory by using less stack space, it can also provide a slight performance boost to your programs. Because the compiler doesn't have to generate as much code to manipulate the data on the stack, the program executes faster. If a function needs to change the contents of a structure, consider using a pointer to the structure instead of passing the entire structure to the function.*

Once the two arguments are placed on the stack, program control is transferred to the get_item() function, which asks for the item number to be entered. The gets() and atoi() functions get and convert the input to a numeric value.

The statement

```
(*bill_ptr).item[item_number] = atoi(gets(buff));
```

shows how indirection is performed on a structure. Because the dot operator (.) has higher precedence than the indirection operator (*), you must parenthesize the indirection operator.

The expression

```
(*bill_ptr).item[item_number]
```

that causes the indirection looks a bit intimidating, but it's nothing you haven't used before. It simply says to use the rvalue of bill_ptr as the starting memory address for the structure. The compiler, however, does not have the correct memory address yet. It knows where the bill structure starts in memory, but it hasn't calculated where the item[] member is stored.

The compiler automatically calculates how many bytes it must add to the lvalue in **bill_ptr** to find **item[10]**. Given the two character array members and ten elements stored in front of item[10], the compiler calculates the offset to **item[10]** as 152 bytes. If the bill structure defined in **main()** is stored at memory address 1000, then **item[10]** is stored at address 1152. Once the address is calculated, the compiler uses indirection to store the new item value into the proper item[] element in memory.

The expression should make sense to you now. In the expression

```
(*bill_ptr).item[item_number]
```

the pointer name (everything in parentheses) simply gets the lvalue where the structure starts in memory. Everything to the right of the dot operator is used to calculate an offset that is added to the lvalue to find the exact memory location being referenced. You can view the expression as two parts:

```
(*bill_ptr).item[item_number]
   lvalue   +    offset
```

The sum of the two parts yields the memory address to use for the indirection operator.

Using the Arrow Operator

C programmers use pointers to structures a lot. In fact, it is so common that the creators of C devised a special operator to indicate indirection involving pointers to structures. This special operator is called the arrow operator. *The arrow operator is used to indicate indirection on a pointer to a structure.*

The arrow operator is formed by placing the minus sign (–) and the greater-than operator (>) next to each other. The arrow operator can only be used for indirection with pointers to structures. Also, like the dot operator, the arrow operator can only appear between the structure name and a member name of that structure.

For example, the expression

```
(*bill_ptr).item[item_number]
```

can be written using the arrow operator as

```
bill_ptr->item[item_number]
```

Either expression can be used for indirection on a pointer to a structure. The only difference is that the parentheses, indirection operator, and dot operator are replaced by a single arrow operator. The two expressions yield exactly the same results.

Of the two forms to indicate indirection on a structure pointer, you will see the arrow operator used most often.

PROGRAMMING TIP. *It's easy to remember the arrow operator. Just keep in mind that "The arrow always points to a structure member."*

Arrays of Structures

You can create arrays of structures. Suppose you wish to create an array of ten invoice structures. The definition might be

```
struct invoice bill[10];
```

This statement causes the compiler to allocate space for ten structures of type **invoice** and give it the identifier named **bill[]**. Program 19.6 shows how you might use an array of structures.

Notice how we have defined **bill[]** to be an array of invoice structures. The program enters a for loop and asks for a client's name to be entered.

Program 19.6   **Using an Array of Structures**

```c
#include <stdio.h>
#include <string.h>
#include <stdlib.h>

#define MAXBILLS    10
#define MAXITEMS    20

#define END         '#'

struct invoice {
   char name[30];
   char address[100];
   int item[MAXITEMS];
   double price[MAXITEMS];
   };

int main(void)
{
   char buff[20];
   int entered, i, item_number;
   struct invoice bill[10];

   for (entered = i = 0; i < MAXBILLS; i++, entered++) {
      printf("\nEnter clients name (# = END): ");
      gets(buff);
      if (buff[0] == END) {
         break;
      }
      strcpy(bill[i].name, buff);
   }
   printf("\n\n");
   for (i = 0; i < entered; i++) {
      printf("\n  name = %s", bill[i].name);
   }
}
```

The program stays in this loop until either a sharp sign (#) is entered instead of a name or MAXBILLS names have been entered.

The statement

```
strcpy(bill[i].name, buff);
```

copies the name into the proper element of the bill[] array. Using **strcpy()** with a structure member is no different from the other examples you have seen using this function.

After the names have been entered, a second for loop displays the names that were entered. The variable **entered** is used to keep track of the number of names that were entered.

Improving Code When Using Arrays of Structures

Usually you create an array of structures and fill in the elements as the program runs. Program 19.6 used the variable **entered** to monitor how many elements of **bill[]** were filled in and to later display the contents of the array of structures. You can eliminate **entered** if you initialize all members of the array to 0 prior to their use. The statement

```
memset(bill, 0, sizeof(struct invoice) * MAXBILLS);
```

initializes MAXBILLS elements of the bill[] array to 0. As each element is filled in, only the unused elements contain 0s. You can use that information when you wish to display the contents of the array.

If you change the second for loop statement to

```
for (i = 0; bill[i].name[0]; i++) {
```

the program displays only those elements of the array that have been filled in with a name. The reason this works properly is because each element of an unused array has a value of zero. Because zero is viewed as logic False, the for loop terminates when an empty name[] array is read. This does away with the need for the **entered** variable in Program 19.6.

Initializing Arrays of Structures

If you know all or part of the list of items that you want stored in the bill[] array, you can use an initializer list to fill in the array. The following code fragment shows an example of how this can be done:

```
struct invoice bill[MAXBILLS] = {
    {"Don Dudine",                        /* bill[0] */
        "CCI",
        1000,0,0,0,0,0,0,0,0,0,0,0,0,0,0,0,0
```

```
            9999.95
        },

        {"Carl Landau",                          /* bill[1] */
            "c/o Seattle Mariners",
            3000,0,0,0,0,0,0,0,0,0,0,0,0,0,44,0,0,0,0
            49.95, 22.0
        }
    };
```

In this code, the initializer list is changed slightly from our earlier example. *When arrays of structures are initialized, each initialized element in the array is surrounded by its own set of braces.* This allows the compiler to determine when the initializer list for one element ends and the next one begins. If the braces were not required, you would be forced to fill in every value for every element in the price[] member (just as we had to do for every item[] member).

The code fragment shows how the first two elements of the bill[] array might be initialized. The same form can be used to initialize the rest of the elements, or the program might allow the empty elements to be filled in from the keyboard.

Just remember, each element of the array in an initializer list of structures must be surrounded by a pair of braces.

Understanding Unions

A *union is a small chunk of memory that can hold different types of data.* The general form for a union is almost identical to that used for structures. Figure 19.4 shows an example of how a union is declared.

Figure 19.4
A **union** declaration

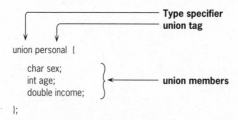

Although the union appears to be the same as a structure, there is an important difference, shown in Program 19.7.

Program 19.7   **Comparing Structures and Unions**

```c
#include <stdio.h>

struct sperson {
   char sex;
   int age;
   double income;
   };

union uperson {
   char sex;
   int age;
   double income;
   };

int main(void)
{
   struct sperson s1;
   union uperson s2;

   printf("\n size of structure = %d", sizeof(s1));
   printf("\n size of     union = %d", sizeof(s2));

}
```

Program 19.7 defines a structure and a union, each of which has the same members. Notice that the syntax for defining a union is exactly the same as that for a structure. The general form is

```c
union union_tag union_variable;
```

The **union_tag** tells the compiler which union "cookie cutter" to use and defines the variable named **union_variable**. So far, the declaration and definition of a union look just like that of a structure.

When you run the program, however, the output may be different than you expected. The output is

```
size of structure = 11
size of     union = 8
```

(You may get different values if your compiler aligns data on even memory addresses.) The union requires less storage than the structure, even though they contain identical members. The reason is because *a union can hold only one of its members at one time.* That is, given the union's definition in Program 19.7, it is capable of holding a **char**, an **int**, or a **double**, but only one of the members can reside in the union at any given time.

When the compiler sees the definition of a union variable, it scans the list of members, noting the size of each member. When it finishes scanning the member list, *the compiler picks the member with the largest storage requirements and allocates enough storage for this member.* In Program 19.7, the income member requires more storage than any other member, so the compiler allocates eight bytes of storage for the **double** variable named **income**. This explains why the output of Program 19.7 shows different storage requirements for a structure and a union with identical member lists.

Now you know why we said a union is like a small buffer. A union is a small portion of memory where you can store any one of the union's members, but only one member at a time. How does the compiler know which member is in the union? It doesn't. You are responsible for storing and retrieving a member from the union.

Using a Union with Interrupt Programming

A very common use for a union is with MS-DOS interrupt programming. Most PC compilers provide a special header file named dos.h that defines several unions that are useful in programming interrupts. The following code fragment shows how the REGS union in the dos.h header file is usually defined.

```
struct WORDREGS {
    unsigned int ax, bx, cx, dx, si, di, cflag, flags;
};

struct BYTEREGS {
    unsigned char al, ah, bl, bh, cl, ch, dl, dh;
};

union REGS {
    struct WORDREGS x;
    struct BYTEREGS h;
};
```

The WORDREGS structure simulates the registers found in the 80x86 CPU. The structure has the structure tag WORDREGS because the members of the structure represent the two-byte register pairs of the CPU. Each member of the BYTEREGS structure represents the single-byte registers of the CPU.

The union named REGS contains two members: a WORDREGS structure and a BYTEREGS structure. The storage requirements for a WORDREGS structure is 16 bytes (eight **unsigned int** members times two bytes each). The BYTEREGS structure requires only eight bytes of storage for its members. A variable capable of storing a union named REGS requires enough storage to hold the larger of the two structure members in the union. Therefore, a union of type REGS will require 16 bytes of memory.

The statement

```
union REGS ireg;
```

causes the compiler to allocate 16 bytes of storage to **ireg**. You can place either a WORDREGS or a BYTEREGS structure in **ireg**. Keep in mind, however, that it is an either-or situation. That is, **ireg** can hold either a WORDREGS or a BYTEREGS structure at any given moment.

Program 19.8 shows how we can use a union with an MS-DOS interrupt to position the cursor on the screen.

The code in **main()** simply sets up the call to the cursor positioning function. The interesting code is in the set_cursor() function. In **set_cursor()** a union of type REGS is first defined with the name **ireg**. Therefore, **ireg** is capable of storing either a BYTEREGS or WORDREGS structure. For your convenience, we will repeat the REGS declaration here:

```
union REGS {
    struct WORDREGS x;
    struct BYTEREGS h;
};
```

Let's see how the compiler views the statement

```
ireg.h.ah = 0x02;
```

When the compiler sees the **ireg.h** portion of the lefthand expression, it knows that you want to use the BYTEREGS structure. (The **h** tells it so.) The compiler now knows that only eight bytes of the register are meaningful and that each member is one byte long.

Next, the compiler sees the **.ah** portion of the expression and now knows that you wish to access the **ah** member of the **h** structure. Therefore, after reading the expression

```
ireg.h.ah
```

the compiler needs to reference the **ah** member of the BYTEREGS structure that is now being stored in **ireg**. The rest of the statement

```
ireg.h.ah = 0x02;
```

Program 19.8   **Cursor Positioning Using an MS-DOS Interrupt**

```c
#include <stdio.h>
#include <dos.h>

#define VIDEO_INTERRUPT    0x10
void set_cursor(int row, int col);

int main(void)
{
   cls();                 /* See Program 19.9 */
   set_cursor(15, 10);
   printf("This starts at row 15, column 10");
   set_cursor(24,1);
}
/*****
                   set_cursor()
   This function sets the cursor at the row-column
coordinates given by row and col. A row-col pair at 1,1
sets the cursor to the upper left corner of the display.

   Argument list:   int row     the row position, 1 - 25
                    int col      " column " , 1 - 80

   Return value:   void

*****/

void set_cursor(int row, int col)
{
   union REGS ireg;

   ireg.h.ah = 0x02;  /* Video interrupt function # 2 */
   ireg.h.bh = 0;     /* Video page # 0              */
   ireg.h.dh = row - 1;
   ireg.h.dl = col - 1;
   int86(VIDEO_INTERRUPT, &ireg, &ireg);
}
```

causes the compiler to store the value 2 in the second byte in the **union**. (Programming interrupts for MS-DOS normally loads the **ah** register of the CPU with the function number of the interrupt. In this example, we wish to use function 2 of the video interrupt.)

The statement

```
ireg.h.bh = 0;
```

says to assign the value of 0 into the fourth member of the BYTEREGS member. (For function 2 of the video interrupt, **bh** is loaded with the video page number. The default video page is page 0, which is the page you normally see on the screen. Most PCs have up to eight pages of video in the text mode.)

The statements

```
ireg.h.dh = row - 1;

ireg.h.dl = col - 1;
```

load the **dh** and **dl** members of the **h** BYTEREGS structure with the row-column position for the cursor. Figure 19.5 shows how the union **ireg** looks at this point in the program.

Figure 19.5

Memory image of **ireg**

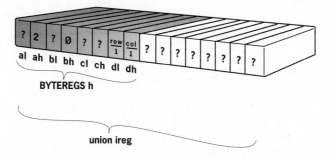

Figure 19.5 shows that the second, fourth, seventh, and eighth bytes of the union **ireg** have been assigned values in the set_cursor() function. The question marks indicate bytes that do not have a known value.

Notice that the last eight bytes in Figure 19.5 are not used at all because the union is using the BYTEREGS structure. If we had placed a WORD-REGS structure in **ireg**, each two-byte pair would represent one of the two-byte CPU registers.

The call

```
int86(VIDEO_INTERRUPT, &ireg, &ireg);
```

is an interrupt call to the int86() interrupt processing function. The symbolic constant VIDEO_INTERRUPT is set to 0x10, which is the MS-DOS interrupt number for all video interrupts. The function number of the interrupt tells which function of the interrupt you want to use. Function 2 is used for cursor positioning. (There are 20 documented functions for the video interrupt.)

The second argument to **int86()** is a pointer to the union that contains the values the compiler will use to load the CPU registers before processing the call to the video interrupt. Because **int86()** expects a pointer to a union, you must use the address-of operator with **ireg**.

The last argument to **int86()** is also a pointer to a REGS union. This union is used to retrieve any register values that might be needed after the interrupt is processed. However, since we do not care about any values returned from the interrupt call, we simply "reuse" the **ireg** union. After all, once the video interrupt is processed, all of the values in **ireg** have already done their work. There is no reason to pass a different union to **int86()**. (Most of the time, you don't care what the registers contain after a video interrupt call.)

After **int86()** has been called, control returns to **main()**. At this point, the cursor in Program 19.8 will be sitting at row 15, column 10. The call to **printf()** then displays a message starting at these screen coordinates. Voilà! You have a cursor-positioning function using interrupts and a union.

Writing Your Own Clear Screen Function

Program 19.9 illustrates another video interrupt function that uses a union.

Actually, Program 19.9 is not a program, but simply a function that you can use in your programs. The **ah** member is set to the video interrupt number. Actually, function 0 of the video interrupt is used to set the video mode (for example, text or graphics) of the display screen. However, as part of that video function, the display screen is also cleared.

It is important to notice that the **al** member is loaded with the video mode being set. The value of 0x03 sets the screen for 80 x 25 color text while 0x02 sets the screen to 80 x 25 monochrome (black and white) text. Use the value that is appropriate for your needs. Once the two members are initialized, the int86() function is called to perform the interrupt.

Interrupt programming on a PC is fascinating. Given the need to load registers with specific values prior to an interrupt call, the union provides a perfect solution to this type of programming.

Program 19.9 **A Clear-Screen Function for Program 19.8**

```
/*****
                                    cls()

    This function clears the display screen

    Argument list:    void

    Return value:    void
*****/

void cls(void)
{
   union REGS ireg;

   ireg.h.ah = 0x00;  /* Video interrupt function # 0 */
   ireg.h.al = 0x03;  /* Color text mode              */

   int86(VIDEO_INTERRUPT, &ireg, &ireg);
}
```

You can also have pointers to union if you need them. You can use the arrow operator just as you did with structures to reference a union member via a pointer. In fact, all of the syntax for a structure applies to the union, with one exception: When you use an initializer list for a union, only one member of the union can be initialized. This makes sense if you think about it. Because a union can only hold one member at a time, trying to initialize more than one member won't work anyway.

You probably won't use unions nearly as often as structures, but they do impart a bit of elegance to certain programming tasks.

Conclusion

In this chapter you learned how to declare, define, and use both structures and unions. Structures provide a means by which you can organize and group your data into useful objects. Kim Brand once called structures "arrays for adults." This is a great way to view structures. Structures provide a way to organize dissimilar data items into one unit.

The union is fairly unique to C. It provides an efficient way to temporarily store information. If C didn't have unions, the alternative would be to define a character buffer and use the cast operator to store and retrieve the data stored in the buffer. Although unions are used less frequently than C's other data types, they are used heavily in interrupt and some types of I/O programming.

Checking Your Progress

1. What is a structure?

A structure is a C data type that allows you to group dissimilar data types into a data structure that can be referenced as a single unit.

2. What is the purpose of a structure tag?

A structure tag is a name given to a structure. Its purpose is to create a reference name for the structure so that it can be used to define a structure variable.

3. What is the purpose of the dot operator?

The dot operator is used to reference a member of a structure. The dot operator always appears between the name of the structure variable and one of its members, as in **mystruct.member_name**.

4. How is indirection accomplished with a pointer to a structure?

Indirection with a structure pointer can be accomplished with two syntactic forms: a parenthesized indirection operator, as in

```
(*mystruct).member
```

or using the arrow operator, as here:

```
mystruct->member
```

Either form can be used for indirection.

5. In Chapter 18, you learned that arrays are not passed to a function, only the lvalue of the array is passed. If you need to pass an entire array to a function, how would you do it? (Assume the array is an **int** array named **data[]** with MAXDATA elements.)

The following code fragment will pass **data[]** to **func1()**:

```
struct {
   int data[MAXDATA];
} mydata;

func1(mydata);
```

The code above copies the mydata structure on the stack and passes it to **func1()**. This means the entire data[] array is passed to the function.

6. What is a union?

A union is a small buffer in memory that is capable of holding different types of data. Only one member of the union can reside in it at any one time. It is the programmer's responsibility to keep track of what is in the union.

7. Explain the following statement:

```
myunion.personal.sex = 'M';
```

The union named **myunion** must have a structure named **personal** that is part of the union. In the personal structure, there is a character field named **sex**. The statement above is assigning the character 'M' into the structure member **sex**.

8. You need to write a program that will allow the user to enter a series of integers into an array. However, the number of integers that will be entered is not known until the program is run. Write a code fragment that shows how you would organize the data to address the problem. Assume the array is **int data[]** and the variable **num** is set to the number of elements needed.

```
struct mydata {
    int num;
    int *data;
};

struct mydata mystruct;

/* After num is set to elements needed... */

mystruct.data = (int *) calloc(mystruct.num,
    sizeof(int));
```

When the statements above have executed, you have an array of **mystruct.num** integers. You can reference the array with

```
mystruct.data[i]
```

as needed. By using a pointer for **data**, you can use **calloc()** to request the desired storage needed and assign the pointer into **mystruct.data**.

20

Miscellaneous Data Types

YOU HAVE ALREADY LEARNED ABOUT MOST OF THE DATA TYPES THAT C provides. This chapter discusses the remaining data types, including **enum**, **typedef**, bit fields, **const**, and **volatile**. Although some of these data types are rarely used, they can be very useful in certain programming situations. The enum, const, and volatile data types are the result of the ANSI standard, and may not be available if you are not using an ANSI-compliant compiler. All compilers should support the typedef and bit field data types.

Using the enum Data Type

The enumerated (enum) data type was added to the C language as part of the ANSI standard. It provides stronger type checking for named constants in C. As you will learn, the enum data type is significantly different from named constants that you might use with the **#define** preprocessor directive.

The general form for the enum data type is

```
enum enum_name {econst1, econst2, ..., econstN};
```

where *enum_name* is the name of the enumeration, and *econst1* through *econstN* represents a list of enumeration constants. It is the enumeration constants that are the named constants for the enum data type. Figure 20.1 shows an example of an enum declaration.

Figure 20.1
An enum declaration

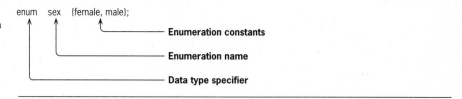

enum sex {female, male};

— Enumeration constants

— Enumeration name

— Data type specifier

The statement in Figure 20.1 declares an enumeration type name **sex**. Like a structure declaration, the enum declaration does not define an enum type. The declaration simply creates a model from which you can create enum variables. The member list of the sex enumeration type consists of two enumeration constants named **female** and **male**. These two enumeration constants are int data types and can have any value that is within the range of an int data type.

Default Values for Enumeration Constants

Unless otherwise stated, the value of the first enumeration constant in an enum member list has the value of 0. The second member in the list has a value of 1. Therefore, the default values for enum constants start with 0 for the first enum constant in the list and increase by 1 for each subsequent enum constant in the list. In Figure 20.1, **female** has a default value of 0 and **male** has a default value of 1.

You can override the default values by assigning values when the **enum** is declared. For example, consider

```
enum speeding {near_city = 55, rural = 65, canada = 62};
```

In this declaration, the speeding enum data type has three members. The enum constant named **near_city** has a value of 55, while **rural** is initialized to 65, and **canada** has the value of 62. These initialized values for the speeding **enum** represent the speed limit for interstate driving and may be used as named constants in your program.

The statement

```
enum speeding {near_city = 55, rural = 65, canada = 62,
other};
```

appends a new enum constant named **other** to the list. **other** is assigned a default value of 63; one greater than the previous enum constant. By default, the current enum constant assumes a value of one greater than the previous constant. (If the constant is the first in the enumerated list of constants, its default value is 0.)

Defining an enum Variable

The statement

```
enum speeding {near_city = 55, rural = 65, canada = 62};
```

only declares an enumeration type named **speeding**; no enum variable has been defined. To define a speeding enumerated variable, you would use

```
enum speeding arrest;
```

This statement creates an enum variable named **arrest** of type **speeding**.

An assignment into an enum variable might resemble the following statement:

```
arrest = near_city;
```

In a strict sense, only values from the enumerated list should be allowed into an enumerated variable. (Alas, as you will soon see, that's not always the case.)

You can omit the enumeration name if the variable is defined as part of the statement. For example, the statement

```
enum {near_city = 55, rural = 65, canada = 62} arrest;
```

defines an enumerated type named **arrest**, but gives no enumeration name. This means that you cannot create any additional variables of this enum type without repeating the entire enumeration list. (Note how the enumeration name is similar in these respects to a structure or union tag.)

Program 20.1 shows an example of an **enum** in a program. It also shows why the enum data type may not live up to your expectations.

The program declares a speeding enumeration type and then defines **arrest** as a variable of this type. The program requests a speed value. The while loop forces the speed to fall within the range of 40 through 65.

The remainder of the program uses the enumerated constants to check the driving speed and display an appropriate message based on the value of **speed**.

The last two statements in the program also show why the enum type is a bit disappointing. Notice that you can assign the value 70 into **arrest** even though that value is inconsistent with the purpose of the **enum**'s use in the program. The enum data type would be more useful for type checking if the enum variable could only assume the values registered in the enumerated list. That is, **arrest** would have strict type checking if the only values it could have are those associated with **min**, **near_city**, **rural**, and **canada**.

The good news is that you cannot change the value of an enumerated constant. For example, the statement

```
near_city = 100;
```

should be flagged as an error by the compiler. This prevents you from changing the value of an enumerated constant once its value is set in the enumeration list.

Comparing enum and #define

You don't seem to gain much by using an **enum** rather than a **#define**. For example, you could modify Program 20.1 to use

```
#define MIN        40
#define NEAR_CITY  55
#define RURAL      65
#define CANADA     62
```

Program 20.1   **Using the enum Data Type**

```
#include <stdio.h>

#include <stdlib.h>
#define BELL       7

int main(void)
{
   char buff[20];
   int speed;

   enum speeding {min = 40, near_city = 55, rural = 65,
      canada = 62};

   enum speeding arrest;
   while (1) {
      printf("\nEnter a speed between 40 and 65: ");
      speed = atoi(gets(buff));
      if (speed > (min - 1) && speed < (rural + 1) ) {
         break;
      } else {
         printf("\n  *** Pay attention to range ***%c\n",
            BELL);
      }
   }
   printf("\n\n");
   if (speed <= near_city) {
      printf("Safe speed for city interstate driving\n");
   } else {
      if (speed > near_city && speed < rural) {
         printf("Speed is safe for ");
         if (speed > canada) {
            printf("US");
         } else {
            printf("US and Canadian");
         }
      } else {
         printf("US only");
      }
      printf(" driving\n");
   }
   arrest = 70;
   printf("\narrest = %d\n", arrest);
}
```

and use these values in the program with the same effect as the enum data type. However, there is one important difference. The enum constants are stored in memory while the program runs, but the symbolic constants disappear after the preprocessor is finished. In other words, the enumerated constants (**min**, **near_city**, and so on) have lvalues and can be used by a debugger.

Symbolic constants created with a **#define** do not have lvalues and cannot be used in variable expressions under the control of a debugger. In this context alone, the enum type has value to the C programmer.

Understanding typedef

A **typedef** allows you to consolidate a complex data declaration into a single word. That is, *a typedef is shorthand for a previously declared data item's attribute list*. For example, suppose you need three integer arrays, each with five elements. Perhaps each of these arrays holds information about three automated machines. Using a **typedef**, you can define the three arrays with the following statements.

```
typedef int MACHINES[5];
MACHINES machine1, machine2, machine3;
```

The attribute list for the MACHINES **typedef** is "an array of five **int**s." (The right-left rule discussed in Chapter 18 shows you how to construct the attribute list.) To determine the attribute list for data items *machine1*, *machine2*, and *machine3*, simply add the attribute list of the **typedef** to the end of the variable name. Therefore, you can say, "the attribute list for *machine1* is an array of five **int**s."

The statement

```
MACHINES machine1, machine2, machine3;
```

is the same as

```
int machine1[5], machine2[5], machine3[5];
```

Notice that the **typedef** does *not* represent a new C data type. (You can always create the same data type without a **typedef**.) Rather, a **typedef** is simply shorthand for the attribute list that a data item can assume. A **typedef** is most often used with fairly long and complex data declarations.

Advantages of Using a typedef

There are three advantages to using a **typedef**. First, it allows you to consolidate complex data types into a single word that you can use in subsequent data definitions. This can help minimize typing mistakes when you use long data definitions frequently in a program.

A second advantage is that you can write the **typedef** in a way that helps to indicate what the data type is or does. For example,

```
typedef char *STRING;
     .
     .
STRING message, prompt;
```

makes it clear that **message** and **prompt** are string data types.

PROGRAMMING TIP. *C programming style conventions call for uppercase letters for **typedefs**. In some ways this is unfortunate, because the reader may assume that the **typedef** is a symbolic constant. If you are unsure whether a **typedef** or **#define** applies to a data item, look near the start of the program and in the #include files to see what the data item is. If you have a debugger, you can use it to display the rvalue and lvalue of the data item in question. If it has an lvalue, it must be a **typedef**.*

Finally, a **typedef** makes it easier to change an attribute list when needed. For example, suppose you create a complex data type and define many variables with that attribute list throughout the program. Later you discover a bug in the attribute list and need to change all of the variable definitions that use that attribute list. If you used a **typedef**, you would only need to change the **typedef**. All of the variables that use the **typedef** would automatically be changed when you recompiled the program.

typedefs versus #define

This last advantage—being able to easily change an attribute list—also applies to a **#define**. There is a difference between a **typedef** and a **#define**, however. Consider the following code fragment:

```
#define STRING    char *

STRING message, prompt;
```

When the preprocessor finishes, the source code appears as

```
char *message, prompt;
```

Notice that **message** does get the proper attribute list, but **prompt** does not. **prompt** has an attribute list of **char**, not pointer to **char**. A **typedef** represents an attribute list; a **#define** does not.

In Chapter 21 you will learn about a **typedef** named **FILE** that is used with almost all programs that use disk files. If you program under the Microsoft Windows operating system, you will find that virtually every data item is a **typedef**.

Type Qualifiers: const and volatile

The ANSI standard added the keywords **const** and **volatile** to the C language. You can add these two type qualifiers to a normal data definition to change the attribute list of the data item. They are called type qualifiers because they appear before a data item's type specifier.

Using the const Type Qualifier

The const type qualifier indicates that the item cannot be changed once it is defined. For example,

```
const int port = 0x380;
```

creates a variable named **port** whose value cannot be changed from its initial defined value of 0x380. This means that a statement like

```
port = newport;
```

is illegal because port has been defined as a variable with the const attribute. In essence, the const keyword creates a read-only type of variable.

If you use the const type qualifier without a type specifier, as in

```
const port;
```

the type specifier for **port** defaults to **int**. Note that this kind of definition for **port** is not very useful since it contains an unknown value that cannot be changed by the program. It follows that a const definition for local data must have an initializer list if it is to be useful in the program.

Upon seeing the const keyword in a data definition, the compiler makes a special mark in the symbol table noting that this variable has an unchangeable rvalue. As such, it cannot be used as the left expression in an assignment statement.

Although you may not have realized it, you have used const variables in several programs already. For example, if you look at the documentation for **strcpy()**, you will see it declared as

```
char *strcpy(char *dest, const char *source);
```

This declaration says that the string (**source**) to be copied into **dest** cannot be changed by **strcpy()**. Many of the standard library string-processing functions use the const type qualifier. It ensures the integrity of a variable throughout the program.

You should use Program 20.2 to check how strict your compiler is about the const keyword.

Program 20.2   **Checking const for Your Compiler**

```
#include <stdio.h>

int main(void)
{
   const int port = 0x380;
   int *iptr;

   port = 0x300;

   iptr = &port;

}
```

The two statements

```
   port = 0x300;

   iptr = &port;
```

are both illegal. The first statement attempts to change the const value of **port** by direct assignment. The second statement is an attempt to sneak up on **port** so it can be changed by process of indirection. Some compilers flag these statements with warning messages and others flag them as errors.

Try this short program to see how your compiler reacts to these two statements. If you don't at least get warning messages from the compiler, you should note this fact if you use the const type qualifier. Even though it may do no good right now, it might prove useful later if you switch to another compiler.

Using the volatile Type Qualifier

The volatile qualifier says that the variable being defined has an rvalue that may be controlled by something outside of the program. For example, a variable might be fed data from a serial port that causes some special form of

interrupt processing. In such cases, the variable might be changed by factors that are not obvious by looking at the program source code.

The definition statement

```
volatile int interrupt_vector;
```

tells the compiler that any statement that uses the variable named **interrupt_vector** should not be optimized in any way that might alter a reference to this variable. For example, suppose you have code similar to this:

```
for (i = 0; i < MAXITERS; i++) {
    pulse = interrupt_vector;
    value = pulse * data[i];
}
```

An optimizing compiler might look at the for loop and reorganize it for its own use during compilation. Because **interrupt_vector** is never assigned a new value in the for loop, the compiler might optimize the code so it *appears* as though the source code were written like this:

```
pulse = interrupt_vector;

for (i = 0; i < MAXITERS; i++) {
    value = pulse * data[i];
}
```

However, the value of **interrupt_vector** may be controlled by forces that the compiler cannot discern simply by reading the code. Using the volatile type qualifier in the definition of **interrupt_vector** tells the compiler: "I know you are clever, but don't optimize or otherwise alter the way I've written any line of code that references this variable." The volatile qualifier is most often used in systems programming or for interfacing to external devices.

Using Bit Fields

C was originally designed so that it could be used in systems programming. C's creators wanted to be able to write an operating system that could be moved from one computing environment to another with a minimum of re-writing. Because of that original design objective, bit fields have always been part of the C language.

In systems programming, it is desirable to store information in as little memory as possible. Bit fields allow programmers to pack information into less memory than the compiler would normally require. If you have assembly language programming experience, you already know about such byte packing.

The syntax for a bit field is similar to that for a structure, except each member of the bit field is defined for a specific number of bits. For example, the definition

```
struct flags {
  unsigned int flag1 : 1;
  unsigned int flag2 : 3;
  unsigned int flag3 : 4;
} status;
```

defines a variable named **status** with three bit fields. The first bit field (**flag1**) is defined to use a single bit. The second bit field (**flag2**) is defined with three bits, and the last bit field (**flag3**) has four bits. Because the first bit field uses a single bit, it can only assume the values 0 or 1. **flag2** can have any value within the range 0 through 7 because it is defined with three bits. **flag3** can have any value from 0 through 15.

Notice that *the syntax for each bit field is the type specifier, followed by a colon, followed by the number of bits assigned to this bit field.* The valid type specifier originally was limited to **unsigned**, but ANSI now permits **unsigned int**, **signed int**, or **int**.

Program 20.3 illustrates how your compiler actually stores the bit fields. When I ran Program 20.3, the output was

```
sizeof status = 1

flag1 = 0 flag2 = 3 flag3 = 5
```

(The output of the program may be different for your compiler.) That the size of **status** is 1 indicates that all three bit fields were stored in a single byte of memory. If you add up the bit requirements for all three bit fields, you'll find that a total of eight bits are needed for **status**. If you increase the number of bits for any field and recompile the program, the size of **status** will increase.

In addition, notice that the output for **flag1** is zero. We assigned it a value that is greater than can be stored in a single bit. The compiler is not required to warn you if you attempt to assign a value too large to fit in the bit field.

PROGRAMMING TIP. *If you try to assign a value into a bit field with too few bits, the behavior of the bit field is* implementation defined. *This is a polite way of saying that ANSI did not specify the rules for such behavior and anything can happen to your data.*

The alternative to using bit fields is to use a **char** or **int** for the equivalent of each bit field. The advantage of the bit fields is that they permit you to store the same information in less memory.

Program 20.3   **Using Bit Fields**

```c
#include <stdio.h>

int main(void)
{
    struct {
        int flag1 : 1;
        int flag2 : 3;
        int flag3 : 4;
    } status;

    printf("\nsizeof status = %d\n", sizeof(status));

    status.flag1 = 2;
    status.flag2 = 3;
    status.flag3 = 5;

    printf("\n\nflag1 = %d flag2 = %d flag3 = %d",
        status.flag1, status.flag2, status.flag3);

}
```

The actual limit to the size of a bit field, what happens if the size is exceeded, and how a bit field is stored in memory are all implementation defined parameters. You will need to consult your compiler's documentation to answer these questions.

Conclusion

This chapter discussed several new type qualifiers and data types. You will probably use the **typedef** most often. The next chapter introduces the **FILE typedef**, which is an integral part of virtually all disk file programming. In fact, you should think about using a **typedef** almost any time you write a **#define**. A **typedef** may be a better way of creating the symbolic constant.

The const modifier is used frequently in the definition of library functions. You will find **const** used often to define function arguments, but rarely to define auto variables within the function body.

Bit fields and **volatile** are infrequently used in applications programming. They are more often used in systems programming or specialized programming (for example, embedded systems) where communication with an external device is necessary.

Checking Your Progress

1. What is an enum data type?

An enum data type is a variable whose value should be restricted to the values in the enumerated list. Unfortunately, most compilers allow you to assign any value into the enumerated value that is consistent with the **enum**'s underlying data type (the default is usually **int**).

2. What is a major advantage of using an **enum** versus a **#define**?

Enumerated types are true variables. As such, they have both lvalues and rvalues. Symbolic constants do not have lvalues; they are not variables that exist in memory when the program is run. Rather, symbolic constants are used by the preprocessor to create pure constants for the compiler. Therefore, enumerated data types can be used with a debugger because they have an lvalue that can be tracked by the debugger. Most debuggers cannot track a symbolic constant.

3. What is a **typedef** and when is it normally used?

A **typedef** is a shorthand form of an attribute list. The **typedef** is often used for complex data definitions. A **typedef** is generally written in uppercase and has a descriptive name (for example, the STRING **typedef** discussed in the text).

4. What does the const type qualifier mean?

If a data item is defined with the const type qualifier, its rvalue is constant during program execution. This permits the compiler to monitor any attempt to change its value and flag any statement that attempts such a change.

5. Explain the volatile type qualifier.

Today's optimizing compilers often rearrange the code you've written to exact the greatest performance possible. Compilers often let you decide whether to optimize for speed, size, or both. During optimization, the compiler may actually change your source code to meet the selected optimizing goal.

The volatile keyword tells the compiler to leave all statements that reference a volatile variable as they are written, preventing the compiler from altering the code.

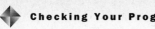

6. What is a bit field and when might it be used?

A bit field is a way of packing data into a smaller amount of storage than the compiler would otherwise allocate. If memory is at a premium (as in an electronic watch with only one pico acre of space), bit fields provide an efficient way to store data.

Each bit field is defined to use only as many bits as it needs to store its information. Multiple bit fields can thus be stored in a single byte of memory.

21

High-Level File I/O

C PROVIDES FOR BOTH HIGH- AND LOW-LEVEL FILE INPUT AND OUTPUT (I/O). High-level and low-level file I/O are very similar, but low-level file I/O is often performed as direct calls to the operating system. The topics in this chapter include creating, reading, and writing disk files using high-level functions. (Low-level file I/O is covered in Chapter 22.)

We start our discussion of disk files with high-level file I/O because the ANSI standard library supports only those functions. You can do just about anything you wish with the high-level file functions. Indeed, the only reason the low-level file operations are discussed at all is because there is so much pre-ANSI C code that uses them.

Understanding I/O Streams

Books and magazine articles on C programming frequently talk about I/O streams. Simply stated, *an I/O stream refers to a collection of data that can be written to or read from an I/O device*. Streams come in two flavors: text and binary.

A text stream is simply a sequence of text characters (often ASCII) grouped into lines. Each line consists of zero or more characters terminated by a newline ('\n') character. A text stream may have zero or more lines in the stream.

A binary stream is a sequence of "raw" data. That is, it does not have to be represented in the host character set (for example, ASCII). A binary stream might represent hexadecimal numbers, floating-point numbers in either BCD (Binary Coded Decimal) or IEEE format, or any other form that might be useful. A binary stream may contain ASCII data in text form as well as binary data.

Opening a Disk File

Before you can do anything with a stream, you must open a disk file that is to be used with the stream. When you open a disk file, your program and the disk operating system must share certain information about the file. That is, certain overhead information about each file must be available before a program can access the file.

The FILE Structure

The overhead information about a disk file is stored in a structure. The declaration of this structure is found in the stdio.h header file supplied with your compiler. If you load your stdio.h header file into your text editor, you should find something very similar to that shown in Figure 21.1.

Figure 21.1
The FILE structure

```
#define OPEN_MAX     10

struct _buffer {
    int _fd;         /* A file descriptor          */
    int _left;       /* Characters left in the buffer */
    int _mode;       /* How you will use the file  */
    char *_nextc;    /* Next character location     */
    char *_buff;     /* Base of file buffer         */
};

typedef struct _buffer FILE;
extern FILE __iob[OPEN_MAX];
```

The FILE structure defined in Figure 21.1 contains all of the overhead information necessary for your program to communicate with the operating system. Because each disk file that might be used needs its own FILE structure, stdio.h normally defines an array of these structures.

Each FILE structure contains the information shown in Figure 21.1, although some compilers may maintain additional information. The member named **_fd** is called a file descriptor. This is an integer number that is returned from the operating system that references the file with which this structure is associated.

The member named **_left** is a count of the characters left in the file's I/O buffer. Rather than read or write one character from or to the disk at a time, the characters are stored in a buffer in memory. If a buffer was not used, your program would constantly be turning the disk drive on and off (a process sometimes called "thrashing the disk"). Using a buffer minimizes disk thrashing during file I/O operations.

The **_mode** member tells the operating system the mode in which the file will be used. The most common file modes are read and write, but other modes exist. (You will learn about the different modes later in this chapter.)

The next two members, **_nextc** and **_buff**, are character pointers that reference the buffer that prevents disk thrashing. The member **_buff** always points to the starting lvalue of the buffer. The member **_nextc** moves through the buffer, always pointing to the next character position to be used.

On a write operation, when all of the characters have been read from the buffer, **_nextc** points to the end of the buffer and **_left** will equal 0. When the buffer is refilled with data, **_left** once again will contain a count of the characters in the buffer and **_nextc** will point to the start of the buffer. (Do you think that **_nextc** and **_buff** point to the same memory location when the buffer is filled? Yes, they do.)

PROGRAMMING TIP. *Notice how the members of the structure and the FILE definition use variable names that begin with a leading underscore. The compiler vendor does this to prevent any definitions in stdio.h from colliding with any data you might define in your programs. We mentioned this variable naming convention in Chapter 4. This also illustrates why you must be careful when using the leading underscore when you define your own variables.*

As you can see, the FILE structure contains all of the information necessary for your program and the operating system to work with disk data files. The best part is that almost all of these details are hidden from you. You don't need to worry about the actual values of the members in the FILE structure. Figure 21.1 uses the symbolic constant OPEN_MAX to set the number of elements to 10. The actual number of FILE elements defined for your system may vary from that shown in Figure 21.1. (The number set in your stdio.h header file might be set by constraints of the compiler or the operating system.) This symbolic constant is important because it determines the maximum number of files that can be open at one time in the program.

Predefined FILE Structures

Every C program automatically opens at least three, and more often four, streams. If you look further in your stdio.h header file, you will probably find something similar to this code:

```
#define stdin    (&_iob[0])
#define stdout   (&_iob[1])
#define stderr   (&_iob[2])
#define stdprn   (&_iob[3])
```

The first **#define** says that one of the FILE structures is dedicated to an I/O stream named **stdin**. This stream is normally dedicated to the standard input device (hence, **stdin**). For most programs, this is the keyboard. The second I/O stream is dedicated to the standard output device (**stdout**). Usually, this is the display screen. The third I/O stream is the standard output error device (**stderr**). Normally, this is also the display screen. The fourth I/O stream is the standard printing device (**stdprn**). This is usually the system's printer. (Some compilers may use the name **stdlst** instead of **stdprn**.)

It is important for you to understand that these three or four standard output devices are opened automatically for you for every C program. It also follows that the maximum number of files your program can actually use is OPEN_MAX minus the number of standard output devices. For example, if OPEN_MAX is 10 and your compiler opens four standard devices, your programs can have only six files open at the same time.

For most programs, six open files is more than adequate because you can open, close, and reopen files as often as you need. Also, today's modern computer systems with 640k or more of memory set OPEN_MAX to a number greater than 10 (15 or 20 is common).

PROGRAMMING TIP. *If your program opens a lot of files and you start getting disk file errors, you may be exceeding the limit imposed by OPEN_MAX. If you suspect this is the source of the problem, consult your compiler documentation to see if you can increase the value of OPEN_MAX. If OPEN_MAX can be increased, make sure the operating system documentation also permits a higher number of open files. If you use MS-DOS, you may also need to adjust the files and buffer statements in the CONFIG.SYS file.*

Using the fopen() Standard Library Function

The standard library function **fopen()** can be used to open a disk file. The function declaration for **fopen()** is

```
FILE *fopen(char *filename, char *mode);
```

The fopen() function returns a pointer to a FILE structure. When you call **fopen()**, two processes occur. First, **fopen()** communicates with the operating system to fill in an empty FILE structure. Having done that, it returns a FILE pointer to your program.

The FILE pointer returned from **fopen()** becomes the communications link between your program and the operating system. Therefore, you need to define a FILE pointer for use in your program. The statement

```
FILE *fpin;
```

defines a FILE pointer named **fpin** (input file pointer).

The first argument to the function is the name of the file you wish to open. The second argument to **fopen()** is the mode in which you wish to open the file. The permissible modes are presented in Table 21.1.

The first thing to notice is that all of the modes passed to **fopen()** are character strings, not character constants. As Table 21.1 suggests, there are four basic mode strings. These strings are: "r" for reading a file, "w" for writing to a file, "a" for appending to a file, and "+" for updating a file. By default, the file is assumed to be a text file. If you wish to work with a binary file, a "b" must be part of the mode string.

PROGRAMMING TIP. *Most of the fopen() modes are fairly benign, but "w" is not. Most of the entries in Table 21.1 that use the "w" mode have the ability to truncate a file to zero length. This is a polite way of saying that anything that was in the file is lost. You should only use the "w" by itself when you are sure no file by the name specified already exists.*

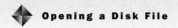

Table 21.1   High-Level Modes for fopen()

Mode	Interpretation
"r"	Open for reading.
"w"	Truncate to zero length, or create for writing.
"a"	Open for writing at the end of the file or, if the file does not exist, create for writing.
"r+"	Open existing file for reading-writing.
"w+"	Truncate to zero length or create for updating.
"a+"	Open for appending or (create and) open for updating at the end of file.
"rb"	Open binary file for reading.
"wb"	Create and open binary file for writing.
"ab"	Open binary file for writing at the end of the file or, if the file does not exist, create from writing.
"rb+"	Open existing binary file for reading and writing.
"wb+"	Create and open binary file for updating.
"ab+"	Open binary file for appending or (create and) open for updating at the end of file.

Let's assume that you wish to open a text file for reading. Let's further assume the file is named TEST.TXT. The following statement attempts to open the text file name TEST.TXT for reading:

```
fpin = fopen("test.txt", "r");
```

In this example, we have used a string constant for the file name. The file name can also be a variable, as shown in the following code fragment:

```
char filename[20];

printf("Enter the file name to open: ");
gets(filename);
fpin = fopen(filename, "r");
```

You could also change the second argument to **fopen()** (the file mode) to a variable, but most C programmers seem to prefer using a string constant.

Coping with fopen() Errors

Just because you call **fopen()** doesn't mean the file can be opened. All kinds of things can go wrong. The disk might be full, the drive door might be open, or there might be bubble gum on the read-write head. Because things can go wrong, you need to check and verify that the file was opened successfully.

The following code fragment shows how you can check to see if the file was opened without any errors:

```
if ( (fpin = fopen("test.txt", "r")) == NULL) {
    printf("Could not open the file\n");
    exit(EXIT_FAILURE);
}
```

The call to **fopen()** returns a FILE pointer that is assigned into **fpin**. A **#define** for a null pointer (NULL) is in the stdio.h header file. In Chapter 17 you learned that a null pointer is guaranteed not to point to anything useful. Therefore, if **fpin** equals the NULL pointer, something went wrong and the file was not opened succcessfully. If **fpin** is NULL, the code fragment above tells the user the file couldn't be opened and the call to **exit()** performs a graceful shutdown of the program. (The symbolic constant named EXIT_-FAILURE is found in the stdlib.h header file.)

*You should always test the pointer returned from **fopen()** to see if the file was opened successfully.* What you do after sensing a null pointer is up to you. You might simply shut the program down as was done in the code fragment, or you could try to continue with some other aspect of the program. The choice depends on the program. One thing is certain, however, and that is that you can't do anything with the file that you tried, but failed, to open.

If **fpin** does not contain the NULL pointer, you can assume the file was opened successfully.

Reading a Disk File

Now that the file is opened successfully, you can read the data in the file. There are several different ways to read the data in the file. We will use the fgetc() function to read the file one character at a time. The function declaration for **fgetc()** is

```
int fgetc(FILE *fpin);
```

The only argument to fgetc() is the FILE pointer that was obtained during the **fopen()** call, or **fpin** in our example. (See how the FILE pointer becomes your communications link to the file.)

The value returned from **fgetc()** is an **int**, even though only one byte is read from the file. The reason for making the return value an **int** is so **fgetc()**

can return an end-of-file marker after all of the data has been read from the file. The end-of-file marker is represented by the symbolic constant EOF and is defined in the stdio.h header file. Usually, EOF is defined with the value of -1, but it is not required to be that value. Because the preprocessor translates EOF to an **int** value, the check of **c** against EOF does not need to have a cast.

Program 21.1 presents a program that will read and display an ASCII text file on the screen.

Program 21.1   **Reading and Displaying an ASCII Text File**

```c
#include <stdio.h>
#include <string.h>
#include <stdlib.h>

void main(void)
{
    char filename[20];
    int c;
    FILE *fpin;

    printf("Enter the file name of the file to read: ");
    gets(filename);

    if ((fpin = fopen(filename, "r")) == NULL) {
        printf("\nCould not open %s. Abort.\n", filename);
        exit(EXIT_FAILURE);
    }

    while ( (c = fgetc(fpin)) != EOF) {
        putchar(c);
    }
    fclose(fpin);
}
```

Let's assume you write the program with your text editor and save it as fileread.c. After you compile and run the program, it first asks you to enter the name of the file to be read. Type in **fileread.c**. The program calls **fopen()** with the file name equal to "fileread.c" and attempts to open the file in the read mode.

If you supply a file name that does not exist, the error message is displayed and the program ends. This happens because **fpin** equals the NULL pointer.

If you supply a file name that does exist, program control begins to execute the while loop. The first call to **fgetc()** retrieves the first character from the file and assigns it into **c**. Next, the program checks to see if **c** equals the EOF marker. If not, the call to **putchar()** displays the character on the screen. Program control then returns for another call to **fgetc()**. The while loop continues to read and display characters until **c** returns the EOF marker.

PROGRAMMING TIP. *It seems strange for fgetc() to return an **int** when you are reading characters from the file. Intuition tells you that the return value should be a **char**. Perhaps, but* always *assign the return value from* **fgetc()** *into an **int** variable. If you use a **char**, it is possible that the variable cannot sense a negative value. This would put the program into an infinite loop.*

Closing a Disk File

After all characters have been read from the file, **c** equals the EOF marker. This makes the while test on **c** logic False, and the while loop ends. The program then executes the statement

```
fclose(fpin);
```

which closes the file. The argument to **fclose()** is the FILE pointer, **fpin**. The call to **fclose()** tells the operating system that we are finished using this file and it is okay to close it. The actual code in **fclose()** will vary according to the requirements of the operating system. The important thing to remember is that once you call **fclose()**, **fpin** no longer points to a valid FILE structure. If you wish to use the file again, you must call **fopen()** to reinitialize **fpin** to point to a valid FILE structure.

The good news is that once you close a file, you can reuse **fpin** to open a different file if you wish. Therefore, even though you are restricted to a limited number of open files (by OPEN_MAX), you can open and close as many files as you need during the course of the program's execution. Just remember to call the fopen() and fclose() functions each time you wish to work with a new file.

Reading Text Files One Line at a Time

The performance of Program 21.1 is not too bad even though we are reading the file one character at a time. Let's modify Program 21.1 so that we can read the file one line at a time instead of character by character. Before you can do this, though, you need to understand how **fgets()** works.

The fgets() standard library function is used to read a text file line by line. The function declaration for **fgets()** is

```
char *fgets(char *buffer, int max_num, FILE *fpin);
```

The first argument (**buffer**) is the location where the data read from disk is stored. This must be a pointer so the function receives the lvalue of where it should put the data.

The second argument (**max_num**) is the maximum number of characters to be read, minus one. **fgets()** reads characters from the file until either **max_num - 1** characters are read or a newline character is read, whichever comes first. As you probably guessed, the "minus one" is used to store the null termination character that **fgets()** appends to the line just read. This allows you to treat **buffer** as a string. The last argument is the FILE pointer that was used to open the file. As always, the file must be opened successfully before the file can be read. (This also means that **fpin** cannot be a NULL pointer.)

The value returned by **fgets()** is a pointer to the characters just read. In other words, if the file is read successfully, you get back the same character pointer you passed to **fgets()**. The return value, therefore, should be equal to the lvalue of **buffer**. After all characters have been read from the file, **fgets()** returns the NULL pointer.

Now that you understand how **fgets()** works, let's revise Program 21.1 so you can read the text file one line at a time. The changes are quite simple. First, place this **#define** just before the main() function:

```
#define MAXSTRING    128
```

There is nothing fixed about this number, but very few text files have lines longer than this. You could also set it to 80 if you wish.

Inside **main()** you need to define a buffer to hold the line of characters that is read from the disk. Add the following line near the top of **main()**:

```
char buffer[MAXSTRING];
```

This definition allows us to read up to 127 characters from the file, with the remaining byte used for the null termination character.

Finally, you should modify the while loop to use the fgets() function shown in this code fragment:

```
while (fgets(buffer, MAXSTRING, fpin) != NULL) {
   printf("%s", buffer);
}
```

The rest of the program code need not be changed. Notice that the test for the end of file has been changed from EOF to NULL. As long as **fgets()** continues to read valid data from the file, it returns a pointer to **buffer**. After all characters are read, **fgets()** returns a null pointer and the while loop ends. Because **buffer** is null terminated, **printf()** is used to display the data instead of the putchar() call in Program 21.1.

Reading Files in Convenient Chunks

Sometimes you will want to read a file where character and lines don't make sense. For example, if a file contains binary floating-point numbers, reading characters or lines probably won't work at all. In these situations, you need a way to read the data in a form that is convenient for the task at hand. The fread() function can be used for such tasks.

The function declaration for **fread()** is

```
size_t fread(char *buff, size_t big, size_t num, FILE
    *fpin);
```

where **buff** is a pointer to where the data is to be read, **big** is the size of the item to be read, **num** is the number of items to be read, and **fpin** is the FILE pointer for the file to be read.

The return value is a count of the number of items that should be read. The size_t type specifier is a standard **typedef** contained in stdio.h. **size_t** is usually an **unsigned int**. If the read is successful, the value returned from **fread()** equals **num**. If the return value and **num** are equal, you know you read what you tried to read. If the return value is EOF or 0, an error occurred.

Suppose you want to read a series of **double** data types from a file. Assuming you opened the file for binary reading, the following code fragment shows how to read the file:

```
int got_back;
double x;

while ( (got_back = fread(&x, sizeof(double), 1, fpin)) !=
    0) {
    printf("%f ", x);
}
```

The code reads the file one **double** at a time, using **x** as the place to store the **double**. Think about what this means. The fread() call says you want to read one **double** (eight bytes) from **fpin**. The second argument tells **fread()** the size (in bytes) that you wish to read. Because you want to read a **double**, why not just use a **double** as the storage place? After all, **x** is eight bytes long and we are only reading one **double** at a time. Using **&x** as the first argument to **fread()** ends up passing an eight-byte "buffer space" to **fread()**—a perfect fit for the **double**!

You could, of course, use a larger buffer if you wish but the program works fairly efficiently without increasing the buffer size. If you're not happy with the performance, try increasing the size of the first and third arguments. It may make a small difference in performance.

PROGRAMMING TIP. *There is a close relationship between the first, third, and return values when using **fread()**. Some beginning programmers think you can increase the number of items read (the third argument) without increasing the size of the space used to store the data. This won't work and can lead to unpredictable results. Also, the return value is the number of items read, not the number of bytes. The value returned from **fread()** should equal the number of items read unless there is an error or end of file is read.*

Reading and Writing a Data File: A Sample Program

Let's write a program that generates a series of random numbers and writes them to a disk file. Let's also have the program reopen the file and display the numbers that were written. Program 21.2 presents the program code.

Getting Ready to Write the Data

Program 21.2 begins with several function declarations for the function in the program followed by two global FILE pointer definitions. Because most of the functions used in the program need access to these FILE pointers, we decided to make them globals.

Notice how **main()** is little more than a series of function calls. This is the way a **main()** should look. **get_filename()** gets a file name from the user and attempts to open the file for writing. If the file cannot be opened, an error message is displayed and the program aborts. Otherwise, **fpout** is assigned a FILE pointer by the fopen() call.

Notice that the program uses the "wb" mode for opening the file. This is done because the data that you are about to write consists of binary values. Be sure that you open a file with the correct mode argument.

The write_random() function simply writes a series of random integers to the file just opened. In the statements

```
if ( (fwrite(&val, sizeof(int), 1, fpout)) == 0) {
    printf("Disk write error");
    exit(EXIT_FAILURE);
}
```

each call to **fwrite()** writes one random integer to the file. If the write fails, an error message is displayed and the program aborts. Note how the address-of operator is used in the call to **fwrite()**. The code treats **val** as though it were a small two-byte buffer from which the data is written to the disk file. After MAXVALS random integers are written, the file is closed and control returns to **main()**.

Program 21.2   **Reading and Writing a Data File**

```c
#include <stdio.h>
#include <stdlib.h>

#define MAXVALS   100

void get_filename(char *filename),
     open_file(char *filename),
     read_random(void),
     write_random(void);

FILE *fpin, *fpout;

int main(void)
{
   char filename[20];

   get_filename(filename);
   write_random();

   printf("\n\nData written. Press any key:\n");
   getch();

   open_file(filename);
   read_random();

}

void get_filename(char *filename)
{
   printf("Enter the file name of the file to write: ");
   gets(filename);

   if ((fpout = fopen(filename, "wb")) == NULL) {
      printf("\nCould not open %s. Abort.\n", filename);
      exit(EXIT_FAILURE);
   }
}
```

Program 21.2   **continued**

```c
void write_random(void)
{
    int i, val;

    for (i = Ø; i < MAXVALS; i++) {
        val = rand();
        if ( (fwrite(&val, sizeof(int), 1, fpout)) == Ø) {
            printf("Disk write error");
            exit(EXIT_FAILURE);
        }
    }
    fclose(fpout);
}


void open_file(char *filename)
{
    if ((fpin = fopen(filename, "rb")) == NULL) {
        printf("\nCould not open %s. Abort.\n", filename);
        exit(EXIT_FAILURE);
    }
}


void read_random(void)
{
    int i, val;

    for (i = Ø; i < MAXVALS; i++) {
        if (i % 1Ø == Ø)
            printf("\n");
        if ( (fread(&val, sizeof(int), 1, fpin)) == Ø) {
            printf("Disk write error");
            exit(EXIT_FAILURE);
        }
        printf("%6d ", val);

    }
    printf("\n\n");
    fclose(fpin);
}
```

COMMON TRAP. *Don't forget to close a disk file when you are finished writing to it. If you don't close the file, there is no guarantee that the data will be written to disk.*

Reading the Data

The open_file() function is used to reopen the disk file that was just written. If the file is opened successfully, **fpin** contains a valid FILE pointer. If the file cannot be opened, an error message is displayed. The mode argument used to open the file is the "rb" mode. This tells the compiler that you want to read binary data from the file.

The final function call simply displays the MAXVALS random integers on the screen. As always, you should close the file when you are finished with it. If there had been additional function calls in the program that needed to use the file, you can leave the file open. However, when you have finished with the file, you should close it immediately.

PROGRAMMING TIP. *The reason for closing a file as soon as you are finished with it is because **fclose()** tidies up things for you. For example, when your program is writing data to a disk file, it may or may not be actually transferring the data to disk. To minimize disk thrashing, your program is actually writing to the buffer shown in Figure 21.1. Only when the buffer is filled does the data actually get transferred to disk. If the buffer is not filled, **fclose()** "flushes the buffer" contents to disk. (You can use **fflush()** to force a disk flush.) This process doesn't work well if the buffer is half filled and, before you can close the file, someone kicks the power plug out of the socket. Don't leave open files hanging around—close them.*

Writing to the Printer

Some programming tasks require that program output be sent to the printer rather than the screen or a disk file. As you will see in this section, you can use the high-level file routines to direct output to the printer as well as to disk files.

The PRN File in MS-DOS

Microsoft's disk operating system has a predefined file named PRN. This file is logically connected to the system's printer and provides a means of communication with the printer. If you are using some other operating system, check its documentation for the logical file name for the printer.

When you wish to direct output to the printer, you still need a FILE pointer to the logical PRN file. If the printer is opened successfully, you can write to it just as though it were a file. Program 21.3 shows you how to do this.

Program 21.3   **Writing to the Printer**

```c
#include <stdio.h>
#include <stdlib.h>

#define MAXSTRING 80

FILE *fpout;

int main(void)
{
    char buff[MAXSTRING + 1];
    int len;

    printf("\nEnter a maximum of %d characters: ",
        MAXSTRING);
    gets(buff);
    len = strlen(buff);

    if ((fpout = fopen("prn", "w")) == NULL) {
        printf("Can't open printer");
        exit(EXIT_FAILURE);
    }
    fwrite(buff, sizeof(char), len, fpout);
    fclose(fpout);
}
```

Everything in Program 21.3 should look familiar. The only new element in the program is the call to **fopen()** using "prn" as the file name. If the printer is opened successfully, the call to **fwrite()** writes the contents of **buff[]** to the printer.

Errors can occur when opening the printer. For example, the printer could be off-line, out of paper, or be experiencing some hardware difficulty. Therefore, you still need to check that the FILE pointer returned from **fopen()** is not the NULL pointer.

PROGRAMMING TIP. *Some operating systems create an additional standard output device named* **stdaux.** *This is the auxiliary output device. Sometimes* **stdaux** *is connected to a serial printer while* **stdprn** *is connected to a parallel printer. If you are having trouble printing with your programs, check your compiler and operating system documentation to see if* **stdaux** *might be the active printer device.*

Writing Formatted Output to the Printer

You may need to write the output to the printer in some specific format. Perhaps it's a column of numbers or equally spaced strings. When you need to write formatted output to the printer, you have several options available. Let's modify Program 21.3 so we can use formatted output. See Program 21.4.

Program 21.4   **Writing Formatted Output to the Printer**

```c
#include <stdio.h>
#include <stdlib.h>

#define MAXSTRING 80

FILE *fpout;

int main(void)
{
   char buff[MAXSTRING + 1];
   int i, len, val;

   if ((fpout = fopen("prn", "w")) == NULL) {
      printf("Can't open printer");
      exit(EXIT_FAILURE);
   }
   for (i = 0; i < 10; i++) {
      val = rand();
      len = sprintf(buff, "\npass %d: val = %d", i, val);
      fwrite(buff, sizeof(char), len, fpout);
   }
   fclose(fpout);
}
```

Program 21.4 writes a series of ten random numbers to the printer. A slight complication is that the length of each number is unknown because the numbers are different. The **sprintf()** function is virtually identical to **printf()**, except the output is written to a character array rather than the screen. The return value from **sprintf()** is the number of characters that were written to the screen. This is exactly the information we need to use **fwrite()**.

The program calls **sprintf()** with the appropriate conversion characters in the string of its second argument. Instead of the output going to the screen, however, it is sent to **buff[]**. The number of characters written to **buff[]** is assigned into **len**. The call to **fwrite()** then writes the contents of **buff[]** to the printer.

One More Formatted Printer Output Option

There is yet another way that you can write formatted output to the printer. Replace the statements

```
len = sprintf(buff, "\npass %d: val = %d", i, val);
fwrite(buff, sizeof(char), len, fpout);
```

in Program 21.4 with

```
fprintf(fpout, "\npass %d: val = %d", i, val);
```

The fprintf() function is used to produced formatted output to a file (FILE **printf()**). The only difference between **fprintf()** and **printf()** is that its first argument is the FILE pointer to the output device being written to. The program will function exactly as it did before, but uses one less statement and you could do away with **buff[]**.

As a final change to Program 21.4, add the statement

```
fprintf(fpout, "\f");
```

just before the call to **fclose()**. This statement uses **fprintf()** to send an escape sequence called the *vertical form feed* to the printer. When this escape sequence is written to the printer, it causes the current page being printed to be ejected from the printer. If you do not use the vertical form feed, the page in the printer is not ejected until the printed page is filled. The vertical form feed allows you to eject a page before it is filled.

Command Line Arguments

Many utilities provided with your computer's operating system require that information be entered at the command line. For example, to copy one file to another file, the COPY command must be followed by the input and output file names. The two file names that follow the COPY command are called *command line arguments*. Command line arguments provide a means by which information can be passed to a program before it starts executing.

Let's write our own COPY command, but use command line arguments rather than prompting for the file names after the program starts executing. See Program 21.5.

Program 21.5　**A Copy Program Using Command Line Arguments**

```c
#include <stdio.h>
#include <stdlib.h>

void check_args(int argc),      /* Function declarations */
     check_name(char *argv[]),
     do_copy(void),
     do_open(char *argv[]);

FILE *fpin, *fpout;

int main(int argc, char *argv[])
{
   char buff[MAXSTRING + 1];
   int i, len, val;

   check_args(argc),       /* Correct number of arguments? */
   check_name(argv),       /* Proper file names?           */
   do_open(argv),          /* Can we open them?            */
   do_copy(),              /* If so, do copy               */

   printf("\nCopy completed\n\n");
}

void do_copy(void)
{
   int c;

   while ( (c = fgetc(fpin)) != EOF) {
      fputc(c, fpout);
   }
   fclose(fpin);
   fclose(fpout);
}
```

Program 21.5   continued

```
void do_open(char *argv[])
{
   if ((fpin = fopen(argv[1], "rb")) == NULL) {
      printf("Can't open input file %s", argv[1]);
      exit(EXIT_FAILURE);
   }
   if ((fpout = fopen(argv[2], "wb")) == NULL) {
      printf("Can't open output file %s", argv[2]);
      exit(EXIT_FAILURE);
   }
}

void check_args(int argc)
{
   if (argc != 3) {
      printf("\nuse:\n\n  program infile outfile\n\n");
      exit(EXIT_FAILURE);
   }
}

void check_name(char *argv[])
{
   if (strcmp(argv[1], argv[2]) == 0) {
      printf("\nfile names must be different\n\n");
      exit(EXIT_FAILURE);
   }
}
```

If Program 21.5 is named mycopy, it assumes that the command line is entered as

```
mycopy inputfile  outputfile
```

The command to the operating system to run the mycopy program takes three command line arguments. The first argument is always the name of the program being run: mycopy in this example. Any subsequent arguments are normally information used in the program itself. For this example, therefore, there are three command line arguments: the program name, the input file name, and the output file name. The argument count is three.

Understanding argc and argv[]

Now let's examine the main() function. The line

```
int main(int argc, char *argv[])
```

is different from any **main()** you have used. All other program examples had no arguments to **main()** (it had **void** arguments). In Program 21.5 there are two arguments to **main()**. The first argument is called the argument count (**argc**). *The argument count tells the program how many arguments were supplied on the command line before the program started running.* The argument count is stored as an **int**. For mycopy, the argument count should be three if the program was invoked correctly.

Using the Right-Left rule from Chapter 17, you can see that the second argument is an array of pointers to **char**. This second argument is called the argument vector. *The argument vector is an array of pointers to **char** that point to the command line arguments.* Figure 21.2 shows how both **argc** and **argv[]** might look in memory. It assumes that the command line was entered as

```
mycopy test.c newtest.c
```

Figure 21.2 assumes that the operating system stored the information starting at memory address 200. The first two bytes (an **int**) hold the argument count. If the program is invoked with the correct number of command line arguments, **argc** will have the value 3.

Figure 21.2
Memory image of
argc and **argv[]**

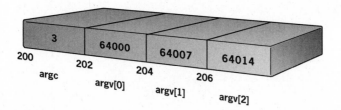

The next two bytes (address 202) holds a pointer to **char** of the first command line argument. Using the value shown in Figure 21.2, we should find the program name stored starting at memory address 64,000. The next two bytes (address 204) is also a pointer to **char**. It says you should find the input file name (test.c) stored at a starting address of 64,007. Finally, the last two bytes (address 206) holds the starting address of the output file name starting at address 64,013. As shown in Figure 21.2, **argv[0]** through **argv[2]** follow **argc** in memory and point to the command line arguments.

Figure 21.3 shows how the command line arguments might be stored in memory.

Figure 21.3

Memory image of the command line arguments

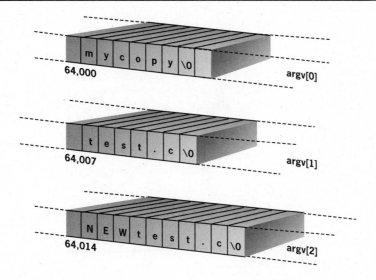

Notice how the rvalues for **argv[]** in Figure 21.2 are the lvalues of the command line arguments in Figure 21.3. Because each command line argument in Figure 21.3 is null terminated, you can use these command line arguments as strings in your program. In Program 21.5, the check_name() function uses **strcmp()** to check the last two arguments to see that the input and output file names are different. This shows you that the argument vector can be used like regular strings in your programs.

PROGRAMMING TIP. *There are no guarantees about the integrity of **argv[0]** once the program begins execution. Some compilers and operating systems thrash **argv[0]** when executing the program's startup code. You might want to write a short program that tries to use **printf()** to display **argv[0]** to see if it is thrashed by the startup code. You can, however, rely on the integrity of **argv[1]** through **argv[n]** in your programs.*

Program 21.5 contains little new program code; most of it simply draws on other concepts you've learned in this chapter. The statements

```
if ((fpin = fopen(argv[1], "rb")) == NULL) {
```

and

```
if ((fpout = fopen(argv[2], "wb")) == NULL) {
```

show how you can use the argument vector to open the files. They are opened for binary reading and writing because you may not know whether they contain text.

The last thing to notice about Program 21.5 is how **main()** is little more than a series of function calls. In fact, the sequence of function calls in **main()** parallels the five program steps you learned in Chapter 2. Functions **check_args()**, **check_name()**, and **do_open()** correspond to the initialization and input steps. The **do_copy()** function combines the processing, output, and shutdown steps. (You can think of the **fclose()** function calls in **do_copy()** as the shutdown step.)

Limiting **main()** to a sequence of function calls makes it easier to debug a program because the program control flow is easier to see. Try to keep **main()** as uncluttered as possible.

File Positioning

All of the disk file programs studied so far have used sequential access methods. That is, the programs have started at the beginning of the file and read sequentially through the data. In some instances, however, you will want to locate a specific item in the data file. While you could start at the beginning of the file and read it sequentially until you find the desired item, sequential access techniques are not very efficient.

Random Access File Positioning

Random access file techniques allow you to jump to a specific position in a file. For example, suppose a data file contains a list of 100 **double** data types and you wish to read the 50th item. In essense, random access techniques allow you to pick up the disk drive head, skip over 49 items, and drop the head down at the start of the 50th item. You can then use a high-level file read function to read the eight bytes associated with the item.

Program 21.6 is a modified version of Program 21.2 and it uses random access techniques to read a specific value from the file.

| Program 21.6 | **Using Random Access File Techniques** |

```c
#include <stdio.h>
#include <stdlib.h>

#define MAXVALS   100

void get_filename(char *filename),
     open_file(char *filename),
     read_val(int item),
     write_values(void);

FILE *fpin, *fpout;

int main(void)
{
   char buff[20], filename[20];
   int item;

   get_filename(filename);
   write_values();

   printf("\n\nWhich item number would you like: ");
   item = atoi(gets(buff));
   open_file(filename);
   read_val(item);

}

void get_filename(char *filename)
{
   printf("Enter the file name of the file to write: ");
   gets(filename);

   if ((fpout = fopen(filename, "wb")) == NULL) {
      printf("\nCould not open %s. Abort.\n", filename);
      exit(EXIT_FAILURE);
   }
}
```

Program 21.6   **continued**

```c
void write_values(void)
{
    int i, val;

    for (i = 0; i < MAXVALS; i++) {
        if ( (fwrite(&i, sizeof(int), 1, fpout)) == 0) {
            printf("Disk write error");
            exit(EXIT_FAILURE);
        }
    }
    fclose(fpout);
}

void open_file(char *filename)
{
    if ((fpin = fopen(filename, "rb")) == NULL) {
        printf("\nCould not open %s. Abort.\n", filename);
        exit(EXIT_FAILURE);
    }
}

void read_val(int item)
{
    int i, val;
    long offset;

    offset = (item - 1) * sizeof(int);
    fseek(fpin, offset, SEEK_SET);
    fread(&i, sizeof(int), 1, fpin);

    printf("\n\nitem %d has the value %d\n\n", item, i);

    fclose(fpin);
}
```

Most of the code in Program 21.6 is the same as Program 21.2, so we will concentrate only on the differences between the two programs. Program 21.6 begins by getting a file name to hold a sequence of MAXVALS integers. (We chose to write a sequential series of values so you can tell whether the value read later in the program is correct.)

Using the fseek() Function

After the values are stored in the data file, the program asks for a specific item number to locate in the file. Let's assume you enter the value 25. The program then calls **read_val()** to read the 25th item in the file. The statement

```
offset = (item - 1) * sizeof(int);
```

calculates how many bytes must be skipped over to find the desired item. Because the file contains nothing but **int** values, the code must skip over (25 - 1) * 2, or 48 bytes to be in a position to read the 25th item in the file. When this statement is resolved, **offset** equals 48. Note that *offset must be a long data type*.

The next statement

```
fseek(fpin, offset, SEEK_SET);
```

calls the standard library function **fseek()** with three arguments. The first argument is the FILE pointer. The second argument is a **long** that tells how many bytes to skip over before placing the disk head down. The last argument determines the reference point for skipping **offset** bytes of data.

SEEK_SET is a symbolic constant that is defined in the stdlib.h header file. There are three of these constants that may be used with the fseek() function:

SEEK_SET   Seek from the start of the file

SEEK_CUR   Seek from the current position in the file

SEEK_END   Seek from the end of the file

Table 21.2 presents some examples of how these constants can be used.

Notice how we have used the L modifier in Table 21.2 after each offset constant. This ensures that the compiler generates the constant as a **long** rather than an **int**. The compiler should get cranky if you try to pass an **int** as the second argument to **fseek()**. If it doesn't, **fseek()** will not work correctly.

Table 21.2   **Using SEEK_SET, SEEK_CUR, and SEEK_END**

fseek() Call	Interpretation
`fseek(fpin, 100L, SEEK_SET);`	Seek into the file 100 bytes.
`fseek(fpin, 100L, SEEK_CUR);`	Seek 100 bytes further into the file from the current position.
`fseek(fpin, 0L, SEEK_END);`	Seek 0 bytes from the end of the file. (This puts the disk head at the end of the file.)
`fseek(fpin, -2L, SEEK_END);`	Seek 2 bytes short of the end of the file.
`fseek(fpin, -10L, SEEK_CUR);`	Back up 10 bytes toward the start of the file from the current file position.
`fseek(fpin, -1L, SEEK_SET);`	Illegal. This tries to seek 1 byte before the start of the file.

The second thing to notice in Table 21.2 is that certain calls (or combinations of calls) are illegal. The last entry in the table is an example. It tries to position the disk head one byte in front of the first byte in the file. This can't be done. The statements

```
fseek(fpin, 10L, SEEK_SET);
fseek(fpin, -11L, SEEK_CUR);
```

illustrate another illegal combination. The first call says to advance 10 bytes into the file and the second call says to back up 11 bytes from this current file position. This is another attempt to seek one byte before the start of the file, which is illegal.

It is legal, however, to seek past the end of the file and write new data. For example, if the file contains 200 bytes, the statement

```
fseek(fpout, 100L, SEEK_END);
```

positions the disk head 300 bytes into the file. You can then write any new data at this location in the file. Keep in mind, however, you now have an "unused" gap in the file from position 200L to 300L. If you try to read the file sequentially, you will get either an error message or garbage if you try to read between these two positions.

Using the ftell() Function

Sometimes you need to know where you currently are in a file. Perhaps you've been writing a series of data of unknown length and you need to know the current position of the disk head in the file. You can do this with the ftell() function. The declaration for **ftell()** is

```
long ftell(FILE *fp);
```

The return value is a **long** data type that tells you the number of bytes between the start of the file and the current file position. It's easy to forget that the value returned from **ftell()** is a **long**.

Conclusion

In this chapter you have learned how to create, open, read, and write both text and binary data files. You have also seen how to use the standard library file functions to write to the printer. The last part of the chapter showed you how easy it is to skip around in a file using random access file techniques.

Most nontrivial programs involve disk data files. One of the great advantages of C is that you are not constrained by a fixed set of file I/O keywords common to other languages. All I/O in C is done through library functions. If you are not happy with the file I/O functions provided with your standard library, you can always write your own. If you have very specific file requirements, you can also build specialized functions from the functions that do exist.

You may wish to examine your library documentation to see if your compiler supports other high-level file functions. The compiler's designers may have already written exactly what you need.

Checking Your Progress

1. What is the purpose of a FILE pointer?

   The FILE pointer serves as the communications link between your application and the operating system when working with disk data files. The FILE pointer points to a structure that contains the information necessary to use the disk file in your program.

2. Suppose you've just written a complex database program and a customer calls saying he cannot access all of his data files. You have checked the software using more files than your customer is using. What might be one of the areas you would have him check?

First, recall that every C program opens three files automatically when the program starts (stdin, stdout, and stderr). Earlier versions of DOS default to as few as eight open files, leaving only five possible FILE structures. Because this default number of open files can be changed with the FILES= command in the CONFIG.SYS file, you should ask your customer to list his CONFIG.SYS file. If there is no FILES command, tell him to set the FILES command to accommodate the files that need to be opened in the program.

3. Suppose you need to write a text file that contains a columnar table. What function might you use to write the data?

The easiest way to write formatted data is with **fprintf()**. The statement

```
fprintf(fpout, "%10.2f  %10.2f %10.2f", x, y, z);
```

would write the values stored in **x**, **y**, and **z** as three columns, each of which is ten columns wide. Two decimal places would be shown for the three values.

4. Inadvertently opening an existing file in the "w" mode is one of the bad things that can happen with high-level file I/O. If the file already exists, it is truncated to zero length. In other words, you just destroyed the file. Write a function that creates a new file only if it doesn't already exist. Assume the function has one argument: the name of the file to open. The function should return a NULL FILE pointer if the file open failed and a non-NULL FILE pointer if the file can be created safely.

One way to write the function is

```
FILE *safe_open(char *filename)
{
    FILE *fpout;

    if ((fpout = fopen(filename, "r")) != NULL) {
        printf("\nFile %s already exists\n\n", filename);
        fpout = NULL;
    } else {
        if ((fpout = fopen(filename, "w")) == NULL) {
            printf("\nCould not create %s\n\n", filename);
            fpout = NULL;
        }
    }
    return fpout;
}
```

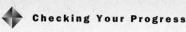

First we try to open the file for reading. This is safe because reading never truncates a file. If we can open the file for reading, the file must already exist. In this case, we do not want to attempt to create the file for writing because we would destroy the contents of the existing file. Therefore, the function displays an error mesage and assigns the NULL pointer into **fpout**.

If the first call to **fopen()** fails, it failed either because the file does not already exist (which is good for us) or because there was some other type of failure (not so good for us). Either way, the second call to **fopen()** is executed.

Assuming there was no hardware failure, the function attempts to create the file for writing using the "w" file mode. If the file is created, a valid FILE pointer is assigned into **fpout**. If there was a hardware or other disk problem, this second call to **fopen()** will also likely fail and **fpout** is NULL.

Because the function type specifier is a FILE pointer, you can assign the return value into a FILE pointer where the function was called. The FILE pointer returned will be NULL if the file exists or we could create the file. If the file was created successfully, the return value is a valid FILE pointer that can be used in the rest of the program.

5. If you open a file under MS-DOS using the file name PRN, what happens to output used with the high-level file I/O functions?

The FILE pointer actually points to a structure associated with the printing device. Therefore, all output is directed to the printer instead of a disk file.

6. What is the difference between using sequential methods to read a disk file and using random access methods?

A sequential read starts at the beginning of a disk file and reads every byte in the file to the desired point (or end of file). Random access methods allow you to position the disk read head to any location in the file by skipping over any unwanted bytes in the file. Although random access methods require that you know how and where the data is stored in the file, it is faster at accessing any given piece of data.

7. A file consists of structures (**yourstruct**) that have been written to a disk file. You now want to update the second-to-last structure in the file. What statement(s) would you use? You can assume that the file is properly opened and **fpout** is a valid FILE pointer.

One method is with the following two statements:

```
fseek(fpout, (long) (sizeof(yourstruct) * -2), SEEK_END);
fwrite(&yourstruct, sizeof (yourstruct), 1, fpout);
```

The fseek() statement has the effect of seeking to the end of the file, minus the number of bytes in two yourstruct structures. (Notice the cast on the second argument to a **long**.) This statement positions the disk head at the beginning of the second-to-last structure in the file. The call to **fwrite()** then writes the updated information in the structure to the file.

22

Low-Level File I/O

Using Low-Level Disk Files

Random Access with Low-Level File I/O

Using Low-Level I/O for the Screen

N THIS CHAPTER YOU WILL LEARN ABOUT LOW-LEVEL FILE I/O. THIS TOPIC IS covered here more for completeness than as a recommendation. The ANSI standard library does not include any low-level file I/O functions. Many operating systems, such as UNIX, include the low-level functions. Requiring the same functions in the standard library would be a duplication of resources. However, some operating systems do not provide the low-level file functions. MS-DOS is one example. Therefore, compilers that work with operating systems that are missing the low-level file functions normally provide them in their bundle of library functions.

Over time, use of the low-level library routines will become less common. Because you can use either high- or low-level file routines, you are better off using the high-level routines. The ANSI standard just about guarantees that the high-level file functions will be around for a long time. The low-level routines may simply fade away over time.

Still, there is much existing code that uses low-level routines and it can't hurt to know how they work.

Using Low-Level Disk Files

Working with low-level files is much the same as working with high-level files. All files must be opened or created, then read or written, and then closed. The functions that perform these tasks are different, however. Many of the low-level functions have names similar to their high-level counterparts, without the leading *f* character. For example, instead of the fopen() function you saw in Chapter 21, you will learn about the low-level open() function in this chapter.

Opening a Low-Level File

The first step in using low-level disk files is to open the file. The declaration of the open() function is

```
int open(char *filename, int cflag[, int mode]);
```

The open() function might appear similar to **fopen()**, but there are some important differences. First, the type specifier for the function is an **int** rather than a FILE pointer. The return value from **open()** is called a file descriptor. A *file descriptor is an integer value that serves as an index number to describe the file*. The file descriptor becomes your program's communication link with the operating system, just as a FILE pointer did with high-level file I/O.

The first argument to **open()** is a pointer to a character string that contains the name of the file that you wish to open. This argument is the same as that used with **fopen()**.

The second argument is an activity variable. This variable describes the type of activity that will be permitted on the file. A list of permissible activites appears in Table 22.1.

Table 22.1   **Permissible Activities for open()**

Symbolic Constant	Interpretation
O_RDONLY	Read-only file
O_RDWR	Read-write file
O_WRONLY	Write-only file
O_BINARY	Binary file
O_TEXT	Text file
O_APPEND	Append to file
O_CREAT	Create file if it doesn't exist
O_EXCL	Return error if file does exist
O_TRUNC	Create a zero length file

The definitions for the symbolic constants in Table 22.1 are stored in a header file named fcntl.h (the file control header). You can use the bitwise OR with the symbolic constants in Table 22.1 to form more complex types of activity on the file. For example,

```
open("test.txt", O_TEXT | O_RDWR);
```

opens a file named test txt for reading or writing text.

When certain activity flags are used together, you must supply a third argument to **open()**. (This is why the third argument in the open() function declaration seen earlier is enclosed in brackets.) If you use O_CREAT with O_WRONLY or O_RDWR, the third argument is required. This third argument is often called the *permission mode*.

These two symbolic constants are normally used with the permission mode:

```
S_IWRITE            Create a file for writing
S_IREAD             Create a file for reading
```

The symbolic constants are usually stored in the stat.h header file. Some compilers provide additional mode constants. (Because **open()** does not have a standard design, compiler vendors can add any bells and whistles they wish. Check the stat.h header file and your compiler documentation for more information.)

The following statement shows how you might create a file using **open()**:

```
fd = open(filename, O_WRONLY | O_CREAT | O_EXCL, S_IWRITE);
```

This statement will create a file named **filename** only if it does not already exist.

Some compilers may supply a simple creat() function. The declaration for **creat()** is

```
int creat(char *filename, mode);
```

In this example, the mode has a different interpretation. The mode value is compiler specific, but typical values are as follows:

```
0          Creates an ordinary read-write file
1          Creates a read-only file
2          Creates a hidden file
4          Creates a system file
```

For most programs, the mode value would be 0. Again, you must check your library documentation to see if this function is supported for your compiler. In addition, you must check the permissible values and interpretations of the mode value. They can vary and may have different meanings.

(Although you may have a creat() function in your library, this chapter proceeds as though it is not available. You can duplicate its actions using the open() function anyway.)

If an error occurs when **open()** is called, the value returned from **open()** is usually –1. Therefore, the code fragment

```
#define ERR  -1

/* Other statements */

if ((fd = open(argv[1], O_RDONLY)) == ERR) {
    printf("Cannot open %s. Abort.", argv[1]);
    exit(EXIT_FAILURE);
}
```

attempts to open the file pointed to by **argv[1]** as a read-only file. If the file descriptor (**fd**) equals ERR (–1), an error message is given and the program aborts. If the call to **open()** is successful, **fd** contains a valid file descriptor.

This file descriptor is then used to manipulate the file pointed to by **argv[1]** in the rest of the program.

Writing with Low-Level File Functions

Start by writing a binary file using low-level file I/O. Consider Program 22.1.

The program begins by requesting a file name. The statement

```
if ((fd = open(filename, O_BINARY | O_CREAT | O_WRONLY |
                         O_EXCL, S_IWRITE))  == ERR) {
```

attempts to create a binary data file named **filename**. However, the file is only created if it does not already exist. If the file is successfully created, you can only use it for writing. If the file already exists or some other error occurs, the return value is –1 (ERR). An error message is displayed and the program aborts. Notice that we had to use the S_IWRITE constant because we used the O_CREAT constant as part of the open() statement.

PROGRAMMING TIP. *It is easy to forget to include the optional mode argument (for example, S_IWRITE) when opening a low-level file. If you omit this argument, your only clue will be that you cannot successfully create the file, even if it does not already exist. Also, don't forget to include the stat.h and fcntl.h header files. They contain several symbolic constants that you will need to use low-level file I/O.*

Just to make things a little more interesting, suppose you want the file to hold a series of integer (binary) values. Specifically, you want the file to store a value, its square, and its cube. Because these values are related to one another, it makes sense to use a structure to organize them together.

A for loop is used to write the values from 0 through 9. The values are calculated and the statement

```
write(fd, (void *) &powers, sizeof(powers));
```

writes the information to disk. The first argument is the file descriptor that you obtained when the file was created. The second argument is a pointer to where the data is stored. The program uses the lvalue of the powers structure for the pointer to the data. The third argument tells how many bytes are to be written.

Notice the advantage of using a structure. You could use three separate calls to **write()**, one to write the value, another to writes its square, and a third to write the value cubed. However, by using a structure, you can save all of the data to disk with one call to **write()**.

Program 22.1   **Writing a Binary File with Low-Level File I/O**

```c
#include <stdio.h>
#include <stdlib.h>

#include <fcntl.h>      /* Needed for activity modes  */
#include <stat.h>       /* Needed for permission mode */

#define ERR    -1

struct table {
   int val;
   int square;
   int cube;
   };

int main(void)
{
   char filename[20];
   int fd, i;
   struct table powers;

   printf("\nEnter a file name: ");
   gets(filename);

   if ((fd = open(filename, O_BINARY | O_CREAT | O_WRONLY |
                           O_EXCL, S_IWRITE))  == ERR) {
      printf("\nCould not create %s", filename);
      exit(EXIT_FAILURE);
   }

   for (i = 0; i < 10; i++) {
      powers.val = i;
      powers.square = powers.val * powers.val;
      powers.cube = powers.square * powers.val;
      write(fd, (void *) &powers, sizeof(powers));
   }
   close(fd);
}
```

Closing a Low-Level File

The call to **close()** performs the same function that **fclose()** did with high-level file I/O. Any data stored in the file buffer is flushed to the disk, the file is marked closed, and the file descriptor (**fd**) is released. (The operating system may perform some additional housekeeping chores, but these are tranparent to both the programmer and the user.) If you fail to close a file, there is no guarantee that *any* data will be written to disk.

Once a file is closed, the **fd** is no longer valid for any file I/O. Only after another call to **open()** can **fd** again be used with a disk file.

After Program 22.1 ends, you should see a new 60-byte file stored on your disk.

Reading a Low-Level File

Now let's see if the numbers stored in Program 22.1 did end up in the disk file as planned. Program 22.2 simply modifies Program 22.1 so that you can read rather than write the file.

Program 22.2 is identical to Program 22.1, except the file is opened for reading rather than writing. The statement

```
read(fd, (void *) &powers, sizeof(powers));
```

shows how the powers structure is used as a buffer to store the data read from the disk. A for loop starts at the beginning of the file and reads it one structure at a time. Each member is displayed by the call to **printf()**. The call to **close()** closes the file and the program ends.

Random Access with Low-Level File I/O

Low-level file I/O provides **lseek()** and **tell()** as replacements for the high-level functions **fseek()** and **ftell()**. Program 22.3 illustrates how each function is used.

Program 22.3 uses random-access file techniques to read a specific record created with Program 22.1. The program begins by finding which series the user wishes to see. Because this question is asked before the file name, **filename** can be used as a general-purpose input buffer to get the keyboard response.

Program 22.2 **Reading with Low-Level File I/O**

```c
#include <stdio.h>
#include <stdlib.h>

#include <fcntl.h>
#include <stat.h>

#define ERR    -1

struct table {
    int val;
    int square;
    int cube;
    };

void main(void)
{
    char filename[20];
    int fd, i;
    struct table powers;

    printf("\nEnter the file name: ");
    gets(filename);

    if ((fd = open(filename, O_BINARY | O_RDONLY))  == ERR)
    {
        printf("\nCould not open %s", filename);
        exit(EXIT_FAILURE);
    }

    for (i = 0; i < 10; i++) {
        read(fd, (void *) &powers, sizeof(powers));
        printf("\n%-3d squared = %-4d cubed = %-4d",
            powers.val, powers.square, powers.cube);
    }
    close(fd);
}
```

Program 22.3   **Random Access Files**

```c
#include <stdio.h>
#include <stdlib.h>

#include <fcntl.h>
#include <stat.h>

#define ERR    -1
#define BELL   7

#define EVER  ;;

struct table {
   int val;
   int square;
   int cube;
   };

void main(void)
{
   char filename[20];
   int fd, i, which;
   long where;

   struct table powers;

   for (EVER) {
      printf("Which power do you wish to see (0 - 9): ");
      which = atoi(gets(filename));
      if (which > -1 && which < 10) {
         break;
      }
      printf("\n\nThe range is - through 9%c", BELL);
   }
   printf("\nEnter the file name: ");
   gets(filename);

   if ((fd = open(filename, O_BINARY | O_RDONLY))  == ERR)
   {
      printf("\nCould not open %s", filename);
      exit(EXIT_FAILURE);
```

Program 22.3   **continued**

```
     }
     lseek(fd, (long) (which * sizeof (powers)), SEEK_SET);
         read(fd, (void *) &powers, sizeof(powers));
         printf("\n%-3d squared = %-4d cubed = %-4d",
             powers.val, powers.square, powers.cube);
         where = tell(fd);
         printf("\n\nThe file is now positioned at %ld\n\n",
             where);
         close(fd);
     }
```

The program then asks for the name of the data file that was created with Program 22.1. This is stored in **filename**, which is then used in the open() call. Next, the statement

```
     lseek(fd, (long) (which * sizeof (powers)), SEEK_SET);
```

positions the disk read head at the beginning of the structure to be read. For example, if the user enters 9, the statement becomes

```
     lseek(fd, (long) (9 * 6), SEEK_SET);
     lseek(fd, (long) (54), SEEK_SET);
```

which sets the disk read head down 54 bytes into the file. A little quick arithmetic shows that this is the proper position. A printf() call displays the contents of the structure.

After reading the structure from the disk, the disk head has advanced to the start of the next structure (or EOF). The statement

```
     where = tell(fd);
```

returns a byte count of the current position of the disk read head. For example, if you select structure number 9, the final **printf()** displays

```
     The file is now positioned at 60
```

which is the end of file. Notice that the value returned by **tell()** is a **long**.

The low-level file I/O functions for reading and writing behave much like the high-level file I/O functions. If you perform timing tests on the two methods, their performance should be about the same. However, given the endorsement of high-level file I/O by the ANSI standard, you will probably be ahead in the long run if you use the high-level functions exclusively.

Using Low-Level I/O for the Screen

Today's computers, with their vast amounts of memory, permit the programmer to be somewhat cavalier about memory usage. However, you may be programming something other than a standard computer. After all, someone's got to program those microprocessors that control everything from your microwave oven to the pulse monitor on your new exercise machine.

You can save some memory by using the low-level file routines to replace some aspects of **printf()**. Program 22.4 shows how you might do this.

Program 22.4   **Replacing printf() with Low-Level File I/O**

```c
#include <stdio.h>

#define MAXSTRING 128

#ifndef fileno
    #define fileno(fp) ((fp)->fd)
#endif

int main(void)
{
    char buff[MAXSTRING + 1];

    write( fileno(stdout), "Enter a string: ", 16);
    gets(buff);
    write(fileno(stdout), buff, strlen(buff));
}
```

The program simply gets a string and displays it on the screen. The write() function is used instead of **printf()** to display both the input prompt and the response. The fileno() function is really not a function, but something called a parametrized macro. You will learn about parametrized macros in Chapter 23. For now, all you need to understand is that **fileno()** converts a (high-level) FILE pointer into a (low-level) file descriptor.

The statement

```c
write( fileno(stdout), "Enter a string: ", 16);
```

takes the standard output FILE pointer, **stdout**, and converts it into a file descriptor. If you're inquisitive, you will probably figure out that the macro extracts the file descriptor from the FILE structure. (You can see this by referring back to Figure 21.1 and the **_fd** member of the FILE structure.) The write() function then uses the file descriptor associated with **stdout** to display the information on the screen. If you didn't see the code, you wouldn't know that **printf()** was not being used.

What is noticeable, however, is how much smaller the executable file is than when you use **printf()**. I checked two different compilers. The two **printf()** versions of Program 22.4 were 9,674 and 6,371 bytes. The **write()** versions were 7,331 and 4,469 bytes. This represents a memory savings of approximately 25 to 30 percent.

Conclusion

Low-level file functions behave very much like the high-level file functions. While the performance of the low-level routines may be slightly better, that advantage pales compared to the portability advantage of the high-level file functions. The ANSI standard is firmly entrenched and you can expect to find those functions in future compilers. The low-level file functions are already starting to fade away. Fewer and fewer articles, for example, use the low-level routines.

Checking Your Progress

1. What is meant by the "activity flags" with respect to the open() function?

   The activity flags detail the ways in which a file can be opened with the open() function. You can use the bitwise OR operator with these flags to produce a variety of activities for the file. (See Table 22.1.)

2. What is a file descriptor?

   A file descriptor is the file I/O link between your application and the operating system. Under MS-DOS, all file manipulation is done by BDOS (Basic Disk Operating System) through a file descriptor. In essence, the file descriptor used in your application is the same file descriptor used to manipulate the file in the BDOS.

3. What are the low-level file equivalents for the high-level **fgetc()** and **fputc()**?

   The low-level equivalents are **getc()** and **putc()**. A number of high-level file functions (most of which start with the letter *f*) have low-level equivalent functions. Consult your compiler's standard library documentation for additional information.

4. In the following statements, what does **where** equal?

```
lseek(fd, ØL, SEEK_END);
where = tell(fd);
```

The call to **lseek()** positions the disk file head at the end of the file. The call to **tell()** returns the number of bytes between the current file head position and the start of the file. Therefore, **where** equals the total number of bytes in the file.

5. Is the following statement legal?

```
lseek(fd, 25L, SEEK_END);
```

Yes. It positions the disk file head 25 bytes past the current end of the file. This is perfectly legal in C. However, the 25-byte gap between the previous end of file and the new position should be viewed as garbage data. An attempt to read data in this gap may or may not work.

6. Which file routines should you use, high- or low-level?

Unless you are programming digital wristwatches, the better choice is high-level file I/O. Its future seems secure. The same cannot be said for the low-level functions.

23

Preprocessor Directives

N THIS CHAPTER YOU WILL LEARN ABOUT THOSE PREPROCESSOR DIRECTIVES that we have not yet discussed. The preprocessor can do much more than process #include and #define directives. It can also be used to control the way the code appears to the compiler. You will also learn about parametrized macros and how they are used. When you have finished this chapter, you will have learned virtually everything you need to know to tackle even the most complex programming projects.

Understanding the Compilation Process

The preprocessor behaves like a program that is separate from the compiler. Most programmers refer to a distinct operation on a program's source code as a *pass*. Although it may not be obvious as the compiler processes your source code, there are several distinct passes made on your code.

Compiler Passes

The first pass on your program code is the preprocessor pass. Its primary responsibility is to process all preprocessor directives. However, it is also responsible for converting constants into their required data types.

The second pass is normally the syntax pass. It is responsible for checking the syntactic and semantic constructs of your program. Most of the error messages you see are produced by this pass. If the code passes the syntactic and semantic checks, most compilers generate an intermediate file that consists of tokens that are associated with specific fragments of code. The tokens in this file (often called tuples or quads) are input data for the actual code generation produced by the compiler.

The third pass may optimize and generate the code at the same time, or these tasks may be split into two separate passes. The output of the third pass is an object file (OBJ) that can be used by the linker to produce an executable program.

The Preprocessor Pass

It is important for you to understand that the preprocessor pass can significantly alter your code. For example, when you include a header file in your program, the code in that file becomes part of your program code. Likewise, when you write something like

```
#define BELL 7

/* some code */
printf("Error condition %c", BELL);
```

the preprocessor produces a textual substitution to your code. What the compiler actually sees is

```
printf("Error condition %c", 7);
```

Notice that the compiler doesn't even know about the **#define** or the symbolic constant BELL. This is because the preprocessor created its own symbol table containing all of the symbolic constants defined in the source file. The preprocessor substitutes the ASCII characters in BELL with the ASCII character 7.

When the preprocessor pass is finished, it generates a new ASCII source code file that may differ substantially from the source file you wrote. It is very important that you understand that most of the preprocessor's work involves two types of *textual substitution*. First, it is responsible for substituting the ASCII text found in all header files in place of the #include directives. Second, the preprocessor is responsible for substituting one set of ASCII characters (BELL) for a different set of ASCII characters (7). Almost all of the preprocessor's work involves substituting one set of ASCII text for a new set of ASCII text.

The rest of this chapter is devoted to understanding the many preprocessor directives that are available to you. In some cases, preprocessor directives present you with alternative ways to accomplish a given task. Other directives simply enable you to write your code to be more flexible, and, perhaps, more portable.

Using Parametrized Macros

With the one exception in Chapter 22, you have always used the #define directive to define a symbolic constant. The #define directive, however, can also be used to create a parametrized macro. A *parametrized macro is similar to a symbolic constant, except the definition can contain one or more arguments, or parameters*. Most programmers refer to parametrized macros more simply as "macros." We will do the same from now on.

For example, suppose your program needs to produce the square of different variables at many different points in the program. You could define a function to do the job, or you could use a macro instead. The square macro might be defined as follows

```
#define square(x)  ( (x) * (x) )
```

Notice that there is no semicolon at the end of the line. If a macro definition will not fit on one line, you can use a backslash (\) at the end of the line. The backslash tells the compiler that the macro definition continues on the next line. For example,

```
#define series(a, b, c)  ( (a * 5) + (b * 10) \
                            + (c * 20))
```

allows the series macro to span more than a single line.

It should also be obvious that a macro definition must occur in the source file before it is used in the program. This ensures that the compiler knows how to use the macro when it appears in the program code.

Let's use the square macro as an example of how the preprocessor treats the macro. Suppose the following statement appears after the macro definition:

```
total = square(y);
```

When the preprocessor has finished processing this statement, the source code is changed by the preprocessor so it looks like

```
total = ( (y) * (y) );
```

to the compiler. This statement takes the value in **y** and multiplies it by itself to produce its square, which is then assigned into **total**.

Couldn't you write the macro without all of the parentheses? That is, could you simplify the macro as follows:

```
#define square(x)  x * x
```

Well, you could, but it may not always work properly. For example, suppose you now use the macro in the statement

```
total = square(5 + 1);
```

When the preprocessor finishes, the statement becomes

```
total = 5 + 1 * 5 + 1;
```

This statement causes **total** to equal 11, but you probably wanted it to equal 36 (the square of 6). If we put the parentheses back in as they were originally, the statement becomes

```
total = ( (5 + 1) * (5 + 1) );
```

which produces the correct value of 36 for **total**. You should always parenthesize the parameters in a macro to prevent the kind of bug shown above. If you always remember that the preprocessor simply substitutes one series of ASCII text (**square(5 + 1)**) with a new series of ASCII text ((**((5 + 1) * (5 + 1))**), it will help you understand exactly what the preprocessor is doing.

Advantages and Disadvantages of Macros

If you can write **square()** as either a function or a macro, what's the advantage of using a macro? Like everything else, tradeoffs are involved when using macros versus functions. Let's see what these tradeoffs involve.

First, each time you use a macro in a program, the macro is replaced with the code that performs the macro's task. This means there is no function to call. The compiler does not have to push any arguments on the stack or generate code to get them off the stack in the function. Nor does the compiler have to generate code to push the result back on the stack and pop the answer back off in preparation for assignment into a variable. All of this stack pushing and popping is *function overhead code* that takes time and code space.

Macros don't have any function overhead code. All of the code to perform the macro's function is generated as inline code. As a result, macros perform slightly faster than do function calls. That's the good news.

The bad news is that macros *do* generate inline code. This means that, if you use a macro a hundred times in your program, the compiler generates a hundred copies of the same code and places it in the program. If you had used a function, there would only be one copy of the code in the program. Therefore, macros tend to bloat the size of a program compared to an equivalent function call.

The tradeoff with macros versus function calls, then, is slightly faster performance using macros against larger code size. If you are programming for a very restricted memory environment, you may be forced to use functions. If memory limitations are not a problem and performance is critical, a macro may be the better solution.

Another advantage of a macro is that it is data inspecific. That is, the macro

```
#define square(x)  ( (x) * (x) )
```

can square any data type. The parameter **x** can be a **char**, **int**, **long**, **double**, or any other type and the square macro generates its squared value. If **square()** were a function call, you would need to write separate functions for each data type that needed to be squared. The reason is because a function must know the type of data being passed to it. Otherwise, the function would not know how many bytes to pop off the stack. A macro, therefore, can prevent you from writing several different functions that accomplish the same task.

Header Files and Macros

If you look through the stdio.h header file, you will find a number of macros defined there. In Chapter 22, you used the macro found in the stdio.h header file

```
#define fileno(f)        ((f)->fd)
```

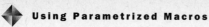

in conjunction with the **stdout** FILE pointer. Therefore, the statement

```
myfd = fileno(stdout);
```

became

```
myfd = ((stdout)->fd);
```

when the preprocessor pass finished. If you look at Figure 21.1 in Chapter 21, you will see that this code retrieves the file descriptor stored in **stdout**'s FILE structure and assigns it into **myfd**. The fileno macro allowed you to use a high-level FILE pointer to retrieve a low-level file descriptor.

You have also used other macros in earlier programs, although you were not aware of it. For example, you used the toupper macro, but thought it was a function named **toupper()**. The macro is defined in the ctype.h header file as something similar to

```
#define _toupper(c)   ((c) + 'A' - 'a')
```

If you work through the code, you will find that it does convert **c** to an upper-case letter. You may wish to take the time a browse through your compiler's header files looking for macros. You might be amazed to see how many you find there.

Forcing Function Calls over Macro Substitution

Suppose you are facing a memory constraint and are concerned about the amount of memory that macro substitutions cause in your program. What alternatives does C provide you to conserve memory?

Some C programmers don't know that the ANSI standard requires, whenever possible, that all macros have a corresponding function in the standard library. (The assert macro cannot be written as a function.) Therefore, you do have a choice in most cases between a function call and a macro. Now the question becomes: How can you force a function call instead of a macro substitution? Several options exist.

You could simply not include the header file that contains the macro definition. The linker would then be forced to search the standard library for the missing function code. The down side is that there may be other macros, symbolic constants, function declarations, and information in the header file that your program needs.

A second alternative is to undefine the macro definition. You will learn about the #undef directive later in this chapter. This would work, but it's not the most elegant solution to the problem.

A third alternative is to write the function yourself. Because your code for a function takes precedence over all other code with the same function name, the linker would not use the macro definition. This approach requires you to reinvent the wheel. You would have to write, test, and debug the function, which is a terrible waste of time.

We can arrive at a better solution by carefully reading the ANSI specification of a macro definition. It says that the name of a parametrized macro *must* be followed either by a white space character, such as a blank space, or by the opening parenthesis that starts the parameter list. Nothing else is legal in the definition of a parametrized macro.

With this macro rule in mind, what happens if you write

```
letter = (toupper)(c);
```

as a statement in your code? Because a closing parenthesis appears between the "r" in **toupper** and the opening parenthesis of the parameter list, **toupper()** cannot cause macro substitution. Because you can parenthesize function names but not macro names, the compiler knows it must use the toupper() function rather than the toupper() macro found in ctype.h.

The method described here allows you to include whatever header files you need without worrying that macro substitution will take place. Because parenthesizing the name forces a function call instead of macro substitution, your program's code size will be smaller.

Conditional Preprocessor Directives

The preprocessor recognizes a variety of conditional directives. The conditional directives are presented in Table 23.1.

Table 23.1　Conditional Preprocessor Directives

Directive	Interpretation
#if	conditional if
#elif	else-if
#else	else
#endif	end of if or elif
#ifdef	if defined
#ifndeg	if not defined

The general form for the conditional directives is

```
#if expression
```

where *expression* is a constant expression. For example,

```
#if MOOD == 1
    #define FEELING    "Good"
#else
    #define FEELING    "Lousy"
#endif
```

In this example, if MOOD equals 1 when the preprocessor reads the conditional directive, FEELING is defined to equal the string "Good". Any other value for MOOD causes FEELING to equal "Lousy".

Notice how the **#if-#else-#endif** above is similar to a regular if-else statement. Braces are not used with the conditional directives. Everything between the **#if** and the **#else** in the example is viewed as part of the MOOD == 1 block. Likewise, multiple lines can appear between the **#else** and the **#endif**.

Controlling Compilation with Conditional Directives

A number of header files do not have set names under the ANSI standard. For example, if you are using memory allocation functions in your code, one compiler might call the associated header file memory.h while another compiler calls it mem.h. You can use the conditional directive to control which header file is read into the program during compilation. For example,

```
#if COMPILER == 1
    #include <memory.h>
    #define COMPANY   "ABC"
#else
    #include <mem.h>
    #define COMPANY   "XYZ"
#endif
```

If the directive

```
#define COMPILER    1
```

appears before the conditional directives, memory.h is included in the source file and COMPANY equals the string "ABC". If COMPILER is any value other than 1, mem.h is included and COMPANY equals "XYZ".

You can cascade the conditional directives using **#elif**. For example,

```
#if COMPILER == 1
    #include <memory.h>
    #define COMPANY  "ABC"
#elif COMPILER == 2
    #include <mem.h>
    #define COMPANY  "XYZ"
#elif COMPILER == 3
    #include <m.h>
    #define COMPANY  "MNO"
 #else
    #include <memory.h>
    #define COMPANY  "CDE"
#endif
```

The use of **#elif** permits you to create conditional compilation that is as complex as the situation demands.

Using Conditional Directives as a define-declare Toggle

Suppose you write a program that uses the following list of global variables:

```
FILE *fpin, *fpout, *fptemp;
```

Let's further assume that there are several source code modules that comprise the program and they all need access to the global variables. The problem is that the three variables must be defined in only one module (usually the module with **main()** in it), but declared in all other modules. You can use the #ifndef conditional directive to solve the problem.

First, place the directive

```
#ifndef MAIN
    extern
#endif
    FILE *fpin, *fpout, *fptemp;
```

in a header file named globals.h. In the source file that contains **main()**, add the lines

```
#define MAIN 1
#include "globals.h"
```

In all of the other files, add only the line

```
#include "globals.h"
```

and then compile the program. What does the preprocessor do with these changes?

The preprocessor directive

```
#ifndef MAIN
```

says: "If MAIN is not defined in this model, include the following line in this source file." Therefore, when you compile all the files that don't contain **main()**, the directive

```
#ifndef MAIN
     extern
#endif
     FILE *fpin, *fpout, *fptemp;
```

is processed so that the source code ends up with

```
extern FILE *fpin, *fpout, *fptemp;
```

This *declares* the three global variables in every file other than the source file that contains **main()**.

When the file that contains **main()** is compiled, the directives

```
#define MAIN 1
#include "globals.h"
```

expand to

```
#define MAIN 1
#ifndef MAIN
     extern
#endif
     FILE *fpin, *fpout, *fptemp;
```

MAIN is defined in this module, so when the preprocessor finishes its job, the source code with **main()** becomes

```
FILE *fpin, *fpout, *fptemp;
```

which *defines* the three variables. You now have an easy way to toggle the definition and declaration of global variables across multiple source files.

The **#ifdef** performs a similar function, but is verbalized as: "If something is defined, do what follows." For example,

```
#ifdef UNIX
    #include "unix.h"
#else
```

```
    #include "msdos.h"
#endif
```

If there is a **#define** for UNIX appearing before these directives, the unix.h header file is included in the source file. Otherwise, the msdos.h header file is included.

The conditional directives existed in C long before ANSI set the standard. ANSI did, however, add some variations to the list of conditional directives. Instead of using

```
#ifndef
```

you may also use

```
#if ! defined
```

Likewise, you can replace

```
#ifdef
```

with

```
#if defined
```

An ANSI-compliant compiler should treat these variations exactly the same as the original **#ifdef** and **#ifndef**.

Predefined Macros

ANSI added several macros that you can use in your programs. These predefined macros appear in Table 23.2.

Table 23.2   ANSI Predefined Macros

Macro	Interpretation
__DATE__	The calendar date as a string with the form mmm dd yyyy.
__FILE__	A string that holds the name of the source code file in which the directive appears.
__LINE__	An integer equal to the current line number of the source file.
__STDC__	A decimal constant that is 1 if the compiler is fully ANSI-compliant.
__TIME__	A string equal to the time of compilation with the format hh:mm:ss.

Try entering the code in Program 23.1 to see how these macros are used.

Program 23.1   **Testing the Predefined ANSI Macros**

```c
#include <stdio.h>

int main(void)
{
    printf("\nTime: %s\n", __TIME__);
    printf("\nDate: %s\n", __DATE__);
    printf("\nLine: %d\n", __LINE__);
    printf("\nFile: %s\n", __FILE__);

#ifdef __STDC__
    printf("\nstdc: %d\n", __STDC__);
#endif

}
```

Notice how we used a **#ifdef** to control the final **printf()** call. The reason is because many vendors do not define the __STDC__ macro at all if the compiler is not fully ANSI compliant. If __STDC__ is defined for your compiler, the last **printf()** is included in the source file. If not, it is left out of the program code.

The technique using conditional compilation shown in Program 23.1 can also be used to toggle debugging code into and out of a program. For example,

```c
#ifdef DEBUG
    for (i = 0; i < MAXVAL; i++) {
        printf("val[%d] = %d \n", i, val[i]);
    }
#endif
```

If DEBUG is defined earlier in the program, the code is toggled into the program. If DEBUG is not defined, the code is omitted. If you wish, you can leave the debugging code (sometimes called *scaffolding* code) permanently in the source file and use the DEBUG constant to toggle it into and out of the program.

Using the #undef Directive

The #undef directive allows you to undefine a previously defined macro. For example, you could use

```
#undef toupper
```

and, if the **toupper** macro was in the preprocessor macro symbol table, it is removed. Unless you redefine **toupper** using a **#define** later in the program, any call to **toupper** is changed from a macro to a function call. (**toupper()** still exists in the program, and the linker will still need to resolve its reference.)

Because ANSI provides functions for most macros, there are not many situations where you need to undefine an ANSI macro. A more likely use is to undefine a macro that you've defined to disable it in subsequent code.

Other Preprocessor Directives

There are three other preprocessor directives that may prove useful: **#line**, **#error**, and **#pragma**.

Using #line

The **#line** directive has the general form

```
#line line_number "filename"
```

where **line_number** is taken to be the next line number in the source file named **filename**. The **filename** token is optional. If you omit **filename**, it is assumed to be the last filename that was used with the #line directive. If **#line** does not appear elsewhere in the program, **filename** is ignored. In this case, the directive appears as if it was written

```
#line line_number
```

The #line directive is most often used in debugging. For example,

```
#line 1 "myfile1.c"
```

sets the next line in the source to line 1 and the source file name is taken to be myfile1.c.

Using #error

The #error directive has the general form

```
#error message
```

where **message** is a string constant. For example,

```
#include "globals.h"

#ifndef COMPILER
    #error "You forgot to set the compiler type"
#endif
```

It is interesting that **#error** produces a compile-time error message rather than a runtime error message. This means you won't see the error message when the program runs, but you may see it while the file is being compiled. **#error** provides a means by which you can check for inconsistencies during compilation.

Using #pragma

The #pragma directive has the general form

```
#pragma   implementation_defined_action
```

The compiler vendor is free to define the action that occurs with any #pragma directive. ANSI created the #pragma directive so vendors could add a new feature without violating the ANSI standard. Unfortunately, there is no way for us to know what the #pragma directives (if any) do with your compiler. You will need to examine your compiler's documentation to see what #pragma directives are available and any actions they might cause.

Using the assert Macro

The assert macro is defined in the assert.h header file. This macro is used to test an expression in a program at run time. The general form of the assert macro is

```
assert(expression)
```

where *expression* is an integral data type. Any time *expression* evaluates to a logic False condition, a message is displayed by the assert macro. The form of the message is

```
Assertion failed: (expression), file (filename), line (nnn)
```

After the message is displayed, the program is stopped by calling the abort() function. (A non-ANSI compiler would call **exit()**.) The **assert** can be turned off by placing the directive

```
#define NDEBUG
```

in the file. This has the effect of turning the assert macro off. It also means that you can leave all assertions in the source, but disable them with a single **#define**.

Program 23.2 shows an example of how the assert macro might be used.

Program 23.2   **The assert Macro**

```
#include <stdio.h>
#include <assert.h>

#define MAXVAL 50

void func1(int i);

int main(void)
{
    int i;

    for (i = 0; i < MAXVAL; i++) {
        func1(i);
        printf("i = %d\n", i);
    }

}

void func1(int i)
{
    assert(i >= 0 && i < 12);   /* Check arg range */

    /* Execute code if okay */
}
```

Program 23.2 executes a for loop, calling **func1()** on each iteration of the loop. In **func1()** the value of **i** is checked by the assert macro. Had this been an actual function, the body of the function would have been executed if the assertion did not fail. The **assert** expression in **func1()** fails after **i** reaches the value of 12. At that point, the assertion fails and the assertion message is displayed. Some compilers may also state that the program had an abnormal termination before the program aborts.

Conclusion

The preprocessor provides control over the compilation process that would not be possible otherwise. The wise use of conditional compilation can greatly simplify how global variables, include files, and other data items are processed by the compiler. Always remember, however, that it is textual substitution that is done by the preprocessor pass.

If you stuck to it this long, you should be very comfortable with C now. Perhaps C is not the perfect language, but it is sure way out in front of whatever is in second place. Enjoy!

Checking Your Progress

1. Can a header that is included in a program contain a #include directive itself?

   Yes. The level of nesting of includes is defined by the implementation, which means ANSI set no fixed depth. However, you can expect most compilers to allow includes to be nested at least four or five levels deep.

2. What does the preprocessor set STRING to in the following code fragment?

   ```
   #define GOOD
   #ifdef GOOD
      #define STRING "Good"
   #else
      #define STRING "Bad"
   #endif
   ```

   STRING equals "Good". Even though GOOD is not defined to be any specific token, the preprocessor places GOOD in its symbol table. It may not have anything associated with it, but GOOD is still in the symbol table.

3. Suppose you are writing code for a machine where an **int** is four bytes. You know that the program will eventually be moved to a system where **int**s are only two bytes. How could you use the preprocessor to make your code more portable? Refer to the machines as BIG (four-byte **int**s) and SMALL (two-byte **int**s).

   All you need to do is make sure all **int**s are promoted to **long**s when the code is moved to the SMALL machine. One approach might be

```
#ifdef SMALL
    #define int long
#endif
```

This assumes that SMALL is only defined when the code is being compiled on the small machine.

4. What is the difference between a macro and a function call?

A macro generates inline code; there is no function overhead. This also means macros execute somewhat faster than function calls. Another advantage of macros is that they are data inspecific; one macro serves all. A disadvantage of macros is that, because inline code is generated, multiple macro invocations generate more code than do the same number of calls to a function.

5. Can __FILE__ and similar macros be used directly in program code, or are they available only during the preprocessor pass?

You may use the predefined macros just as you would any other data item in your program.

The ASCII Character Set

This appendix displays the ASCII character set, which extends from 0 through 127 inclusively. A control character is abbreviated as ^. For example, Ctrl-C is shown as ^C. The values from 128 through 255 are the IBM extended character set. (These are not part of the ASCII character set and may not be portable.)

Decimal	Hexadecimal	Octal	Binary	ASCII Character
0	0x00	0	00000000	null (NUL)
1	0x01	1	00000001	^A (SOH)
2	0x02	2	00000010	^B (STX)
3	0x03	3	00000011	^C (ETX)
4	0x04	4	00000100	^D EOT
5	0x05	5	00000101	^E ENQ
6	0x06	6	00000110	^F ACK
7	0x07	7	00000111	^G (bell) BEL
8	0x08	10	00001000	^H (backspace) BS
9	0x09	11	00001001	^I (tab) HT
10	0x0a	12	00001010	^J (linefeed) LF
11	0x0b	13	00001011	^K (vertical tab) VT
12	0x0c	14	00001100	^L (formfeed) FF
13	0x0d	15	00001101	^M (carriage return) CR
14	0x0e	16	00001110	^N SO
15	0x0f	17	00001111	^O SI
16	0x10	20	00010000	^P DLE
17	0x11	21	00010001	^Q DC1
18	0x12	22	00010010	^R DC2
19	0x13	23	00010011	^S DC3
20	0x14	24	00010100	^T DC4
21	0x15	25	00010101	^U (NAK)
22	0x16	26	00010110	^V (SYN)
23	0x17	27	00010111	^W (ETB)
24	0x18	30	00011000	^X (CAN)
25	0x19	31	00011001	^Y (EM)
26	0x1a	32	00011010	^Z (SUB)
27	0x1b	33	00011011	Escape
28	0x1c	34	00011100	FS
29	0x1d	35	00011101	GS
30	0x1e	36	00011110	RS

Decimal	Hexadecimal	Octal	Binary	ASCII Character
31	0x1f	37	00011111	US
32	0x20	40	00100000	Space
33	0x21	41	00100001	!
34	0x22	42	00100010	"
35	0x23	43	00100011	#
36	0x24	44	00100100	$
37	0x25	45	00100101	%
38	0x26	46	00100110	&
39	0x27	47	00100111	'
40	0x28	50	00101000	(
41	0x29	51	00101001	)
42	0x2a	52	00101010	*
43	0x2b	53	00101011	+
44	0x2c	54	00101100	,
45	0x2d	55	00101101	-
46	0x2e	56	00101110	.
47	0x2f	57	00101111	/
48	0x30	60	00110000	0
49	0x31	61	00110001	1
50	0x32	62	00110010	2
51	0x33	63	00110011	3
52	0x34	64	00110100	4
53	0x35	65	00110101	5
54	0x36	66	00110110	6
55	0x37	67	00110111	7
56	0x38	70	00111000	8
57	0x39	71	00111001	9
58	0x3a	72	00111010	:
59	0x3b	73	00111011	;
60	0x3c	74	00111100	<
61	0x3d	75	00111101	=
62	0x3e	76	00111110	>
63	0x3f	77	00111111	?
64	0x40	100	01000000	@
65	0x41	101	01000001	A
66	0x42	102	01000010	B

Decimal	Hexadecimal	Octal	Binary	ASCII Character
67	0x43	103	01000011	C
68	0x44	104	01000100	D
69	0x45	105	01000101	E
70	0x46	106	01000110	F
71	0x47	107	01000111	G
72	0x48	110	01001000	H
73	0x49	111	01001001	I
74	0x4a	112	01001010	J
75	0x4b	113	01001011	K
76	0x4c	114	01001100	L
77	0x4d	115	01001101	M
78	0x4e	116	01001110	N
79	0x4f	117	01001111	O
80	0x50	120	01010000	P
81	0x51	121	01010001	Q
82	0x52	122	01010010	R
83	0x53	123	01010011	S
84	0x54	124	01010100	T
85	0x55	125	01010101	U
86	0x56	126	01010110	V
87	0x57	127	01010111	W
88	0x58	130	01011000	X
89	0x59	131	01011001	Y
90	0x5a	132	01011010	Z
91	0x5b	133	01011011	[
92	0x5c	134	01011100	\
93	0x5d	135	01011101	]
94	0x5e	136	01011110	^
95	0x5f	137	01011111	_
96	0x60	140	01100000	`
97	0x61	141	01100001	a
98	0x62	142	01100010	b
99	0x63	143	01100011	c
100	0x64	144	01100100	d
101	0x65	145	01100101	e
102	0x66	146	01100110	f

Decimal	Hexadecimal	Octal	Binary	ASCII Character
103	0x67	147	01100111	g
104	0x68	150	01101000	h
105	0x69	151	01101001	i
106	0x6a	152	01101010	j
107	0x6b	153	01101011	k
108	0x6c	154	01101100	l
109	0x6d	155	01101101	m
110	0x6e	156	01101110	n
111	0x6f	157	01101111	o
112	0x70	160	01110000	p
113	0x71	161	01110001	q
114	0x72	162	01110010	r
115	0x73	163	01110011	s
116	0x74	164	01110100	t
117	0x75	165	01110101	u
118	0x76	166	01110110	v
119	0x77	167	01110111	w
120	0x78	170	01111000	x
121	0x79	171	01111001	y
122	0x7a	172	01111010	z
123	0x7b	173	01111011	{
124	0x7c	174	01111100	l
125	0x7d	175	01111101	}
126	0x7e	176	01111110	~
127	0x7f	177	01111111	Del
128	0x80	200	10000000	Ç
129	0x81	201	10000001	ü
130	0x82	202	10000010	é
131	0x83	203	10000011	â
132	0x84	204	10000100	ä
133	0x85	205	10000101	à
134	0x86	206	10000110	å
135	0x87	207	10000111	ç
136	0x88	210	10001000	ê
137	0x89	211	10001001	ë
138	0x8a	212	10001010	è

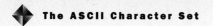

Decimal	Hexadecimal	Octal	Binary	ASCII Character
139	0x8b	213	10001011	ï
140	0x8c	214	10001100	î
141	0x8d	215	10001101	ì
142	0x8e	216	10001110	Ä
143	0x8f	217	10001111	Å
144	0x90	220	10010000	É
145	0x91	221	10010001	æ
146	0x92	222	10010010	Æ
147	0x93	223	10010011	ô
148	0x94	224	10010100	ö
149	0x95	225	10010101	ò
150	0x96	226	10010110	û
151	0x97	227	10010111	ù
152	0x98	230	10011000	ÿ
153	0x99	231	10011001	Ö
154	0x9a	232	10011010	Ü
155	0x9b	233	10011011	¢
156	0x9c	234	10011100	£
157	0x9d	235	10011101	¥
158	0x9e	236	10011110	℞
159	0x9f	237	10011111	ƒ
160	0xa0	240	10100000	á
161	0xa1	241	10100001	í
162	0xa2	242	10100010	ó
163	0xa3	243	10100011	ú
164	0xa4	244	10100100	ñ
165	0xa5	245	10100101	Ñ
166	0xa6	246	10100110	ª
167	0xa7	247	10100111	º
168	0xa8	250	10101000	¿
169	0xa9	251	10101001	⌐
170	0xaa	252	10101010	¬
171	0xab	253	10101011	½
172	0xac	254	10101100	¼
173	0xad	255	10101101	¡
174	0xae	256	10101110	«

Decimal	Hexadecimal	Octal	Binary	ASCII Character
175	0xaf	257	10101111	»
176	0xb0	260	10110000	▓
177	0xb1	261	10110001	▓
178	0xb2	262	10110010	█
179	0xb3	263	10110011	│
180	0xb4	264	10110100	┤
181	0xb5	265	10110101	╡
182	0xb6	266	10110110	╢
183	0xb7	267	10110111	╖
184	0xb8	270	10111000	╕
185	0xb9	271	10111001	╣
186	0xba	272	10111010	║
187	0xbb	273	10111011	╗
188	0xbc	274	10111100	╝
189	0xbd	275	10111101	╜
190	0xbe	276	10111110	╛
191	0xbf	277	10111111	┐
192	0xc0	300	11000000	└
193	0xc1	301	11000001	┴
194	0xc2	302	11000010	┬
195	0xc3	303	11000011	├
196	0xc4	304	11000100	─
197	0xc5	305	11000101	┼
198	0xc6	306	11000110	╞
199	0xc7	307	11000111	╟
200	0xc8	310	11001000	╚
201	0xc9	311	11001001	╔
202	0xca	312	11001010	╩
203	0xcb	313	11001011	╦
204	0xcc	314	11001100	╠
205	0xcd	315	11001101	═
206	0xce	316	11001110	╬
207	0xcf	317	11001111	╧
208	0xd0	320	11010000	╨
209	0xd1	321	11010001	╤
210	0xd2	322	11010010	╥

Decimal	Hexadecimal	Octal	Binary	ASCII Character
211	0xd3	323	11010011	⊑
212	0xd4	324	11010100	⊨
213	0xd5	325	11010101	⊩
214	0xd6	326	11010110	⊓
215	0xd7	327	11010111	‡
216	0xd8	330	11011000	‡
217	0xd9	331	11011001	⌋
218	0xda	332	11011010	⌈
219	0xdb	333	11011011	█
220	0xdc	334	11011100	▄
221	0xdd	335	11011101	▌
222	0xde	336	11011110	▐
223	0xdf	337	11011111	▀
224	0xe0	340	11100000	α
225	0xe1	341	11100001	β
226	0xe2	342	11100010	Γ
227	0xe3	343	11100011	π
228	0xe4	344	11100100	Σ
229	0xe5	345	11100101	σ
230	0xe6	346	11100110	μ
231	0xe7	347	11100111	τ
232	0xe8	350	11101000	Φ
233	0xe9	351	11101001	Θ
234	0xea	352	11101010	Ω
235	0xeb	353	11101011	δ
236	0xec	354	11101100	∞
237	0xed	355	11101101	φ
238	0xee	356	11101110	ε
239	0xef	357	11101111	∩
240	0xf0	360	11110000	≡
241	0xf1	361	11110001	±
242	0xf2	362	11110010	≥
243	0xf3	363	11110011	≤
244	0xf4	364	11110100	⌠
245	0xf5	365	11110101	⌡
246	0xf6	366	11110110	÷

Decimal	Hexadecimal	Octal	Binary	ASCII Character
247	0xf7	367	11110111	≈
248	0xf8	370	11111000	·
249	0xf9	371	11111001	·
250	0xfa	372	11111010	·
251	0xfb	373	11111011	√
252	0xfc	374	11111100	η
253	0xfd	375	11111101	2
254	0xfe	376	11111110	•
255	0xff	377	11111111	

Precedence and Associativity of Operators

This appendix lists the operators available in C and their precedence and associativity. In the "Associates" column you'll see that some entries have numbers in parentheses. These numbers refer you to notes about these entries that appear at the end of the table.

As you can see, there are quite a few operators available to you. Rather than view the table as something formidable to memorize, think of it as a list of tools, each of which is crafted to make your job easier.

Brian Kernighan tells a story about bumping into Dennis Ritchie (the creator of C) in the halls at Bell Labs. As part of the informal conversation, Brian asked Dennis whether a certain operator had higher precedence than some other operator. In essence, Ritchie's response was: "I can't remember, go look it up." If Brian Kernighan and Dennis Ritchie haven't memorized the precedence of every operator, there's no reason to think you should.

Operator	Precedence	Associates
var_name	17	(1)
[]	17	left (2)
var_name()	17	left (3)
()	17	left (4)
.	17	left
->	17	left
++ --	16	left (5)
++ --	15	right (6)
sizeof	15	right
~	15	right
!	15	right
- +	15	right (7)
&	15	right
*	15	right (8)
(type)	14	right (9)
* / %	13	left (10)
+ -	12	left (11)
<< >>	11	left
< <= >= >	10	left
== !=	9	left
&	8	left (12)
^	7	left
		6	left

Operator	Precedence	Associates
&&	5	left (13)
||	4	left (14)
? :	3	right
= += -= *= /= %= <<= >>= &= ^= |=	2	right
,	1	left

1. Associativity does not apply to variable names.
2. Brackets for array subscripts.
3. Function call.
4. Parentheses.
5. The postincrement and postdecrement operators.
6. The preincrement and predecrement operators.
7. Unary negation and plus.
8. Indirection operator, not multiplication.
9. The cast operator.
10. Multiply, divide, modulus.
11. Add, subtract.
12. Bitwise AND, not address-of operator.
13. Logical AND, not address-of operator or bitwise AND.
14. Logical OR, not bitwise OR.

INDEX